CURRICULUM DEVELOPMENT FOR STUDENTS WITH MILD DISABILITIES

ABOUT THE AUTHOR

Dr. Carroll J. Jones received her Ph.D. in Special Education Administration and Learning Disabilities from Kansas State University, and her M.Ed. in Reading and B.A. in Elementary Education from The University of Arizona. Dr. Jones was the Coordinator of the Inclusive Early Childhood Program (undergraduate, dual licensure) and Coordinator of the Special Education Program (graduate) at Southern Arkansas University in Magnolia, Arkansas. In addition to developing new programs, Dr. Jones' primary interests include curriculum-based assessment and programming for students with mild disabilities. Dr. Jones has previously published twelve special education teacher education textbooks and many articles; made numerous professional conference presentations; and served as a consultant in developing dual licensure teacher education programs.

Cover Design: Chris Gross is a graphics artist from Dubuque, IA. Her design depicts the joy and freedom that comes from learning.

Second Edition

CURRICULUM DEVELOPMENT FOR STUDENTS WITH MILD DISABILITIES

Academic and Social Skills for RTI Planning and Inclusion IEPs

By

CARROLL J. JONES, PH.D.

CHARLES C THOMAS • PUBLISHER, LTD.
Springfield • Illinois • U.S.A.

Published and Distributed Throughout the World by

CHARLES C THOMAS • PUBLISHER, LTD.
2600 South First Street
Springfield, Illinois 62794-9265

©2010 by CHARLES C THOMAS • PUBLISHER, LTD.

ISBN 978-0-398-07911-6 (spiral/paper)

Library of Congress Catalog Card Number: 2009036385

With THOMAS BOOKS *careful attention is given to all details of manufacturing
and design. It is the Publisher's desire to present books that are satisfactory as to their
physical qualities and artistic possibilities and appropriate for their particular use.*
THOMAS BOOKS *will be true to those laws of quality that assure a good name
and good will.*

Printed in the United States of America
TS-R-3

Library of Congress Cataloging in Publication Data

Jones, Carroll J.
  Curriculum development for students with mild disabilities : academic and
social skills for RTI planning and inclusion IEPs / by Carroll J. Jones. -- 2nd
ed.
      p. cm.
  Includes bibliographical references.
  ISBN 978-0-398-07911-6 (spiral)
    1. Children with disabilities--Education--Curricula--United States. 2.
Individualized education programs--United States. 3. Individualized instruc-
tion--United States. 4. Curriculum planning--United States. I. Title.

LC4031.J575 2010
371.9'043--dc22

                                                                2009036385

In memory of Lola Scheuerman

CONTRIBUTOR

Dr. Tandra Tyler-Wood received her Ph.D. and Masters' degrees in Special Education from The University of North Carolina at Chapel Hill. Her Bachelors' degrees in Psychology and Special Education are from Converse College in Spartanburg, South Carolina. Currently, Dr. Tyler-Wood is an Associate Professor in the Technology and Cognition Department at the University of North Texas in Denton, and Coordinator of the Educational Diagnostician Program. Her research interests are in the areas of appropriate assessment and effective teaching strategies for exceptional learners. She is the chairman of the Assistive Technology Division of the Society for Information Technology and Teacher Education. She is the coordinator and principal researcher on a research project, Simulation Enhanced Training for Science Teachers (SETS), funded by the Research in Disabilities Education Division of the National Science Foundation.

FOREWORD

Curriculum, assessment, and instruction are irrevocably linked elements in the pursuit to ensure that students with disabilities in today's schools benefit from the attention provided them. Without a highly specified curriculum, there is no target for the learning process. Indeed, the whole curriculum development issue has long been troublesome for special education, as teachers have struggled to address broader state level curriculum guidelines while providing the degree of specificity needed to teach students with special needs. Without means of assessing detailed levels of students'progress toward their goals, teachers are left to guess what to teach. Without knowledge of what to teach derived directly from students' performances on real-life skills, the best instructional practices may be wasted.

Dr. Jones has produced a text that offers a highly useful road map through the minefield of educating students with disabilities in the general curriculum alongside their peers as much as possible while still addressing their individual needs as indicated on their Individualized Education Plans (IEPs). Curriculum-based instruction used widely and skillfully has immense implications for strengthening the curriculum, assessment, and instruction links. It is useful for identifying students in need through a Response-to-Intervention approach. It also provides critical support to educators serious about ensuring their students are learning as a result of teacher input into the classroom.

With special education teachers in short supply and the demands on their time so great, this book can provide a valuable resource for cutting the clutter and moving to the heart of the teaching process--determining what skills students need to move effectively to the next level. In this revised edition, Dr. Jones has expanded the usefulness of the text in both breadth of skills addressed and in applied examples of the curriculum-based assessment process.

Congratulations, Dr. Jones, on making a great resource even better!

Virginia J. Dickens, Ph.D.
Professor of Special Education
Fayetteville State University
Fayetteville, North Carolina

PREFACE

When we discuss curriculum for students with mild disabilities, we are talking about the contents of Individual Education Programs (IEPs) which should contain the outline of the specialized and adapted general education curriculum for children and adolescents with disabilities. Since 1975 and the passage of P.L.94-142, the Education for All Handicapped Children's Act, when Individual Education Programs (IEPs) were mandated for all students with disabilities, there has been controversy about the contents, form, and length of IEPs.

The required curriculum for IEPs was changed in the 1997 Individuals with Disabilities Education Act (formerly Education for All Handicapped Children's Act), and continued in the IDEA 2004 reauthorization. The mandated curriculum for students with disabilities is the "general education curriculum," modified as needed. This book focuses primarily on the basic academic and social skills in the general education curriculum in the form of scope and sequence charts that can be used as objectives for the State Frameworks (goals and benchmarks) in preparing IEPs for children and youth with mild disabilities.

For the most part Individual Education Programs have focused on form rather than on curricular content. There have been nearly as many forms for writing IEPs as there are school districts in the United States. A number of State Departments have adopted IEP forms to provide some consistency across school districts. Often designers of IEP forms have been more concerned about complying with legal requirements, providing accountability, and avoiding lawsuits than with designing appropriate curricula for students with disabilities. The curriculum part of IEPs has varied from small checklists to huge computer banks of skills to state specified minimum competencies handwritten into yearly program outlines. Many school districts use computer programs that generate IEPs for teachers to use as curriculum guides. Many of the IEPs today are the specific state standards written into goals and benchmarks.

A number of problems make writing IEPs very difficult and time-consuming for beginning special education teachers even with access to computer programs. The extreme shortage of special education teachers has resulted in large numbers of teachers with emergency or alternative licenses who possess inadequate experience in teaching, lack a foundation in the general education curriculum of academic skills and sequences associated with each grade level, and possess little, if any, experience in modifying and teaching curriculum for at-risk and special needs students. Writing IEPs also requires a knowledge of the theoretical foundations of both general education and special education, and the instructional techniques and assessment procedures associated with each major approach.

The traditional IEP form relates assessment results on one page, goals on another page, and objectives on additional separate pages. This form is difficult for new IEP writers to see the relationship between assessment results, and goals and objectives. The specific IEP form used in this text is concerned only with the curriculum development part of the IEP. This form was designed to illustrate clearly to students the relationships among assessment results in the Present Level of Performance, the Annual Goals, Instructional Objectives, and Evaluation Methods and Materials sections of the IEP.

In order to reduce the paperwork load on inexperienced as well as experienced teachers according to IDEA 2004, many states are having special education teachers use the state academic framework goals to create IEPs. The Frameworks do not task analyze subject areas to indicate a sequence of basic skills to be taught. Obviously, writing goals only, and primarily those specified in the State Frameworks requires much less time and curricular knowledge.

However, teachers are often asked to write Individual Implementation Plans (IIPs) composed of the objectives or scope and sequences of skills to be taught, which may or may not be included in the IEP, but provides the individual skills that teachers must teach to assist special needs students in reaching their goals. Perhaps there was a reduction in curricular information included in the IEP, however, teachers still must write IIPs or something similar, and lesson plans with skills for teaching and monitoring progress.

This book for preservice teachers and special education teachers was designed to provide a foundation in the general education academic curriculum and the generic skills sequences at each grade level. It provides information on the new process of identification of children with disabilities through their responses to intervention (RTI). The scope and sequence charts should assist teachers in pinpointing the specific deficits a child/youth experiences, in modifying the general education curriculum for each student with mild disabilities, and in writing complete Individual Education Programs (IEPs) and Individual Implementation Programs (IIPs).

This new edition of *Curriculum Development for Students With Mild Disabilities* has been reorganized so the first three chapters focus on historical curriculum development and primary theorists in early childhood education curriculum, general education curriculum, and special education curriculum. An additional focus is on the impact of federal laws (IDEA and NCLB) on the curriculum and assessment in schools today including the new methods of identifying children and youth who need special education services. The current focus on the education of preschoolers who are at-risk and/or disabled has changed the curriculum of this population of children. Also, developing the IEP is presented from a number of different perspectives including the use of norm-referenced testing scores, criterion-referenced scores, and curriculum-based assessment results.

The chapters have been updated and several chapters have been included in a different sequence to provide the major generic theory in the first three chapters. The scope and sequence charts were modified to include current national education standards and benchmarks, and the scope and sequence of skills in each of the academic areas that require annual state assessment. The book has been reorganized into ten chapters as follows: Historical Perspectives of Curriculum (Chapter 1); The Curriculum Development Process (Chapter 2); Early Childhood Special Education Curricula (Chapter 3); Oral Expression Curricula (Chapter 4); Reading and Listening Curricula (Chapter 5); Written Expression Curricula (Chapter 6); Mathematics Curricula (Chapter 7); Educational Technology Curricula K-12 (Chapter 8); Social and Self Competence Curricula (Chapter 9); Science Curricula (Chapter 10); and Evaluation Reports: Case Studies (Appendix).

Thanks to Dr. Tandra Tyler-Wood, Associate Professor, Department of Technology and Cognition at the University of North Texas, for revising the technology chapter and writing the new Science chapter. A special thanks to Dr. Virginia Dickens, Professor of Special Education, Fayetteville State University, who serves as a sounding board and provides insight; and for writing the Foreword.

This book is dedicated in memory of a dear friend, Lola Scheuerman, who was one of the finest public elementary school reading teachers in our nation, and who worked with at-risk and disabled learners in the Shawnee Heights School District in Topeka, Kansas and in the Shawnee Mission School District in Shawnee Mission, Kansas for over thirty years. Lola Scheuerman was the consummate "Master Teacher."

C.J.J.

CONTENTS

TABLES

CURRICULUM DEVELOPMENT FOR STUDENTS WITH MILD DISABILITIES

Chapter 1

HISTORICAL PERSPECTIVES OF CURRICULUM

Special education is different today in many dramatic ways than it was in the not-too-distant past. Today, standards-based education drives what schools do, how teachers function, and how students respond.
(Polloway, E., Patton, J. & Serna, L., 2008, 3)

Curriculum for children and youth with mild disabilities must be developmentally-appropriate and age-appropriate to prepare them intellectually, academically, and socially to function in society. The curriculum or content of instruction reflects the historical development of general and special education, as well as the legal impact of general education and special education laws. Inclusion and Response-to-Intervention for students with mild disabilities frequently require modification of the general education curricula. Individual Education Programs (IEPs), mandated by special education laws, are the documents that contain the specially planned curricula for students with disabilities.

WHAT IS CURRICULUM?

The public school system is a small microcosm of society which mirrors society's cultural, social, political, economic, ethical, moral, religious, professional, intellectual, legal, historical, and personal beliefs and problems. The curriculum of the public schools is intended to prepare students to succeed in society as responsible citizens, therefore, is reflective of society and often sensitive to the concerns of society.

Curriculum has been defined in many different ways, however, curriculum is the content, the what we teach, the age-appropriate and developmentally appropriate life tasks (Adelman & Taylor, 1993). The curriculum or content of instruction is built on the goals of education set forth by federal, state and local education agencies. In addition to the planned or static learning experiences and competencies, curriculum, also, includes the dynamic and unplanned learnings and experiences (Shepherd & Ragan, 1992). In further delineating curriculum, it has been described as (1) a series of courses, (2) documents (teacher guides and manuals), (3) sequential learning objectives, and (4) experiences (Shepherd & Ragan, 1992).

Curriculum Guides

All states have a state adopted curriculum, often referred to as curriculum frameworks, which outline the instructional program in each subject at each grade level. The elementary school general education curriculum is often divided into the following broad categories: language arts and reading, science, mathematics, social studies, health and physical education, the arts, and optional subjects such as computer technology, foreign language, and instrumental music (Jarolimek & Foster, 1989). The secondary curriculum is separated into discrete courses in each field such as mathematics: algebra, advanced algebra, geometry, trigonometry, calculus.

Previously, the states' required minimum competency testing program provided a "remedial curriculum" in basic subject areas for children and youth who did not pass these tests. The minimum competency tests in most states have been discontinued. All states now have state curriculum standards or frameworks for each grade level which are the goals of the state academic program. Progress is now monitored through a state required grade-level testing program that is aligned with the state required curriculum. Currently, testing is required in the curriculum areas of language arts, mathematics, and science as a result of the mandates of the No Child Left Behind Act 2001.

The state adopted commercial textbooks for each subject, the most widely used curriculum documents, are utilized to instruct students. The teachers' editions or curriculum guides of these commercial textbook series contain structured and sequential learning outcomes (scope and sequence charts of skills and concepts to be developed), lesson objectives, suggested teaching approaches, provisions for evaluation, suggestions for enrichment activities, and educational media available (Shepherd & Ragan, 1992). Thus, most of the state adopted curriculum (state curriculum frameworks) is contained in the students' state adopted textbooks and the teachers' curriculum guides or manuals.

U.S. GENERAL EDUCATION CURRICULUM DEVELOPMENT

Over the past 350 years, educational curriculum in the United States has changed considerably in response to the changing forces of economics, politics, religion, and social forces.

Historical General Educational Periods

Colonial Period

For the first 150 years (1625–1775), the schools in the United States adhered to religious purposes evidenced by the Puritans who established schools to teach children to read the Bible to guide their personal salvation (Shepherd & Ragan, 1992). Discipline was considered to be a very important part of education. New England, at that time, was controlled in both public and private life by the Puritan ministers. The Puritans were encouraged to beat and punish their children in an effort to drive out the inborn sin or willfulness, especially in the school situation (Lascarides & Hinitz, 2000). The education of children during the early years of the settlement was conducted by the family and the church rather than through any school. The goal of education was to instill the habits of obedience, reverence, and industry, which were fundamental for the adult Christian life of a Puritan (Lascarides & Hinitz, 2000, 186). Reading was taught on a one-to-one basis by a parent or a literate neighbor's wife, who set up a Dame School. Most children learned their adult roles as apprentices in their own homes (Lascarides & Hinitz, 2000). The Puritans set the scene for schools of the future when they passed the "Old Deluder Satan" Act in 1647 requiring that children be provided schooling at the expense of the community (Shepherd & Ragan, 1992).

The reading curriculum for colonial children was contained primarily In the *Hornbook, The New England Primer*, and the *Bible*. The first book from which colonial children learned was the *Hornbook* which contained their letters (upper and lower case), and how to spell. It also included simple syllables and The Lord's Prayer. The *New England Primer*, the most used book in colonial schools for more than one-hundred-fifty years, was evidence of the religious motive for education as the content was primarily religious (Lascarides & Hinitz, 2000). The basic curriculum of the colonial period included the three R's (reading, writing, and arithmetic), catechism, prayers, and hymns (McNergney & Herbert, 1995). When the children advanced beyond The *New England Primer*, they entered grammar school. The texts for grammar school were written in Latin. The curriculum was the same as the curriculum taught in private schools in England (Lascarides & Hinitz, 2000).

The sons and some daughters of Southern plantation owners had private tutors during the colonial period. The curriculum for the boys included Greek and Roman classics, mathematics, spelling, reading, writing, dance, literature, music, art, breeding of fine horses (as a young adult), riding horses and hunting game. The curriculum for the girls included speaking French, reading, writing, spelling, basic mathematics, household management, social graces, domestic skills of a housewife, needlework, dancing, and playing a musical instrument (Lascarides & Hintz, 2000).

During the next one hundred years (1776–1876), the schools were influenced greatly by politics which supplanted the previous religious focus of the schools (McNergney & Herbert, 1995). Prominent citizens pressed for a system of education that was free, state-controlled, nonsectarian, tax supported, and open to all. In addition to the three R's (prayers, catechism, and hymns were eliminated), the curriculum was expanded to include history and geography, agriculture, physiology and hygiene, grammar and composition, drawing and music. The *public school revival* (1823–1876) resulted in an increased awareness of the importance of public education, an enriched curriculum, increased school appropriations, establishment of state departments of education, and improved teacher education programs (Shepherd & Ragan, 1992).

Progressive Educational Movement Period (1876–1929)

The public school system, during the next 50 years (1876–1929), were affected by economics as the United States expanded in business and industry, in territory, and in influence on world affairs. The agricultural-based economy changed to a complex industrialized economy. The social reforms in the treatment of children, child labor, and the *progressive educational movement* led to a focus on the development of a skilled labor force (McNergney & Herbert, 1995). The school curricula were changed to include domestic science, manual training, and a correlated basic curriculum.

The humanist-based progressive educational movement, focused on the whole child (physical, mental, emotional, and social development), and the attainment of self-actualization and self-realization. Methods of teaching were changed from rote memorization to "learning by doing," concrete experiences, individualized instruction, self-directed activities, and practical-living skills (McNergney & Herbert, 1995). From the humanist perspective, problems are evident in individuals who demonstrate inappropriate social and emotional behaviors, negative self-concepts, and extreme anxiety. Humanist instructional methods and curriculum were designed to address areas of basic needs, enhance the self-concept, develop social skills, and reduce extreme anxiety and stress (Slavin, 1994).

National government policies during two periods of national emergency, the Great Depression and World War II, placed increased responsibility on the public schools to ameliorate the social and economic situation and prepare for a war-time economy (Shepherd & Ragan, 1992). The effects of the progressive educational movement began to be felt with the correlation of subjects into broad fields—language arts, social studies, and the emphasis on physical fitness (Shepherd & Ragan, 1992). The emphasis on democracy stimulated teachers to operate more democratic classrooms with students working in groups, identifying their own learning goals, and evaluating the success of their work. The curriculum expanded to include democratic living skills, and increased the focus on science to develop "scientists" to help with the war effort and to meet the increased demands for improved technology (McNergney & Herbert, 1995).

Post-War Period: Mid-1940s–1960s

After World War II, the economic, political and social forces in the United States exploded with changes which impacted the public schools. Increased industrial productivity stimulated by industrial automation launched the United States as a world leader in manufactured goods. Social dynamics changed as population shifted from rural to urban to suburban areas; and southern blacks moved to the north and west with increased racial integration. Many states were beginning to offer state-supported kindergarten classes. This period saw the building of many new schools to meet the needs of educating the postwar baby boom. New elementary school buildings were one-level designs with school libraries, automated instructional media, and multiple sources of media. Major changes in curriculum emphasized speaking a second language, studying current world affairs, and air-age education (Shepherd & Ragan, 1992).

In 1957, the launch of the first artificial earth satellite, Sputnik, by Russia resulted in nation-wide concern for improvement in the public schools. Curriculum reforms were funded by a tremendous increase in public school money including Head Start in 1964 and the Elementary and Secondary Education Act of 1968. These reforms included increased math and science requirements with reforms in physics, biology, and chemistry; and "new math" and "inquiry science" (McNergney & Herbert, 1995). Curriculum reforms also included special curricula for gifted students.

Early 1970s to Mid–1980s

The 1970s was a period of civil unrest in the United States when the courts focused on constitutional rights of individuals and used the public schools to enforce social change (i.e., *PARC v. PA*, 1972). It was a period when school buildings and buses were bombed and burned, and school-bond propositions were voted down. Curriculum during this period reflected a humanist influence on learning how to learn, developing social skills and a positive self-concept, values clarification, and teaching students to be self-actualizing individuals (McNergney & Herbert, 1995).

During the mid- 1970s to mid-1980s, the theoretical emphasis in curriculum (i.e., academics, social and behavioral skills) and instruction shifted to behavioral psychology. For the most part behaviorism effects methodology rather than curriculum content. Many commercial and noncommercial programs were designed to enhance behavior and classroom management abilities of teachers through using time-out, reinforcement, contingency contracting, and token economies (Shea & Bauer, 1994). The behavioral approach to academics utilized the direct instruction method, daily direct measurement with charting, task analysis, precision teaching, scope and sequence charts of academic skills, and highly sequenced functional academic skills. Computer assisted instruction (CAI) for drill and practice, a behavioral instructional approach with immediate feedback for correct and incorrect answers, began to be popular.

Additionally, there was a call for a "return to the basics" in academics. Early childhood and after school programs were created to offset the effects of poverty and meet the needs of working parents. The influx of immigrants resulted in increased funding for bilingual programs and a focus on multicultural education. Improved technology and the development of personal computers led to a significant demand that all students become computer literate.

In 1983, the National Commission on Excellence in Education published, *A Nation At Risk: The Imperative of Education Reform.* The Commission cited America's schools as being mediocre, short-sighted, and having a bureaucracy structure with debilitating functions (McNergney & Herbert, 1995). Politicians jumped on the "bandwagon" and demanded school reform, so state legislatures created accountability systems for teachers requiring them to take Teacher Effectiveness Training courses and pass teacher competency examinations for certification. Students were required to pass minimum competency tests for graduation. However, the double-digit inflation and high unemployment led the federal government to take an increased role in managing the economy including school budgets which received 10 percent less federal funding during this period (Shepherd & Ragan, 1992).

Mid-1980s to Late 1990s

The major theoretical focus of this period has been cognitive psychology which includes concerns regarding the ways students process information, a renewed interest in Bloom's cognitive taxonomies, Gardner's multiple intelligences, problem-based learning, critical reasoning, and metacognition. Cognitive instruction from the information processing perspective includes programming to remediate problems in areas of attention, perception, memory, and language. Cognitive strategists emphasized metacognitive approaches to learning which include self-planning, self-organization, self-questioning, self-monitoring, self-evaluation, and self-reinforcement. Learning strategies is an important area of cognitive curriculum; and the criteria for judging instructional effectiveness is generalization of skills to other settings, materials, and teachers (Reid, Hresko, & Swanson, 1991).

Constructivism, a cognitive learning theory popular in the United States from mid-1980s to the end of the 1990s, was based on the idea that children learn by connecting new knowledge to previously learned knowledge (Reyhner, 2008). Constructivism was based on the cognitive theories of Piaget (Raymond, 2008); and on the social constructivism and language focus as a foundation of learning of Vygotsky (Raymond, 2008). Whole language is a constructivist approach applied to the teaching of reading (Weaver, 1996). The whole language approach is a meaning-based approach with little emphasis on the direct development of meaning, reading skills such as phonics, and writing mechanics of grammar, spelling, capitalization and punctuation (Reyhner, 2008). The whole language approach uses literature and textbooks from other subject areas, guided reading, sustained silent reading, and daily journalwriting.

The 1990s saw statistically significant declines in student achievement nationwide on the "National Assessment of Education Progress." Much of the blame for these declines was attributed to the use of the whole language approach. Throughout the 1990s and into the early 2000s, whole language skeptics generated considerable research that cast considerable doubt on features of whole language that de-emphasized skills, especially in phonics Cromwell, (1997). Whole language is currently considered a controversial approach to teaching reading.

Behavioral psychology continues to influence the curriculum with a focus on minimum basic skills, minimum competency testing, the use of computers to aid drill and practice, and particularly in the area of classroom management with the use of extrinsic reinforcement. Behavioral psychology provided the scope and sequence charts of learning strategies as well as academic and social skills instructional content. Behavioral instructional strategies are primarily utilized to teach literal level skills requiring rote memory and recitation such as memorizing basic math facts. Teachers continued to rely on behavior management, contingency contracting, and token economy systems to maintain discipline within their classrooms.

The humanist movement of the 1990s continues to embody basic humanist principles including open schools and learning centers, team teaching and teachers as facilitators, multiage groupings, student selection of learning pace and learning materials, no grades (pass/fail), no standardized testing (Slavin, 1994). The current humanist movement focuses on self-regulated learning, affective education, authentic assessment (i.e., portfolio assessment, curriculum-based assessment), self-motivation, and moral development. Typical instructional procedures utilized in schools of the 1990s included cooperative learning strategies as peer tutoring, jigsaw learning, and team-assisted individualization (Slavin, 1994). The aim of the humanist education movement of the 1990s was to help students seek self-actualization, self-fulfillment, and self-motivation. A renewed focus on community service has resulted in recommendations to add a Service Learning curriculum to the already full daily schedules.

In 1994, the "National Center for Education Statistics" reported that in the previous decade substantial gains in education had been made including higher proportion of high school students taking academic core courses and advanced placement classes, fewer dropouts between tenth and twelfth grades, and increased college enrollments. The call for reform continued with the passage of the National Educational Reform Act (Goals 2000) in March 1994. Many of the goals of Goals 2000 were impossible to measure or to achieve such as: (1) all children will arrive at school ready to learn; (2) high school graduation rates will increase to at least 90 percent; (3) every school shall be free of drugs and violence; and (4) U.S. students will be first in the world in math and science.

State legislatures supported by state courts beginning with Kentucky mandated reconstruction of school systems with a focus on accountability. Public schools experimented with various teacher accountability programs, principal accountability, and student accountability systems. Also, at the university level there has been focus on accountability resulting in changes in how teachers and principals are trained, and continued experimentation on which models to utilize. Schools again were called upon to help solve or eradicate the social problems of high rates of teen pregnancies, AIDS and other sexually transmitted diseases, school-dropouts, at-risk children (i.e., poverty, "crack" babies, gangs, violence, teen suicide). Many of these social topics have been added to the public school curriculum or have become the responsibility of the schools.

In the face of indecision, change, spiraling social problems, and violence in the public schools, increasing numbers of parents have turned to alternatives to public schools including home schooling, charter schools, and private schools to avoid many of the social problems impacting public schools. The education of students with disabilities is a volatile subject area in which some people want to "restructure" the public schools with the "inclusion" of all students with disabilities in the general education classroom regardless of the level of intellectual functioning; while others rally for nongraded and multi-age classes, distance learning, increased computer and technology skills. The emphasis on a functional life curriculum for students with disabilities resulted in a similar requirement for all students with school-to-work skills added to the curriculum at each grade level.

Current General Education Curriculum Focus

The early 2000s have been impacted significantly by the reauthorization of the No Child Left Behind Act (NCLB, 2001), originally the Elementary and Secondary Education Act of 1965. Historically, this federal program was known as the "Title I" program which provided supplemental support, primarily in reading and mathematics, to economically disadvantaged children and youth. The NCLB (2001) focused on several areas of considerable concern to public schools: (1) preparing, training and recruiting highly qualified teachers and principals; (2) making the education system accountable; (3) helping all children learn to read; and (4) helping children with disabilities (U.S. Department of Education, 2004).

Highly Qualified Teachers

NCLB (2001) required that all teachers of core academic subjects, especially reading and mathematics, must be highly qualified by the end of the 2004–2005 school year. A "highly qualified" teacher (HQT) must (1) hold a bachelor's degree or better in the subject(s) he/she teaches; (2) hold full teacher certification in the subjects taught in the state of his/her employment; and (3) demonstrate knowledge of the subject he/she teaches U.S. Department of Education, 2004). Under the President's 2005 budget, teachers received $5.1 billion in support through training, recruiting incentives, loan forgiveness, and tax relief (U.S. Dept. of Education, 2004).

Accountable Education System

The No Child Left Behind Act (NCLB 2001) holds schools and school districts accountable for making sure that all children are learning. Every state is required to have a State Plan including a timeline for determining whether a school, district, and the state are making "adequate yearly progress" (AYP) toward the goal of 100 percent of students meeting state standards by 2014. Every state is required to (1) set standards for grade-level achievement, and (2) develop a system to measure the progress of all students and subgroups of students in meeting those state-determined grade-level standards. The U.S. Department of Education (2004) has required that the accountability plan gradually be put in place beginning with grades 1–3 and moving to high school. The timeline includes the following:

2003:	Standards developed in reading/language arts, and mathematics.
2004:	Baseline Year.
2005–2006:	Annual assessments in reading/language arts and mathematics in grades 3–8, and high school.
2005–2006:	Science standards developed in grades 3–5, 6–9, 10–12.
2007–2008:	Science assessments at one grade at each of three grade levels (3–5, 6–9, 10–12). Disaggregate test data.
2008–2009:	Disaggregated science assessment data will be used in state accountability calculations.
2010–2011:	Standards developed for 2 years of high school English and 2 years of high school mathematics.
2012–2013:	States will administer assessments aligned with the high school English and mathematics standards.
2013–2014:	All students will be functioning at grade level in reading and mathematics.
2019–2020:	All students will achieve proficiency in science at grade level.

For fiscal year 2005, President Bush requested $410 million to support the development and implementation of state assessments (U.S. Department of Education, 2004).

Helping Children Learn to Read

The goal is for every child to know how to read at grade level by the third grade. This goal is supported by a request for $1.4 billion for the Early Reading First Program (pre-kindergarten program), Reading First Program (early grades program), and Striving Readers Program (upper grade students program) (U.S. Department of Education, 2004). No Child Left Behind Act of 2001 puts emphasis on determining which educational programs and practices have been proven effective through rigorous scientific research. Federal funding is targeted to support these programs and teaching methods that work to improve student learning and achievement.

The ultimate goal of NCLB is that all children will be proficient in all subject matter by the year 2014 and will be taught by qualified teachers highly trained in the subjects they teach (U.S. Dept. of Educ., 2004). This important program serves more than 15 million students in nearly all school districts and more than half of all public schools including two-thirds of the nation's elementary schools at an annual cost of $13–$15 billion (U.S. Department of Education, 2004).

Helping Children with Disabilities

In 1997, the reauthorization of the Individuals with Disabilities Education Act (IDEA) required that students with disabilities be included in State and district-wide assessment programs. No Child Left Behind Act of 2001 builds on this requirement by ensuring that these assessments measure how well students with disabilities have learned required grade level material in reading and math.

5th Anniversary Achievements of NCLB 2001

In January 2007, Education Secretary Margaret Spellings, indicated achievement toward the goals of No Child Left Behind Act of 2001 include the following areas:

• All 50 states and D.C. have accountability plans in place.
• All 50 states and D.C. assess students in grades 3–8 and once in high school in reading/language arts and math.

- The percentage of classes taught by a highly qualified teacher has risen to over 90%.
- Nearly 450,000 eligible students have received free supplemental educational services (tutoring) or public school choice (*5th Anniversary Achievements,* Jan. 2007).
- More reading progress was made by 9-year-olds in 5 years than in the previous 28 years combined (*Nation's Report Card,* January 2007).
- Reading and mathematics scores for 9-year-olds and 4th graders have reached all-time highs (*Nation's Report Card,* January, 2007).

No Child Left Behind Act of 2007

U. S. Education Secretary, Margaret Spellings, Press Release on July 12, 2007 on the No Child Left Behind Act of 2007 as follows:

> This new act retains the solid foundation we've laid and incorporates lessons we've learned in the past five years. Now that we've identified struggling students and schools, we can provide them with the extra tools and resources they need to get back on track. We can give educators more credit for student improvement and give principals and superintendents more resources to reinvent chronically underperforming schools. Thanks to annual assessments and the abundance of data we now have on student performance, we can give states and schools more flexibility without sacrificing accountability for results.

In 2007, President Bush's budget request for 2009, drew on the data and experience gathered during the first five years of NCLB implementation to develop a reauthorization proposal designed to build on the success of NCLB and address new challenges. This proposal, which was shared with the Congress in late summer 2007, focused on (1) increasing flexibility for states and school districts to turn around low-performing schools, (2) improving the academic achievement of students in our high schools, and (3) expanding choice options for students in chronically low-performing schools (U.S. Department of Education, February 4, 2008). In summary the 2009 budget requests for elementary and secondary education programs under NCLB 2007 includes the following:

- $14.3 billion for Title I Grants to Local Education Agencies for high-school programs and restructuring low-performing schools.
- 491.3 million for a reauthorized Title I School Improvement Grants program identified for restructuring.

- $408.7 million for State Assessment Grants to fund state assessment systems, and support the development and implementation of 2 years of high school assessments.
- $1 billion for Reading First State Grants to improve reading skills of students in high-poverty, low-performing elementary schools.
- $100 million for the Striving Readers program to improve skills of teenaged students who are reading below grade level.
- $800 million for 21st Century Learning Opportunities for high-quality after-school and summer school programs.
- $300 million for new Pell Grants for Kids (K–12) to transfer to local private schools or high-quality school.
- $200 million for the Teacher Incentive Fund as a reward to those who will work in hard-to-staff schools, and close achievement gaps.
- $175 million for programs aimed at improving math and science instruction in K–12 schools.
- $730 million for English Language Acquisition State Grants to serve disadvantaged populations and LEP students.
- $452.7 million for Title I Migrant Education and Neglected and Delinquent State agency programs.

This budget request combined with the $1.1 billion increase in 2007 would make available a total of $1.5 billion in new funds to implement the reauthorization proposal for Title I (Fiscal Year 2009 Budget Summary, February 4, 2008).

The No Child Left Behind Act of 2007 is the major force in general education driving not only the curriculum being taught, but also, determining the methods used in teaching, and sometimes even specifying the specific programs or commercial books and materials to be used in the classroom. The success of a school is determined by the students' scores on the state standards tests. Often a teacher's success is determined by the scores his or her students achieve. There are numerous pros and cons to such an all-inclusive educational mandate which never considers the intelligence levels or the life environment of children/youth in the general education classroom.

These NCLB (2001, 2007) requirements also apply to the majority of students with disabilities.

HISTORY OF SPECIAL EDUCATION CURRICULUM

Prior to the end of the eighteenth century, there were few attempts to educate children and youth with disabilities. The majority of physicians and professional educators felt that efforts to educate students with mental retardation were futile. Children and youth diagnosed mentally ill (emotionally disturbed) were treated like animals, beaten and chained, kept in small cells with no light, and with no concerns for their education. Treatment of persons with mental illness and mental retardation focused on rendering them subservient and obedient by almost any means (Scheerenberger, 1983).

Historical Special Education Periods 1800s–1900

Students with Mental Retardation

Educating children and youth with disabilities has focused as much on specialized teaching techniques as it has on specialized curriculum. The earliest history relating to special education is found primarily in the early 1800s with European physicians who attempted to discriminate and to educate "idiotic" and "insane" children (Patton et al., 1990). Jean Marc Itard, a French physician considered the father of modern special education, and his student Edouard Seguin, who became a famous educator of children with mental retardation in Europe and in the United States, pioneered revolutionary curriculum and instructional procedures that are still evident in our regular education and special education programs today. These curriculum and Instructional procedures included the following:

1. **A Developmental Approach to Instruction:** Curriculum was based on the individual's functioning level(s) in the normal developmental sequence;
2. **Sensory Stimulation:** Curriculum was based on the remediation of deficits in basic sensory systems including vision, hearing, tactile, smell, kinesthetic, and taste;
3. **Functional-Life Curriculum:** Curriculum that focused on developing living skills within the immediate environment (e.g., self-care, social communication, academic instruction related to daily life);
4. **Individualized Instruction:** Instructional approach based on the needs, characteristics, and functioning levels of the individual;
5. **Systematic Instruction:** Instructional approach based on task-analyzed sequences of skills beginning with real-life and concrete tasks at the child's functioning level (Hardman et al., 1990).

In Europe and in the United States, Seguin used his physiological curriculum and methods of teaching children and youth with mental retardation which involved five areas: (1) training the muscular system; (2) training the nervous system; (3) educating the senses; (4) acquiring general ideas; and (5) developing the ability to think in abstract terms and acquiring a strong understanding and practice of moral (social) precepts (Scheerenberger, 1983).

In the late 1800s in England, John Langdon Down proposed a comprehensive curriculum for students with mental retardation including physical activities to ensure strength and coordination; intellectual training including senses, basic self-care, use and value of money, gardening, and vocational training; speech and language training; moral training including obedience, and right from wrong (Scheerenberger, 1983). The first institutions in the United States for persons with mental retardation were schools and treatment centers to educate higher functioning "feebleminded" individuals so they would be capable of supporting themselves (Sloan & Stevens, 1976). The curriculum programs at these training schools included industrial, custodial, and farming skills.

Students with Emotional Disturbance

Generally, the early treatment of mentally ill and insane persons falls into two pre-1900 periods: the Supernatural period and the Illness Period. During the Supernatural period (prior to the late 1700s), the causes of emotional disturbances were attributed to beliefs in magic or possession by an evil spirit (Peterson, 1991). There were few attempts to educate the mentally ill (behavior disordered) children and youth. However, they were frequently beaten and chained to drive out the evil spirits.

During the Illness Period in the eighteenth century in Europe, the work of medical doctors in different countries (Philippe Pinel' of France, William Tuke of England, and Benjamin Rush of America) worked to improve the lives of the mentally ill. These physicians fought for more humane treatment of the mentally ill including good food, clean surroundings, no chains, and no beatings. Although Pinel' believed that children with insanity were incurable, he was a proponent of more humane treatment (Haring et al., 1994).

The education of children and youth with mental illness included a focus on managing their behavior, but also work therapy and skills (McKown, 1961). In the United States, Dorothea Dix and colleagues campaigned for better treatment, rehabilitation, and educational programs in Massachusetts' state hospitals, however, within ten years these facilities became custodial rather than educational. The early professionals in the field of mental illness achieved only modest success in changing the life conditions of the mentally ill and had little to no success in their education (Paul, 1991).

Students with Learning Disabilities

The emergent period in the field of learning disabilities began in the early 1960s, however, major historical antecedents can be traced to the 1980s to the brain research that identified the three major categories of learning problems of children and youth with specific learning disabilities today. These three categories of problems concerned: (1) disorders of perceptual and motor processes; (2) disorders of spoken language; and (3) disorders of written language (Weiderholt, 1974).

These early physician scientists described the behavioral characteristics of their adult patients and attempted to localize sensory, perceptual motor, and language (spoken and written) functions to precise parts of the brain (Weiderholt, 1974). They also conducted autopsies on the brains of deceased patients to determine if the loss of specific functions was related to a specific part of the brain (Lerner, 1993). Later, the researchers worked with educators to interpret the results of the brain studies and to create remediation programs (curriculum and instruction methods) for children who demonstrated the specific characteristics and disabilities in perceptual-motor processes, disorders of spoken language, and disorders of written language.

The development of the field of specific learning disabilities was significantly affected by the revolutionary teaching methods and curriculum that Itard, Sequin, and Montessori used with children who had mental retardation in the middle to late 1800s. Their curriculum and instruction procedures were, also, very helpful for students with perceptual-motor problems who did not have mental retardation.

Historical Special Education Periods: 1990s–1960

This historical period was extremely important in laying down the foundation for educating students with mild disabilities. The development of a mental scale of intelligence by Alfred Binet and Theodore Simon was used in French schools to screen those students who were not benefiting from the regular classroom experience and who might need special education (Patton et al., 1990). The intelligence scale also allowed mental functioning to be divided into various categories including gifted and mild mental retardation. The brain researchers teamed with teachers in translating research results into tests, remedial materials, and teaching procedures.

Students with Mental Retardation

In the early 1900s, the training schools for students with mental retardation became institutions for custodial care as it became obvious that retardation could not be cured with education. In 1905, M.W. Barr proposed the first classification system of retarded persons based on education and the methods of training needed for the different levels of feeblemindedness (Sloan & Stevens, 1976).

The years between 1930 and 1950 saw gradual renewal in the education of persons with mental retardation. Wallace, 1930 President of the American Association of Mental Deficiency, recommended that school for the feeble-minded be extended to 12 months; and that curriculum coordinate areas of academics and social skills with hand training activities (i.e., playground, agricultural) and field trips to community-based factories and stores (Sloan & Stevens, 1976). During this period several important research centers were established at major institutions serving individuals with mental retardation: Letchworth Village in New York, Vineland Training School in New Jersey, and the Wayne County Training School in Michigan (Sloan & Stevens, 1976).

Beginning in the 1930s the developmental method became important focusing on curriculum composed of hierarchies of task-analyzed normal developmental skills in cognition, fine and gross motor, communication, social and behavioral, self-help, and adaptive skills (Lascarides & Hinitz, 2000). Primary theoretical foundations of the developmental curriculum included Gesell's (1928) early childhood skill sequences, Piaget's cognitive developmental skills, Erikson's psychosocial developmental skills, and Kohlberg's moral developmental skills.

A number of other factors contributed to the education of students with disabilities during this period. Edgar Doll (1939) wrote the **Vineland Social Maturity Scale** which in revised forms is still very valuable today in determining the social skills of students with mental retardation. David Wechsler (1949) published the first edition of the **Wechsler Intelligence Scale for Children**, which has been revised several times, is the most frequently used intelligence test in the United States. Skeels & Dye's (1939) research revealed that an inadequate environment could be a cause of mental retardation. This research became the foundation for the creation of many preschools for children from low-income homes.

Another important event in the education of students with mental retardation was the passage of the Vocational Rehabilitation Act (PL84-566) in 1953 in which Congress attempted to meet the employment needs of adults with mental retardation. This act required the state vocational agencies to subsidize vocational rehabilitation training for persons with mental retardation.

Students with Emotional Disturbance

Prior to the 1960s, the mental health system was the primary service provider for children with emotional disturbance, utilizing medical or pharmacological, and psychodynamic or psychological treatment (Whelan, 1988). There was little effort to educate children and youth with emotional disturbance. When behaviors interfered with their learning and the learning of other students, these students were excluded from the public schools.

However, by 1922 concern regarding students with mental illness resulted in the establishment of child guidance clinics presided by psychiatrists with psychologists and social workers.

Students with Learning Disabilities

The development of the field of learning disabilities was significantly affected by the revolutionary curriculum and teaching methods that Itard, Seguin, and Montessori used in teaching children with mental retardation. Historically, almost all of the pioneers in the field of learning disabilities were advocates of the process approach, a multisensory approach to diagnosis and intervention. Most early interventions for students with learning disabilities involved the integration of multisensory teaching techniques with a specialized curriculum. In the 1920s, Grace Fernald developed a multisensory approach (VAKT) known as the Fernald Method to remediate reading and writing deficits.

This period was a foundation period for the field of learning disabilities as the researchers paired with teachers to create remediation programs for students who had normal intelligence but were experiencing difficulties in acquiring academic skills: (1) disorders of perceptual motor skills (i.e., researcher: Strauss, teacher: Lehtinen), (2) disorders of written language (i.e., researcher: Samuel Orton, teachers: Gillingham & Stillman), and (3) disorders of spoken language (i.e., researcher: Myklebust, teacher: Johnson).

In the 1940s, Heinz Strauss, a psychiatrist and director of Cove School, and Laura Lehtinen, a teacher, concerned with controlling the neurologically-based problems exhibited by brain-injured children (i.e., hyperactivity, impulsivity, short attention span, distractibility) designed a carefully controlled individual learning environment without distractions; and directed learning responses through motor activity and carefully sequenced tasks to be learned (Lovitt, 1989). William Cruickshank (1950s-1990s) utilized the general techniques of Strauss and Lehtinen, integrating the controlled environment with the multisensory approach, and modification of the learning materials to increase the instructional stimulus (Lerner, 1993). Cruickshank, also, stressed a readiness curriculum prior to academics that used concrete objects (i.e., puzzles, blocks, stencils) to teach perceptual tasks to students with learning disabilities (Lovitt, 1989).

Historical Special Education Period: 1960s–1980s

During the late 1960s and 1970s, both regular and special education began to be influenced by teaching techniques based on principles of behavioral psychology. These specialized behavioral teaching procedures included Skinner's operant conditioning (i.e., reinforcement, contingency contracting, time-out, token economies); Bandura's social learning theory (observational learning); and Meichenbaum's cognitive behavior modification. Behavioral techniques were more concerned with educational procedures than with specific curriculum. Direct teaching with structured modeling using concrete materials and increased focus on performance rate has been used successfully as a method of teaching concrete skills to students with mild disabilities.

Students with Mental Retardation

A common approach to instructing children and youth with mental retardation during the late 1960s and 1970s was using behavioral teaching techniques to implement developmental curricula. Age-appropriate behaviors in a developmental curriculum included the following: (1) **Infancy and Early Childhood Ages**: Sensory motor skills, communication, self-help skills, socialization skills; (2) **Childhood and Early Adolescence**: Application of basic academics in daily life activities, application of reasoning and judgment in mastering the environment, social skills; (3) **Adolescence and Adult Life**: Vocational and social responsibilities and performances (Grossman, 1973).

During the 1980s, the education of individuals with mental retardation focused on essential living skills which included daily living activities, social skills, and work skills. Two frequently used curriculum programs were Brolin's (1986) The *Life Centered Career Education* (LCCE), and the *Hawaiian Transition Project* (1987).

Students with Emotional Disturbance

During the 1960s the psychodynamic perspective dominated programs for children and youth with behavior disorders (Shea & Bauer, 1994). Psychoeducational interventions included milieu therapy, clinical teaching, Life-Space Interviewing, Reality Therapy, and the various therapies used with children including play, puppetry, dance, drama, music, art, and physical education. Milieu therapy is total environmental control usually in a hospital or institution with consistent expectations and consequences for students (Reinert, 1980). Clinical teaching (Shea & Bauer, 1994), Life-Space Interviewing (Redl, 1959), and Reality Therapy (Glasser, 1965) were school-based counseling techniques to help students sort out problems, behave responsibly, and make sound decisions when confronted with a problem.

When the public schools began to assume responsibility for teaching children and youth with emotional and behavior disorders, there were difficulties translating psychodynamic therapies into educational practices (Paul, 1991). Norris Haring and E. Lakin Phillips combined Cruickshank's structured environment classroom with Skinner's operant conditioning to develop educational programs for students with behavior disorders (Henley et al., 1993). Thus, the techniques for teaching students with behavior disorders focused on integrating structure and behavior management techniques rather than on specific educational curriculum.

Students with Learning Disabilities

During the 1960s and early 1970s, learning disabilities was defined (EHA, 1975) and remediated as basic psychological process deficits resulting in disorders in academics. Educational programming focused on process training or multisensory approaches to teaching academics. The behavioral approach became very popular with teachers of students with learning disabilities in the mid-1970s and early 1980s with a focus on task-analyzed skills, literal level academics, concern with rate of response, direct instruction of skills (Mercer, 1997). However, behaviorism was primarily an instructional approach applied to curriculum rather than a specific curriculum.

In the 1970s, a number of university research centers were established to create curriculum for students with learning disabilities: University of Kansas, learning strategies curriculum for secondary students; University of Illinois-Chicago, social competence and communication; University of Virginia, cognitive theory and controlling attention; Columbia University, improving basic skills. The results of these research centers significantly impacted the learning disabilities curriculum of the 1980s and 1990s.

During the 1970s–1980s, the education curriculum received by students with mild disabilities depended on the philosophy of the school district and the perceived purpose of special education. The most popular elementary school models used were the resource room for children with learning disabilities; separate self-contained classrooms for students with behavior disorders;

and separate self-contained classrooms for students with mental retardation depending on their functioning levels.

Many elementary schools used the resource room to remediate basic skills, and enable the students to "fit" into one of the three reading or math groups within their elementary classroom. The special education curriculum in this instance was the general education curriculum, but at a modified or lower level in the district adopted textbooks. The self-contained classroom for students with learning disabilities was used when students were not able to "catch up" enough to fit into one of the elementary classroom groups. The curriculum in the self-contained classroom for students with learning disabilities often did not use district level textbooks, but specially designed remedial textbooks to achieve in core academics and functional skills. The special education teachers were not concerned with grade level skills only, but with skills hierarchies in various academic fields.

At the secondary levels, the models most often selected by the school district were (1) basic academic remediation model, (2) tutorial model, (3) functional academics model, (4) learning strategies model, (5) work- study model, and (6) life skills model (Mercer & Mercer, 2000). The basic academic remediation curriculum focused on developing reading and mathematics usually at elementary grade levels. General education classroom teachers saw little benefit of this model in their classrooms. The most popular model used was the tutorial model in which students attended regular classes briefly and then went to the resource classroom for 1:1 or 1:3 teacher assistance with assignments. General education teachers preferred the tutorial model because the students with disabilities handed-in completed assignments without additional work on the part of the general education teacher.

Students needing functional curriculums and work-study curriculums usually attended self-contained programs. The learning strategies model resource classroom approach requires extensive training of the special education teacher and students prior to being able to use the strategies to access knowledge across the general education curriculum. Ultimately, the learning strategies model provides the students the greatest benefit as they learn strategies that teach them how to learn (access, retain, produce) information from the class texts.

At the secondary level, parallel educational systems often resulted in a mini-high school for students with disabilities where they changed classes just like the students in general education, however, they changed from one class to another that were taught only by special education teachers. The curriculum was often based on the state's minimum competency skills derived from the state's minimum competency test results. Students who passed minimum competency tests would receive a diploma; other students received a "certificate of attendance."

Historical Special Education Period: Early to Mid–1990s

Students with Mental Retardation

The 1990s revealed a new definition of mental retardation by the American Association on Mental Retardation (AAMR) with a focus on the degree of support needed to function appropriately in an environment. The definition of mental retardation concerned four dimensions: I. Intellectual Functioning and Adaptive Skills; II. Psychological and Emotional Considerations; III. Physical and Health; and IV. Environmental Considerations (Luckasson, 1992). Some of the AAMR 1992 definition changes were positive including classifying individuals in terms of the levels of support needed to achieve, and the reconceptualization of adaptive behavior into ten specific adaptive skill areas. However, there has been considerable dissatisfaction with the AAMR 1992 definition (Bierne-Smith, Ittenback, & Patton, 2002). IDEA, however, continues to use the 1973 AAMR definition which was republished with minor working changes in 1983 (Heward 2006).

Another positive result of the 1992 AAMR definition change was the development of a functional curriculum based on the ten adaptive behavior areas involved in daily life functions (i.e., self-care, home living, self-direction, health and safety, functional academics); and socially appropriate behavior (i.e., social skills, communication, leisure, work) (Luckasson, 1992). In addition, most students with mild-to-moderate mental retardation also need self-determination curriculum skills (Heward, 2006).

Students with Emotional Disturbance

The 1990s has seen a resurgence of humanist psychological theory focusing on four major principles: self-regulated learning, affective education, authentic assessment, and self-motivation. These principles have been applied to students with emotional disturbance in assisting them to control their severely aggressive or withdrawn behaviors. Several social and metacognitive curricular programs (overlapping humanist and cognitive theories) have been used successfully in modifying and changing students with behavior disorders including the following: *The Metacognitive Approach to Social Skills Training* (Sheinker et al., 1988); *Social Skills for Daily Living* (Schumaker et al., 1988); *Skill Streaming the Elementary School Child* (McGinnis & Goldstein, 1997); and *Skill Streaming in Early Childhood* (McGinnis & Goldstein, 2003).

Students with Learning Disabilities

The learning disabilities research centers established in the 1970s began to have significant impact in the 1980s and on into the 1990s in educating students with learning disabilities. Cognitive psychology and the research regarding perception, attention, memory, metacognition, and cognitive problem-solving greatly influenced both general education and special education teachers and students. **The Learning Strategies Curriculum**, a metacognitive approach developed at the University of Kansas research center, has proved to be effective in teaching students with learning disabilities, especially adolescents. The Strategies Curriculum teaches students how to learn or the acquisition and storage of information, and demonstration of competence. Its purpose is to teach students to gain more from their academic curriculum. Humanist and cognitive constructivist theories, methods, and curriculum have overlapped with the focus on cooperative learning, whole language, literature-based reading, literature-based mathematics, and inquiry science.

HISTORICAL SPECIAL EDUCATION LAW AND CURRICULUM

The majority of special education legislation and litigation since 1975 and the passage of Education for All Handicapped Children Act has been more concerned with free public education, least restrictive environment, due process, and nondiscriminatory evaluation than with curriculum for learners with disabilities. "Appropriate education" in the past was seldom litigated due to the lack of specific definition. However, embedded in the special education laws are curriculum requirements, especially in IDEA 1997 and IDEA 2004.

Education for All Handicapped Children Act of 1975

Six major principles of law now exist as a result of the passage of Special Education Laws including the following (Turnbull, 2006):

1. **Principle of Zero Reject**: Schools must educate all children 0–21 years with disabilities, regardless of the nature or severity of the disability.
2. **Principle of Nondiscriminatory Evaluation**: The student is evaluated in all areas of suspected disability and in a way that is not biased by race, language or cultural characteristics or disabilities. Evaluation must be administered by a trained multidisciplinary team using nonbiased, multifactored methods of evaluation. No single evaluation

procedure may be used as the sole criterion for placement or planning.

3. **Principle of Least Restrictive Environment**: The student with disabilities must be educated in the least restrictive environment consistent with his or her educational needs and, insofar as possible, with students without disabilities. Each school district is required to provide a continuum of placement and services alternatives.

4. **Principle of Appropriate Education**: All children with disabilities will be provided a free, appropriate public education. An Individualized Education Program (IEP) is written for each student with a disability including levels of functioning, long-term (annual) goals, short-term objectives (optional), extent to which student will not participate in the general education classroom and curriculum, and the special education and related services to be provided including transition services, as needed.

5. **Principle of Procedural Due Process**: Schools must provide safeguards to protect the rights of children with disabilities and their parents. Parents have rights to information and informed consent before their child is evaluated, labeled, or placed; and the right to an impartial due process hearing if they disagree with the school's decisions.

6. **Principle of Parent Participation**: Schools must collaborate with the parents of students with disabilities in the design and implementation of special education services.

The Education for All Handicapped Children Act of 1975 (EHA) specifically required that each student with disabilities have an Individualized Education Program (IEP), in other words, a specific individual educational curriculum which would include goals and objectives (Haring et al., 1994). The EHA amendments, also, required the development of an IEP that contains an appropriate educational program outline, a modified general education curriculum when appropriate, and supplemental aids and services (Shea & Bauer, 1994; Haring et al., 1994).

In 1986 <u>PL99-476</u>, Congress included mandated provisions in the Education of Handicapped Children Act Amendments to expand educational services through the public schools for disabled children ages 3–5 years beginning in academic year 1991–1992; and provided grants for services to infants and toddlers ages birth–2 years.

In 1990 PL101-476, an amendment to PL94-142,was passed which changed the name of Education for All Handicapped Children Act (EHA, 1975) to Individuals with Disabilities Education Act (IDEA, 1900). This change was because the law provided services for individuals with disabilities from birth–21 years, rather than just to children. Another change was the recommendation of the use of the term "disabled or disabilities" rather than the term "handicapped." Additional major changes specified in IDEA 1990 included the following:

1. IDEA 1990 required transition services for disabled teens and an Individualized Transition Plan (ITP) by age 14 years.
2. Two new categories of disabilities were added to the previous list of disabilities served by IDEA: Autism, and Traumatic Brain Injury.
3. States are not immune from lawsuits by private citizens if the state violates the law under IDEA, as a result of a U.S. Supreme Court decision.
4. Early intervention programs are to be developed to address the needs of children prenatally exposed to maternal substance abuse.

In 1991, Congress passed an amendment to IDEA to provide services to disabled and at-risk preschoolers ages 3–5 years; to infants birth–2 years with developmental delays, established risk such as medical diagnosis of a disability, biological risk conditions such as premature birth or low-birth-weight syndrome, and to children with environmental risks such as poverty and its correlates, child abuse or neglect (Heward, 2006).

Individuals with Disabilities Education Act 1997

Most of the basic requirements of the reauthorization of Individuals with Disabilities Education Act 1997 have been in the law since the 1977 Federal regulations (CEC: A Primer. . . , 2005). However, the mandated changes have had significant effect on the curriculum, assessment, teaching methodology, and monitoring of students with disabilities. Congress mandated that school districts must document that students with disabilities have access to the general education curriculum, and they must, also, document the students involvement with and the progress in the general education curriculum. Additionally, students with disabilities are required to participate in the state wide and district-wide testing programs.

Additional requirements of IDEA 97 included the following:

1. School districts must report achievements (i.e., report cards) to parents of students with disabilities regarding the progress of their child/youth at least as often as teachers report to parents of students in general education.
2. Charter schools must serve children with disabilities.

3. Young children experiencing developmental delays and who need special education and related special education services may be designated as "children with a disability," thus, they do not need a categorical label in order to receive special education services.

4. Children with a diagnosis of attention deficit disorder or attention deficit hyperactivity disorder may be eligible for special education services under the "Other Health Impairment" category.

5. New IEP Requirements:
   • A statement of the child's present levels of educational performance, including how the child's disability affects her involvement and progress in the general education curriculum.
   • For preschool children, the IEP must describe how the disability affects the child's participation in appropriate activities.

6. List any modifications in the administration of state-wide or district-wide assessments that are needed for the child to participate in the assessment.

7. If the child was involved in drugs, brought weapons to school, or engaged in behavior that would result in injury to self or others, the school may change placement to a more restrictive placement for immediate intervention.

DISCIPLINE. There were significant additions in IDEA 1997 that concerned discipline of students with disabilities. A major focus was that the student with disabilities could be disciplined, however, the student must continue to receive educational services even in a temporary alternative setting. If a student with disabilities violates a school rule there are a number of procedures that must take place to ensure that the student's due process rights have been covered including the following: (1) convening the IEP team immediately; (2) manifestation determination; (3) functional behavioral assessment; (4) behavioral intervention plan; (5) change of placement considered; and (6) behavior plan added to IEP.

After a child/youth with disabilities has violated a school rule, the IEP team reviews the child's file to determine if there is a current Behavior Intervention Plan, and was the current behavior indicated on it. The team must consider the misbehavior to determine if it is a manifestation of the student's disability. If there is no current Behavior Intervention Plan, the team will conduct a Functional Behavior Assessment and prepare a Behavioral Intervention Plan.

Schools may remove the student from his/her current placement for a period of up to 45 days in an Interim Alternative Educational Setting (IAES) at which time he/she participates in general education academics (although in another setting) and his/her inappropriate behavior will be addressed so that it does not occur again.

Current Special Education Law and Curriculum

The education of children and youth with disabilities changed dramatically with the passage of IDEA 97 which required that all students with disabilities use the general education curriculum, with the exception of 1–3 percent of the students with disabilities. Additionally, all children and youth with disabilities, except 1–3 percent of the most severely disabled, must take the state standards-based test given to all non-disabled students. IDEA 2004 was aligned with NCLB 2001/2007 to reinforce the mandates of IDEA 1997.

Individuals with Disabilities Education Improvement Act 2004

The new Individuals with Disabilities Education Improvement Act (IDEA, 2004) includes several areas related specifically to curriculum: (1) IEP changes, (2) early intervention Services, (3) discipline, (4) accessible instructional materials for children with disabilities, and (5) changes in identifying students with learning disabilities.

IEP CHANGES. In an effort to reduce paperwork, special education teachers are required to only write measurable goals. Short-term objectives are only required for a very small percentage of children, generally less than 1 percent of students with disabilities/who are taking alternate assessments aligned to alternate achievement standards (CEC, 2005, A Primer on IDEA 2004). However, even if short-term objectives are not mandated by law, all parents can still request that their child's team identify short-term objectives. Without short-term objectives parents will have virtually no way of measuring whether their children are making progress in achieving their annual goals; and teachers will not have a guide as to the intervening steps that should be taken towards achieving these goals and when they should be taken. Without short-term objectives, teachers will have difficulty developing meaningful progress reports to parents (IDEA 2004).

EARLY INTERVENTION SERVICES (EIS). Under IDEA 2004 (CEC 2005, A Primer on IDEA 2004; IDEA Partnerships, undated), school districts can develop early intervention services for students in grades K–12. These services are provided for students who have not been identified as needing special education but who require academic or behavioral support to succeed in general education classes. EIS reduces the need to determine that a child has a disability before providing support. EIS provides for educational and behavioral evaluations, services, supports, and scientifically-based literacy instruction, as well as professional development. Districts that experience substantial disproportionate representation must use the maximum amount of funds to provide EIS, particularly for groups that were significantly overidentified for special education. At any time, a child can be referred for evaluation and the right to a free, appropriate public education. Children previously identified as disabled can receive EIS (CEC, 2005, A Primer on IDEA 2004).

DISCIPLINE. The IDEA 2004 regulations expand the school's discretion as well as give additional guidance on disciplining students with disabilities. Some of the topics the regulations address include change of placement, the school's basis of knowledge of a disability, and manifestation determination: (1) school personnel have new authority to consider unique circumstances on a case-by-case basis when determining whether a placement change is appropriate for a child with a disability who violates a code of student conduct; and (2) the school has the ability to move a child to an Interim Alternate Educational Setting (IAES) for up to 45 days. If a child's removal from his or her present educational setting is a change of placement, the IEP team determines appropriate services for the child. The change in placement is for more than 10 consecutive school days and the behavior is not a manifestation of the disability, the removal is a change of placement. The removal for special circumstances is related to drugs, weapons, or serious bodily injury.

A child who has not been determined to be eligible for special education and has violated a code of student conduct has all the IDEA protections if the school knew the child had a disability before he or she committed the behavior. In other words, if the child has a history of behavioral problems, the child's parents have requested an evaluation of the child, other teachers or district personnel have expressed specific concerns about the child's behavior patterns, then the child falls under the IDEA protections (CEC, 2004, A Primer on IDEA 2004). The burden of proof for the manifestation determination review has now been shifted to the parents who have to prove that the behavior was caused by or had a direct substantial relationship to the disability (FAPE, IDEA Partnerships, undated).

ACCESSIBLE INSTRUCTIONAL MATERIALS FOR CHILDREN WITH DISABILITIES. Under IDEA, public schools must provide children with disabilities with timely access to appropriate and accessible instructional materials. The IDEA 2004 regulations state that (CEC, 2005, A Primer on IDEA 2004):

- States must adopt the **National Instructional Materials Accessibility Standards,** which were published on July 19, 2006.
- States must establish a definition of "timely access" to accessible instructional materials.

• States must take all reasonable steps to provide these materials to children with disabilities at the same time nondisabled children receive instructional materials.

• School districts must ensure that all children with disabilities who need instructional materials in accessible formats receive them in a timely manner, regardless of whether or not the children receive special education services.

Changes in Identifying Students with Learning Disabilities. IDEA 2004 included a special rule for the identification of specific learning disabilities. It provided that an LEA (local education agency) is not required to take into account whether the student has a "severe discrepancy between achievement and intellectual ability." The LEA may use a "severe discrepancy standard", but it is not required to do so. The LEA may, but is not required to use a "process that determines if the child responds to scientific, research-based intervention" which is referred to as Response-to-Intervention (RTI) (Turnbull et al., 2006, p. 33).

Response-to-Intervention System of Tiers

Response-to-Intervention is in the early stages of development and is still being researched. On October 18, 2007, the Council for Exceptional Children published its "Position on Response to Intervention" which Deviated from the generic statements in IDEA 2004 that Response-to-Intervention was a special rule for the identification of students with specific learning disabilities. CEC has insisted on a number of specifications Regarding RTI including the following:

1. RTI is a process designed for early identification of and intervention for children at-risk for academic failure (not just for children with specific learning disabilities).
2. RTI must be a school-wide initiative.
3. RTI must be a multitiered problem-solving process with at least three tiers.
4. RTI must provide data on how a child responds to scientifically-based intervention.
5. The RTI process is part of a comprehensive evaluation required for identification of any disability and not a substitute for a comprehensive evaluation.
6. RTI must not delay the referral for a comprehensive evaluation of a child who is suspected of having a disability (CEC, October 18, 2007).

There are a few RTI models that are being piloted. "The RTI models have several components in common: RTI uses tiers of intervention for struggling students, relies on research-based instruction and interventions, uses problem-solving to determine interventions for students, and monitors students regularly to determine if they are progressing as they should academically and/or behaviorally" (CEC, Nov. 9, 2007, Response to Intervention).

Response-to-Intervention combines important features of assessment and instruction. Professionals have specified that the core features of RTI must include the following:

I. Assessment Features:
    1. School-wide initiative (CEC, 2007)
    2. Assessment aligned with state standards (James, F. 2004)
    3. Multi-tiered problem-solving process (CEC, 2007)
    4. Pre-identification strategy (James, F., 2004)
    5. Diagnostic-prescriptive learning system (Mellard, 2003)
    6. Universal Screening (Mellard, 2003)
    7. Assessment in general education (Mellard, 2003)
    8. Continuous progress monitoring during interventions (Mellard, 2003)
    9. Classroom teachers design and complete student assessments (Mellard, 2003)
II. Instruction/Intervention Features:
    1. High quality classroom instruction (Mellard, 2003)
    2. Research-based interventions (Mellard, 2003)
    3. Research-based instruction (Mellard, 2003)
    4. Multi-tiered intervention (CEC, 2007)
    5. Progress monitoring during interventions (CEC, 2007)
    6. Fidelity measures (Mellard, 2003)

The Response-to-Intervention System of Tiers (see TABLE 1) was created to illustrate the RTI process and the use of the assessment features and intervention features in a Three-Tier RTI System.

Tier I: General Education

Tier I: General Education is the first step in the district-wide Response-to-Intervention initiative. During Tier I all students are receiving state standards-based curricula in the state-adopted textbooks in the general education classrooms, and on a scheduled basis all students receive state standards-based assessment. Tier I indicates that the state standards-based assessment will be considered the Universal Screening for **Tier III: Special Education**.

Records are kept on the scores students achieve on the Universal Screening or the scores students earn in the various core curriculum courses including language arts/reading, math and science which are tested and monitored as part of the No Child Left Behind Act (NCLB 2001).

A final expectation of **Tier I: General Education** was suggested by Mellard (2003) that classroom teachers design and complete the monitoring assessments. Curriculum-Based Assessments (CBAs) prepared using the state adopted textbooks are perfect to be used in assessing and monitoring student progress in the general education curriculum. A text that provides teacher-friendly directions to creating and using CBAs and a District-Wide CBA System is by Carroll Jones (2008): **Curriculum-Based Assessment: The Easy Way to Determine Response-to-Intervention** (2nd edition). Springfield, IL: Thomas. The preparation of a District-Wide CBA System for Response-to-Intervention Process is ideal for the Universal Screening Assessments.

Pre-Tier II: Conferences

The **Pre-Tier II Conferences** serve as an important part of the RTI problem-solving process. Conferences should be held frequently considering the progress of students who are experiencing significant difficulties in general education. The Committee(s) will consider students general academic functioning levels, grades in the core curriculum courses, and their functioning on the Universal Screening Test (state standards-based assessments). The Committee(s) will determine if the student needs more intensive intervention as provided in Tier II interventions. One significant concern regarding the RTI Tier System is the lack of consideration of the cognitive functioning of the students performing below grade level as related to low scores on the Universal Screening assessment in Tier I and Tier II.

Tier II: General Education + Tier II Interventions

The school district will need to have predetermined functioning levels or scores that are used to determine when low functioning students will move from one Tier to the next. Students who function below grade level and meet the school district requirements for **Tier II Interventions** will be referred to Title I Reading and/or Mathematics programs, or other individual or small group compensatory remediation (see TABLE 1). These students will receive research-based instruction and intervention using a diagnostic-prescriptive approach.

After a predetermined time (such as 8–12 weeks) with frequent progress monitoring (using the District-Wide CBA System) indicating that the student has not made adequate progress with instruction in the general education classroom plus intensive remediation in Tier II, teachers will begin the next RTI problem-solving stage. However, school districts will need to determine how many interventions a child may receive before going to the next Tier. Prior to being moved to **Tier III: Special Education**, the school district will need to implement the special education evaluation process which will be covered in three stages: **Pre-Tier III: Pre-Referral Conference**, **Pre-Tier III: Special Education Comprehensive Evaluation**, and **Pre-Tier III: Individual Education Program Conference** (see TABLE 1).

Pre-Tier III: Pre-Referral Conference

During the second problem-solving conference, a special education teacher and/or school psychologist will explain to the classroom teacher that the CBA-RTI will be put into place. The special education teacher or classroom teacher will individually administer the District-Wide CBA System in the areas in which the student experiences difficulty. These scores will be used as a baseline for the 8–12 weeks (or other specified time) of intensive core instruction with frequent monitoring using the CBA System. At the end of the intervention period, the student will again be administered CBAs from the District-Wide CBA System (probably Form B).

After the 8–12 weeks of intensive core instruction, the Pre-Tier III: Pre-Referral Conference Committee will consider the student's performance, the scores on the CBA System assessment (pre-and-post tests), scores on the frequent monitoring assessments, scores on the Universal Screening test (state standards-based tests), and decide if the student should be referred for Special Education Evaluation.

Pre-Tier III: Special Education Comprehensive Evaluation

At this point the Committee has completed the required steps including the Referral Form for a comprehensive evaluation and parent permission. The evaluation team will administer a standardized comprehensive test battery including intelligence testing, language testing, academic testing, social/emotional testing, and other assessments as needed in a comprehensive evaluation. The evaluation team will prepare report(s) that include the standardized test battery information, the results of the District-Wide CBA System evaluation (state adopted textbook-based), and the results of the intervention (see TABLE 1).

Pre-Tier III: IEP Conference

The IEP Committee will consider all of the information presented to determine if the student meets the eligibility criteria to qualify for special education and related services. In addition to the new information from the comprehensive evaluation and the District-Wide CBA System evaluation, the committee will also consider the student's educational history including **Tier I: General Education** information from the Universal Screening and the student's progress in the standards-based curriculum, Tier II information from Title 1 and/or compensatory instruction, and the results from the CBA monitoring; as well as the assessment information from the **Pre-Tier III: PreReferral Conferences** regarding the 8–12 weeks of intensive core instruction and monitoring (see TABLE 1).

Once the committee determines that the student meets special education eligibility requirements and is determined to be a child with a disability, the Individual Education Program (IEP) will be developed and instructional placement(s) will be determined. The IEP will be developed from the District-Wide CBA System results which provides textbook-specific and skill-specific information regarding educational functioning in the district's textbooks; and other services as needed. The student then moves to **Tier III: Special Education** and is provided the special education and related services by special education teachers.

Tier III: Special Education

In **Tier III: Special Education**, the student with a disability will spend a specified amount of time usually in the special education resource classroom where special education teachers provide intensive intervention in areas of deficiency using diagnostic-prescriptive instructional methods, direct instruction, research-based interventions, and frequent progress monitoring using the District-Wide CBA System that provides textbook specific and skill specific information on the student's performance. Most students with exceptional needs also spend a majority of the day in the general education classroom receiving instruction with peers. The District-Wide CBA System referred to in **Tier 1: General Education** will be used by special education teachers for short-term (daily or weekly) monitoring of progress toward goals and objectives on the Individual Education Program, and annual pre-and-post testing for updating the IEP.

Special Education Curriculum Comments

Until the passage of IDEA 1997, general education and special education curricula selected for a student with disabilities was not concerned with the grade level expectations for a student his/her age/grade level, but the functioning level of the student in a hierarchy of academic skills and other areas of need. Each IEP was prepared specifically for one student based on that student's strengths and weaknesses, and disability-specific concerns.

Prior to IDEA 97, curriculum was selected from numerous available task analyzed curricula on the basis of a child's needs and preferences, and integrated by the special education teacher for the IEP. Special education teachers considered a student's skills and needs from a life-time perspective.

The curriculum (IEP) concerned age-appropriate, developmentally-appropriate, and functionally-appropriate skills. Students with mild disabilities used the general education textbooks either modified or at lower reading levels, and any of the other curriculums as needed such as adaptive behavior skills.

Additionally, students with disabilities often used books and materials other than the ones used in the general education classrooms. Examples of the types of curricula used in educating students with disabilities included the following: Functional Academics, Adaptive Behavior Skills, Community Living, Behavior Modification, Learning Strategies, Developmental Skills, Work-Study Curricula, Self-Determination Curricula, Basic Academics, Essential Living Skills, Pre-Vocational and Vocational Training, and a Modified General Education. Each of these curriculums had books and materials designed specially for students with disabilities.

Today, all children regardless of disability, intelligence level, and academic functioning level, are expected to use the specific books and materials used by the students in the general education curriculum and to make progress in the general education curriculum as a result of changes in the Individuals with Disabilities Education Act 1997. If this was possible most children/youth would not have needed special education or been found eligible for it.

When IDEA 1997 was aligned with the No Child Left Behind Act (2001), there was an unprecedented shift in special education policy from an accountability mechanism based on procedural compliance with federal and state law to one based on the academic performance of students with disabilities on state standards-based tests (Skrtic et al., 2005, Preface ix). This policy shift used support and funding from two different groups of special needs children, those from low socioeconomic environments (NCLB) and disabled students (IDEA) to force a standards-based reform (SBR) movement in general education. There is much concern among educators about the special needs students who are being held accountable for their progress in the general education curriculum, as are their teachers, principals, and schools when it was known previously that they probably could not accomplish the general education academic standards. Is this appropriate education for students with disabilities or for students from low socioeconomic environments who are all functioning below grade level?

SUMMARY

The public school system is a small microcosm of society which mirrors society's cultural, social, political, economic, ethical, historical, and personal beliefs and problems. The curriculum or content of instruction is built on the goals of education set forth by federal, state, and local education agencies.

Throughout history the curriculum of schools in the United States has reflected society's needs. During the colonial period (1625–1775), the basic curriculum reflected the religious influences and was composed of reading, writing, arithmetic; catechism, prayers, and hymns; and home living. The political influence of 1776 to 1876 on curriculum added history, geography, agriculture, physiology and hygiene, grammar and composition, drawing and music to the "3 R's." The religious influences were eliminated. The latter part of this period saw the beginning experimentation with teaching children with mental retardation using Itard and Seguin's revolutionary curriculum, some adaptive behavior skills and home living skills.

Social and economic influences of 1876–1929 resulted in curriculum changes with correlated basic curriculum, domestic science, manual training, and democratic living skills. The Post War 1940s–1960s placed importance on current affairs, studying a second language, and an air-age education with increased requirements in math and science. Special education for students with mental retardation focused on developmental skills and adaptive behaviors. The curriculum for the new field of learning disabilities stressed remediation of disorders of perceptual motor skills, disorders of written and spoken language.

The 1970s and 1980s affected by civil unrest and social change stressed a "return to basics" (3 R's), appropriate social and behavioral skills, and computer literacy in general education. The behavioral approach was used in teaching students with emotional disturbance; a developmental curriculum, essential living skills and work skills was the curriculum focus for students with mental retardation. The students with learning disabilities were taught information processing skills, learning strategies, and a modified general education academic curriculum.

Accountability has been a significant focus since the 1980s and has continued to build in support. Using a standards-based academics curriculum focus, politicians have pressed for accountability from teachers, principals, and students. The standards-based reform of general education curriculum is currently being driven by the alignment of IDEA and NCLB forcing all students into the general education curriculum and standards-based tests.

Although few debate the importance of standards-based curriculum, there are many professionals concerned with the appropriateness of forcing all students from low socioeconomic backgrounds and almost all students with disabilities to use the general education curriculum, the general education standards-based testing, and judging schools by the scores all students make on high stakes testing. There has been concern about appropriate alternate assessment for students with disabilities, but so far this is reserved for only about 2 percent of the most severely disabled students.

TABLE 1

RESPONSE-TO-INTERVENTION SYSTEM OF TIERS

TIER III: SPECIAL EDUCATION
* Intensive Special Education Intervention
* Annual Updating IEPs Using CBAs
* Annual Pre- & Post-Testing Using CBAs
* Monitoring IEP Progress Using CBAs

Pre-Tier III: IEP Conference
* Determine eligibility
* Determine placement
* Write IEP using District-
  Wide CBAs

PRE-TIER III: SPED COMPREHENSIVE EVALUATION
* Standardized Test Battery
* Results of 8-12 weeks of intensive instruction
* District-Wide CBA System

Pre-Tier III: Pre-Referral Conference
* CBA Screening & RTI Intervention
* 8-12 weeks of intensive instruction
* Universal Screening for Tier III

TIER II: GENERAL EDUCATION + TIER II
* Title I Reading/Math/etc. in small groups
* Compensatory Remediation in small groups
* Continuous Progress Monitoring using CBAs

Pre-Tier II: Conference
* General Class Functioning (Grades, etc.)
* Functioning Levels in Core Curriculum
* Universal Screening Results

TIER I: GENERAL EDUCATION
* State Standards-Based Curriculum
* State Standards-Based Assessment
  (Universal Screening for Tier III)
* Progress Monitoring (whole class)
* Create District-Wide CBA System

Jones, C.J. (2008): <u>Curriculum-Based Assessment: The Easy Way to Determine Response-to-Intervention</u>. Table 55, page 179. Springfield, IL: Thomas.

Chapter 2

THE CURRICULUM DEVELOPMENT PROCESS

CBAs are very useful as they incorporate the best characteristics of informal tests and criterion-referenced tests, and directly assess students' mastery of the curriculum. With this information, teachers can write skill specific IEPs for students with mild disabilities.

(Jones, 2008, 11)

IDEA IEP Requirements
Special Education Assessment
IEP Development Process Using NRTs
　　Evaluation Report Information
　　Writing Michael's IEP
IEP Development Process Using CBAs
IEP Development Process Using State Standards
Summary
Curriculum Development Process: Tables 2–6

One of the most difficult, time-consuming, and important responsibilities of a special education teacher is the preparation of Individual Education Programs for each of his/her students with disabilities. This task requires the special education teacher to possess in-depth knowledge of: (1) the general education curriculum; (2) state curriculum frameworks; (3) assessment and evaluation; (4) state standards-based tests; (5) interpreting the results of the multidisciplinary evaluation to determine a student's functioning levels and global strengths and weaknesses; (6) scope and sequence charts; (7) pedagogy or teaching methods and strategies for modifying the general education curriculum, and (8) teaching and assessment materials.

IDEA IEP REQUIREMENTS

An Individual Education Program (IEP) is a specially designed curriculum for a specific child or adolescent with disabilities. Usually the curriculum for students with mild disabilities is a modified general education curriculum. PL94-142 (IDEA 1975) required that the IEP include at minimum the following information: (1) current levels of educational performance; (2) annual goals and short-term instructional objectives; (3) specific special education and related services to be provided and the extent of participation in general education programs; (4) projected dates for initiation and the anticipated duration of services; and (5) appropriate evaluation procedures, criteria, and schedules for measuring attainment of objectives on at least an annual basis (Federal Register, 1977).

IDEA 1997 IEPs

The IDEA 1997 mandated several changes to the Individual Education Program. "The IEP will move from a deficit-based educational plan to one that is strength-based. IDEA 1997 is based on the belief that the majority of students with disabilities can participate in the general education curriculum to varying degrees" (CEC, 1998, 3). All children and youth (except for 1%) will be involved in and make progress in the general education curriculum (CEC, 2005, A Primer on IDEA 1997 Regulations). The IEP should include documentation and an explanation of how the student will progress toward achieving short-term objectives and the annual goals, and how the student will be monitored throughout the year. The IEP must also include how progress information will be reported to parents (CEC, 1998, 3). Further, parents of children with disabilities must be informed of their child's progress at least as regularly as parents of nondisabled students, as to how well the student is benefiting and moving toward meeting his/her annual goals (CEC, 1998, 4). An additional requirement of IDEA 1997 is that transition services must be addressed when the student reaches 14 years-of-age rather than 16 years of age.

IDEA 2004 IEPs

In addition to the previous mandated information regarding IEPs (IDEA 1975 and IDEA 1997), IDEA 2004 indicated some additional changes. The IDEA 2004 regulations specify changes to IEPs that make them more relevant to student progress and to reduce paperwork. IEPs must include a statement of the student's present levels of academic achievement in the general education curriculum and in functional performance. IEPs must have measurable goals statements including academic and functional goals (CEC, 2006, A Primer on the IDEA 2004 Regulations). A primary departure from IEP regulations in previous years is that teachers may omit writing measurable benchmarks and short-term objectives in order to reduce paperwork (CEC, 2006, A Primer on the IDEA 2004 Regulations).

Since benchmarks and short-term objectives are very important steps in determining progress toward the goals, many parents and teachers will want them included on the IEP or on a supplemental program development sheet called the Individual Implementation Plan (IIP). States may continue to use the benchmarks and short-term objectives for all students, but they must inform the districts and the U.S. Department of Education (CEC, 2006, A Primer on the IDEA 2004). Also, parents may request that teachers add short-term objectives to their child's IEP to assist them in determining the progress their child is making toward achieving his/her goals.

Benchmarks and short-term objectives are required for the children who take alternate assessments (CEC, 2006, A Primer on the IDEA 2004 Regulations). There must be a statement in the IEP indicating why the child cannot participate in general education assessments and why the alternate assessment selected is appropriate for the child.

Transition services must be included in the IEP when the student is 16 or younger. When the IEP team meets to discuss the student's post-secondary goals and transition services, the student must be invited to the meeting, and his/her interests must be considered. Measurable post-secondary goals must be developed for each student based on age-appropriate transition assessments related to his or her training, education, employment, and independent living skills (CEC, 2006, A Primer on IDEA 2004 Regulations).

SPECIAL EDUCATION ASSESSMENT

Assessment is intricately interwoven with all special education procedures dealing with providing an appropriate education. Assessment refers to the process of gathering information about the cognitive, academic, social/emotional, and developmental functioning of a student. In special education there are five types and purposes for assessment:

Type	Purpose	Instruments
1. Screening	Early Detection	Group NRTs, Informal
2. Evaluation	Eligibility	Individual NRTS
3. Programming	Writing IEPs	CBAs, CRTs, Informal
4. IEP Monitoring	Determining Progress	CBAs, CRTs, Informal
5. Program Evaluation	Annual IEP Update	CBAs, CRTs, Informal

(Jones, 2008, 11).

The focus of this book is programming and writing IEPs. Assessment for programming involves using the results of assessment to plan a curriculum or curriculum modifications to use as the annual curriculum outline (IEP) for teaching a specific student with disabilities. The types of assessment instruments which should be administered to gain information regarding programming include criterion-referenced tests (CRTs), curriculum-based assessment (CBAs), informal tests, and state curriculum standards tests because they are related to the skills and content that teachers teach in the classroom.

Criterion-referenced tests (CRTs) are tied to generic hierarchies of skills in academic areas rather than specifically tied to the district or school curriculum. CRTs generally are not normed, but they provide specific information on exactly which skills in the hierarchy a student knows and does not know, and on which skill in the sequence to begin instruction.

Informal tests are usually teacher-made and related directly to classroom instruction, such as weekly social studies or science tests. Unlike CRTs, the scope of the informal tests is not usually great enough to plan sequential skill development for a year. However, there are some generic commercial informal tests such as an Informal Reading Inventory which may have 8–12 different levels of difficulty to use in estimating a student's reading functioning level.

Curriculum-based assessment (CBAs) may include characteristics of CRTs and informal tests (Jones, 2008). Like informal tests, CBAs are based on the content of the district or state-adopted curriculum. Similar to CRTs, CBAs are based on kindergarten through twelfth grade skills hierarchies (scope and sequence charts). However, the content of CBAs are the skills hierarchies embedded in the district or state-adopted textbooks. An important use for CBAs is to determine the student's specific skill knowledge and which level of textbooks the student needs to use for instruction. Thus, CBAs are valuable in planning textbook level specific Individual Education Programs (IEPs) and in determining a child's specific skills for inclusion in the general education classroom curriculum.

State curriculum frameworks contain the state-adopted curriculum standards which become IEP goals in appropriate subject areas (see TABLE 2). The state-adopted curriculum standards are imbedded in the state-adopted textbooks used by students and teachers. The mandated state standards-based tests that must be administered annually to determine student progress (NCLB 2007) are based on the state curriculum frameworks. Curriculum skills hierarchies (subject area scope and sequence charts) are embedded in the state-adopted textbooks and in IEP objectives (see TABLE 2). The CBAs prepared from the state-adopted textbooks are designed to be used more frequently than the annual tests to measure progress in acquiring IEP objectives.

Unfortunately in most cases, the special education teacher is expected to prepare the IEP based on the results of the evaluation for eligibility for special education. Evaluation usually uses norm referenced tests (NRTs) in order to compare a student's functioning to other students of the same age or grade, and are not designed to provide specific information regarding the curriculum. Writing IEPs from NRTs results provides a very rough estimate of the student's annual curriculum. Since this is a task frequently expected of special education teachers, the procedure will be illustrated in this chapter.

IEP DEVELOPMENT PROCESS USING NRTs

In a majority of school districts, the first Individual Education Program (IEP) written for a student utilizes the results of the multidisciplinary evaluation (NRTs). In demonstrating this process, frequent references will be made to Michael's (case study) functioning levels, strengths and weaknesses which were taken from his evaluation report (see TABLE 3) and typed on his Individual Education Program (see TABLE 4). The IEP form used in this chapter for demonstration purposes focuses on the curriculum development aspect and does not include the many other aspects usually included for legality purposes and accountability.

Although Michael has learning disabilities in several academic areas, the IEP will be prepared in many academic areas for demonstration purposes. Therefore, in some areas Michael's curriculum (IEP) will indicate remedial (R) skills needed, and in some areas in which he is functioning on grade level the skills will be age/grade appropriate developmental (D) skills. This process, however, is valuable for three reasons: (1) to provide IEP samples in many academic and social areas for practice; (2) to indicate the remedial skills which will be Michael's actual IEP, usually taught in the resource room; and (3) to indicate grade specific skills or developmental skills that Michael will be taught in the general education classroom.

Additionally, a major purpose of using scope and sequence charts that specify skills taught at various grade levels in general education classrooms is to familiarize special education teachers with the skills students with disabilities need in order to function in the general classroom. Special education teachers usually focus on the criterion-referenced approach with hierarchies of skills in academic areas rather than by grade level. The generic scope and sequence charts in this text were designed to assist special education teachers who need grade specific skills (objectives) in order to prepare IEPs. Most state curriculum frameworks are goals.

Evaluation Report Information

Background and Educational Concerns

Although test interpretation and methods of determining eligibility for special education services are beyond the scope of this book, we will refer to test scores (see TABLE 3) in determining functioning levels in order to write the IEP. The first three pages of the IEP (see TABLE 4) were completed from information in Michael's evaluation report (see TABLE 3). As we proceed, you will need to flip back and forth between Michael's Evaluation Report (see TABLE 3) and the curriculum part of the IEP (see TABLE 4).

a. **Identification Information** (TABLE 4). Find this in TABLE 3.

b. **Reasons for Referral: Cognitive** (TABLE 4). Where did you find this information? (TABLE 3, lst paragraph, last sentence). Cognitive information does not just include intelligence but also characteristics that affect cognition such as attention, perception, memory, metacognitive skills. Intelligence information was not provided in the **Background and Educational Concerns**.

c. **Reasons for Referral: Academic** (TABLE 4). Where did you find this information in the **Background and Educational Concerns**? Find this in TABLE 3, lst and 2nd paragraphs.

d. **Reasons for Referral: Behavioral** (TABLE 4). Where did you find this information in the **Background and Educational Concerns**? Find in TABLE 3, under the **Behavior** heading.

e. **Find the Medical Information** (TABLE 4). Find this information in TABLE 3 in **Background and Educational Concerns**.

f. Read **Speech/Language Screening** (TABLE 4). Use only information in TABLE 3, **Background and Educational Concerns**.

g. Read **Cultural/Economic Disadvantage**, and **Family/Home Information** (TABLE 4). Locate this information in TABLE 3, **Background and Educational Concerns**.

Norm-Referenced Test Scores

The norm-referenced test scores reported are generally grade equivalency (GE), age equivalency (AE), and standard scores (SS). The GEs are compared to Michael's actual grade level (2.9) in school to determine if he is functioning below grade expectancy. The AEs are compared to Michael's chronological age of 8 years 3 months to determine if he is functioning below age expectations. The standard scores (SS), which are probably the most accurate of the norm-referenced test scores, are compared to Michael's Full Scale IQ score to determine if he is functioning as expected for cognitive or intellectual ability. Standard scores are test scores with a mean of 100 and a standard deviation of 15. Tests that have these same characteristics can be compared:

Standard Scores: 131 ↑ Above Average

116-131 High Average

85-115 Average

70-84 Low Average

69 ↓ Below Average (McLoughlin & Lewis, 2008, 67)

Current Evaluation

Michael's Case Study **Psychological Report** (TABLE 3) indicates that he was administered the **Wechsler Intelligence Scale for Children-Revised (WISC-R)** to determine his intellectual functioning. The WISC series of tests is the most frequently used intelligence tests to assess general intellectual performance of school-aged children (McLoughlin & Lewis, 2008, 196). This example is not the most recent version of the test. The WISC-R is divided into two domains, Verbal and Performance; a Full Scale IQ; and under each domain is a list of subtests and scores. Michael's test scores are indicated on the third page of the IEP (see TABLE 4). This information is provided to give a brief explanation of the intelligence test scores and does not suggest the contents of the test or the methods in which the trained tester or school psychologist determines the student's specific abilities.

Wechsler Scores:	IQ Scores		Scaled Scores
	130 +	Very Superior	16-19
	120-129	Superior	14-15
	110-119	High Average	12-13
	90-109	Average	8-11
	80-89	Low Average	6-7
	70-79	Borderline	4-5
	69 & Below	Mentally Deficient	1-3

(Pierangelo and Giuliani, 1998, 34,35).

Read the **Psychological Report** (see TABLE 3) and Intelligence Testing Summary (see TABLE 4). Note that Michael's overall cognitive ability (Full

Scale IQ 112) falls within the high average range. His verbal expressive skills were average (Verbal IQ 107) and his psychomotor skills were high average (Performance IQ 115). His subtest scaled scores ranged from 10 to 14, or from average to superior.

Michael's **information processing test results** (TABLE 3) were listed on the 3rd page of the IEP (see TABLE 4). The school psychologist administered two tests to assess Michael's skills in information processing: **Bender Gestalt Test** and some subtests from the **Detroit Test of Learning Aptitude** (see TABLE 3). On the **Bender Gestalt Test**, Michael's chronological age of (CA 8–3) 8 years 3 months was compared to his age equivalent (AE 9–0 to 9–11) or performance test scores of 9 years to 9 years and 11 months indicating that his ability to draw designs was above expectancy for his age. On the **Detroit** Michael's Age Equivalency (AE) for both subtests were above his chronological age (CA) expectancy. Read the last paragraph of the **Psychological Report Test Interpretation** and find, "on the Detroit both visual memory for letters, and auditory memory for complex oral directions were above age expectancy."

Refer to TABLE 3, **Psycho-Evaluation Report** and to TABLE 4, **Information Processing Scores** which indicate two more information processing tests: **Slingerland Screening Test: Form B** (informal test) and two subtests of the **Woodcock-Johnson: Tests of Cognitive Abilities**. The test interpretation for these tests (see TABLE 3) is under TESTING INTERPRETATION: Learning Modality. Read these test summaries, then turn to TABLE 4 and find the test summaries. **The Slingerland Screening Test** (see TABLE 4) shows scores divided into two categories: Adequate and Inadequate. The Inadequate skills of visual memory, and visual memory with a written response could cause many problems such as learning math facts and steps in algorithms as well as remembering sight words, and doing any written activity. The **Woodcock-Johnson** test scores, perceptual speed (SS 105) and auditory memory (SS 103) compared to his Full Scale IQ 112 are a little low, but still within the average range. Refer to the **Psycho-Evaluation Report**, under Testing Interpretation Summary (TABLE 3) last sentence, for the summary statement for the **Learning Modality** summary (see TABLE 4) under **Information Processing Scores**.

Thus, we have completed the first three pages of Michael's IEP (see TABLE 4) with information from Michael's Evaluation Report (see TABLE 3). We know why Michael was referred for evaluation; his strengths and weaknesses in cognitive, academic, and behavioral areas noted in the classroom; and results from his intelligence evaluation and his information processing evaluation. We know that in spite of having high average range intelligence, he experiences information processing deficits in visual memory and visual memory with a written response, and his academics skills are very weak.

Writing Michael's IEP

In preparing Michael's IEP using NRTs the following process will be followed: (1) determine the current functioning level (see TABLE 3); (2) decide on a goal, usually one year's growth; (3) refer to the appropriate scope and sequence charts for skill areas in the chapters of this textbook at the goal level; (4) transfer the skills to the Instructional Objectives section of the IEP distributed across the number of grading periods (see TABLE 4); and (5) determine possible evaluation materials and methods, the criteria, reporting to parents, assistive technology, as needed. Let's walk through how to complete Michael's IEP to use as a model for completing future similar assignments.

Basic Reading Skills

On the IEP (see TABLE 4), we will first consider the Basic Reading Skills. Basic Reading Skills are divided into two categories of skills: Word Recognition Skills (also called Word Identification Skills) and Word Analysis Skills (also called Word Attack Skills). Word recognition includes two categories of words: (1) high frequency words or sight words that are not decodable and must be memorized; and (2) new words children learn in the stories and content subject areas (e.g., science, social studies) that they read. Word Analysis Skills include strategies for decoding words: Phonics Analysis, Structural Analysis, Contextual Analysis, and Dictionary Analysis Skills.

PRESENT LEVEL OF PERFORMANCE. Michael's performance level scores in word recognition and word analysis from the **Woodcock Reading Mastery Test** results (see TABLE 3), under the Psycho-Educational Report), were previously transferred to the IEP (see TABLE 4) under the **Present Level of Performance** column. The scores indicated are GE (grade equivalency) and SS (standard scores). Strengths and weaknesses are found in the Evaluation Report (see TABLE 3) under the Testing Interpretation: **Reading/Listening** section, first paragraph. Let's look for strengths. The second sentence indicates, "Letter identification skills appear adequate," and is written under Strengths (see Table 4). Michael uses "context clues to aid comprehension and self-corrects word identification" (see TABLE 3) is also a strength, and is written under **Strengths** (see TABLE 4).

The third sentence (see TABLE 3) under **Reading/Listening** states, "Reading skills of word attack (analysis) and word identification (recognition) are significantly weak." This information is stated under **Weaknesses** in the

IEP (see TABLE 4). The fourth sentence also indicates weaknesses: "Michael has a tendency to substitute, omit, and transpose sounds" (see TABLE 3). This is a word analysis problem in phonics, also, written under **Weaknesses** (see TABLE 4).

ANNUAL GOALS. In preparing the annual goal (GOAL 1) for Word Recognition, (see TABLE 4), it should be noted that Michael is functioning at GE 1.9 level, and the current date is May 25, 2008 (page 1, TABLE 4) which is the ninth month of the second grade school year or 2.9 grade level. The IEP will be prepared for the next academic year or to the end of third grade or 3.9 grade level. Note that an "R" was placed above **Basic Reading Skills** in the **Present Level of Performance** column (see TABLE 4) to indicate that this is a remedial instruction area for Michael. Although, he is functioning a year behind grade level and has a high average IQ, it is unreasonable to plan for more than a year's growth in word recognition during an academic year. Thus, the word recognition goal targets the end of second grade skills (see TABLE 4).

Goals need to be positive, thus, the goal is stated using the verb "improve." For simplicity, in Michael's sample IEP, I've used the acronyms TSW (the student will) and TSWBAT (the student will be able to) which allows us to focus on the content of the goals and objectives. In a "REAL" IEP, we would use the student's name: **GOAL I: Michael will improve basic reading skills in word recognition to the end of 2nd grade level** (see TABLE 4). Word Analysis will be planned in the next section.

SHORT TERM OBJECTIVES. Short-term objectives are the task specific, sequential, measurable skills or the benchmarks that must be mastered in order to attain the annual goal. Planning instructional objectives is facilitated if the skills are grouped according to the number of grading periods in the school year (i.e., 4 nine-week grading periods or 6 six-week grading periods). For illustrative purposes, Michael's IEP (see TABLE 4) has been divided into four grading periods.

The next step is to turn to **Chapter 5, "Reading and Listening Curricula." Scope and Sequence Charts for Basic Reading Skills: Sight Words and Basal Vocabulary**, Second Grade Level (see TABLE 27) from which we will derive the specific grade level skills for Michael to master. The Scope and Sequence Chart indicates that by the end of second grade a student should be able to read 300 new second grade reading textbook vocabulary words, and 100 new high frequency words.

In planning the short-term objectives, the amount of information to learn is divided into four grading periods (see TABLE 4). Since there are a total of 400 words to learn at the second grade level that means there are 100 new words to learn in each grading period. In Michael's case, during the first grading period, it is reasonable to review 100 reading textbook vocabulary words (here called basal vocabulary) from the first grade Primer (the highest first grade reading book), and study 100 high frequency words at the second grade level. Note the other three objectives each have 100 of the new second grade basal vocabulary words, and other content words that second grade students will need to know in science, social studies, health. Begin each objective with verbs that tell what the student should be able to do in the specific skills category, and list the individual skills (see TABLE 4). This form is easier to see at a glance the skills hierarchies in each area.

The **Evaluation Materials and Objective Criteria** section (see TABLE 4) includes three types of information. The Evaluation Materials list is a collection of possible ways the teacher may evaluate Michael to check his mastery of the word recognition skills. Since the IEP is prepared for a year in advance, the teacher does not know precisely what materials or methods will be used, so provides a sample from which to select for evaluation. These materials will also be used for instruction, so they will be familiar to the student during the assessment periods. The Criteria is the standard criteria for instructional level reading word recognition which is 95 percent accuracy. In order to ensure that mastery did occur the teacher needs to periodically retest Michael at least three times during the grading period. As per IDEA 1997 requirements parents' reports will be sent at the middle of each grading period and at the end of a grading period or about every 4–5 weeks. Also, every student receiving special education services must be considered for assistive technology. At this point, the IEP team has decided that Michael does not need assistive technology services.

WORD ANALYSIS SKILLS. In preparing Michael's goal (GOAL II) for word analysis skills, find the Woodcock-Reading Mastery Test, Word Analysis skills (see TABLE 3). Note that GE 1.7 and SS 84 are his scores on this subtest. Again, even though Michael will be in the third grade next year his goal should aim for the end of second grade functioning in word attack skills. Thus, the Word Attack Goal (GOAL II) states, "TSW improve word analysis skills in the following: Phonetic analysis, structural analysis, contextual analysis, dictionary analysis to the end of second grade level" (see TABLE 4). It would not be incorrect to aim for third grade level, you would have to combine second and third grade skills.

The instructional or short-term objectives will be planned using the second grade level of the **Scope and Sequence Charts: Basic Reading Skills: Word Analysis** (see TABLES 28, 29, 30) in Chapter Five. The second grade word analysis or word attack skills include a large number of phonics and structural analysis skills, and very few contextual analysis and dictionary skills. At higher grade levels it works very well to have the focus of the first grading period to be phonics skills (TABLE 28), the second grading period to be structural analysis skills (TABLE 29), the third grading period to be contextual analysis (TABLE 30), and the fourth grading period to focus on dictionary skills (TABLE 30). However, in this case, there are numerous second grade phonics skills, so these skills were divided across the first three grading periods of the IEP (see TABLE 4). The structural analysis, contextual analysis, and dictionary skills were included in the fourth grading period (see TABLE 4).

There is no specific right or wrong method of determining which of the skills to put in each grading period except that they are sequential. Since there are four grading periods the skills that need to be mastered are divided in some logical manner into four groups. Two IEP pages (see TABLE 4) were needed to indicate the specific word analysis or word attack skills.

A wide range of possible word attack evaluation materials were indicated under **Evaluation Materials** (see TABLE 4). Since instructional level criteria for almost all academic subjects except for word recognition is represented as a range from 75 to 85 percent accuracy, 80 percent was indicated here as the middle of that range. As with the previous section of the IEP, **Parent Reports** were indicated as being due every 4–5 weeks in a system using 4 nine-week grading periods. No assistive technology is needed at this time.

REMAINING ACADEMIC AND SOCIAL SKILLS AREAS. A number of academic area examples are included in the IEP (see TABLE 4), and the process is the same as previously described. Remember to continue to compare the test scores and interpretations on the Evaluation Report (see TABLE 3) to the model IEP sections (see TABLE 4), then find the appropriate academic scope and sequence charts in this book to use as objectives. Michael has several academic areas that are developmental (D) (age/grade scores appropriate level or higher) such as oral expression, mathematics calculation and reasoning, and social skills. The academic areas of reading and written expression are remedial (R) (below grade level functioning). The mathematics reasoning IEP section (see TABLE 4) provides an example of grouping several skills areas in the same grading period. Note the oral expression, social skills, and written expression require different types of criteria than the traditional percentage accuracy. However, the "4 out of 5 times" is equivalent to 80 percent. "Average" is the target accuracy level on a rubric which depends on how many levels the rubric contains.

IEP DEVELOPMENT PROCESS USING CBAS

In order to explain the IEP development process using CBAs, it is necessary to discuss the preparation of Scope and Sequence Charts as well as Curriculum-Based Assessment.

Scope and Sequence Charts

The Scope and Sequence Charts (see TABLES 16–47) in this text are generic because they are a composite of many sources including several textbook series, several states' scope and sequence charts, historical basic skill outlines, and national association recommended skills for various subject areas. The school district scope and sequence charts would be composed primarily of the various publisher-made scope and sequence charts for the district-adopted textbooks. For example, assume that the K–6th grade-adopted math series was **Addison-Wesley Mathematics**, the language series was **World of Language** by Silver Burdett & Ginn, Zaner-Bloser Spelling and Handwriting; and **Innovations in Science** by The Wright Group. Each publisher has prepared a Scope and Sequence Chart of skills to be taught in their textbook series by grade level. Organized in one document or in one notebook with subject area dividers, these are part of the school district's scope and sequence charts.

Curriculum-Based Assessment

In order to use CBAs in program planning or writing Individual Education Programs (IEPs), it is necessary to have CBAs with characteristics of criterion-referenced tests (CRTs) and/or informal diagnostic tests. Often the textbook publisher will prepare CBAs to accompany the text series, for example, the End-of-Year Tests, chapter tests, and unit tests that accompany the mathematics, social studies, science, language textbooks adopted by your school district are CBAs. Reading textbook publishers often provide an Informal Reading Inventory with their textbook series. These CBAs provide teachers information on which level of textbook in the series is the student's functioning level, if the teacher uses several levels in the assessment process.

Sometimes CBAs must be prepared by teachers based on the specific district-adopted textbooks. Basal vocabulary word lists can easily be prepared using the new words introduced at each grade level, usually found in the back of each Teacher's Edition (TE) of the reading series. Word attack skills CBAs can be prepared by selecting questions from the workbooks and worksheets at each grade level. An informal reading inventory can be prepared by photocopying selections of 100–200 words from each of the basal reader levels with student text copies for students to read, and the matching TE copies with comprehension questions. For in-depth information on how to prepare Curriculum-Based Assessments refer to Jones, C. J. (2008).

Assessment for Programming

Assessment for programming or writing IEPs should utilize the tests that accompany district textbooks and/or teacher prepared CBAs. The student should be assessed in all of the academic areas usually tested with NRTs. However, the student may be given several levels of End-of-Book Tests or CBAs before instructional level is determined. On the sample **CBA Test Results** for Betsy (see TABLE 5a, 5b, 5c) mathematics, reading, and written expression. Since Betsy was administered CBAs, there are no statistical or derived test scores. On CBAs usually three levels are determined: Independent Level, Instructional Level, and Frustration Level. Instructional Level is the level of the textbooks that she will use in the classroom, and the level where the student scores 75-85 percent accuracy. Notice how much different Betsy's **CBA Test Results** (see TABLE 5a) look from Michael's norm-referenced test results included in his IEP (see TABLE 4).

Writing IEPs Based on CBAs

The process for writing IEPs based on CBAs is the same as the process for writing IEPs based on NRTs and generic scope and sequence charts, except that the IEPs based on NRTs are estimates. The IEPs based on CBAs are much more accurate since the student's scores come from the district curriculum content area tests. The IEPs prepared from NRTs and generic Scope and Sequence Charts (the focus of this text) are not specific to the district curricula, but are specific to content or subject areas. Since NRTs are not based on content sequences but on comparisons of the test performances of other students the same age and grade, the test results are not necessarily comparable to textbook levels.

Writing short-term objectives helps to plan the academic year and prepare for instruction for specific strengths and weaknesses, and monitor progress. Although, generic scope and sequence charts like the ones in this book can be used to prepare short-term objectives. The school district should prepare their own scope and sequence charts P–12, and use those skills specific to their adopted textbooks and to the CBAs. We have previously indicated how to prepare district scope and sequence charts.

SAMPLE CASE STUDY: BETSY: Betsy was administered two types of Math CBAs: Survey CBAs and specific skills CBAs (see TABLE 5a). She was first administered three End-of-Year Math tests–second grade, third grade, and fourth grade (although not all at the same time). The scores that Betsy received in math calculation and math reasoning, and the total test scores were recorded on the Mathematics Scoring Sheet (see TABLE 5a). Considering the criteria at the top of the chart we can analyze we can analyze the scores and determine functioning levels. At the second grade level Betsy scored 95 percent in all survey tests, which reveals Independent functioning at the second grade level. On the third grade math test scores on the Survey tests, Betsy scored 80–85 percent accuracy indicating Instructional level. At the fourth grade level, Betsy scored 55-60 percent accuracy indicating Frustration level functioning. So Betsy's overall Instructional level in math appears to be at the third grade level based on the math survey tests.

Betsy was administered Specific CBAs (see TABLE 5a) in mathematics calculation and problem-solving to pinpoint specific areas of difficulty. At the second grade level she scored 95 percent in addition and subtraction indicating Independent level skills in those areas. Also, note that at the third grade level in addition and subtraction, she scored 90 percent, also indicating Independent functioning. At the fourth grade level in addition and subtraction, Betsy scored 80 percent in addition and subtraction which is on grade Instructional level. Thus, addition and subtraction are areas of strength for her.

In analyzing Betsy's performance in multiplication and division with 75 percent accuracy in each area, her Instructional level is at the second grade level. The amount of multiplication and division studied at the second grade level is minimal. At the third grade level in multiplication (40%) and division (20%), Betsy shows a severe deficit in these areas, and at the fourth grade level the testing was discontinued. So, Betsy can work on grade level with her fourth grade class in addition and subtraction, but needs second and third grade level instruction in multiplication and division.

Goal 1: Betsy will improve math calculation skills in multiplication and division to the end of 3rd grade level in (district textbook, district scope and sequence charts, and/or CBAs).

The district scope and sequence chart in multiplication and division would be used to write short-term objectives. We don't have the district's scope and sequence math charts so we will refer to Chapter 7 Mathematics and find the second and third grade math skills in multiplication and division. Skills such as these would be used in writing the short-term objectives.

Betsy's scores in problem-solving indicate Instructional level functioning at the third grade level (see TABLE 5a) reflecting that she cannot calculate word problems in multiplication and division, and other areas may be revealed by analyzing the test. If we had only considered her Survey Test results, we would not have known that Betsy had difficulties in calculation in multiplication and division because the high scores in addition and subtraction camouflaged her weaknesses.

Thus, Betsy's math assessment indicates overall Instructional functioning at the third grade level with fourth grade level performance in addition and subtraction, and second grade functioning in multiplication and division. Betsy may need additional goals and objectives in fourth grade math areas except calculation in addition and subtraction, if she cannot "catch up" to the classroom level instruction.

Next, we will analyze Betsy's test performance in Reading (see TABLE 5b). We are most interested in her performance at the Instructional level, which is fourth grade. Her reading assessments indicate fourth grade Instructional level in sight words word recognition in context, and word analysis; and fifth and sixth grade level in reading and listening comprehension which are above her grade level. The only area in which she is experiencing difficulty in reading is basal words, or the new words introduced in her reading textbooks, where her instructional level is at the early third grade level. Betsy needs remedial work in vocabulary at the third and fourth grade levels. Since her scores are at the 90 percent accuracy, it should not take long for her to reach 4th grade Instructional level at 95 percent.

Betsy's Written Expression Scoring Sheet (see TABLE 5c) indicates that her Instructional level in written expression is fourth grade level in all areas assessed: Handwriting, Spelling, Composition Skills, and Written Composition (creative stories and functional reports). Therefore, Betsy needs no additional assistance in written expression.

Thus, CBAs provide specific information on how a student is progressing in the general education curriculum. This is very valuable information for including students with mild disabilities in the general education classroom. Writing IEPs based on CBAs and the district scope and sequence charts are very helpful to teachers in remediating problem areas and in helping students progress in the general education curriculum. CBA data is also very important in monitoring all students to determine when additional assistance may be needed to prevent severe deficits.

IEP DEVELOPMENT PROCESS USING STATE STANDARDS

The implementation of the No Child Left Behind Act (NCLB, 2001), reauthorization of the Elementary and Secondary Education ACT (ESEA, 1965), has required States to develop "a single statewide accountability system applied to all public schools and LEA's" (Spellings, Lead and Manage. July 24, 2002). This accountability system required each State to develop challenging academic content, student achievement standards, and an aligned assessment system that measures student progress toward meeting these standards (Letter to Chief State Officer, Oct. 22, 2004). "All public school students are included in the State accountability system" (Spellings, Lead and Manage, July 24, 2002) with the exception of 1 percent of the most severely cognitively disabled.

In response to the USDE mandate, national education organizations such as the **National Council of Teachers of Mathematics** began creating educational standards or guidelines to be used on a national level (Education World, 1996–2008). Currently, there are National Standards in numerous academic areas including: Fine Arts, Language Arts, Mathematics, Physical Education and Health, Science, Social Science, and Technology (Education World, 1996–2002).

Although, each state has developed their own standards, they have been based on the standards created by the special professional associations. Currently, states have developed standards and aligned assessments in reading/ language arts, mathematics, and science (Spellings, July 24, 2002). Some states have specific standards for each grade level, and some states have standards that span three grades such as K–3, 4–6, 7–9, and high school.

Previously, we discussed the **IEP Development Process Using NRTs** (Michael's IEP) in which the NRT scores were used as performance indicators (estimated functioning levels) in writing the IEP Goals. The generic scope and sequence charts from this book were used for short-term objectives. We have, also, discussed the **IEP Development Process Using CBAs** (Betsy's IEP) in which the CBA scores from state-adopted textbooks were used as performance indicators (grade specific textbooks for specific functioning levels) in writing the IEP Goals. The curriculum scope and sequence charts from the state-adopted textbook series (discussed how to create) would be used to write short-term objectives.

The **IEP Development Process Using State Frameworks** follows a similar procedure (see TABLE 2). The scores on the **Annual State Standards Tests** are used as performance indicators or functioning levels. Since students with disabilities must have access to and show progress in the general education curriculum, the state curriculum frameworks and the annual state standards tests results meet that requirement. Actually, there are several ways in which the IEP could be created using frameworks and standards tests. Teachers could use scores from the annual state standards test scores as performance indicators to write goals, and (a) write no short-term objectives; or (b) use textbook specific skills from the district scope and sequence charts to write short-term objectives; or (c) use CBAs prepared from the skills in the textbooks to write short term objectives; or (d) use textbook specific skills from the Teacher's Editions to write short-term objectives.

For our example, we will use the **Arkansas English Language Arts Curriculum Frameworks: Standard 9: Reading Comprehension** (see TABLES 6a and 6b) and the grade level variety of strategies to finish the goal. We will use Jeffrey, as a hypothetical student with special needs placed in the second grade general education classroom.

Sample of Jeffrey's IEP

Goal 9: Reading Comprehension: Jeffrey shall apply a variety of strategies to read and comprehend printed material at the 2nd grade level (see Table 6a).

Second Grade Goals: (see Table 6b)

1. Using prior knowledge to make meaning, activate prior knowledge by using features of text and/or knowledge of the author. (R.9.2.1.)

2. Using connections to make meaning, make connections from different parts of the same text. (R.9.2.2)

3. Using visualization to make meaning, form mental pictures from text independently including sequence of a process (R.9.2.3) etc.

If the teacher needs/wants to prepare short-term objectives, they may use the District Scope and Sequence Chart: Reading Comprehension. If the teachers have not yet created a District Scope and Sequence Chart for all subject areas, they may use the generic reading comprehension skills and the content reading skills indicated in Chapter 5: Reading and Listening Curricula in preparing short-term objectives. Teachers may wish to use specific grade level textbooks for short-term objectives. Regardless of the method, short-term objectives are very important in lesson planning and in monitoring progress toward goals.

SUMMARY

Developing IEPs for students with mild disabilities is a time-consuming task. Whether using NRT scores and generic curriculum scope and sequence charts; using CBA scores and district-specific scope and sequence charts; or using state standards testing scores and state curriculum standards and goals, the process of preparing the curriculum part of an IEP is essentially the same.

The IDEA requirements for IEPs include mandates from IDEA 1975, IDEA 1997, IDEA 2004, and indirectly from NCLB 2007. A current difference is allowing teachers to write only annual goals. While it sounds like omitting short-term objectives would reduce paperwork, monitoring progress and keeping parents informed of their children's progress is difficult without specific short-term objectives. In addition to annual goals on the formal IEP, some states require short-term objectives on the Individual Implementation Plans (IIPs), which does not result in less paperwork. The current IEPs must be related to the state's standards and state standards assessment to determine the students' progress in the general education curriculum.

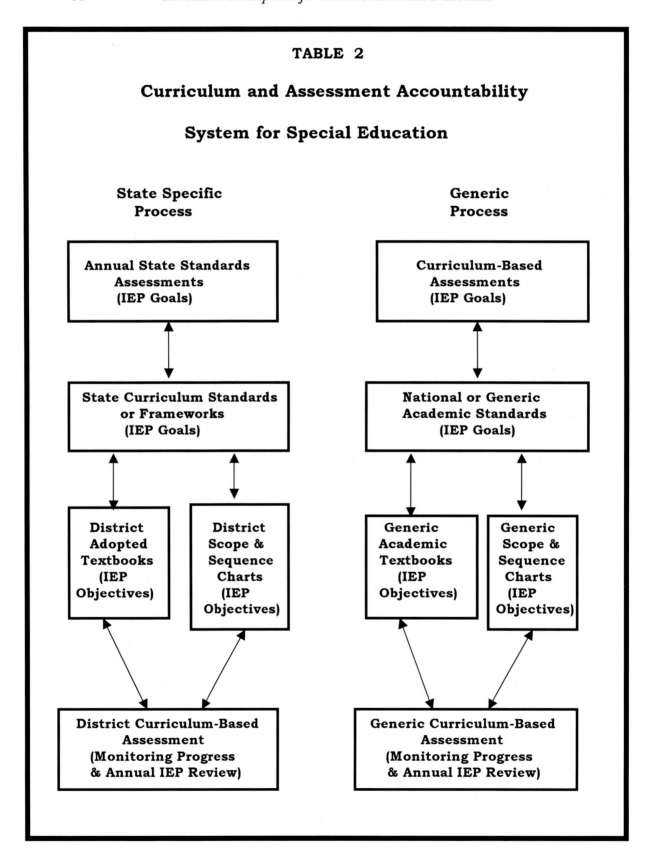

TABLE 2

Curriculum and Assessment Accountability

System for Special Education

TABLE 3

EVALUATION REPORT: MICHAEL

Age: 8 years, 3 months
Grade: 2nd grade
Date: March   , 20__

BACKGROUND AND EDUCATIONAL CONCERNS

REASON FOR REFERRAL:
Michael is an eight-year, three-month-old second grade student at Jefferson Elementary School, which he has attended since kindergarten. The primary reason for the school's request to have Michael evaluated is that he is functioning significantly below grade level. He has a short attention span, is easily distracted, and has difficulty following directions.

Michael is functioning in the lower third of his class in all academic areas. He has not retained sight words for his grade level. He has great difficulty comprehending what he has read. He cannot sound out new words. Michael does not know the basic math facts required for second grade. He has a hard time grasping new math skills. His written expression skills are also weak. Michael failed reading and language the second quarter.

HEALTH:
Michael is under the care of an ENT (ear, nose, throat doctor) because of a hole in his left eardrum. There are no other medical concerns.

VISION AND HEARING SCREENING:
School screenings indicate that visual and auditory acuity are satisfactory.

SPEECH AND LANGUAGE SCREENING:
School screenings indicate that speech and language are within normal limits.

BEHAVIOR:
In the classroom, Michael is difficult to understand and has difficulty making eye contact. His attention span is extremely short. He cannot stay on a given task. He does not work well independently. Michael needs one-to-one with the teacher the majority of the time. When working in a group, Michael likes to talk but does not wait for his turn.

SOCIOECONOMIC AND HOME INFORMATION:
English is the language of the home. Michael's mother is a homemaker, and his father is a bricklayer. Michael has two preschool-aged sisters. The family lives in a nice moderate-sized brick home in an average working class neighborhood. There are no obvious social or economic environmental concerns.

Mother often dresses Michael for school because he tends to play instead of getting dressed. He does not have specific household chores.

TABLE 3 (cont.)

Michael reacts to frustration with anger, and is very sensitive to corrrection at home. Michael likes to color, draw, and make things from paper. He collects many things, and takes care of his possessions within normal limits. He complies with family rules and gets along in the neighborhood. He plays with neighborhood children, but also enjoys playing imaginary games alone.

CURRENT EVALUATION

This evaluation includes assessments in the areas of intelligence, perception, speech and language, academic achievement, and behavior.

PSYCHOLOGICAL REPORT

<u>Wechsler Intelligence Scale for Children-Revised (WISC-R):</u>

Verbal IQ	107	Performance IQ	115	Full Scale IQ 112
Information	10	Picture Completion	14	
Similarities	13	Picture Arrangement	10	
Arithmetic	10	Block Design	14	
Vocabulary	11	Object Assembly	11	
Comprehension	12	Coding	12	
Digit Span	11			

<u>Bender Gestalt Test:</u>   CA 8-3   AE 9-0 to 9-11

<u>Detroit Test of Learning Aptitude:</u>

Visual Attention Span for Letters	AE 9-6 to 9-9
Oral Directions	AE 9-0 to 9-3

TESTING INTERPRETATION:

   Michael, an appealing eight-year, three-month-old second grader, seemed preoccupied when he initially entered the testing situation. However, he quickly became involved in the tasks presented and motivation, task focus, and perseverance were excellent throughout. A mild articulation problem which did not interfere with the intelligibilityof speech was noted.

   Results of the <u>WISC-R</u> indicate that Michael's overall cognitive ability falls within the high average range. Verbal expressive skills were average, while psychomotor skills were high average. Very little variability among subtest scores was noted with the mean scaled score at the 75th percentile. Relative strengths were noted in both verbal and nonverbal abstract conceptualization abilities. No true weaknesses were noted on this instrument. On the verbal scale, subtests measuring acquired knowledge such as general information and numerical reasoning were relatively weaker than those measuring abstract reasoning abilities.

   Results of the <u>Bender</u> and <u>Detroit</u> were consistent with the <u>WISC-R</u>. On the <u>Detroit</u>, both visual memory for letters, and auditory memory for complex oral directions were above chronological age expectancies and were in keeping

TABLE 3 (cont.)

with overall measured ability on the <u>WISC-R</u>. The <u>Bender</u> indicated well-developed visual perception and visual perceptual motor integration. While not scored as errors, some unusual aspects of Michael's <u>Bender</u> record were noted. His designs were generally of small size, crowded at the top of his page, and in some cases colliding with each other. Heavy pencil pressure was also noted.

———————————

School Psychologist

SPEECH AND LANGUAGE REPORT

SPEECH:
<u>Fisher-Logemann Test of Articulation Competence:</u>
Articulation: Misarticulations include consistent lateralization of "s, z, sh, zh, ch, j"; and inconsistent substitution of W for L.
Rhythm: Within normal limits
Voice Quality: Hoarse, somewhat hyponasal, pitch normal, intensity normal, intonation adequate.
Oral Peripheral Examination: Speech mechanism was atypical, but adequate for speech production.

LANGUAGE:
<u>Informal Language Assessment:</u> Michael speaks in complete grammatical sentences.
<u>Stephens Oral Language Screening Test:</u> No language concerns.

TESTING INTERPRETATION:
A formal test of articulation revealed that Michael consistently distorts the "s, z, sh, zh, ch, j" sounds, and occasionally substitutes "w" for "l" in conversation. These errors are considered to be maturational in nature at this time and do not affect overall intelligibility. Although dentician is atypical, the speech mechanism appeared to be adequate for speech production.

Fluency of speech was within normal limits. Voice quality was noted to be moderately hoarse and somewhat hyponasal; when asked if he had a cold, Michael said, "Yes." Pitch, intensity, and intonation were within normal limits. Michael is currently under the care of an ENT for ear problems.

Receptive and expressive language skills appeared to be adequate based on the screening test administered and informal assessment.

———————————

Speech/Language Pathologist

TABLE 3 (cont.)

PSYCHO-EDUCATIONAL REPORT

INFORMATION PROCESSING:

<u>Slingerland Screening Test:</u> Form B
Far Point Copying	adequate
Near Point Copying	adequate
Visual memory	inadequate
Visual Discrimination	adequate
Visual Memory/Written Response	deficient
Auditory Memory/Written Response	adequate
Visual Discrimination	adequate
Auditory Visual Association	weak

<u>Woodcock-Johnson Psycho-Educational Battery: Tests of Cognitive Abilities</u>
Perceptual Speed:	GE 3.0 AE 8-4	%ile 64	SS 105
Auditory Memory:	Ge 2.3 AE 7-7	%ile 59	SS 103

READING/LISTENING:

<u>Woodcock Reading Mastery Test:</u>
Letter Identification	GE 2.5	%ile 35	SS 94
Word Identification	GE 1.9	%ile 17	SS 86
Word Attack	GE 1.7	%ile 15	SS 84
Word Comprehension	GE 2.0	%ile 25	SS 90
Passage Comprehension	GE 2.4	%ile 38	SS 95
Total	GE 2.1	%ile 21	SS 88

<u>Durrell Analysis of Reading Difficulty:</u>
Subtest	Level	Reading Rate	Comprehension
Oral Reading	2	M2 (4 errors)	100%
	3	H1 (errors)	100%
Silent Reading	2	L2	46% (below grade l)
	3	M2	29% (grade l)
Listening			
Comprehension 3			100% (grade 3)

WRITTEN EXPRESSION:

<u>Slingerland Screening Test:</u> Form B
Handwriting (Manuscript): Good spatial organization and spacing
        Adequate letter formation
        Uniform letter size
        Adequate alignment

TABLE 3 (cont.)

Test of Written Language (TOWL):
Word Usage	Scaled Score	8	SS	90
Style	Scaled Score	9	SS	95

Informal Written Expression Assessment:
1. Writes simple complete sentences using a given noun or verb.
2. Experience difficulty writing a sentence using a given adjective.
3. Constructs questions.
4. Recognizes when to use periods and question marks.
5. Does not use capitalization consistently when writing from memory.
6. Reverses letters when writing from memory.

Test of Written Spelling:
Predictable Words	Unpredictable Words	Total
GE 1.6	GE below 2.4	1.6
SA 6-11	SA below 7-5	6-10
SQ 83	SQ below 89	82

MATHEMATICS:

Key Math Diagnostic Arithmetic Test:

At or Above Grade Expectancy	GE	%ile	SS	Below Grade Expectancy	GE	%ile	SS
Numeration	2.8	50	100	Fractions	1.2	9	80
Addition	3.5	75	110	Symbols	2.1	21	88
Subtraction	2.7	49	100	Multipl.	2.1	21	88
Mental Comp.	4.0	84	115	Division	2.4	34	94
Numerical Reasoning	3.3	59	103	Money	2.2	25	90
Word Probs.	2.9	56	102	Time	2.1	21	88
Measurement	2.6	45	98				

TESTING INTERPRETATION:

Learning Modality:

The Woodcock-Johnson indicates that Michael's auditory memory skills are developed to a seven-year, seven-month-old age level which is average development for age and grade level expectations. Michael displayed a strength in his ability to remember, organize and repeat number sequences up to five digits presented orally. Although sentence imitation (auditory memory) appears weak, errors are due to small word substitutions (i.e., "a" for "the," etc.) and omissions. Sentence meanings are maintained.

The Slingerland reveals that Michael is able to auditorally discriminate

TABLE 3 (cont.)

and has sound/symbol associations for initial and final consonants. Michael's performance on the Slingerland supports adequate auditory memory. His auditory memory with a written response for unrelated letter and number sequences was also adequate. Although he was able to remember dictated phrases, errors are due to weak visual memory for spelling. During test administration Michael sat quietly until the phrases and spelling words were presented. He then stood up and down, knelt on the chair and repeated the phrases over and over while writing.

While visual discrimination of letter and number sequences appears adequate for age and grade level expectations, the Slingerland results support evidence of deficient visual memory abilities both with and without a written response. Michael has a tendency to reverse "b" and "d," and transpose and invert letters. This tendency was evident throughout the educational assessments. The Auditory Visual Association subtest indicates that Michael's good auditory performance weakens when visual associations are required.

Michael's performance on both the near and far point copying subtests reveals that visual motor integration skills are within grade level expectations. Manuscript handwriting is characterized by adequate letter formations, uniformity of letter size, alignment and spatial organization. Michael's test behavior indicates that he experienced difficulty with memory for the written words as he copied only two letters at a time, subvocalized letters, squeezed his pencil and frowned.

Mathematics:

Key Math Test scores indicate that overall mathematics achievement is within grade level expectations and is a relative strength. Calculation in addition and subtraction are at or above grade expectancy, while multiplication and division skills are below grade expectancy. Mathematics reasoning skills of mental computation, numerical reasoning, word problems, and measurement are at or above grade level expectations, while skills in fractions, money, and time are below expectations.

Reading/Listening:

Reading performance on the Woodcock indicates below grade and cognitive expectations in all areas. Letter identification skills appear adequate. Reading skills of word attack and word identification are significantly weak. Michael has a tendency to substitute, omit, and transpose sounds (i.e., she/see, cup/cap, who/how). When context is not available he does not always attempt to sound out unfamiliar words unless urged to do so.

Word and passage comprehension are stronger skill areas than word attack and word identification in isolation. When reading sentences, Michael has a tendency to substitute words but uses context clues to aid in comprehension and self corrects. Therefore, word identification improves in context. Comprehension during oral reading reveals a strength at the third

TABLE 3 (cont.)

grade level on the <u>Durrell</u>, however, on silent reading passages Michael's comprehension falls to below the 1st grade level. Michael's listening comprehension for short passages is at least the third grade level. This performance substantiates his adequate auditory memory skills and deficient visual memory skills.

<u>Written Language:</u>

Michael's overall written language skills appear to be somewhat weak for grade expectancy. He is able to write simple complete sentences and questions using correct punctuation. His performance on the <u>TOWL</u> indicated weak word usage skills, and average style (capitalization and punctuation) skills. During the informal writing sample he did not consistently use capitalization.

Spelling is a significant weakness for use of phonics skills during spelling (predictable words), and poor use of visual memory (unpredictable words). Errors included reversals, omissions, and additions of sounds (letters). During the spelling test he was very nervous, stood up and down, knelt on the chair, and said, "okay," immediately after writing each word. During the informal writing sample he also reversed letters.

<u>Summary:</u>

In summary, this psycho-educational evaluation reveals the auditory channel to be a consistent strength, while visual memory is a consistent processing weakness. Michael's processing difficulties appear to interfere with his academic achievement in spelling and basic reading skills. Adaptive behavior difficulties appear to be directly related to Michael's processing weaknesses.

_____
Educational Diagnostician

BEHAVIOR

<u>Quay Timed Observations:</u>

Michael was observed during two different sessions. The first session was during independent boardwork in which he was on task 18 out of 32 segments or 56% of the time. The second session was during his classroom reading group in which he was on task 24 out of 32 segments or 75% of the time.

<u>Informal Observations:</u>

Michael seemed to have a lot of difficulty staying on focus even during the structured reading group activity. He had difficulty staying in one place throughout the sessions. He engaged in self-distracting activities such as turning around in his seat, playing with his pencil, looking around the room, sitting with his knees on the chair.

_____
Resource Room Teacher

TABLE 3 (cont.)

EVALUATION SUMMARY

Michael is functioning in the high average range of intelligence. He demonstrates significant weaknesses in the area of visual memory skills with and without a written response. His auditory channel appears to be a consistently strong learning modality.

Speech assessment indicates maturational articulations problems which do not interfere with overall intelligibility. Fluency of speech, pitch, intensity, and intonation were within normal limits. Voice quality was hyponasal due to a cold. Receptive and expressive language skills appeared adequate for age expectancy.

The academic assessment indicates that Michael's skills range from below 1st grade level in silent reading to third grade level in listening comprehension. The language arts areas of reading and written expression especially spelling all seem significantly weak for age and ability expectations. These weaknesses appear directly related to visual memory deficits.

During testing Michael demonstrated good motivation and cooperation. He was restless and needed structure during the test sessions. He displayed good perseverance in one-to-one settings. In the classroom, Michael had difficulty with task focus and frequently engaged in self-distracting behaviors.

_____

Chairperson

Diagnosis: _____

TABLE 4

INDIVIDUAL EDUCATION PROGRAM

IDENTIFICATION INFORMATION:

Student's Name: ___Michael___   Date: __May 25, 2000__

Birthdate/Age: __March 3, 2000 / 8 yrs. 3 mo.__   Parents' Name(s): _____

School: ___Jefferson Elementary School___   Address: _____

Grade/Placement: ___2nd Grade___   Phone (Home): _____ Business: _____

Diagnosis: LD in Basic Reading Skills, Reading Comprehension, Written Expression

REASONS FOR REFERRAL:

Cognitive	Academic	Behavioral
* Short attention span. * Easily distracted. * Difficulty following directions (receptive language).	* Functioning below grade level. * Failed reading and language. * Basic Reading Skills: Not retained sight words; Problems sounding out words (phonics). * Problems with reading comprehension. * Math Calculation: Does not know 2nd grade basic math facts. * Math Reasoning: Problems grasping new math concepts. * Written expression skills weak	* Difficulty with social skills: conversation & eye contact. * Can't stay on task. * No independence skills (needs 1:1 teacher help). * In group, talks, but does not wait turn.

MEDICAL INFORMATION:

Vision Screening: __Satisfactory__   Hearing Screening: __Satisfactory__
                                                    Hole in eardrum, under care of ENT.
Medication: __None indicated.__   Health: __No other medical concerns.__

TABLE 4 (cont.)

Speech/Language Screening:

* Within normal limits.
* English is the language of the home.
* Speech is difficult to understand.

Cultural/Economic Disadvantage or Deprivation:

* No obvious economic concerns.

Family/Home Information:

* Mother dresses Michael for school because he plays (immaturity).
* Michael reacts to frustration with anger; sensitive to criticism.
* Complies with family rules.
* Gets along well in neighborhood.

Date of Beginning Service: _____

Projected Ending Date: _____

Date IEP Initially Approved: _____

Review Date: _____

Committee Members:

Role/Title	Name
_____	_____
_____	_____
etc.	

TABLE 4 (cont.)

INTELLIGENCE & PROCESSING TESTING RESULTS

INTELLIGENCE TESTING SCORES

WISC-III

VIQ 107   PIQ 115   FS IQ 112

I 10	PC 14
S 13	PA 10
A 10	BD 14
V 11	OA 11
C 12	COD 12
D 11	

Summary:

* Overall cognitive ability falls within high average range.
* No true weaknesses were noted.

INFORMATION PROCESSING SCORES

* Bender Gestalt Test: CA 8-3   AE 9-0 to 9-11

* Detroit Tests of Learning Aptitude:
  Visual Attention Span for Letters   AE 9-6 to 9-9
  Oral Directions   AE 9-0 to 9-3

* Slingerland Screening Test: Form B

Adequate	Inadequate
Far Point Copying	Visual Memory
Near Point Copying	Visual Memory/
Visual Discrimination	Written Response
Auditory Memory/	Auditory-Visual Assn.
Written Response	

* Woodcock-Johnson Psycho-Educational Battery: Tests of Cognitive Ability

Perceptual Speed	GE 3.0	%ile 64	SS 105
Auditory Memory	GE 2.3	%ile 59	SS 103

Learning Modality:

Michael has a definite strength with the auditory channel with oral or written responses. Visual memory especially with a written response is an area of weakness.

TABLE 4 (cont.)

Present Level of Performance	Annual Goal	Instructional Objectives	Evaluation Materials & Objective Criteria
R BASIC READING SKILLS **Performance Levels:** Word Recognition: GE 1.9 SS 86 Word Attack: GE 1.7 SS 84 **Strengths:** Michael uses context clues to aid comprehension and self correct word identification. Letter identification is adequate. **Weaknesses:** Word attack and word identification are significantly weak. He has a tendency to substitute, omit, & transpose sounds.	**GOAL I:** TSW improve basic reading skills in word recognition to the end of 2nd grade level.	**1st GRADING PERIOD** TSWBAT read orally the following word recognition skills: a. 100 basal vocabulary (1st grade Primer). b. 100 high frequency words (2nd grade). **2nd GRADING PERIOD** TSWBAT read orally the following word recognition skills: a. 1st 100 basal words (2nd grade). b. Read rhyming words. **3rd GRADING PERIOD** TSWBAT read orally the following word recognition skills: a. 2nd 100 basal vocabulary (2nd grade). b. Read word families. c. Read content area words: Math and health (2nd grade). **4th GRADING PERIOD** TSWBAT read orally the following word recognition skills: a. 3rd 100 basal vocabulary (2nd grade). b. Read content area words: Social Studies (2nd grade).	**Evaluation Materials:** Response lists, flash cards, sight word probes, language master oral responses, teacher-made tests, workbook pages, worksheets, CBAs, CRTs. Criteria: 95% accuracy on 3 successive data days. **Parent Reports:** Due every 4-5 weeks. No Assistive Technology Needed.

TABLE 4 (cont.)

Present Level of Performance	Annual Goals	Instructional Objectives	Evaluation Materials & Objective Criteria
R BASIC READING SKILLS (cont.)	**GOAL II:** TSW improve Word Attack skills in the following: Phonetic Analysis, Structural Analysis, Contextual Analysis, Dictionary Analysis to the end of 2nd grade level.	**1st GRADING PERIOD** TSWBAT decode and read unknown words using the following Phonics Analysis skills: a. Initial, medial, final consonant blends. b. 2-3 letter initial consonant blends. c. Final consonant blends in isolation. d. Words with consonant blends. e. Substitutes initial consonant blends to form new words. **2nd GRADING PERIOD** TSWBAT decode and read unknown words using the following Phonics Analysis skills: a. Initial, medial, final consonant digraphs. b. Sounds of "g" (hard and soft). c. Words with long and short vowels. d. Decoded words with VC silent E pattern. e. Decodes consonant variants /s, g, c/. **3rd GRADING PERIOD** TSWBAT decode and read unknown words using the following Phonics Analysis skills: a. Long /e/ and long /i/ sounds of /y/. b. Vowel diphthongs /oi, ou, ow, ew/. c. Sounds of /a/ followed by /l/, /w/, /u/. d. Multiple sounds of long /a/ (ei--weigh; ai--straight; ay--day; ey--they). e. Vowel digraph or vowel team irregularities.	**Evaluation Materials:** Worksheets, games, Teacher-made tests, informal word analysis test, phonics worksheets, CBAs, dictionary skills worksheets, CRTs, workbook pages. Criteria: 80% accuracy on 3 successive data days. Parent Reports: Due every 4-5 weeks. No Assistive Technology Needed.

TABLE 4 (cont.)

Present Level of Performance	Annual Goal	Instructional Objectives	Evaluation Materials & Objective Criteria
BASIC READING SKILLS (cont.)		**4th GRADING PERIOD** TSWBAT decode and read unknown words using the following Word Analysis Skills: STRUCTURAL ANALYSIS: a. Forms compound words with 2 known words. b. Identifies root/base words in inflected forms of known words. c. Decodes words in which the final silent /e/ is dropped before adding endings (ing). d. Decodes words with prefixes: un, re, dis, pre, pro, en, ex. e. Decodes words with suffixes: less, full, ness, er, est, ly, y. f. Known meanings of contractions. g. Identifies plural endings, irregular plurals, and 's possessives. h. Divides words into syllables. CONTEXTUAL ANALYSIS: a. Uses context clues to determine meaning of new words. DICTIONARY ANALYSIS: a. Alphabetizes words using 1st and 2nd letters of words. b. Recognizes accents in 2 syllable words.	<u>Evaluation Materials:</u> **Worksheets, games, teacher-made tests, informal word analysis test, phonics worksheets, CBAs, dictionary skills worksheets, CRTs, workbook pages.** <u>Criteria:</u> **80% accuracy on 3 successive data days.** <u>Parent Reports:</u> **Due every 4-5 weeks.** **No Assistive Technology Needed.**

TABLE 4 (cont.)

Present Level of Performance	Annual Goal	Instructional Objectives	Evaluation Materials & Objective Criteria
R READING COMPREHENSION **Performance Levels:** **Word Comprehension:** GE 2.0 SS 90 **Passage Comprehension:** GE 2.4 SS 95 **Strengths:** Reading comprehension is a relative strength. Comprehension with oral reading is a strength. **Weaknesses:** Comprehension after reading silently is a weakness. Reading comprehension is below expectancy.	**GOAL III** TSW improve reading comprehension (literal, inferential, evaluative, appreciation) to the end of 2nd grade level.	**1st GRADING PERIOD** TSWBAT comprehend (written or oral), after reading, literal level skills including the following: a. Identify the main idea and supporting details. b. Rephrase the main idea. c. Arrange sentences in sequence. d. Sequence within sentences. e. Answer questions regarding key words. f. Indicate cause and effect relationships. g. Find proof in text. h. Follow printed directions. i. Tell story previously read. j. Skim for information. **2nd GRADING PERIOD** TSWBAT comprehend (written or oral), after reading, inferential level skills including the following: a. Indicate main idea by providing a title. b. Identify the speaker. c. Compare and contrast ideas. d. Understand figures of speech. e. Predict outcomes. f. Describe feelings, motives, reactions to story characters.	**Evaluation Materials:** Teacher-made tests, workbook pages, CBAs, CRTs, worksheets, IRI. **Criteria:** 80% accuracy (acquisition level) on 3 successive data days. **Parent Report:** Due every 4-5 weeks. No Assistive Technology Needed.

TABLE 4 (cont.)

Present Level of Performance	Annual Goal	Instructional Objectives	Evaluation Materials & Objective Criteria
READING COMPREHENSION (cont.)		**3rd GRADING PERIOD** TSWBAT comprehend (written or oral), after reading, evaluation level skills including the following: a. Draw conclusions. b. Recognize stereotyping of people in stories. c. Makes judgments from given facts. **4th GRADING PERIOD** TSWBAT comprehend (written or oral), after reading, appreciation level skills including the following: a. Recognize tone, feelings, humor. b. Recognize an emotional reaction. c. Indicate author's opinion/interest. d. Dramatize/illustrate stories previously read. e. Interpret feelings of characters in stories.	**Evaluation Materials:** Teacher-made tests, workbook pages, CBAs, CRTs, worksheets, IRI. Criteria: 80% accuracy (acquisition level) on 3 successive data days **Parent Report:** Due every 4-5 weeks. No Assistive Technology Needed.

TABLE 4 (cont.)

Present Level of Performance	Annual Goal	Instructional Objectives	Evaluation Materials & Objective Criteria
D **LISTENING COMPREHENSION** **Performance Levels:** 3rd grade 100% **Strengths:** Listening Comprehension is above grade level expectations on understanding short passages. **Weaknesses:** No problems indicated.	**GOAL IV** TSW improve listening comprehension skills (literal, inferential, evaluative, appreciative) to the end of 3rd grade level.	**1st GRADING PERIOD** TSWBAT comprehend, after listening, (oral or written) literal level skills including the following: a. Identify the main idea and supporting details. b. Rephrase the main idea. c. Arrange sentences in sequence. d. Sequence within sentences. e. Answer questions regarding key words. f. Indicate cause & effect relationships. g. Find proof in text. h. Follow oral directions. i. Tell story previously read. j. Skim for information. **2nd GRADING PERIOD** TSWBAT comprehend, after listening, (oral or written) inferential level skills including the following: a. Identify main idea by providing a title. b. Identify the speaker. c. Compares and contrasts ideas. d. Understand figures of speech. e. Predict outcomes. f. Describe feelings, motives, reactions to story characters.	**Evaluation Materials:** Worksheets, IRI, CBA, CRT, teacher-made test, listening center test. **Criteria:** 80% accuracy on 3 successive data days. **Parent Report:** Due every 4-5 weeks. No Assistive Technology needed.

TABLE 4 (cont.)

Present Level of Performance	Annual Goal	Instructional Objectives	Evaluation Materials & Objective Criteria
LISTENING COMPREHENSION (cont.)		**3rd GRADING PERIOD** TSWBAT comprehend, after listening, (oral or written) evaluation level skills including the following: a. Draw conclusions. b. Recognize stereotyping of people in stories. c. Make judgments from given facts. **4th GRADING PERIOD** TSWBAT comprehend, after listening, (oral or written) appreciation level skills including the following: a. Recognize tone, feeling, humor. b. Recognize an emotional reaction. c. Indicate author's opinion/interest. d. Dramatize or illustrate stories previously heard. e. Interpret feelings of characters in stories.	**Evaluation Materials:** Worksheets, IRI, CBA, CRT, teacher-made test, listening center test. **Criteria:** 80% accuracy on 3 successive data days. **Parent Report:** Due every 4-5 weeks.

TABLE 4 (cont.)

Present Level of Performance	Annual Goal	Instructional Objectives	Evaluation Materials & Objective Criteria
D ORAL EXPRESSION **Performance Levels:** **Speech:** Within Normal Limits **Language:** Within Normal Limits **Strengths:** Fluency of speech, pitch, intensity, and intonation were within normal limits. Speech mechanism was adequate for speech. Receptive and expressive language skills were adequate. He speaks in complete sentences.	**GOAL V:** TSW improve oral expression in syntax, semantics, and pragmatics to the end of 3rd grade level.	**1st GRADING PERIOD** TSWBAT utilize oral expressive language during informal conversation and formal drills including the following syntax skills: a. Comprehend and use interrogative sentences (i.e., who what, when). b. Comprehend and use negation (explicit and implicit) in sentences. c. Comprehend and use reversible passive sentences. d. Comprehend and use the conjunctions "If. . then" and "Neither. . .Nor". e. Use correct nouns, verbs, plurals in sentences. **2nd GRADING PERIOD** TSWBAT utilize oral expressive language during formal language drills including the following semantics word meaning skills: a. Use concrete vocabulary related to physical attributes (size, color, shape, composition), and to functional attributes. b. Use relational vocabulary including temporal concepts (i.e., yesterday) and temporal sequencing (i.e.. months). c. Use relational vocabulary such as temporal relationships (i.e., first, second) and spatial relationships (i.e., on, in, over, under). d. Use quantitative concepts including cardinal numbers, ordinal numbers, and comparative concepts.	**Evaluation Materials/ Methods:** Oral exercises, drills, role play, informal conversations, small group & individual oral activities, CBA, CRT. **Criteria:** 4 out of 5 expressive events on 3 successive data days. **Parent Report:** Due every 4-5 weeks. No Assistive Technology Needed.

TABLE 4 (cont.)

Present Level of Performance	Annual Goal	Instructional Objectives	Evaluation Materials & Objective Criteria
ORAL EXPRESSION (cont.) Weaknesses: Maturational articulation errors: distortions of /s, z, sh, zh, ch, j/ sounds, and occasional substitutions of /w/ for /l/. Speech mechanism was atypical. Voice quality was hoarse; he had a cold.		**3rd GRADING PERIOD** TSWBAT utilize oral expressive language including the following semantics sentence meaning and nonliteral meaning skills: a. Use sequential vocabulary (i.e., size, item, degree, value) in sequencing every day situations, by retelling the plot of movie or TV program, and events in a book. b. Choose appropriate synonym, antonym, homonym to complete given sentences. c. Answer "Wh" questions: Who, what, when, where, why. d. Locate and explain absurdities in pictured and verbal material. **4th GRADING PERIOD** TSWBAT utilize oral expressive language including the following pragmatics skills: a. Request information such as asking questions. b. Convey information such as answer questions. c. Express attitudes and emotions such as dealing with fear. d. Regulate social interactions such as displaying courtesy. e. Select appropriate conversation topics. f. Interpret others' emotions by noticing facial expressions, body language, etc.	**Evaluation Materials/ Methods:** Oral exercises, drills, role play, informal conversations, small group & individual oral activities, CBA, CRT. **Criteria:** 4 out of 5 expressive events on 3 successive data days. **Parent Report:** Due every 4-5 weeks. No Assistive Technology Needed.

TABLE 4 (cont.)

Present Level of Performance	Annual Goal	Instructional Objectives	Evaluation Materials & Objective Criteria
D WRITTEN EXPRESSION **A. HANDWRITING:** **Performance Levels:** Manuscript **Strengths:** Manuscript handwriting is characterized by adequate letter formation, alignment, and spatial organization. **Weaknesses:** Michael experienced difficulty with memory for written words and letters (reversals).	**GOAL VIII:** TSW improve handwriting in manuscript and cursive forms to the end of 3rd grade level.	**1st GRADING PERIOD** TSWBAT write using a pencil in manuscript including the following skills: a. Write using appropriate writing posture, pencil grip, paper position for manuscript and hand preference. b. Write words, sentences, and paragraphs in manuscript handwriting on standard 3rd grade writing paper. c. Write in manuscript using appropriate letter formation, letter size, proportion, alignment, spacing, line quality, slant, and rate for 3rd grade. **2nd GRADING PERIOD** TSWBAT write in cursive and read cursive handwriting including the following skills: a. Match manuscript to cursive letters (lower and upper case). b. Read paragraphs in cursive writing from chalkboard or paper. c. Write lower and upper case cursive letters in groupings reflecting similar letter formation: <u>Cursive Lower Case</u> (i, v, w, t, r, s) (n, m, v, x) (e, l, b, h, k, f) (c, a, g, d, q) (o, p, j) (y, z) <u>Cursive Upper Case</u> (C, A, E) (T, F, Q, Z, L) (S, G) (O, I, J, Y) (N, M, P, R, B, D, U, V, W, K, H, X)	**Evaluation Materials:** Handwriting exercises, worksheets, Zaner-Bloser handwriting evaluation exercises, lesson overlays. **Criteria:** Average on a 3rd grade handwriting rubric. **Parent Report:** Due every 4-5 weeks. No Assistive Technology Needed.

TABLE 4 (cont.)

Present Level of Performance	Annual Goal	Instructional Objectives	Evaluation Materials & Objective Criteria
WRITTEN EXPRESSION HANDWRITING (cont.)		**3rd GRADING PERIOD** TSWBAT write using pencil on standard 3rd grade paper the following cursive writing skills: a. Write upper & lower case cursive letters on standard 3rd grade writing paper using appropriate letter formation. b. Write cursive letters using appropriate size, proportion, and alignment. c. Write in cursive with consistent spacing between letters within words, between words, and sentences. d. Write in cursive with confident strokes and consistent line quality. **4th GRADING PERIOD** TSWBAT write using pencil on standard 3rd grade writing paper the following cursive writing skills: a. Write in cursive letters and words using uniform slant. b. Write all cursive letters from memory. c. Maintain overall neat paper appearance and legibility. d. Evaluate cursive letters and words using overlay sheets.	**Evaluation Materials:** Handwriting exercises, worksheets, Zaner-Bloser handwriting evaluation exercises, lesson overlays. **Criteria:** Average on a 3rd grade handwriting rubric. **Parent Report:** Due every 4-5 weeks. No Assistive Technology Needed.

TABLE 4 (cont.)

Present Level of Performance	Annual Goal	Instructional Objectives	Evaluation Materials & Objective Criteria
R WRITTEN EXPRESSION B. SPELLING: Performance Levels: <u>Predictable Words</u> GE <u>1.6</u> SS <u>83</u> <u>Unpredictable Words</u> GE <u>-2.4</u> SS <u>-89</u> Strengths: No strengths indicated. Weaknesses: Michael revealed poor use of phonics skills during spelling, and poor use of visual memory (unpredictable words). Errors included reversals, omissions, and additions of sounds.	GOAL IX: TSW improve in spelling words and spelling skills to the end of 2nd grade level.	**1st GRADING PERIOD** TSWBAT spell the 1st 75 second grade spelling words, other words (i.e., content words, homonyms, high frequency words) and the following phonics spelling skills: CONSONANT PHONEMES: a. Spell words with regular consonants. b. Spell words with consonant digraphs. c. Spell words with initial and final consonant blends. d. Spell words with /x/ spelling of /ks/. e. Spell words with /k/ spelled /c/ /k/ /ck/ f. Spell words with /s/ spelling of /s/ & /z/ g. Spell words with silent consonants. **2nd GRADING PERIOD** TSWBAT spell the 2nd 75 second grade spelling words and the following phonics spelling skills: VOWEL PHONEMES: a. Spell words with a short vowel in initial or medial position. b. Spell words with schwa sound. c. Spell words with long /a/ sound spelled a-C-e; /ai/ or /ay/. d. Spell words with long /e/ sound spelled /ea/ or /ee/.	<u>Evaluation Materials:</u> Spelling book exercises, phonics tests, dictated tests, proofing spelling tests, teacher-made tests, CBA, CRT, Weekly and Unit tests. <u>Criteria:</u> 80% accuracy on 3 successive data days. <u>Parent Reports:</u> Due every 4-5 weeks.

TABLE 4 (cont.)

Present Level of Performance	Annual Goal	Instructional Objectives	Evaluation Materials & Objective Criteria
WRITTEN EXPRESSION SPELLING (cont.)		**3rd GRADING PERIOD** TSWBAT spell the 3rd 75 second grade spelling words and the following phonics spelling skills: **VOWEL PHONEMES:** a. Spell words with long /o/ sound spelled /o/, /oa/ /ow/. b. Spell words with vowel digraphs: ew, ow. c. Spell words with /oy/ spelling of the /oi/ sound (i.e., boy). d. Spell words with r-controlled vowels sound /or/, /ur/, /ir/. e. Spell words with r-controlled vowels. **4th GRADING PERIOD** TSWBAT spell the 4th 75 second grade spelling words and the following spelling skills: **STRUCTURAL ANALYSIS SKILLS:** a. Spell words with endings /ed, ing, er, est/. b. Spell plural words made by adding /s/ or /es/. c. Spell compound words. **SPELLING RULES:** a. Capitalizes proper nouns in spelling. **DICTIONARY SKILLS:** a. Use a picture dictionary. b. Alphabetize spelling words.	**Evaluation Materials:** Spelling book exercises, phonics tests, dictated spelling tests, proofing spelling tests, teacher-made tests, CBA, CRT, Weekly and Unit tests. **Criteria:** 80% accuracy on 3 successive data days. **Parent Reports:** Due every 4-5 weeks. No Assistive Technology Needed.

TABLE 4 (cont.)

Present Level of Performance	Annual Goal	Instructional Objectives	Evaluation Materials & Objective Criteria
R **WRITTEN EXPRESSION** **C. COMPOSITION SKILLS** **Performance Levels:** Style SS <u>95</u> Word Usage SS <u>90</u> **Strengths:** Michael demonstrated average skills in capitalization and punctuation of skeleton sentences. He wrote simple complete sentences using a given noun or verb. He wrote questions. He recognized when to use periods and question marks. He had low average skills in word usage.	**GOAL X:** TSW improve in composition skills (capitalization, punctuation, word usage, grammar, sentence writing, paragraph writing) to the end of third grade level.	**1st GRADING PERIOD** TSWBAT use and proof composition skills in written work including the following: **CAPITALIZATION** a. Proper names; month, day, common holidays. b. First word in a line of verse. c. First & important words in book titles. d. First word of salutation & closing of informal notes. e. Initials in names. f. Titles of respect: Mr., Mrs., Dr. g. Places and things. **PUNCTUATION** a. Punctuate using a period after initials, after abbreviations. b. Punctuate using commas in a list, in dates, in letter greetings & closings, between day and month, and to separate city, state, and country. c. Use exclamation mark after exclamatory sentence. d. Use apostrophe in contractions. **2nd GRADING PERIOD** TSWBAT use (in writing) word usage and grammar skills including the following: **WORD USAGE** a. Use /there is/ and /there are/. b. Use /let/ & /leave/; /don't/ & /doesn't/. c. Use appropriate verb forms in sentences: throw, threw, thrown; drive, drove, driven.	**Evaluation Materials:** Composition skills exercises, worksheets, skeleton sentences, sentence & paragraph starters, grammar worksheets, teacher made tests, CBA, CRT. <u>Criteria:</u> 80% accuracy on skills in isolation. Average on a 3 level rubric for paragraphs. <u>Parents Report:</u> Due every 4-5 weeks. No Assistive Technology Needed.

TABLE 4 (cont.)

Present Level of Performance	Annual Goal	Instructional Objectives	Evaluation Materials & Objective Criteria
WRITTEN EXPRESSION **C. COMPOSITION SKILLS (cont.)** Weaknesses: He had problems writing a sentence with an adjective. He did not write any paragraphs.		**GRAMMAR:** a. Use singular, plural, possessive nouns. b. Use verbs: action and helping. c. Use article adjectives. d. Recognize conjunctions. **3rd GRADING PERIOD** TSWBAT write sentences using proper capitalization, punctuation, word usage, grammar including the following skills: a. Write exclamatory sentences. b. Write a variety of sentences. c. Combine short, choppy sentences into longer ones. d. Write interesting beginning and ending sentences in a paragraph. e. Avoid run-on sentences (no punctuation). f. Proof own sentences. **4th GRADING PERIOD** TSWBAT write paragraphs with proper punctuation, capitalization, word usage, grammar including the following skills: a. Keep to one idea. b. Keep sentences in order and sequence ideas. c. Find and delete sentences that do not belong. d. Indent first word in paragraphs.	**Evaluation Materials:** Composition skills exercises, worksheets, skeleton sentences, sentence & paragraph starters, grammar worksheets, teacher-made tests, CBA, CRT. Criteria: Average on a 3 level rubric. **Parent Report:** Due every 4-5 weeks.

TABLE 4 (cont.)

Present Level of Performance	Annual Goal	Instructional Objectives	Evaluation Materials & Objective Criteria
R **WRITTEN EXPRESSION** D. **WRITTEN COMPOSITION** <u>Performance Levels:</u> No test administered due to inability to write a paragraph.	**GOAL XI:** TSW improve in written composition, both creative and functional, to the end of 2nd grade level.	**1st GRADING PERIOD** TSWBAT write creative (narrative) stories using appropriate punctuation, word usage, capitalization, grammar, sentence/paragraph structure including the following skills: a. Respond to sensory stimuli with descriptive words. b. Use a variety of descriptive words and phrases in stories. c. Write imaginative stories in which ideas and feelings are expressed. **2nd GRADING PERIOD** TSWBAT write creative (narrative) stories & poetry using appropriate punctuation, capitalization, word usage, grammar, sentence and paragraph structure including the following skills: a. Literacy story elements: plot, setting, characters. b. Write fairy tales and tall tales. c. Write in daily journal. d. Write riddles, songs, and poems. e. Write a variety of poetry: rhyme, rhythm, onomatopoeia, imagery, alliteration.	<u>Evaluation Materials:</u> Story starters, story frames (sequence, character analysis, character comparisons), poetry topics, CBA, CRT, teacher-made tests. <u>Criteria:</u> Average on a 3 level rubric. <u>Parent Reports:</u> Due every 4-5 weeks. No Assistive Technology Needed.

TABLE 4 (cont.)

Present Level of Performance	Annual Goal	Instructional Objectives	Evaluation Materials & Objective Criteria
WRITTEN EXPRESSION D. WRITTEN COMPOSITION (cont.)		**3rd GRADING PERIOD** TSWBAT write expository (functional) products using appropriate punctuation, capitalization, word usage, grammar, sentence and paragraph structure including the following skills: a. Write persuasive paragraphs. b. Write friendly letters and envelopes. c. Write invitations. d. Write Thank You letters. e. Write directions and instructions. **4th GRADING PERIOD** TSWBAT write functional products using appropriate punctuation, capitalization, word usage, grammar, sentence and paragraph structure including the following skills: a. Write book reports. b. Write short science reports (i.e., animals). c. Write short research reports. d. Write math and science activities.	**Evaluation Materials:** Report forms, content webs and maps, letter and envelope forms, CRT, CBA, teacher-made tests. **Criteria:** Average on a 3-level rubric. **Parent Report:** Due every 4-5 weeks. No Assistive Technology Needed.

TABLE 4 (cont.)

Present Level of Performance	Annual Goal	Instructional Objectives	Evaluation Materials & Objective Criteria
D MATHEMATICS CALCULATION Performance Levels: Addition: GE 3.5 SS 110 Subtraction: GE 2.7 SS 100 Multiplication: GE 2.1 SS 88 Division: GE 2.4 SS 94 Strengths: Calculation in addition and subtraction are at or above grade expectancy. Weaknesses: Calculation in multiplication and division are below grade expectancy.	GOAL VI: TSW improve in mathematics calculation in addition, subtraction, multiplication, and division to the end of 3rd grade level.	**1st GRADING PERIOD** TSWBAT compute mathematics calculation problems (written) in addition including the following skills: a. Add 2-digit & 3 digit numbers with & without regrouping. b. Master basic addition facts with sums through 18. c. Use mental computation strategies to add. d. Mentally estimate sums to 3-digits. e. Find the sum of two whole numbers up to 10,000. f. Explain addition & subtraction as opposite operations. g. Explain regrouping in addition of with up to 4 digits. h. Add "0" properly. i. Use addition to check subtraction. **2nd GRADING PERIOD** TSWBAT compute mathematics calculation problems (written) in subtraction including the following skills: a. Write subtraction facts related to known addition facts. b. Explain subtraction regrouping. c. Use addition to check subtraction. d. Subtract 2, 3, & 4 digit numbers with & without regrouping. e. Master basic subtraction facts. f. Subtract 2 whole numbers of 10,000 or less to find differences. g. Subtract with more than one regrouping.	Evaluation Materials: Worksheets, teacher-made tests, End of Unit or Chapter tests. math fact probes, math games. Criteria: 80% accuracy on 3 successive data days. Parent Reports: Due every 4-5 weeks. No Assistive Technology Needed.

Curriculum Development for Students with Mild Disabilities

TABLE 4 (cont.)

Present Level of Performance	Annual Goal	Instructional Objectives	Instructional Materials & Objective Criteria
D MATHEMATICS CALCULATION		**3rd GRADING PERIOD** TSWBAT compute mathematics calculation problems (written) in multiplication including the following skills: a. Master multiplication facts to 10 x 10. b. Multiply by 10, 100, 1000. c. Multiply 2 whole numbers with/without regrouping in which one factor is 9 or less & the other is a multi-digit number up to 3 digits. d. Write numbers in expanded form using multiplication. e. Explain: Multiplication & division as opposite operations; Multiplication as repeated addition. f. Multiply 2-digits by 1-digit; 3-digits by 1-digit; 10-digits by 1-digit. **4th GRADING PERIOD** TSWBAT compute mathematics calculation problems (written) in division including the following skills: a. Master basic division facts to 100 divided by 10. b. Explain: Division rules; Multiplication & division as opposites; Division vocabulary; Division as repeated subtraction. c. Divide 2 & 3 digit dividends by 1-digit divisors. d. Solve division problems with remainders. e. Divide using multiples of 10.	<u>Evaluation Materials:</u> Worksheets, teacher-made tests, End of Unit or Chapter tests, math fact probes, math games. <u>Criteria:</u> 80% accuracy on 3 successive data days. <u>Parent Report:</u> Due every 4-5 weeks. No Assistive Technology Needed.

TABLE 4 (cont.)

Present Level of Performance	Annual Goal	Instructional Objectives	Evaluation Materials & Objective Criteria
D **MATHEMATICS REASONING** **Performance Levels:** **Numeration:** GE _2.8_ SS _100_ **Mental Computation:** GE _4.0_ SS _115_ **Numerical Reasoning:** GE _3.3_ SS _103_ **Word Problems:** GE _2.9_ SS _102_ **Measurement:** GE _2.6_ SS _98_ **Fractions:** GE _1.2_ SS _80_ **Time:** GE _2.1_ SS _88_ **Money:** GE _2.2_ SS _90_	**GOAL VII:** TSW improve mathematics reasoning in numerals, measurement, money, time, story problems, and geometry to the end of third grade level.	**1st GRADING PERIOD** TSWBAT compute mathematics reasoning problems (written) in numerals, money, measurement, time, charts & graphs, and geometry including the following skills: a. Write numbers in sequence 1-999. b. Read & write numbers (digits & words) up to 5 digits. c. Order & compare numbers to 99,999 using signs for greater than, less than, = d. Demonstrate place value up to one hundred thousand. e. Use place value to explain 3, 4, & 5 digit numbers. f. Count by 2s, 4s, 5s, 10s. g. Locate positive and negative whole numbers on a number line. **2nd GRADING PERIOD** TSWBAT compute mathematics reasoning problems (written) in measurement including the following skills: **LINEAR MEASURE:** a. Make linear measurements in feet & inches; centimeters & meters. b. Convert inches, feet, yards. c. Estimate linear measures; measure. d. Measure distances in environment. **WEIGHT (MASS):** a. Compare weights of objects using a balance scale.	**Evaluation Materials:** Teacher-made tests, worksheets, Chapter & Unit tests, CBA, CRT, manipulative activities, games, math probes. **Criteria:** 80% accuracy on 3 successive data days. **Parent Report:** Due every 4-5 weeks. No Assistive Technology Needed.

TABLE 4 (cont.)

Present Level of Performance	Annual Goal	Instructional Objectives	Evaluation Materials & Objective Criteria
MATHEMATICS REASONING **Strengths:** Mental computation and numerical reasoning are significant areas of strength, while numeration & word problems are grade level strengths. **Weaknesses:** Fractions, time, & money are areas of significant weakness.		**2nd GRADING PERIOD (cont.)** b. Estimate weights of objects in pounds & ounces; in grams & kilograms. c. State abbreviations for grams & kilograms. milliliters. **CAPACITY (VOLUME):** a. Convert half pint, quart. b. Estimate & measure liquid capacity in cups, pints, quarts, gallons, liters. c. Compare US Customary & metric measures. **TEMPERATURE:** a. Measure & record temperature in Celsius & Fahrenheit degrees. b. State freezing point of water. c. Read room temperatures on Celsius scale thermometer. **3rd GRADING PERIOD** TSWBAT compute mathematics reasoning problems (written) in money, time, and story problems including the following: **MONEY:** a. Add & subtract money problems. b. Read & write dollars & cents using decimal notation. c. Make change using as few coins as possible. d. Demonstrate equivalence of a dollar with a variety of coins. **TIME:** a. Tell time in 5 minute intervals. b. Tell time in minutes before and after. c. Use AM and PM. d. Use the calendar: week, month, year. e. Tell time on a conventional clock.	**Evaluation Materials:** Teacher-made tests, worksheets, Chapter & Unit tests, CBA, CRT, manipulative activities, games, math probes. **Criteria:** 80% accuracy on 3 successive data days. **Parent Report:** Due every 4-5 weeks. No Assistive Technology Needed.

TABLE 4 (cont.)

Present Level of Performance	Annual Goal	Instructional Objectives	Evaluation Materials & Objective Criteria
		3rd GRADING PERIOD (cont.) **STORY PROBLEMS:** a. Solve written two-step story problems involving addition, subtraction, multiplication, division. b. Compose simple story problems which require using familiar facts & operations. c. Estimate answers to story problems. **4th GRADING PERIOD** TSWBAT compute mathematics reasoning problems (written) in geometry including the following: a. Name spheres, cylinders, rays, planes, right angles, parallel lines. b. Calculate diameter & radius. c. Find lines of symmetry in a figure. d. Determine if figures are congruent. e. Label lines as horizontal, vertical, parallel and perpendicular. f. Label polygons: pentagon, hexagon, octagon. g. Draw a right angle. h. Compute area in square inches and in square centimeters. i. Label solid figures: sphere, cube, pyramid, rectangular solid, cone, cylinder.	**Evaluation Materials** **Teacher-made tests, worksheets, Chapter & Unit tests, CBA, CRT, manipulative activities, games, math probes.** **Criteria:** **80% accuracy on 3 successive data days.** **Parent Report:** **Due every 4-5 weeks.** **No Assistive Technology Needed.**

TABLE 4 (cont.)

Present Level of Performance	Annual Goal	Instructional Objectives	Evaluation Materials & Objective Criteria
R STUDY SKILLS Performance Level: Below grade level. Strengths: None indicated. Weaknesses: Michael experienced weakness in independent board work. He had difficulty staying on task. He engaged in self-distracting behaviors.	GOAL XII: TSW improve in study skills and study behaviors to the end of the 3rd grade level.	1st GRADING PERIOD TSWBAT demonstrate (oral, written) study skills in locating information including the following: a. Use the Table of Contents in a variety of books. b. Find information on charts, maps, pictures, and calendar, dictionary and reference books. c. Use alphabetical sequence (2-3 letter) in locating information. d. Use encyclopedia, dictionary, glossary. 2nd GRADING PERIOD TSWBAT demonstrate (oral, written) study skills in locating information including the following: a. Use subtitles to locate information. b. Locate information in TV schedule. c. Use glossary, title page & index to locate information and answer questions. d. Select specific information in a telephone directory. e. Use a thesaurus to find synonyms.	Evaluation Materials: Locating information worksheets or work-book pages, CRT, CBA, teacher-made test, note-taking forms. Criteria: 80% accuracy on 3 successive data days. Parent Report: Due every 4-5 weeks. No Assistive Technology Needed.

TABLE 4 (cont.)

Present Level of Performance	Annual Goal	Instructional Objectives	Evaluation Materials & Objective Criteria
STUDY SKILLS (cont.)		**3rd GRADING PERIOD** **TSWBAT demonstrate (oral, written) reading study skills including the following:** a. **Skim or reread to find specific information.** b. **Judge sources of information as relevant or irrelevant.** c. **Judge fact or fancy; true or false.** d. **Make generalizations from facts.** e. **Use the appropriate word for context.** **4th GRADING PERIOD** **TSWBAT demonstrate (oral, written) reading study skills including the following:** a. **Follow written and oral directions.** b. **Classify items into categories.** c. **Take notes for preparing report.** d. **Use test-taking strategies including identifying clue words.** e. **Summarize science and social studies lesson.** f. **Organize information for preparing a report.**	**Evaluation Materials:** **Locating information worksheets or workbook pages, CRT, CBA, teacher-made test, notetaking forms.** **Criteria:** **80% accuracy on 3 successive data days.** **Parent Report:** **Due every 4-5 weeks.** **No Assistive Technology Needed.**

TABLE 4 (cont.)

Present Level of Performance	Annual Goal	Instructional Objectives	Evaluation Materials & Objective Criteria
R SOCIAL SKILLS Performance Level: Behavioral Observations Strengths: Plays with other children in the neighborhood. Complies with family rules. Weaknesses: Does not wait his turn. Reacts to frustration with anger. Sensitive to criticism.	GOAL XIII: TSW improve social competence in social perspective-taking moral development social regulation, and social problem-solving to the upper primary grade level.	**1st GRADING PERIOD** TSWBAT demonstrate social competence skills in social perspective-taking including the following: a. Show understanding of his role as student and as a friend. b. Show sensitivity to friends' attitudes. c. Demonstrate ability to observe self and others simultaneously and engage in comparison (social comparison). d. Exhibit empathy and sympathy. **2nd GRADING PERIOD** TSWBAT demonstrate social competence in moral development skills including the following: a. Show eagerness to please teacher, parents, and other role models. b. Demonstrate understanding expectations to conform to several sets of rules regarding moral codes & behaviors. c. Show emerging understanding of social relationships and moral feelings. d. Tell the truth and accept consequences.	Evaluation Materials: Role-playing, teacher-made test, CBA, daily/weekly charting of behavior, self charting, contingency contracting. Criteria: 4 out of 5 situations / classes on 3 successive data days. Parent Report: Due every 4-5 weeks. No Assistive Technology Needed.

TABLE 4 (cont.)

Present Level of Presentation	Annual Goal	Instructional Objectives	Evaluation Materials & Objective Criteria
SOCIAL SKILLS (cont.)		**3rd GRADING PERIOD** TSWBAT demonstrate social competence skills in social regulation including the following: a. Control his temper in conflict situations with peers. b. Follow classroom rules regarding entering the classroom without disruption. c. Follow school building rules for walking in the hallway, waiting in line, using the drinking fountain, using the restroom, and in the cafeteria. **4th GRADING PERIOD** TSWBAT demonstrate social competence skills in social problem-solving including the following: a. Accept consequences for wrong doing. b. Show increasing reasonableness. c. Use problem-solving to reduce dangerous risk-taking (i.e., playground equipment). d. Decide what to do to deal with stress of making a mistake. e. Face reality of situation.	**Evaluation Materials:** Role-playing, teacher-made tests, CBA, daily/weekly charting of behavior, self monitoring, contingency contracting, problem-solving activities. **Criteria:** 4 out of 5 situations/classes on 3 successive data days. **Parent Report:** Due every 4-5 weeks. No Assistive Technology Needed.

TABLE 5a

MATHEMATICS SCORING SHEET

Date: _____   Grade: 4th   Name: Betsy

Criteria:

Independent Level 90% +
Instructional Level 75-85%
Frustration Level -70%

STUDENT PERFORMANCE:

	Survey CBAs:					Specific CBAs:		
	End-of-Year CBAs					Basic Calculation		
Grade Level	Calc.	Reas.	Total	Add.	Sub.	Mult.	Div.	Prob. Solv.
1st	____	____	____	____	____	____	____	____
2nd	95%	95%	95%	95%	95%	75%	75%	80%
3rd	85%	80%	80%	90%	90%	40%	20%	75%
4th	60%	55%	60%	80%	80%	-----	------	--------
5 th	____	____	____	____				
6 th	____	____	____	____				
GRADE LEVEL:								
INDEPEND.	2 nd	2 nd	2 nd	3 rd	3 rd	-----	------	2 nd
INSTRUCT.	3 rd	3 rd	3 rd	4 th	4 th	2 nd	2 nd	3 rd
FRUSTRA.	4 th	4 th	4 th	---	----	3 rd	3 rd	4 th

TABLE 5b

READING SCORING SHEET

Date: _____   Grade: __4th__   Name: __Betsy__

Criteria: Word Rec.   Comp.

Independent   98%   90%
Instructional   95%   75-85%
Frustration   90%   -70%

STUDENT PERFORMANCE:

Grade Level	Graded Word Lists	Basal Words	Sight Words	Word Recog. Context	Word Analysis	Comprehension Reading Lit./Con.		Listening Lit./Con.	
1st	100%	___	___	___	___	___	___	___	___
2₁	100%	___	___	___	___	___	___	___	___
2₂	95%	___	___	___	___	___	___	___	___
3₁	95%	95%	___	95%	___	95%	90%	___	___
3₂	90%	90%	3rd 100%	95%	3rd 93%	95%	90%	___	___
4th	90%	90%	95%	95%	85%	90%	90%	95%	95%
5th	70%	85%	___	90%	___	80%	75%	90%	85%
6th	___	___	___	80%	___	60%	35%	75%	70%
7th	___	___	___	___	___	55%	30%	50%	35%

GRADE LEVEL:

	Graded Word Lists	Basal Words	Sight Words	Word Recog. Context	Word Analysis	Reading		Listening	
INDEPEND.	___	___	3₂	___	3	4	4	5	4
INSTRUCT.	3₁	3₁	4	4	4	5	5	6	5
FRUSTRA.	3₂	3₂	___	5	___	6	-5	-6	6

TABLE 5c

WRITTEN EXPRESSION SCORING SHEET

Date: _____   Grade: __4th__   Name: __Betsy__

Criteria: Rubric:

Independent	90%+	Above Average	3
Instructional	75-85%	Average	2
Frustration	-70%	Below Average	1

STUDENT PERFORMANCE:

Grade Level	Handwriting Man.	Cursive	Spelling Graded List	ISI	Composition Skills (Skills in Isolation) Cap.	Punct.	Gram.	Mean.	Written Composition Crea.	Funct.
1st	___	___	100%	___	___	___	___	___	___	___
2nd	___	___	100%	___	___	___	___	___	___	___
3rd	___	___	90%	90%	90%	90%	85%	90%	___	___
4th	___	2	80%	85%	85%	85%	80%	85%	2	2
5th	___	___	70%	65%	70%	70%	65%	70%	___	___
6th	___	___	50%	___	___	___	___	___	___	___
7th	___	___	___	___	___	___	___	___	___	___
8th	___	___	___	___	___	___	___	___	___	___

GRADE LEVEL:

	Man.	Cursive	Graded	ISI	Cap.	Punct.	Gram.	Mean.	Crea.	Funct.
INDEPEND.	___	___	3rd	3rd	3rd	3rd	___	3rd	___	___
INSTRUCT.	___	2	4th	4th	4th	4th	4th	4th	4th	4th
FRUSTRA.	___	___	5th	5th	5th	5th	5th	5th	___	___

TABLE 6a
Arkansas Department of Education
English Language Arts Curriculum Frameworks

Standards	
Oral and Visual Communications	
1. Speaking	Students shall demonstrate effective oral communication skills to express ideas and to present information.
2. Listening	Students shall demonstrate effective listening skills in formal and informal settings to facilitate communication.
3. Media Literacy	Students shall demonstrate knowledge and understanding of media as a mode of communication.
Writing	
4. Process	Students shall employ a wide range of strategies as they write, using the writing process appropriately.
5. Purpose, Topics, Forms & Audience	Students shall demonstrate competency in writing for a variety of purposes, topics and audiences employing a wide range of forms.
6. Conventions	Students shall apply knowledge of Standard English conventions in written work.
7. Craftsmanship	Students shall develop personal style and voice as they approach the craftsmanship of writing.
Reading	
8. Foundations of Reading	Students shall apply concepts of print, acquire knowledge of spoken words and understand the relationship of speech to print as they develop a foundation for literacy.
9. Comprehension	Students shall apply a variety of strategies to read and comprehend printed material.
10. Variety of text	Students shall read, examine, and respond to a wide range of texts for a variety of purposes.
11. Vocabulary, Word Study & Fluency	Students shall acquire and apply skills in vocabulary development and word analysis to be able to read fluently.
Inquiring/Researching	
12. Research/ Inquiry Process	Students shall engage in inquiry and research to address questions, to make judgments about credibility, and to communicate ideas in ways that suit the purpose and audience.
	Etc.

TABLE 6b
Arkansas Department of Education
English Language Arts Curriculum Frameworks

Strand: Reading
Standard 9: Comprehension K-4
Students shall apply a variety of strategies to read and comprehend printed material.

THE GOAL FOR EACH STUDENT IS PROFICIENCY IN ALL REQUIREMENTS AT CURRENT AND PREVIOUS GRADES.

	Kindergarten	Grade 1	Grade 2	Grade 3	Grade 4
Using prior knowledge to make meaning	R.9.K.1 Preview the selection & use prior knowledge to make reasonable predictions.	R.9.1.1 Access appropriate prior knowledge to enhance & monitor the understanding of the text.	R.9.2.1 Activate prior knowledge by using features of text and/or knowledge of the author.	R.9.3.1 Activate prior knowledge by previewing using text structure. R.9.3.2 Use prior knowledge to determine a purpose for reading.	R.9.4.1 Organize prior knowledge & new information to make meaning of the text.
Using connections to make meaning	R.9.K.2 Make connections from text to self during read aloud. R.9.K.3 Make connections from text to text during read aloud.	R.9.1.2 Make connections from text to self during independent reading. R.9.1.3 Make connections from text to text during independent reading.	R.9.2.2 Make connections from different parts of the same text.	R.9.3.3 Make connections from text to world during reading.	R.9.4.2 Make connections that demonstrate a deeper understanding of text related to self, text, and/or world.
Using visualization to make meaning	R.9.K.4 Form a mental picture text read by teacher, including story elements or descriptions.	R.9.1.4 Form mental picture from text read independently, elements or descriptions.	R.9.2.3 Form mental pictures from text read independently including sequence of a process.	R.9.3.4 Form mental pictures to organize and visualize content of the text.	R.9.4.3 Form mental pictures reflecting vivid details & personal connections with the text.

Etc.

Chapter 3

EARLY CHILDHOOD SPECIAL
EDUCATION CURRICULA

". . . early childhood special education programs need to apply developmentally appropriate practices within an intervention-oriented context." (Safford, 1989, 38)

Learning theorists, philosophers, physicians, psychologists, and educators have been concerned with the education of young children, disabled and nondisabled children, for over four hundred years. The divergent psychological learning theories of humanism, developmental psychology, behaviorism, and cognitive/information processing, constructivism and their various theorists continue to impact early childhood curricula for all children.

HISTORY OF EARLY CHILDHOOD EDUCATION

Early Historical Perspectives

Interest in educating young children and the designation of a specific curriculum can be traced to antiquity (ancient Greece and Rome). Throughout history, until the age of 6 or 7 years old, children were under the care and supervision of their mother (Roles, undated). Young children were educated at home informally, without any formal curriculum, in developmental skills, social skills and manners, appropriate behavior, language understanding and usage. Play has been considered a very important part of a child's learning because through playing games, the children learn to work within a set of rules (Lascarides & Hinitz, 2000).

In the fifteenth and sixteenth centuries, middle-class parents were anxious to have their children obtain an education because it was an avenue to upward mobility and to securing an important government post. Grammar schools with a rigorous classical curriculum (in Latin) were created for the children of aristocratic parents (Roles, undated). However, many children needed an earlier educational experience to be ready for Grammar School.

During the mid-1600s an educational reformer, *Jan Amos Comenius* (1592–1670), was concerned with revising the content and pedagogy of education. Comenius proposed and implemented reforms in a variety of schools that are the foundation of the U.S. educational system today. He implemented the careful grading of the schools so that the skills of one grade level would be the foundation for the next higher grade level. For mental training of the child, Comenius outlined two groups of studies:

1. those providing the materials for thought including nature study, geography, household economy, and
2. those supplying the symbols of thought such as drawing, writing, and language (Lascarides & Hinitz, 2000).

He advocated that education is necessary for all young people of all classes of society, for both sexes, including those who are backward, mentally weak, and of limited intelligence to help them overcome their shortcomings. . . . (Lascarides & Hinitz, 2000, 39).

During the Industrial Revolution (1700–1840) women and children were used as cheap labor in industry. As a result large numbers of the children in Great Britain could neither read nor write; and the education of poor children was almost nonexistent (Nursery Schools, 2008). Infant schools (nursery schools) in England came about as a result of children taking their young siblings to school with them while the parents worked in the mills. During that same period, infant schools flourished in the United States. Their purpose was to provide child care for the young children of the factory workers. Factory owners furnished infant schools for children as young as 18 months old. Many nursery schools were sponsored and financed by churches and charitable organizations, and were often sponsored and affiliated with universities as research schools (Nursery Schools, 2008).

Robert Owen (1771–1858) is generally acknowledged to have opened the first infant school in Britain in 1816 in the Scottish town of New Lanarck (Kwon, 2002). He provided housing for workers in his mills and no longer let the children ages 6, 7, 8 years old work in the mills. Owen built a school for the factory workers' children. The curriculum in his school included: Gymnastic exercises, clapping, counting movements, simple object lessons, easy arithmetic, storytelling, children's prayers and hymns. Owen objected to beating or threatening children and specified that children should be spoken to with a pleasant face, and kind manners and tone of voice. He advocated free and unstructured play (Kwon, 2002). The infant schools that followed were promoted by infant societies. They lacked a uniform purpose, curriculum or pedagogy, but preparation for the subjects taught in elementary schools came to predominate (Nursery Schools, 2008).

The realization that young children needed specialized treatment adapted to their age did not take hold until the ideas and practices of *Johann Pestalozzi* (1745–1827) attracted the attention of a small number of reformers in England (Nursery Schools, 2008). Pestalozzi introduced something new in the field of education, the **Principle of Self-Activity** in acquiring and using knowledge. The application of this concept revolutionized the method of school instruction. Pestalozzi indicated that the traditional subjects for instruction—reading, writing, arithmetic—could not be regarded as the starting point of learning because their elements for understanding—line (form), language, and number—are formed in the child's own mind in order to understand the world. These three elements should be developed in the child before he is taught the traditional subjects (Lascarides & Hinitz, 2000).

During the early to middle 1800s, *Fredrich Froebel* (1782–1852) was the first educator to design an organized curriculum for young children which focused primarily on various activities with no attempt to formally teach reading or math. The kindergartens or "children's gardens" for four-to-six year-olds were developed to bridge between a free early childhood life at home and a highly organized school life (Lawton, 1988). Froebel was concerned about children's moral, spiritual, physical, and intellectual growth. Most significant among Froebel's educational strategies was his emphases on guided play as a method for learning; using manipulative materials that utilize senses; and circle-time which provided an opportunity to sing songs and learn new ideas through discussion (Morrow, 1989). All teaching was based on the self-activity of the pupils, a technique he learned from studying under Pestalozzi. Froebel gave the children experiences instead of instruction.

John Dewey (1859–1952) modified the activity curriculum, but focused on unstructured play, learning by doing, democratic decision-making, social and emotional behavior, independence, and physical development. He continued to encourage various areas of the classroom designated for specific activities—block area, art area, playhouse area, manipulatives and puzzles; and recommended outdoor play and nature exploration when weather permitted (Lawton, 1988).

Historically, European psychologists, physicians and educators influenced curricula for young children in America. Early childhood special education programs and curricula are generally traced back to the late 1800s and to *Maria Montessori* and her school for feebleminded children in Rome (Scheerenberger, 1983). Montessori was heavily influenced by Jean Itard and Edouard Seguin who proposed a developmental approach to instruction, individualized instruction, sensory stimulation, systematic instruction, and functional-life curriculum (Hardman et al., 1990). The Montessori approach differed from most early childhood programs in its emphasis on formalized, prescribed, and especially designed materials which emphasize individual self-directed and self-paced activities (Safford, 1989). Montessori Schools continue to thrive in the United States., however, since most of the schools are private they are attended by middle and upper class children.

Arnold Gesell (1880–1961) was the preeminent authority on child development in the mid-twentieth century United States. In 1924, Gesell instituted the use of cinematography in studying infant and child development (Keith, 2008). He obtained voluminous pictorial records of infant and child behavior throughout early childhood and up to the age of 10 years old. Gesell and his coworkers were able to determine normal ranges of childhood development as well as behavioral patterns from these records (Keith, 2008).

Gesell's interest in the education of the preschool child led him to study infants and young children at the ages of 4, 6, 12, 18, 24, 36, 48, 60 months and establish developmental norms for 1–5 years of age (Keith, 2008). These norms were referred to as Developmental Schedules and organized into four major areas of behavior: motor characteristics, adaptive behavior, language, and personal-social behaviors (Keith, 2008).

Gesell and coworkers, Frances Ilg and Louis Ames, wrote numerous books filled with the child development information they gained from their child research to help parents understand the process of their child's development through the elementary years and into adolescence (Lascarides & Hinitz, 2000). The titles of the books indicated the content such as *Your Five-Year-Old: Sunny and Serene,* and *Your Six-Year-Old: Loving and Defiant* (Keith, 2008). Gesell saw the education of the preschool child in terms of growth instead of in terms of instruction or training. Similar developmental scope and sequence charts can be found in TABLE 7.

The Theory of Cognitive Development, one of the historically influential psychological theories, was developed by Jean Piaget (1896–1980) (Plucker, 2007). He was very interested in studying the evolution of knowledge in children. Piaget's studies and in-depth observations of children resulted in a cognitive developmental model that included four stages of thinking: Sensorimotor (0–2 years), Preoperational (2–7 years), Concrete Operational (7–11 years), and Formal Operational (11+ years) (Boeree, 2003). Each stage is characterized by different ways of thinking and different thinking abilities.

Piaget's theory is known as "constructivist" due to the belief that children construct their own abilities through self-motivated action in the world (Plucker, 2007).

Early childhood education is primarily concerned with the sensorimotor stage (0–2 years) and the preoperational stage (3–5 years). Children acquire the skills in these stages at varying rates, and those with disabilities usually progress at a slower than average rate. During the sensorimotor stage the most crucial skills that children acquire include sensory exploration with a motor response, object permanence, imitation and deferred imitation, mental representation, beginning language acquisition and usage, and ability to use mental combinations to solve simple problems (Boeree, 2003).

Most children at ages 3–5 years will be functioning within the preoperational stage. The primary skills they acquire during this stage concern the use of language symbols to store and retrieve information, use of mental representations, ability to pretend, beginning understanding of past and future, explosive language knowledge and use (receptive and expressive) (Boeree, 2003). Children in this stage are still very egocentric in thoughts and can only focus on one aspect of a problem at a time (Boeree, 2003).

Piaget's basic law of development indicated that the child constructs his own intelligence and knowledge through play. Play becomes the basis for self-initiated activity from which the young child constructs characteristic ways of acting and thinking (Lascarides & Hinitz, 2000). "Play is thought to support the development of such cognitive qualities as curiosity, exploration, logical, mathematical, social knowledge, temporal sequencing, conservation, spatial reasoning, seriation, classification, and perspectivism" (Monighan-Nourot, 1990, 77).

The cognitive-developmental viewpoint is exemplified by Piaget's constructivist theory. The cognitive-developmental/interactionist theories formed the basis for a number of curriculum models: Head Start and Follow Through programs, High/Scope Curriculum, Lavatilli Early Childhood Curiculum, Kami-De Vriss Curriculum, and the Bank Street model (Lascarides & Hinitz, 2000, 132).

Advances Due to Federal Intervention

For the most part, education is not mentioned in the Constitution and is considered a states' rights issue, but there is a history of federal funding for economically disadvantaged children and for children with disabilities. Most of the federal efforts can be tracked through three major laws and their reauthorizations: Head Start for School Readiness Act (1965), Elementary and Secondary Education Act (1965), and Education for All Handicapped

Children's Act (1975). Although, initially started as separate programs with separate budgets, these programs concurrently have many overlapping areas.

Head Start for School Readiness Act

The Head Start for School Readiness Act was originally signed in 1965 to provide a range of services for low income and at-risk children as a preventive to help ensure these children will be ready to learn when they reach kindergarten. Head Start provides educational, health and nutrition, social services, parent involvement, and other services to eligible children from birth through 5 years of age (CCSSO, 2008). This program was expanded to include a number of services: Parent and Child Centers (1967), Head Start for Children of Migrants (1969), Project Follow Through for services continued through third grade (1967–1996), Early Head Start for infants and toddlers (1984), American Indian-Alaska Native Head Start (1965), Home Start (1972–1975) for isolated and rural families (Head Start, 2008). Currently, Head Start serves more than 900,000 children aged 3 and 4 years, and similar services to 63,000 children aged 1–3 years (CCSSO, 2008).

No Child Left Behind

The Elementary and Secondary Education Act of 1965 was reauthorized as the No Child Left Behind Act of 2001 (previously discussed in Chapter One). The Early Childhood Initiative "Good Start, Grow Smart" is a multifactored approach to improve the educational foundation skills of kindergarten children from low income families so they will be successful in first grade. An additional focus is to improve the knowledge base of preschool children from low income families so they will be successful in kindergarten. Children's educational programs will be enhanced through strengthening **Head Start** (3–5 year olds) and **Early Head Start** (0–3 years old) Programs (Early Childhood Initiative, ED.gov, 2008).

The curriculum will be enhanced to focus specifically on reading skills in **Reading First** and **Early Reading First** programs. Due to the ages of the children, the programs must focus on all areas of development, especially early language development, cognition, literacy and pre-reading skills. Children will also need to study the other areas that are the focus of NCLB (2001)–mathematics, science, and social studies. Teachers will use proven research-based materials and research-based instruction to increase skill acquisition (Improve Student Performance, ED.gov, 2008).

The multifactored aspect of this program will provide additional focus areas to enhance children's learning: (1) Professional development for teachers and teacher aides, (2) Conferences with presentations by experts in various academic areas, (3) Use of The Child Care Bureau to provide a network of Technical Assistance, (4) A wide variety of materials and resources for parents and teachers, (5) Numerous research projects will be ongoing to provide information on improved instruction methods and curriculum (Improve Student Performance, ED.gov, 2008).

Special Education

The Handicapped Children's Early Education Act of 1968 was the first federal legislation to specifically recognize the importance of early education for children with disabilities. This law provided grants for the development and implementation of experimental programs in early education for children with handicaps from birth to age six years. The 1991 Early Childhood Amendment concerned provision of services to disabled and at-risk preschoolers ages 3–5 years, and infants and toddlers birth-to-2 years old with established risk: Medical diagnosis, Biological diagnosis (premature, Low-birth-weight syndrome), and/or Environmental risk (poverty and its correlates) (Heward, 2006). This law was eventually merged with IDEA.

The Education for All Handicapped Children's Act of 1975 (P.L. 94-142) established a national policy regarding the education of children with disabilities from ages 3–21 years (Turnbull, 1993). The major impact of the law was the provision of special education services for children with disabilities aged six years and older (Turnbull, 1993). All of the states have a mandatory school attendance law that includes children aged 6 or 7 years old, but not younger (State Compulsory Attendance Laws, 2004). However, P.L. 94-142 provided preschool incentive grants to states that identified and served preschool children eligible for special education services (Turnbull, 1993).

Throughout the past thirty-plus years, this law has been amended five times. We will address only the amendments that specifically concerned early childhood special education. The 1983 Amendment (P.L. 98-199) gave incentives to states to provide services to preschool children with disabilities. The 1986 Amendment (P.L. 99-457) required states to provide free appropriate public education to all 3–5 year-old children with disabilities who were eligible to apply for federal preschool funding (Heward, 2006). Also, it included grants to encourage states to develop services for infants and toddlers. The 1990 Amendment (P.L. 101-476) specified that early intervention programs were to be developed to address the needs of children prenatally exposed to maternal substance abuse (Heward, 2006).

The 2004 Amendment affirmed the nation's commitment to a system of early childhood services for children with disabilities ages 3–5 years old, and early intervention services for children with disabilities birth-to-2 years old (CEC, 2006). States will also serve children ages 0–5 years old with developmental delays or at-risk conditions (medical risk, biological risk, or environmental risk). Currently, all states are providing services to children, birth-5 years with disabilities and those at-risk for disabilities (CEC, 2006).

PRE-KINDERGARTEN CURRICULUM MODELS

An early childhood program curriculum model or framework should include at least the following features: (1) A statement of the **principles** and values that should guide early childhood centers; (2) A summary of **program standards** that parents may expect in the early childhood center; (3) An orientation concerning **content and outputs** that the children will attain; (4) The pedagogical guidelines outlining the process through which the children will achieve the outcomes (play-based programming, group management, theme or project methodology) (UNESCO, 2004).

Several of the historical "curriculum models" were works-in-progress for most of the developer's career. Comenius' preschool curriculum model, at this point, is primarily the scope and sequence outline of subject areas or content that he considered important.

Historical Preschool Curriculum Models

There have been many different curricula designed for young children which adhere to various psychological learning theory perspectives and/or various theorists perspectives. However, most early childhood programs also incorporate the learning center concept into their teaching approaches. Centers include a discovery or science center; dramatic play centers including a home living center, a block-building center, and other dramatic play centers; a learning, language, and readiness materials center; an art center; a book center; a music center; and a center for large muscle activities (Hamilton et al., 1990).

Three of the early historical preschool curriculum models are included here. Two of these curriculum models–Frobel's and Montessori's–continue to be used worldwide today.

Comenius' Curriculum

During the mid-1600s, Jan Amos Comenius designed an educational system of four levels: Infancy, childhood, boyhood, and youth (each lasting six years) (Lascarides & Hinitz, 2000). He called the school for young children (birth-to-six years), the School of Infancy. The curriculum for the School of Infancy, the first formal early childhood curriculum, included the following:

1. Natural Things: Plants, animals, names of things: body parts, etc.;
2. Optics: Difference between light and darkness;
3. Astronomy: Distinguish sun, moon, stars;
4. Geography: Knowledge of where child was born, where he lives: village, town, city;
5. Chronology: Hour, day, week, month;
6. Beginning of history: Yesterday;
7. Household Affairs: Distinguish who belongs to the family and who does not;
8. Politics: State, ministers, legislation (Lascarides & Hinitz, 2004, 41).

These categories form the basis of contemporary early childhood education curriculum. Additional activities were related to music, health, cleanliness, justice, patience, and industriousness. Comenius believed that instruction should be individualized because children learn to speak and reach their developmental milestones at different ages.

Froebel's Kindergarten Curriculum

Froebel (1782-1852) regarded infancy and the preschool years as the most significant period of education, and the time most neglected in conventional education practice. He was concerned about children's moral, spiritual, physical, and intellectual growth (Froebel Web, 2008). To teach these principles, Froebel designed special educational materials that formed the core of the kindergarten curriculum. These were called "gifts," "occupations," and "Mother plays." The *gifts* were a set of geometric shapes such as balls, cubes, cut paper, string, and cylinders. These gifts were used to perform a sequence of highly structured activities called *occupations*. The occupations were highly structured activities such as sewing designs with colored threads, folding paper, weaving mats, stringing beads, and modeling clay. Through the use of the *gifts* and *occupations*, children learned geometric relationships and to understand fundamental principles of knowledge (Kindergarten, 2008). "Mother" plays are a series of finger plays, games, and songs designed to teach children about their bodies, senses, and social relationships. The "Mother" plays also enabled children to practice self-control, cooperation, and taking turns. In addition, Froebel added gardening, nature study, music, and dance to enrich the curriculum (Froebel Foundation, 2002–2007).

Although, the Froebel Kindergarten Curriculum was first designed and used in the mid-1800s, there are still many Froebel schools throughout the world today including schools in the following: St. Louis, MO; Grand Rapids, MI; Rockford, IL; Mississauga, Ontario; Toronto, Ontario; Hull, England; Islamabad, Pakistan; Germany; Honduras; and a Home-School Curriculum. Many Froebel schools have added academic readiness to the curriculum as foundation for first grade in today's academic focus (Froebel Foundation, 2008).

Montessori Schools

The Montessori schools have been proven successful all over the world with children having a variety of functioning levels and disabilities including mental retardation, learning disabilities, behavior disorders, giftedness, sensory impairments (blindness); a variety of socioeconomic backgrounds including wealthy, poor, and middle class; and taught in a variety of environments from refugee camps and slums to elegant schools in beautiful private homes (Stephenson, 2008). The Montessori curriculum designed in the early 1900s included the following:

I. **Practical Life:** Designed to instill independence, self-confidence, self-esteem and self-control. These concepts are developed through activities such as–care of person, care of environment, food preparation, fine motor development, gross motor development.

II. **Sensorial Work:** Exploration, imitation, initiation, and pattern completion are the objectives of this area. The sensorial lessons consist of auditory learning (sound), visual learning (color, size, shape, gradation), tactile learning (texture, weight, temperature), learning through smell (distinguish and match scents), learning, through taste (distinguish salty, sweet, sour).

III. **Language:** Phonics-based approach is used for reading, also includes sight words and whole language. Handwriting is a built-in feature of the language area and children learn to write as they are learning sounds. Child learns the separate skills of reading and writing at his/her own pace.

IV. **Mathematics:** Mathematical materials isolate each concept and introduce it to the child in a concrete form using manipulative equipment. Children first learn to associate each numerical symbol with the proper quantity. The child progresses one step at a time to a more abstract understanding of the concepts of arithmetic.

V. **Science:** Hands-on activity that includes biology, botany, zoology, and physical science. Children have organized time outdoors to study nature and to grow small gardens of flowers and vegetables.
VI. **Geography:** Children use Primary Globes, jigsaw puzzle maps of the world and its continents to study land and water formations (Turtle River Montessori School, 1994). There is a heavy emphasis on the cultural aspects of various countries. Each area has a scope and sequence chart of skills that children master at their own pace (Coppell Montessori Academy, 2008).

The American Montessori Society (AMS) was founded in 1960 with their primary office in New York City. Through numerous websites, one can locate the Montessori schools in America, Montessori schools in the world, various Montessori Associations and Organizations throughout America and International sites. Additionally, there are a number of universities in the United States with Master's degree programs in the Montessori Approach.

Current Popular Curriculum Models

A curriculum model refers to an educational system that has a theory and knowledge base that reflects a philosophical orientation and program content that is supported by child development research and educational evaluation (Michigan Project, 2005). The practical application of a curriculum model includes guidelines on how to set up the physical environment, structure the activities, interact with the children and their families, support staff members in their initial training, and ongoing implementation of the program. In order to provide a preschool program of the highest quality, it is necessary to adopt a research-based curriculum model (Michigan Project, 2005).

Seven "curriculum models" were evaluated using the following criteria to determine how well they met the requirements to be a good PreKindergarten curriculum model: Research-based, theory based, principles, scope and sequence of skills (developmental, academic, both), aligned standards, teacher planning, program materials, student assessment, active involvement of students, disabled or at-risk provisions, any extra teacher training required, and program assessment. These formal "curriculum models" include the following: (1) Montessori Method; (2) The Creative Curriculum; (3) High/Scope Preschool Curriculum; (4) Bank Street Approach; (5) The Pinnacle Curriculum; (6) New Portage Guide; (7) Curiosity Corner. There will be a brief summary of each of the curriculum models here, and in the back of the chapter there is a *Curriculum Model Comparison* (see TABLE 8), and a *Curriculum Comparison* for each of the curriculum models (see TABLES 9–15).

The Montessori Method

The **Montessori Method**, which has over 5000 schools in North America, has been **validated by research** (NAMTA, 1996–2008). It is theoretically based on the theories of Jean Piaget (constructivism); Itard and Sequin (developmental, individualized, systematic, child's functioning level); and Montessori's theories (auto-formation or self-development, auto-education or self-teaching, and self-motivation). The major **principles** of the program include the following: (a) Child must master the prepared environment; (b) Structural learning (concrete to abstract, simple to complex); (c) Cosmic curriculum (multisensory, child's choice); and (d) Auto-education (child learns at his own rate and in his own way). The **scope and sequence** charts focus on child developmental skills (senses), conceptual or academic development, and practical life activities and character development (Coppell Montessori Academy Curriculum, 2008). Teacher requires special training (license) for teaching the Montessori Method. There is a wealth of program materials, developmentally appropriate and specially designed didactic materials used in teaching the Montessori Method. There is **active student involvement** with the self-directed, interactive, materials-centered approach depending on the student's natural motivation to learn. The program is very successful with special needs students due to the active student involvement and self-determined activities. Teachers must be specially trained in the Montessori Method (see TABLES 8 and 9).

The Creative Curriculum for Preschool

The **Creative Curriculum** is the country's leading **research validated** comprehensive curriculum for preschool students. It is **theoretically based** on the constructivist theories of Piaget, and the activity/theme-based theories of John Dewey (Teaching Strategies, 2002–2008). The major **principles** of the program include the following: (a) Active exploration of environment using a hands-on approach; (b) Curriculum relates directly to the academic curricula used in Elementary schools; (c) Curriculum uses goals from all areas of child development. **Scope and Sequence** charts include skills at the preschool level in developmentally appropriate subjects and child development areas. **Standards are aligned** with Head Start Frameworks, and other programs. **Teacher Editions** include information on daily schedules, implementation guidelines, and specific **materials and kits** to integrate academic and developmental skills. A **student assessment** is linked to the curriculum—all assessment materials are provided. The Creative Curriculum provides **professional developmental training** for teachers and **technical assistance**.

The teacher is, also, provided with extensive **outcomes reporting** tools to help the program meet Head Start, OSEP, and state mandates (see TABLES 8 and 10).

High Scope Preschool Program

High/Scope is a comprehensive, **research-based** system with curriculum components from a variety of programs including preschool education. Each individual program consists of a complete system of **teaching practices**, **defined curriculum content areas, assessment tools**, and a **teacher training** model (High/Scope Educational Research Foundation, 2008). The preschool program is theory-based on Piagetian theory, constructivism and active learning. The Preschool curriculum is based on 58 **key development indicators** that are early childhood milestones organized around five **dimensions of school readiness**: (1) Approaches to learning; (2) Language, literacy, and communication; (3) Social and emotional development; (4) Physical development, health and well-being; and (4) The arts and sciences (mathematics, science, technology, social studies) (High/Scope Educational Research Foundation, 2008).

The High/Scope program is based on children's "Active Participatory Learning" and teachers "Intentional Teaching"; additionally "control" is shared between adults and children. The Preschool Program is based on the premises that children construct their own knowledge through discovery and direct experiences; and teachers facilitate learning through scaffolding.

High/Scope's Preschool Curriculum has been aligned with **Head Start Performance Child Outcomes**, and the early childhood standards of numerous states including New Jersey. The materials are highly organized and there are Curriculum Components for each High/Scope program. Extensive evaluation of the effectiveness of the programs exists. **The Preschool Child Observation** Record (COR) is used to **evaluate the children's progress**. The program includes a teacher training model, and **program evaluation tools** are provided (see TABLES 8 and 11) (High/Scope Educational Research Foundation, 2008).

Bank Street Developmental-Interaction Approach

The Bank Street Approach is used in Bank Street College's Demonstration School. Although there is a **modest amount of research** to support the efficacy of the Preschool Program, there is much research done on the theoretical models lending support to the curriculum. The Preschool Curriculum is **theory-based** on the theories of Jean Piaget (constructivism and active learning), Erik Erikson (social/emotional development), and John Dewey (action learning and center themes).

The approach is **based on the premise** that children must be actively involved in acquiring competence through choice, active investigation, independent pursuit, and learning through discovery. The curriculum is flexible within a planned framework encompassing developmentally appropriate knowledge and skills including **Head Start Scope and Sequence** Standards and the Bank Street standards. Teachers promote cognitive development by creating a climate that encourages questioning, exploration, and children's growing understanding of patterns, rhythms and relationships in the ideas and environment around them.

Five key social studies subjects serve as the **core of the curriculum** which integrates developmental skills (physical, emotional, cognitive, social), and academic skills of mathematics, reading, and writing. The arts and sciences help children find meaning in the world around them. The teachers serve as facilitators and create a sense of community in the environment. Students follow daily schedules which help them to become independent learners. Students are evaluated using a **trans-disciplinary play-based assessment**. Teachers observe children in various settings, record data, and notice patterns of behavior.

Students are **actively engaged** in the environment during their explorations. Children with developmental delays and disabilities have the same developmental goals set for all children, however, the goals or objectives may need to be individually modified for their specific difficulty.

The Bank Street Preschool Program requires **extensive teacher training** for curriculum implementation. **Standards are aligned** with other programs such as Head Start Programs, and with state standards. **Program evaluation** is conducted using several prepared assessments (see TABLES 8 & 12).

Pinnacle Curriculum

The Pinnacle Curriculum is **research-based** on the developmental milestones of early childhood. The **theoretical-base** is primarily Piaget's constructivism with focus on Erikson's social-emotional development, and Gardner's multiple intelligences. The Pinnacle appears to be the curriculum part of many early childhood programs such as Head Start, and faith-based prekindergarten programs. Play is a major way that children learn skills and knowledge.

The **scope and sequence** of the curriculum integrates both early childhood normal developmental milestones and the early childhood preacademic skills. The Pinnacle Curriculum has been **aligned with NAEYC** and

Georgia PreKindergarten Standards. The Pinnacle Curriculum has specific **teacher guides** for six levels. There is a teacher guide for each month with lesson plan guides, options for enriching activity centers every day/week, academic options, art patterns for classroom enrichment. **Active learning** is supported with circle time, outside time, dramatic play, art, science and math manipulatives. The program accommodates for children with **varied learning styles**, rates, and patterns. **Special teacher training is required**.

The **program is evaluated** using The Early Childhood Environmental Rating Scale; and a variety of state student evaluations are used to determine student progress. Teachers must take six mini-courses in assessment and use a variety of assessment instruments including portfolio assessment, narrative, performance-based tests, checklists of academic and developmental skills (see TABLES 8 & 13).

New Portage Guide to Early Education

The original Portage Project began as a demonstration project funded by the U.S. Department of Education in 1969 to develop a criterion-referenced checklist of developmental skills to be used for assessment and curriculum planning for children with moderate and severe intellectual disabilities. It has been used in home-based programs in rural areas, and is very popular in Europe in rural areas.

The Portage approach is based on behavioral psychology and is essentially a structured way of teaching new skills working from what a child can actually do. It is based on normal **child development skills** in all domains including social, emotional, cognitive, physical, and communication skills. It is a **home-based program**, so all of the teachers, therapists, and the parents who implement the program must have special training.

The New Portage Guide's **standards have been aligned** with the Head Start Child Outcomes Framework and the Wisconsin Model Early Learning Standards. The teacher uses the child's performance on the Portage assessment to plan the goals and objectives for the child's IEP. The teachers and therapists engage in **weekly planning** and in family partnership planning.

The Portage Kit is an **Activity Card File** that consists of 580 developmentally sequenced behaviors from birth-to-6-years of age in five developmental areas (socialization, self-help, language, cognition, and motor skills) that comprise the major part of the child's educational program. There is a spiral bound activity and resource book that the parents and teachers use in planning. **The student assessment** is a checklist of developmental skills to monitor children's progress. The amount of student involvement depends on the functioning level of the child. There is a significant amount of teacher and therapist, and parent **training** that is involved. The National Portage Association provides the training in workshops and at conferences.

The New Portage Guide (2003) was completely revised due to new research in brain development; the relationship between social and emotional development and early learning; new research on early literacy and pre-math, development of early learning standards; and the new **Head Start Outcomes Framework** (see TABLES 8 & 14).

Curiosity Corner

"Curiosity Corner" is a relatively new early childhood program developed to be used with children at-risk for school failure due to poverty. It focuses on normal childhood **developmental milestones** and **six domains of language literacy outcomes**: oral language, print knowledge, phonological processing, early reading and writing, cognition and math. Success for All Foundation created the Curiosity Corner early childhood program, and are in the process of conducting ongoing research on the success of the program. Early research indicated that compared to other preschool programs, Curiosity Corner three-year-olds showed statistically significant higher expressive language ability and greater positive social interactions than the control children.

Curiosity Corner provides a **balanced developmental approach** emphasizing language and literacy in the context of physical, emotional and interpersonal development; and **subject areas** in math, science, social studies, music, movement, and art. The **Scope and Sequence Chart** shows core skills (goals and objectives) that are targeted by various **activities across themes**. The detailed thematic units are **aligned with state and national** early childhood learning guidelines. The teacher receives a themed structured unit each week (about 30 pages of activities), thus, **very little additional teacher planning is necessary**. The teacher focuses on the instructional processes that are built around cooperative learning, active learning, and detailed supportive structure.

There are two **sets of materials**, one set for 3-year-olds and one set for 4-year-olds, with Teacher's Guides that include concrete, interactive experiences with detailed instructions and materials including games and manipulatives. Students are **actively engaged** in the daily sequence of program components including Greetings and Readings, Clues and Questions, eight different learning labs, Outside/Gross Motor Play, and Questions and Reflections.

Extensive teacher training is provided by the Success for All Foundation, and there is **ongoing program assessment** to determine if the teachers are implementing the program correctly. Using data from the professional onsite observations, the trainer determines if/what additional assistance or training is needed by the teachers, then provides that training in workshops. In addition to program assessment, the students are assessed frequently using specific **Child Assessment Tools** (see TABLES 8 & 15).

Informal Curriculum Models

There are many informal curriculums used in prekindergarten programs. Additionally, many of the informal curriculum models have been added to the formal curriculum models as one aspect of the formal models. The informal models to be discussed include the following: Activity curriculum, subject curriculum, variations of the subject curriculum, developmental curriculums, variations of the developmental curriculums, the project approach, and the theme-based approach.

Activity Curriculum

During the early to middle 1800s, Froebel (previously discussed) was the first educator to design an organized curriculum for young children which focused primarily on various activities with no attempt to formally teach academics (math, reading). Froebel was concerned about children's moral, spiritual, physical, and intellectual growth. In 1837, Froebel established his Play and Activity Institute which he renamed in 1840 as "Kindergarten" (Froebel Foundation, 2002–2007). Most significant among Froebel's educational strategies were his emphasis on guided play as a method for learning; using manipulative materials that utilize senses; and circle time which provided an opportunity to sing songs and learn new ideas through discussion (Morrow, 1989). The activity approach has been included in the High/Scope model; the Creative Curriculum; the Crayola Creative Program; Crossties; PEEK: Peabody Early Experiences Kit; the Portage Classroom Curriculum; and Small Wonder (LSU AgCenter, 2005); Pinnacle Curriculum; Montessori Method; Bank Street Developmental Interaction Approach; and Curiosity Corner.

Subject Curriculum

"The most prevalent form of curriculum organization is by subject, such as math, science, social studies, moral education, health and safety, language arts, and creative expression (art, music, and movement)" (Lawton, 1988, 241). The teacher may utilize a wide variety of teaching strategies from humanist, behavioral, developmental, and/or constructivist teaching methodology, but the subject areas are kept separate. The Early Childhood Charts: Academic Curricula (see TABLE 16) provides examples of subject curricula content for prekindergarten students. Subject curriculum has been included in many of the prekindergarten programs such as Integrated Curricula and Webbed Curriculum.

INTEGRATED CURRICULA. A variation of the subject curricula is the Integrated Curriculum which focuses on the various subject areas, however, the teacher matches subject area content from all subjects for overlapping concepts/content and teaches the overlapping areas during the same time frame. For example, if Chapter 3 in social studies covers occupations of city and health workers, and Chapter 5 in health covers health-related occupations, the teacher teaches these together as a unit rather than going sequentially through the chapters in the books.

Other integrated curricula appear to include among the curricular areas, developmental skills as well as subject areas. An example of this type of integrated curriculum includes the following centers: Art, dramatic play, language arts, large motor, math, music, science, sensory, small motor, social studies, and writing center (Herr & Libby, 1990). Integration of subject areas and developmental skills is very popular at the PreKindergarten level and can be found in the following formal programs (previously discussed): Montessori Method; Creative Curriculum; High/Scope; Bank Street; Pinnacle Curriculum; and Curiosity Corner.

WEBBED CURRICULUM. The Webbed Curriculum is also a variation of the Subject Area Curricula and Integrated Curricula. Webbed Curriculum uses a theme of interest or thematic units around which to structure content in all subject areas. Webbed Curricula require the actual planning of a visual representation of the activities in each subject area around the web theme (Krogh, 1995). "The Web" helps the teacher to achieve a balance of activities in each curricular area, and to integrate the theme across the curriculum (Krogh, 1995).

Using a Planning Web (see TABLE 17, Modified Planning Web), the Teacher writes the curriculum theme in the center circle, then writes subject specific activities (see TABLE 16) related to the theme in the subject area boxes. Thus, the teacher plans across the curriculum. There are many sources of themes (see TABLE 18), and prepared thematic units online such as Anytime Theme Units (Abraham, no date). A basic Planning Web does not include the developmental areas included on the Modified Planning Web (see TABLE 17). The developmental skills (see TABLE 7) should be written in the oval around the academic boxes in the appropriately labeled section.

Developmental Curricula

There are a variety of curricula that have roots in developmental psychology which focuses on the normal maturational process of children, birth-to-six-years old, in the areas of physical, cognitive, communication, sensorimotor, affective, and social skills (see TABLE 7). This life-oriented approach places the emphasis on the child, not on the subject matter (Hendrick, 1990).

DEVELOPMENTAL-INTERACTION CURRICULA. The developmental-interaction curricula is a process approach based on the psychological stage theories which indicate that children pass through a number of predictable, orderly stages in their growth and development. The theoretical foundations of this curriculum include Piaget's cognitive development stages, Erikson's psychosocial developmental stages, Kohlberg's moral development stages, and Gesell's normal child development stages (Hendrick, 1990). This curricular approach views the purpose of Pre-Kindergarten education to foster competence in all aspects of life in a climate of caring. Interaction is seen as occurring between the child and the environment and between various aspects of the selves within the child (Hendrick, 1990). A number of popular PreKindergarten programs use the developmental-interaction curricula including the following: High/Scope Preschool Program; Bank Street Developmental-Interaction Approach; Creative Curriculum; and Pinnacle Curriculum.

EARLY INTERVENTION CURRICULA (0–3 YEARS). Effective programming for children with disabilities requires that the planned program is in harmony with the child's developmental age and performance capabilities (Peterson, 1987). The developmental domains provide a framework for the curricular content of an early childhood special education program: visual activities, auditory activities, phonological awareness, cognitive skills, communication and language skills, fine motor skills, gross motor skills, social skills (Lerner, 1997); self-help skills and daily living skills (play skills, adaptive skills, safety skills, functional living skills) (Peterson, 1987). The Early Childhood Charts: Developmental Curricula (see TABLE 7) provides examples of early childhood intervention curricular skills.

There have been a number of early childhood intervention programs for children with various disabilities including the following: Portage Project (a home-based approach) in Wisconsin; PEECH Project (Precise Early Education for Children with Handicaps) for children with mild to moderate disabilities in Illinois.

However, with the 1997 reauthorization of IDEA, children with disabilities must have access to the general education curriculum and show progress in the general education program (previously discussed in Chapter 1). Almost all prekindergarten programs include some combination of child development skills and pre-academic or readiness skills, which is then tailored to the specific needs of young children with disabilities.

Project Approach

Most national and state standards indicate that all children regardless of age need to learn how-to do research. Project work involves children conducting research on events or things worth learning about in their own environment (University of Illinois, 1994). Usually the whole class divided into small groups is involved in the in-depth investigation (Katz & Chard, 1998). Project work is very beneficial to children as a part of their learning because the teaching-learning process is the opposite of systematic (direct) instruction used by teachers to help children acquire basic knowledge and skills (Kamii, 1991). Working in small heterogeneous groups, children of many functioning levels can also learn life skills including social skills, sharing, and helping others. Project work is based on active learning which (1) provides children with opportunities to apply skills; (2) addresses children's proficiencies; (3) stresses intrinsic motivation; and (4) encourages children to determine what they want to work on, and have a choice in how they will demonstrate their learning (Katz, 1994).

The Project Approach involves processes, content, and products (Clark, 2008). A project has three basic processes or phases: Phase 1: Beginning the Project; Phase 2: Developing the Project; and Phase 3: Concluding the Project (University of Illinois at Urbana-Champaign, 1994). Other authors are very specific that the children choose what to investigate (Katz & Chard, 1998). Probably the age and the experience level of the children needs to be considered. Some topics that the teacher may want to consider for prekindergarten age children include the following: the cafeteria; the hospital; the grocery store; ants; the clubhouse; pets; flowers; trucks; toys (Katz & Chard, 1998). The teacher and children complete a web or concept map as a result of the brainstorming and posing questions during Phase 1.

During the Phase 2 part of the project, the children do direct investigation or research on the topic. The children should be involved in a variety of activities—reading, recording, observing, interviewing experts, collecting samples, drawing while observing target, constructing models (Katz, 1994). Each child is involved in representing what he or she is learning, and each child works at his/her own level in terms of reading, writing, etc. Phase 3 is concerned with the culminating events which include preparing oral and/or written reports, and presenting oral and/or written findings, showing the specific artifacts collected or prepared by each student (Chard, 1998).

Advocates of the Project Approach suggest that it is best used as complementary to the more systematic part of the curriculum, rather than the whole curriculum (Katz, 1994). The Project Approach is an active fun way for children to apply skills previously learned. It is a valuable study skills approach that makes the student, as part of a group, go through the same process they will need throughout their educational career in preparing and writing reports.

Theme-Based Approach

The Theme-Based Approach is a popular way to organize the curriculum for preschool and primary grade students. Themes or thematic units can be added to or incorporated into almost any formal or informal curriculum model. This approach assists children in understanding the connections among the various subjects and assignments in school.

A theme is an idea or topic that a teacher and children can explore in many different ways (Kostelnik, Soderman, & Wilson, 1999). In developing a theme, teachers select topics they believe to be relevant to the curriculum and of interest to the children. The teacher builds a set of lessons around the central idea. The activities selected usually cut across the curriculum and take place simultaneously with the required curriculum or within a relatively condensed period of time throughout the day.

Theme teaching is most effective when teachers incorporate the following principles into the planning and implementation of their themes (Kostelnik, et al., 1991):

1. Themes should relate directly to children's real-life experiences.
2. Each theme should represent a concept for children to discover.
3. All themes should integrate content learning with process learning.
4. Theme related information should be learned through hands-on activities and discussion.
5. The theme should allow for integration of several subject areas in the program (across the curriculum).

There are almost unlimited resources online where teachers can buy or download themes and thematic units on almost any topic imaginable. Teachers must examine these theme-based units carefully to make sure that they build on the standards that need to be included in your state/district curriculum. One source for prepared thematic units online is **Anytime Theme Units** prepared by Cathy Abraham, a retired teacher. Each of her Units (Colors, Community Helpers, Frogs, The 5 Senses, etc.) has at least 20 pages that include songs, poems, fingerplays, field trip suggestions, creative art activity ideas, math activities, book lists, bulletin board ideas, cooking ideas, centers, and so on. Teachers need to examine prepared thematic units and select the most relevant aspects to enhance the topics they are teaching.

The "Pinnacle Curriculum" and the "Curiosity Corner" (Success for All Foundation, 2004) are two popular PreKindergarten curriculum models that incorporate thematic units into their programs. The Pinnacle Curriculum uses themes as monthly add-ons to their curriculum. Each month has themes related to the specific month by weather, holidays, activities, colors, shapes, and letters. For example, November themes are early explorers, Pilgrims, Mayflower, scarecrows, Thanksgiving. The November color is brown; shape: triangle; and letters: p, b, g (Pinnacle Curriculum, 2005).

Preschool programs such as Head Start Programs that use Curiosity Corner are provided all of the materials they will need for their thematic units. Curiosity Corner has integrated the preschool language and literacy goals and objectives with the prepared thematic units. Within each of the ten Global Themes, the students will be doing activities that deal with each of the five Language and Literacy Goals and the 21 Objectives (Curiosity Corner Scope and Sequence, 2004). Curiosity Corner is a theme-based curriculum with weekly theme guides which are the vehicle for teaching the language and literacy goals and objectives.

SUMMARY

There has long been an interest in the education of preschool-aged children. There has, however, been little agreement on the content or curriculum and the methods of pedagogy used in teaching young children. Some early theorists like Froebel thought young children should have guided play, self-chosen activities, special toys to teach concepts actively. However, Montessori recommended formalized, prescribed, and specially designed materials that were self-directed and self-paced. Gesell and colleagues studied children's behavior extensively during the early-to-mid-1900s and this information has been organized into child development schedules, which are still being used today. Piaget developed the theory of the cognitive development of the brain and encouraged "constructivism" whereby children created their own knowledge through their experiences.

Several federal laws, Head Start Act (1965), Elementary and Secondary Education Act (1965), and Education for All Handicapped Children (1975) were authorized a number of times during the past 40 years. Together these laws provide education reforms for all of the nation's children, supported by billions of dollars of funding. A wide range of formal and informal curriculums are being used today to increase the knowledge and skills of PreKindergarten-aged children.

TABLE 7

EARLY CHILDHOOD CHARTS: DEVELOPMENTAL CURRICULA

I. PHYSICAL DEVELOPMENT	GROSS MOTOR:

FINE MOTOR:
String Beads:
4 large beads; 2"; 1".
Scissors Use:
Snip with scissors.
Cut out simple shapes.
Use Crayons:
Hold crayon- -thumb & finger.
Color within lines.
Clay Manipulation:
Roll, pound, squeeze, pull.
Make balls, snakes, cookies.
Complete Puzzles:
3 interlocking pieces.
6 piece puzzle.
Builds Block Towers:
9 small blocks
Wrist & Finger Coordination:
Take apart & put together snap
   toys.
Screw/unscrew threaded
   objects.
Drive nails & pegs.
Drawing:
Imitate circular, vertical,
   horizontal strokes.
Make dots, lines, circular strokes.
Copy circle & imitates a cross.
Draw diagonal line in square.
Draw with pencil and/or crayon.
Draw a person (head, trunk, 4
   limbs).
Draw simple house.
Copy a cross & a square.
Copy triangles.
Trace a diamond.
Painting:
Paint with some wrist action.
Enjoy finger-painting.

GROSS MOTOR:
Standing and Hopping:
Stand on tiptoes momentarily.
Stand on one foot with aid.
Balance- -1 foot for 5 to 10 sec.
Hop one to two times (1 foot).
Cover 2 meters (6'6") hopping.
Walking:
Walk on a line for 3 steps.
Walk on tiptoes.
Walk backward, toe-heel.
Walk up & down stairs alone,
   alternating feet.
Walk on a balance beam.
Running & Skipping:
Run well without falling.
Run around obstacles.
Run smoothly--speed changes.
Run lightly on toes.
Skip on alternate feet.
Jumping & Kicking:
Jump off floor with both feet.
Jump over 6" high object,
   landing on both feet together.
Jump forward 10 times without
   falling.
Gallop, jump, run in rhythm
to tunes.
Jump rope.
Kick ball forward.
Riding Wheeled Toys:
Pushes, pulls, steers toys.
Ride (steers & pedals) bicycle.
Ride bike w/o training wheels.
Skate.
Throwing and Catching:
Catch bounced ball.
Catch ball with both hands.
Toss object toward target.
Throw ball overhand.
Bounces ball and catches it.

TABLE 7 (cont.)

II. EMOTIONAL DEVELOPMENT

Separate comfortably from parents.
Developing good self-concept.
Achieve the basic attitudes of
    trust, autonomy, and initiative.
Remain in contact with feelings
    while maintaining emotional
    self-control.
Face reality.
Empathizes and sympathize w/others.
Demonstrate confidence in abilities.
Experience a wide range of
    emotions.

III. PLAY DEVELOPMENT

Parallel play (plays near other
    children).
On-looker play (watches other
    children, joins in briefly).
Domestic make-believe.
Symbolically uses objects & self.
Begins cooperative play.
Participates in simple group
    activities.
Associative play (joins in play near
    other children; gradually joins in).
Uses dramatic play-acting out
    whole scenes.
Uses imaginative play with dolls.
Enjoys imaginary companions.
Plays simple table games.
Plays competitive games.
Plays games with rules.
Engages with other children in
    cooperative play, fair play, role
    assignments.

IV. SOCIAL DEVELOPMENT

Sharing:
Take turns with assistance.
Shares and asks for wants.
Shares toys.
Finds satisfaction in helping
    others.
Friendship:
Make a special friend.
Show affection for younger
    children.
Play & interacts with other
    children.
Choose own friends.
Show concern & sympathy.
Responsibility:
Sense of property is developed.
Defend own possessions.
Develop ability to stand some
    frustration.
Enjoy doing things for self.
Likes to be trusted.
Wants to do what is expected.
Respects reasonable authority.
Shows responsibility in taking
    care of the classroom.
Shows respect for each other
    and each others' property.
Social Cognition:
Learns to control unsocial
    impulses.
Acquires socially acceptable
    strategies for getting wants.
Learns to function successfully
    as a member of a group.
Understands their place in the
    world, and feels good about
    their gender role and ethnic
    heritage.

TABLE 7 (cont.)

V. <u>COGNITIVE DEVELOPMENT</u>

<u>INITIATIVE AND CURIOSITY:</u>

<u>Observes objects with curiosity:</u>

Examines with attention to detail
   noticing attributes of objects.
Asks questions about similarities
   & differences seeking information.

<u>Approaches problems flexibly:</u>

Finds multiple uses for objects.
Experiments with materials in
   new ways.
Finds alternative solutions to
   solving problems.

<u>Applies knowledge or experience</u>
   <u>to new concept:</u>

Uses daily experiences & applies
   knowledge to similar situations.
Applies new information/vocabulary
   to an activity or interaction.
Generates a rule, strategy, or idea
   from one learning experience
   and applies to a new concept.

<u>LANGUAGE DEVELOPMENT:</u>

Answers question with details;
   a complete thought.
Asks increasingly complex questions
   to further own understanding.
Discusses familiar & new topics
   and continues discussions by
   asking questions or making
   comments.
Follows oral directions with more
   than two steps.

<u>ENGAGEMENT & PERSISTENCE:</u>

<u>Shows persistence in approaching</u>
   <u>and completing tasks.</u>

Continues work on task even when
   facing difficulties.
Maintains concentration over time
   on task, question, set of
   directions or interactions.
Completes a variety of tasks,
   activities, projects and
   experiences (finishes painting,
   before moving to next activity,
   puts toy away before leaving
   the area, etc.).
Asks for and accepts help and/or
   suggestions from teacher or
   peers for problem solving.
Demonstrates ability to set goals
   and follow through on plans
   to completion.

<u>REASONING & PROBLEM SOLVING:</u>

<u>Compares/Measures:</u>

Uses comparative words related
   to number, size, shape, texture,
   weight, color, speed, volume.

<u>Explores cause and effect:</u>

Explains plans for testing cause
   and effect & tests possibilities.
Offers simple, age appropriate
   reasons & ideas for tasks &
   problem solving.
Generates idea in one learning
   experience & applies in new
   context.

TABLE 7 (cont.)

VI. LANGUAGE DEVELOPMENT

RECEPTIVE LANGUAGE:	EXPRESSIVE LANGUAGE:
Semantics:	**Semantics:**
Points to pictures of common objects when they are named. Responds to simple directions (Give me a ball.) Grasps meaning of time words (after awhile, in a minute). Identifies objects when told use. Understands time concepts (tomorrow). Carry out a series of 2-4 related directions. Follow 3 unrelated commands in proper order. Understands "Let's pretend." Incorporates verbal directions into play activities. Understands sequencing of events.	Repeats at least one nursery rhyme & sings a song. Tells content of a story, may confuse some facts.
	Morphology:
	Uses "s" on nouns to indicate plurals. Uses "ed" on verbs to indicate past tense.
Morphology:	**Syntax:**
Understands size comparatives (big, bigger). Understands comparatives (pretty, prettier, prettiest).	Ask "what" and "where" questions. Makes negative statements. Uses sentences of 3 or more words (agent/action/object). Talks about past experiences. Ask "when," "how," "why." Join simple sentences to make compound subjects/predicates. Talk about causality by using "because" or "so."
Syntax:	**Pragmatics:**
Understands questions beginning With "what" & "where." Understands "if. . . .then" and "because" relationships.	Give first and last name. Give and receive information. Communicate with family, friends, and strangers. Basic functional use of language: rituals (greetings & farewells), informing/asking, controlling (asking, promising, negotiating), expressing feelings.

TABLE 7 (cont.)

EXPRESSIVE LANGUAGE (cont.):

Narrative Production:
   (Ages 3-5 years)

Proto-narratives centered around
   a central theme, character, or
   setting.
Proto-narratives include a
   beginning, middle, and ending;
   with no plot or cause-effect.
Children talk about 1 or more
   events and begin to use
   structured components of
   narrative; setting (where);
   events; complications; and
   endings/outcomes.
Sequencing or sentence chaining
   with "and then" is common,
   does not focus on story
   chronology.
Begins to produce primitive
   narratives or stories containing
   a basic episode: Initiating event
   or problem; attempt or action
   by character to solve the problem;
   and consequences or resolution
   of problem.

VII: AUDITORY DEVELOPMENT:

Discrimination of Sound:

Discriminate between two words.
Differentiate commands ("come"
   and "sit down").
Differentiate initial consonants,
   vowel patterns, and number of
   syllables (ball, lollipop).
Differentiate initial consonants
   and number of syllables, similar
   vowel patterns (cat, rattle).

Differentiate vowel patterns and
   syllables, same initial
   consonants (boat, banana).
Same vowel pattern and consonant,
   different number of syllables
   (base, baseball).
Same vowel pattern and syllables,
   different number of syllables
   (bat, cat).

Recognition of Sound:

Match same sound that is given.
 Point to picture of common object
   when named.
Respond to verbal greeting.
Anticipate routine activities
   from sound cues.
Produce two sounds in order
presented.
Recognize intended sound source
   with one distracting sound
   source present.
Recognize intended sound source
   with multiple distracting sounds.

Comprehension of Sound:

Respond correctly when asked
   "where."
Understands prepositions "on,"
   "in," "under".
Follow series of two/three
   related directions.
Listens to story books read and
   requests to be read again.
Understands comparatives.
Understands opposites.
Sequences events verbally.
Understands receptive language
   academic skills.

TABLE 7 (cont.)

VIII. <u>VISUAL DEVELOPMENT</u>

<u>Visual-Motor Development:</u>

Retrieves objects quickly and
    accurately.
Put objects accurately in container
    (eye-hand coordination).
Catch a ball.
Build a 3-block tower.
Demonstrate body awareness by
    matching body parts to those of
    a doll or picture.
Touch body parts on cue (body-
    awareness localization).

<u>Visual Perception:</u>

Recognizes common objects visually.
Visually discriminate by size, shape,
    color.
Match common objects (visual
    classification).
Demonstrate visual directionality.
Complete pegboard, formboard,
    puzzle (visual figure-ground).
Remember pictures shown or
    follows visual directions
    (visual memory).
Sequence 3 objects or pictures
    logically.
Use common objects purposefully
    (visual comprehension).
Duplicate geometric designs/
    letters (visual-motor
    integration).

IX. <u>SELF-HELP SKILLS</u>

<u>Dressing:</u>

Begin to pull down garments.
Button large front buttons.
Open front and side buttons.
Close front snaps.
Dress with light weight garments.
Distinguish between front and
    back of garment.
Button series of buttons.
Learn to buckle belt.
Dress & undress with minimum
    assistance.
Tie single knot with shoe laces.

<u>Grooming:</u>

Attempts to wash hands when
    assisted.
Wipes nose with tissue.
Wash and dry hands.
Dispose of paper towels and
    Tissues.
Bathe self with minimum of
    Supervision.
Wet brush and apply toothpaste.
Attempt to comb hair.
Begin to lace shoes.

<u>Eating:</u>

Hold small cup in one hand.
Use small glass with little
    assistance.
Chew and swallow before
    speaking.
Serve self with finger foods.
Pours liquid from pitcher.
Serves self at table.

TABLE 7 (cont.)

IX. SELF-HELP SKILLS (cont.)

Utensil Use:

Holds fork and spears food.
Spoon inserted without inverting,
    less spillage.
Holds spoon with fingers, less
    spillage.
Spears food with fork and eat with
    fork.
Spreads soft butter with knife.
Eats well with fork and spoon.
Cuts well with knife.

Toileting:

Begins to sit on potty.
Requires assistance with clothes
    and wiping.
Communicates need to use bathroom.
Pulls pants down.
Requires assistance pulling pants
    up and down.
Seats self on toilet.
Attempts to wipe after toileting.
Goes to bathroom alone.
Independent at manipulation of
    simple clothes.
Require assistance with wiping.
Is regularly dry at night.
Independent in toileting (clothing,
    setting, wiping, flushing)---age
    4-5 years.

References: Bailey & Wolery, 1992; Barraga, 1983; Caplan, 1971; Frost,
             1972; Gard et al., 1980; Wadsworth, 1984; Jones, 1988;
             Peterson, 1987; Krogh, 1994 and 1995; Hendrick, 1990;
             Healy et al., 1978; Dummer et al., 1995; Creative Curriculum,
             2005; Head Start, 2003; Nippold, 2006.

			TABLE 8				
			CURRICULUM MODEL COMPARISONS				
			Summary Table: Formal Models				
Curricula Criteria	**Montessori Method**	**Creative Curriculum**	**High Scope**	**Bank Street**	**Pinnacle Curriculum**	**New Portage**	**Ceative Corner**
Research Based	Yes	Yes	Yes	Yes	Yes	Yes	Yes
Theory Based	Yes	Yes	Yes	Yes	Yes	Yes	Yes
Principles/ Character- istics	Yes	Yes	Yes	Yes	Yes	Yes	Yes
Scope & Sequence: Develop./ Academic/ Both	Both	Both	Both	Both	Both	Develop-mental	Both
Standards Aligned	Yes	Yes	Yes	Yes	Yes	Yes	Yes
Teacher Planning	Yes	Provided	Some Required	Yes	Provided	Plans IEPs	Provided
Program Materials	Yes	Yes	Yes	Informal	Yes	Yes	Provided
Student Assess- ment	Informal & formal	Provided	Provided	Informal Provided	Informal	Check-list	Yes
Active Involve- ment	Yes	Yes	Yes	Yes	Yes	Depends on Child	Yes
Disabled/ At-Risk	Yes	Yes	Yes	Yes	Yes	Yes	Yes
Teacher Training	Montessori License	Professional Development	Requires Training	Requires Training	Requires Training	Extensive Training	Extensive Training
Program Evaluation	Requires Outcomes Reporting	Extensive Outcomes Reporting	Requires Outcomes Reporting	Requires Outcomes Reporting	Requires Outcomes Reporting	Requires Outcomes Reporting	Requires Outcomes Reporting

TABLE 9

Curriculum Model Comparisons

Montessori Method

1. **Research-Based:**
   Montessori Method has been validated by a number of research studies in both private and public sectors for program effectiveness.

2. **Theory-Based:**
   Theory-based on Jean Piaget's constructive approach; original theories of Itard and Sequin (developmental, individualized, systematic, child's functioning level); and Montessori's theories of auto-formation (self-development), auto-education (self-teaching), and self-motivation.

3. **Principles and/or Program Characteristics:**
   Major premises of Montessori Method includes the following: (a) children are capable of self-directed learning. (b) It is critically important for teacher to be "observer" not lecturer. (c) Beware of child's "sensitive periods" of learning. (d) Children have an "absorbent mind" from birth to age 6 years". (e) Children are masters of their school room environment. (f) Children learn through discovery, so didactic materials with a control for error are used, so child can self-correct. (g) Children most often learn alone during periods of intense concentration. (h) The hand is connected to the developing brain in children—use hands-on experiences. (i) Children's cognitive processes are inherently different from an adults. (j) 63% of class time is spent in individual activity.

4. **Scope/Sequence (Developmental, Academic, Both):**
   Montessori Method focuses on the child development skills (senses), conceptual or academic development, and practical life activities and character development.

5. **Standards Aligned:**
   When Montessori Schools are part of the public school system, both sets of standards are aligned and assessed.

6. **Teacher Planning:**
   Teacher's primary role is to organize the materials and the classroom, and facilitate the child's choices and learning.

(Montessori Method, cont.)

7. **Program Materials:**
   Wealth of materials that support program (can order online). Materials are specially designed; developmentally appropriate toys, games, tools, etc. Uses sequential didactic materials and exercises for sensory, motor, and intellectual education. Materials proceed from simple to complex, from concrete to abstract.

8. **Student Assessment:**
   In general Montessori Schools use standardized tests for national reference. Examples of the norm-referenced tests used are the Iowa Tests of Basic Skills or the California Achievement Test. Montessori Schools in the public school system are assessed using the district and state assessment system.

9. **Active Student Involvement:**
   Program is developed around hands-on learning environment, child oriented, "self-directed, interactive, materials-centered approach". Relies on natural motivation of the child to learn.

10. **Provisions for Disabled/At-Risk:**
    Special needs children (ADHD, learning or psychological problems) because of individualized program with self-selected and self paced learning.

11. **Teacher Training:**
    Requires Montessori license. There are also materials and courses for professional development.

12. **Program Evaluation:**
    Montessori Programs in the public schools must have the same outcomes-based tests as other district and state programs. Additionally, Montessori objectives are evaluated through observations and notation.

13. **References:**
    NAMTA (North American Montessori Teacher's Association (1991). Montessori Research Summary. <www.montessori-namta.org>

    Olaf, Michael (2008). The Montessori Method. The Montessori Foundation. <www.michaelolaf.net> or <www.Montessori.org>

    Orem, R. C. (1991). <u>Montessori Today</u>. New York: Putnam's Sons.

TABLE 10

Curriculum Model Comparisons

Creative Curriculum

1. **Research-Based:**
   The Creative Curriculum is the country's leading scientifically based, research validated comprehensive curriculum: Programs for Infants; Toddlers and Twos; Family Child Care.

2. **Theory-Based:**
   Theoretically, the program is based on the theories of Jean Piaget (constructivism), and John Dewey (learning through activities, themes).

3. **Principles and/or Program Characteristics:**
   Major principles of the program include the following: (a) The children are involved in the active exploration of the environment using a hands-on approach. (b) This program will assist children to become independent, self-confident, inquisitive, and enthusiastic learners. (c) The curriculum relates directly to the subject area (academic) curricula used in elementary schools, so children's learning in preschool forms the foundation of the learning that follows. (d) The curriculum identifies goals in all areas of child development: Social/emotional, cognitive, physical, and language abilities. (e) Program includes a parenting component.

4. **Scope/Sequence (Developmental, Academic, Both):**
   The scope and sequence charts include skills at the preschool level in developmentally appropriate academic subject areas and in child development areas.

5. **Standards Aligned:**
   The curriculum skills have been aligned with a number of sets of standards including the Head Start Child Outcomes Framework.

6. **Teacher Planning:**
   A variety of teacher instructional materials are available including training manuals, audio-visual resources, planned activities for the children, guidelines on how-to organize the environment, the daily schedule is planned, and a list of toys and materials for the lessons are available. The Teacher's Editions show teachers how to integrate the activities in academic and developmental areas. Very little extra teacher planning is required in this comprehensive program.

(Creative Curriculum, cont.)

7. **Program Materials:**
   A wide range of materials accompany the program including prepared kits; Creative Curriculum Literacy Kits, Creative Curriculum for Preschool Math Kits, Creative Curriculum Science and Social Studies Kits, etc. Materials for eleven different centers, and dozens of activities for teachers to use are provided.

8. **Student Assessment:**
   A student assessment system is linked to the curriculum. The assessment materials are provided including: Literacy Implementation Checklist: Literacy Observation Tools; The Creative Curriculum Development Continuum for ages 3-5 has 50 objectives—this tool has been proven valid and reliable in a wide range of research studies; Individual Child Summary Worksheet; Class Summary Worksheet; and CC-Port The Creative Curriculum Progress and Outcomes Reporting Tool.

9. **Active Student Involvement:**
   Children are actively involved in "learning through play". The Early Childhood staff teaches children academic subjects and functional skills in a play-based environment that is designed to be imaginative, flexible, innovative, and fun.

10. **Provisions for Disabled/At-Risk:**
    The curriculum is inclusive of all learners especially children with disabilities or at-risk because most of the program is individualized.

11. **Teacher Training:**
    Creative Curriculum provides professional development for teachers, and technical assistance.

12. **Program Evaluation:**
    Creative Curriculum provides tools and technical assistance, and extensive outcomes reporting tools to help programs meet Head Start, OSEP, and state mandates.

13. **References:**

    * Creative Curriculum System (2002-2008). Literacy in the creative curriculum for preschool. Teaching Strategies Inc. <http://www.creative curriculum.net>

TABLE 11

Curriculum Model Comparisons

High/Scope Preschool Program

1. **Research-Based:**
   Four decades of research from thousands of programs would-wide have validated the effectiveness in promoting children's development.

2. **Theory-Based:**
   The theoretical base of this program lies with Jean Piaget's constructivist theory and other developmentally appropriate guidelines.

3. **Principles and/or Program Characteristics:**
   Children use active learning in working with materials, manipulation of concrete items, making choices, development of language skills, and the assistance of adult scaffolding. A basic premise of the program is that children learn best by doing. "Control" is shared between adults and children, so that children's creativity is encouraged. Active learning is the central element—children must construct their own knowledge by discovering through direct experiences. This is called "Active Participatory Learning". A central element of the day is the "plan-do-review" sequence in which the children make a plan, carry it out, and then reflect on it. The daily routine also includes time for small and large group experiences and time for outside play.

4. **Scope/Sequence (Developmental, Academic, Both):**
   The program focus is 58 key developmental indicators (KDIs) that are early childhood milestones based around the five dimensions of school readiness identified by the National Education Goals Panel: Approaches to learning; language, literacy, and communication; social and emotional development; physical development, health and well-being; and the arts and sciences (math, technology, social studies, science.

5. **Standards Aligned:**
   High/Scope has been aligned with Head Start Performance Child Outcome Standards and the early childhood standards of numerous states including New Jersey.

(High/Scope cont.)

6. **Teacher Planning:**
   Program includes a set of teaching practices for adult-child interaction, arranging the classroom and materials; curriculum content areas; a teacher training model. Teacher's role is as a facilitator.

7. **Program Materials:**
   Materials are carefully organized for specific play. Computers are a regular part of the program. Curriculum components for numerous programs: Infants and Toddlers; Preschool; Early Literacy; Movement and Music; Elementary; Youth Development. Each individual program consists of a complete system of teaching practices, defined curriculum content areas, assessment tools, and teacher training model.

8. **Student Assessment:**
   Assessment tools are provided. The Preschool Child Observation Record (COR) is used to evaluate the children's program.

9. **Active Student Involvement:**
   Children have direct, hands-on experiences. Children have active involvement with people, materials, ideas, and events. Children are encouraged to make their own choices about materials and activities.

10. **Provisions for Disabled/At-Risk:**
    High/Scope was created for at-risk urban children. It has been used successfully with Head Start programs, effective with children with developmental delays and learning disabilities because it is tailored to each child's individual level and pace.

11. **Teacher Training:**
    Teacher training in "Intentional Teaching", adult scaffolding, etc. program includes a teacher training model with courses and conferences.

12. **Program Evaluation:**
    Extensive evaluation of the effectiveness of the program exists. Program evaluation tools provided include the Preschool Program Quality Assessment (PQA) which assesses the quality of the program and identifies staff training needs.

13. **References:**

High/Scope Educational Research Foundation (2008). High/Scope Preschool Curriculum. <http://www.highscope.org>

TABLE 12

Curriculum Model Comparisons

Bank Street Developmental-Interaction Approach

1. **Research-Based:**
   As a Title 1 school and New York City school, Bank Street has ongoing research as to the effectiveness of the school especially for children at-risk. Much research has been conducted on the theoretical models lending support to the curriculum.

2. **Theory-Based:**
   The Bank Street Program is based on the theories of Jean Piaget (constructivism), Erik Erikson (social/emotional development), John Dewey (action learning and centers/themes).

3. **Principles and/or Program Characteristics:**
   The approach aims for actively involving children in acquiring competence. Making choices, active investigations, independent pursuit of learning through discovery are dominant components of the learning climate. The curriculum is flexible within a planned framework encompassing developmentally appropriate knowledge and skills. Adults relate to each child as a person and as a learner. Bank Street College of Education, also, operates Head Start Programs which integrates the Head Start standards into the Bank Street Developmental-Interaction Approach.

4. **Scope/Sequence (Developmental, Academic, Both):**
   There is a planned framework encompassing developmentally appropriate knowledge and skills—physical, emotional, cognitive, and social. There is a focus on five key social studies subjects: Cultural anthropology, history, political science, economics, and geography. Arts and science education are woven in with the world around them. There are also learning activities in mathematics thinking, language and literacy, and writing that are integrated into the curriculum. Social studies serves as the core of the curriculum. Bank Street Head Start programs also include the Head Start requirements.

5. **Standards Aligned:**
   The Bank Street Preschool Program's developmental standards and their social studies core curriculum are aligned with the Head Start performance standards and performance indicators with a focus on readiness academics. These standards form the base for the curriculum.

(Bank Street, cont.)

6. Teacher Planning:
The Bank Street Preschool Program is less structured than many programs, leaving a lot of discretion to individual teachers and children to decide what they want to work on. Children learn by experimenting and exploring, and making discoveries. Teachers are facilitators of learning; and they create a sense of community. Teachers plan detailed schedules for the children that include written labels, messages, job charts, signals that tell where materials, etc. are found, the events of the day, the choices they have available. Detailed schedules help children become independent.

7. Materials:
Children play with toys and materials that leave a lot to the imagination—blocks, water, art materials, clay, puzzles, etc. Many of the materials are either teacher or parent made or children made. The program has adequate materials to support the learning focus of the curriculum.

8. Student Assessment:
Children are assessed using a trans-disciplinary play-based assessment. Teachers observe children in various trans-disciplinary settings, record observations, and notice patterns of behavior. Bank Street uses assessments that are provided by Head Start and assessments they have created. Students are assessed on all of the standards of the program.

9. Active Student Involvement:
Children engage actively with the environment to increase motivation. They have direct and rich interactions with a wide variety of materials, ideas, and people in their environment. Children go about their work, moving and talking freely.

10. Provisions for Disabled/At-Risk:
Bank Street College's Early Childhood Center believes that programs for disadvantaged children should be geared to the same developmental goals set for all children. However, they modify the methods for reaching the goals by adapting them to the individual child's developmental deficits. In 1986 the landmark program for including the infants, toddlers and preschoolers with developmental delays and/or disabilities was started in the Family Center. Teachers work very closely with therapy staff to meet the needs of the children (IEP or IFSP).

(Bank Street, cont.)

11. **Teacher Training:**
    Bank Street Preschool Program requires extensive training on curriculum implementation and integrating all of the various standards that children must meet. Bank Street College provides much of the training that their teachers need.

12. **Program Evaluation:**
    In program evaluation Bank Street uses A *Tool Kit for Evaluating Initiatives to Improve Child Care Quality* (2006) and *Early Childhood Environmental Rating Scale* (which is aligned to the *Creative Curriculum Implementation Checklist*). They also collect performance data on the children and aggregate it to determine efficacy in learning.

13. **References:**

    * Bank Street Head Start (2006). *A Tool Kit for Evaluating Initiatives to Improve Child Care Quality.* <www.bankstreet.edu/iccc/toolkit.html>

    * Bank Street Head Start (2006): Curriculum and Assessment. <www.bankstreet.edu/headstart/curriculum.html>

TABLE 13

Curriculum Model Comparisons

Pinnacle Curriculum

1. **Research-Based:**
   The Pinnacle Curriculum is research-based on the developmental milestones of early childhood.

2. **Theory-Based:**
   The theoretical base of the Pinnacle Curriculum includes Jean Piaget's constructivist theory, Gesell's normal child developmental skills areas, Erikson's social-emotional development, and Gardner's multiple intelligences.

3. **Principles and/or Program Characteristics:**
   (The Pinnacle Curriculum seems to be the major curriculum part of a number of programs, for example, a Head Start program may be established with their guidelines, then purchase the Pinnacle Curriculum for the organized curriculum standards, materials, etc.) (a) Behavior is a function of structure and humans develop in a patterned predictable way (Gesell). (b) The teacher uses guided discovery, and themes to capture children's interest. (c) Faith-based Pre-Kindergarten programs using Pinnacle Curriculum wish to offer a balance of academic education and developmental standards and instill Christian values. (d) Play is a major way that children learn skills and knowledge. (e) Themes are used to capture children's interest.

4. **Scope/Sequence (Developmental, Academic, Both):** The scope and sequence of the curriculum integrates both early childhood normal developmental milestones (Pinnacle Curriculum) and the early childhood preacademic skills (i.e., Georgia's PreKindergarten Content Standards). This program promotes early literacy, and developmentally appropriate and age-appropriate activities in all areas. There are clearly stated learning objectives in all domains.

5. **Standards Aligned:**
   The standards of Pinnacle Curriculum are aligned with NAEYC and Georgia PreKindergarten Standards, for example. If the Preschool was also a Head Start School, those standards would also be included in the alignment.

6. **Teacher Planning:**
   The teachers are provided with daily resources that make implement-

(Pinnacle Curriculum, cont.)

ing the prepared lesson plans easier to implement. Suggested book lists and monthly supply lists are also provided. Thus, the teachers are provided most of the lesson resources that they will need.

7. **Program Materials:**
The Pinnacle Curriculum has specific teacher guides for six levels: Infants, Toddlers, Twos, Threes, Fours, School-age. There is a teacher guide for each month with lesson plan guides, options for enriching activity centers every day/week, academic options, art patterns for classroom enrichment. ChildCraft Education Corporation has designed classrooms with special child sized furniture, centers, etc. to set up in the classroom, so the teacher does not have to plan centers, etc.

8. **Student Assessment:**
Teachers use Gesell developmental skills checklists. Pinnacle requires teachers to take six courses related to assessment of young children including portfolio assessment, narrative, performance-based, checklists. In addition, they are administered assessments on their academic standards. ChildCare Education Institute has these courses, etc. prepared.

9. **Active Student Involvement:**
The students use hands-on, center-based, multisensory activities that promote the development of emerging skills. Some of the active learning preschool experiences include circle time, outside time, dramatic play, art, science and math manipulatives.

10. **Provisions for Disabled/At-Risk:**
The program accommodates for children with varied learning styles. Each child has a rate and a pattern of growth, and teachers observe each child to determine their rate and pattern of growth. The activities are all multisensory which is helpful to many children who have disabilities or are at-risk.

11. **Teacher Training:**
Teacher Enrichment Training Solutions provide many courses for professional development.

12. **Program Evaluation:**
The Early Childhood Environmental Rating Scale is often used to evaluate the PreKindergarten Programs, and a variety of state student evaluations are aggregated to determine student progress.

(Pinnacle Curriculum, cont.)

When the Pinnacle Curriculum is used in a Head Start program, Head Start assessments are also used.

13. **References:**

Pinnacle Curriculum (2005). Pinnacle early childhood curriculum. ChildCare Education Institute. <http://www.cceionline.com>

TABLE 14

Curriculum Model Comparisons

New Portage Guide to Early Education

1. **Research-Based:**
The Portage Program has been used in home-based programs for children with moderate and severe intellectual disabilities since 1969. Research has not overwhelmingly shown success. However, the developmental skills on which the program is based have been validated by research.

2. **Theory-Based:**
The Portage approach is based on behavioral psychology and is essentially a structured way of teaching new skills working from what a child can actually do. The original Portage Project began as a demonstration project funded by the U.S. Department of Education in 1969 to develop a criterion-referenced checklist of developmental skills to be used for assessment and curriculum planning for children with moderate and severe intellectual disabilities.

3. **Principles and/or Program Characteristics:**
The Portage Program is an intervention program for families with children from 0-6 years-old who have special education needs. It is a home-based program in which teachers and therapists make home visits to train parents in teaching assessing the progress of their child. Services to families are more useful when they support everyday living and are delivered in the child's natural environment.

4. **Scope/Sequence (Developmental, Academic, Both):**
The scope and sequence of skills is based on child developmental skills in all domains including social, emotional, cognition, physical, and communication developmental skills areas with functioning skills from birth-to-six-years.

5. **Standards Aligned:**
The New Portage Guide's standards have been aligned with the Head Start Child Outcomes Framework and the Wisconsin Model Early Learning Standards.

6. **Teacher Planning:**
Teacher uses the child's performance on the Portage assessment to plan the goals and objectives for the child's IEP or IFSP. The teacher and therapists engage in weekly planning and family partnership planning.

(Portage cont.)

7. **Program Materials:**
   The Portage Kit is an Activity Card File that consists of 580 developmentally sequenced behaviors from birth-to-age-six-years in five areas (socialization, self-help, language, cognition, and motor skills) that comprise the major part of the child's educational program. There is a spiral bound activity and resource book that the parents and teachers use in planning.

8. **Student Assessment:**
   Student assessment is a checklist of developmental skills to monitor the child's progress. The parents and teachers assess through observation of the child while performing the specific developmental tasks on the IEP. There are two separate skills assessment packages: (1) Infants and Toddlers, and (2) Preschool 3-6 years. The Tool for Observation and Planning is used for weekly planning and family partnerships.

9. **Active Student Involvement:**
   The amount of student involvement depends on the functioning level of the child. The skills are presented in a direct instruction play-based format.

10. **Provisions for Disabled/At-Risk:**
    The program and materials, etc. were specifically developed for children with moderate and severe developmental delays. The home-based approach of having the teacher and therapists go to the family home and train them was specifically designed for rural parents of moderate and severely disabled children.

11. **Teacher Training:**
    There is a significant amount of teacher training involved. Trainers must have credentials as a trainer to be able to train the therapists, the teachers, and the parents. The National Portage Association provides the training in workshops and at conferences.

12. **Program Evaluation:**
    The New Portage Guide (2003) was completely revised because of new research on brain development; the relationship between social and emotional development and early learning; new research on early literacy and pre-math; development of early learning standards; and the Head Start Outcomes Framework. The Tool for Observation and Planning (TOP) was designed for assessing children's development in programs such as: Head Start, Early Head Start, Child Care,

(Portage cont.)

Preschool Programs, 4-year-old Kindergarten, Early Childhood Special Education, Inclusion Programs, and Home Visitation Programs.

13. **References:**

* The Portage Project (2003). The New Portage Guide Birth-to-Six: The Tool for Observation and Planning (TOP). <www.portageproject.org>

TABLE 15

Curriculum Model Comparisons

Curiosity Corner

1. **Research-Based:**
   There is on-going research by Success for All Foundation including both program assessment and student assessment. The results of the first year assessments in New Jersey indicated that the 3-year-olds in Curiosity Corner showed statistically significant higher expressive language ability and social interactions compared to control children. Another early research showed no discernable effects on oral language and cognition.

2. **Theory-Based:**
   The Curiosity Corner is an early childhood program that is a language and literacy focused problem-solving program based on the normal childhood developmental skills and preschool readiness skills. It focuses on cooperative learning, and active learning within a carefully designed supportive structure.

3. **Principles and/or Program Characteristics:**
   (a) This early childhood curriculum was designed to help children at-risk for later school failure due to poverty. (b) The children's experiences will develop attitudes, skills, and knowledge necessary for later school successes with special emphasis on language and literacy skills. (c) The integrated approach is built on a daily sequence of components: Greetings and Readings, Clues and Questions, Rhyme Time, 8 Learning Labs, Story Tree, Outside/Gross Motor Play, Snack Time, Question and Reflection, and Home Link.

4. **Scope/Sequence (Developmental, Academic, Both):**
   The Scope and Sequence Chart shows core skills (goals and objectives) in child development and readiness skills that are targeted by various activities across themes.

5. **Standards Aligned:**
   The detailed thematic units are aligned with state and national early-learning guidelines.

6. **Teacher Planning:**
   The teacher receives a themed structured unit each week (total of 38). Thus, the teacher can focus on the instructional processes that are built around cooperative learning, active teaching, and detailed supportive structure.

(Curiosity Corner, cont.)

7. **Program Materials:**
    There are two sets of materials one set for three-year-olds and one for four-year-olds of 38 weekly thematic structured units that include concrete, interactive experiences with detailed instructions and materials. The Teacher's Manual has instructional activities, themes, children's activities and games, and manipulatives.

8. **Student Assessment:**
    Student assessment will involve assessing the goals and objectives as the students progress through the various global themes. The Program includes specific Child Assessment Tools.

9. **Active Student Involvement:**
    Daily activities are conducted in a sequential order to provide active learning experiences. Parents are encouraged to actively engage in children's learning though various activities both in and out of the classroom. Students are very active during the daily sequence of components including Greetings and Readings, Clues and Questions, eight different learning labs, Outside/Gross Motor Play, and Questions and Reflections.

10. **Provisions for Disabled/At-Risk:**
    Curiosity Corner is implemented in Head Start centers and various early childhood centers mostly in high poverty neighborhoods with children who are at-risk for academic failure. Each class has one teacher and one assistant for 15 students.

11. **Teacher Training:**
    Extensive teacher training and support are required. The Program provides training, support, and teaching materials for teaching staff. The in-depth professional development is provided by the Success for All Foundation's training staff to support teachers' implementation of the thematic units.

12. **Program Evaluation:**
    The program assessment is very rigorous and actually starts with the initial implementation of the Curiosity Corner. There are two visits to the site that include classroom observations and professional development workshops. Using rubrics outlining what teachers and children should be doing during aspects of the program, the Success for All Foundation (SAF) trainers evaluate the various aspects of the program and its effect on the children. Using the data from the observations, the SAF trainers identify specific pro-

(Curiosity Corner, cont.)

fessional development needs for the teachers, and then conduct targeted workshops.

13. **References:**

* Curiosity Corner Scope and Sequence (2004). Language and Literacy.Success for all Foundation. <CC_Scope_and_Seq.pdf> or <www.successforall.net/early/early-curriculum.htm>

* Curiosity Corner (2004). Success for All Foundation. <http://www.successforall.net/early/early-kindercorner.htm>

TABLE 16

EARLY CHILDHOOD CHARTS: ACADEMIC CURRICULA

I. EMERGENT LITERACY

PHONOLOGICAL AWARENESS:

Aware of speech sounds.
Hear rhyming words.
Can segment a sentence.
Divide words into syllables.
Auditory discriminate relevant
   phonetic sounds.
Engage in auditory blending of
   phonetic sounds.
Identify sounds.
Engage in word segmentation.
Can segment & blend sounds.
Contrast beginning and ending
   sounds.

PREREADING:

Identifies labels & signs in
   environment.
Knows printed words represent
   spoken words.
Comprehends meaning of place,
   quantitative, and descriptive
   words (i.e., in/on, before/after).
Predicts future events.
Shows awareness of print, books &
   purpose of reading.
Visually discriminates letters and
   words.
Matches letters and words.
Identifies letters and words.
Sound-letter match and
   recognition.
Sequence: left to right, top to
   bottom, front to back.
Uses picture clues to identify
   unknown words, clarify concepts,
   and make inferences.
Sequence story events using
   pictures or orally.

WRITING DEVELOPMENT:

Explore writing materials.
Scribble for writing.
Differentiate between drawing
   and writing.
Print numbers 1-5.
Use one hand dominantly.
Copy first name.
Print letters, a few simple
   words, & a few capital letters.
Use adult grasp of pencil.
Use learned letters randomly
   for writing.
Attempt writing in order to
   convey meaning.
Use invented spelling for
   writing.
Dictate stories or sentences
   s/he wants written down.

COMPREHENSION OF STORIES:

Retells familiar stories using the
   pictures in the book.
Retell a story without the help
   of a book or pictures.
Include elements of story:
   structure in the story retellings;
   setting, theme, plot, resolution.
Answers questions about the
   stories that are on the literal,
   inferential & evaluative levels.
When read to, fill in words of a
   story using context & syntax.
Construct inferences about
   outcome of story.
Shows independent interest in
   reading-related activities.

TABLE 16 (cont.)

II. MATHEMATICS CURRICULA

CLASSIFICATION:

Groups objects by function.
Arranges or matches objects by color.
Group objects by size.
Regroup by one attribute.
Selects "large" or "small" objects
   in a group.
Sorts by several criteria at once
    such as color & function, or
    size & shape, etc.

SERIATION:

Linear:

Arranges objects in order of
   increasingly intense color; size.
Select items missing in serial array.

Unit:

State relationships between sets
   of 1, 2, 3, 4, etc.
Develop sequence of objects or
   numerals based on units in each.
Count to 10; 20.
Tell which numeral is greater:
   2 or 6; 3 or 8; etc.
Join sets & counts objects.

Temporal:

States what s/he did first and/or
   last in simple task.
Follow simple directions (First
   put the block in the box, next
   put the penny beside the tray).
Know which task is done after
   recess after being told.

1:1 CORRESPONDENCE:
(Conservation of Number)

States number of pencils required
   for a group of 3 children.
Orders "milk" for class lunch on
   basis of number in attendance.
Distributes milk when received.
Matches 1:1 correspondence.
States which row has more.
Makes equal numbers in unequal
   rows.
Realizes that number of pencils
   is same whether packed in a
   box or scattered on a desk.

SPATIAL RELATIONS:

States which object is over/under,
   in/beside, etc. object.
Matches geometric objects to
   openings into which they fit.
Distinguish between right & left.
Understands vocabulary of space
   and position.

GEOMETRY:

Identifies shapes (circle, triangle,
   square), 2 & 3 dimensional.
Makes graphs and maps.
Matches shapes (circles, squares,
   triangles, diamonds).
Estimate distance, height, and
   quantity.
Order by height.

PATTERNS & MEASUREMENT:

Recognize, duplicate, & extend
   patterns using materials.
Uses standard & non-standard
   Measures for length & area.

TABLE 16 (cont.)

III. SCIENCE CURRICULA

CLASSIFICATION:

Classify categories of animals,
  plants, rocks, etc.
Classify   animals by body parts
  (i.e., 4-legs, wings, 2-legs).
Classify transportation modes.

CONSERVATION

Of Shape:

State why ball of clay has same
  mass whether rolled into a ball
  or a rope.
Show ball of clay can be made
  into a rope & back into a ball.
Break clay into smaller pieces &
  puts back into a ball.
Flatten clay like a pancake &
  puts back into ball.

Of Liquid:

State which glass has more water.
Demonstrated equality by pouring
  water from one glass into
  several smaller ones.

TIME:

Observe seasonal changes.
Marked by clocks & calendars.
Anticipate future events.
Describe or represents past.
Understands time concepts:
  yesterday, today, tomorrow.

SCIENCE SKILLS & METHODS:

 Observes and gathers data.

IV. SOCIAL STUDIES

CITIZENSHIP: My Citizenship.

Recognizes reasons for rules.
Aware of role of leaders.
Recognizes community workers
  & services they provide.
How to be a good classroom citizen.

HISTORY: My Past.

Aware of information about my
  immediate past.

GEOGRAPHY: My Environment:

Locate places in my environment
Express geographic thinking.

PSYCHOLOGY: My Self-Concept.

Aware of differences between
  needs and desires.

SOCIOLOGY: How I Fit In.

Each belongs to a family &
  families differ.

ANTHROPOLOGY: My Culture.

Recognizes similarities &
  differences in people.

POLITICAL SCIENCE:

Voting is a way of making choices.

ECONOMICS: My Financial Support

Use of trade to get goods & services.

TABLE 16 (cont.)

V. CREATIVE ARTS CURRICULA

ART:
Use of Art Media & Materials:
  Woodworking Activities
  Painting: Fingerpainting.
  Clay Activities
Drawing Activities:
Using crayons, markers, chalk.
Construction:
Making collages, sculptures.
Art Appreciation

MUSIC CURRICULA:
Use variety of musical instruments:
  Singing & Playing instruments.
  Explore sounds of rhythm.
Moving to Music:
Walk, run, jump, gallop, clap,
  and freeze to the sound of
  percussion instruments.
Move spontaneously to many types
  of music.

MUSIC THEORY:
Listen attentively to music.
Label printed music as music.
Recognize difference between
  singing and speaking.
Show by movements that they
  recognize beat, tempo & pitch.
Shows music appreciation.
Enjoys listening to music and sounds.

DRAMATIC PLAY:
Participates in variety of dramatic
  play activities.
Shows creativity & imagination
  using materials & roles.

VII. PHYSICAL EDUCATION

BODY MANAGEMENT SKILLS:
Move selected body parts (legs,
  arms, head, elbow, knees).
Perform selected movements of
  torso, arms, legs.
Move body or parts of body
  forward in directional space.
Move body into different shapes.
Move objects: push-pull, lift-
  lower, carry-hold.
Select static balance skills.
Perform dynamic balance skills.
Select stunts & tumbling.

FUNDAMENTAL MOTOR SKILLS:
Select object control skills (roll
  a ball, throw/toss underhand or
  overhand, catch tossed ball, etc.)
Select locomotor skills (run, jump,
  hop, gallop)

SELECT GAMES, SPORTS AND
DANCE SKILLS:
Follow rules in low-organized
  games.
Play ones' position in low-
  organized games.
Use selected equipment during
  games.
Perform selected aquatic skills.
Imitate or create movements
  during dance.
Move body to rhythm or music
  with even & uneven beats.
Activities designed to enhance
  perceptual-motor abilities.
Practice in starting, stopping,
  dodging & changing directions.

References: Krogh, 1995; Ellis, 1977; Wolery & Brookfield-Norman, 1988;
       Dummer et al., 1995; Morrow, 1989; Head Start, 2003.

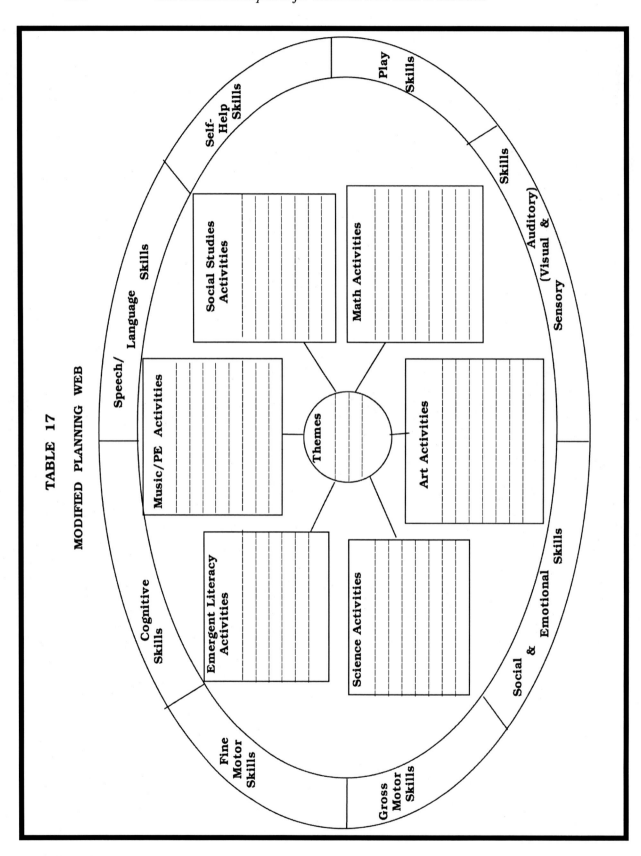

TABLE 17

MODIFIED PLANNING WEB

TABLE 18

EARLY CHILDHOOD CHARTS: CURRICULA THEMES

I. SELF- CONCEPT
All About Me and My Body:
Sight, Smell, Sound, Taste, Touch
I am special.
Dental Health
Living healthy; Food; Exercise
Keeping clean and tidy.

**II. INTRODUCTION TO
          FAMILIES**
Families at Home
Families at Work
Families at Play.

III. FAMILY CELEBRATIONS
Grandparents' Day
New Year's Celebrations Around
     the World
Chinese New Year
Festivals of Merriment
Halloween
Thanksgiving Around the World
Thanksgiving in America
Festivals of Light
Hanukkah
Christmas Around the World
Christmas in America
Valentine's Day

IV. SEASONS AND WEATHER
Winter (ice, snow)
Spring (rain)
Summer (sunshine)
Fall

V. TRANSPORTATION
 Many Ways to Travel
 Air and Space Transportation
 Rail Transportation
 Road Transportation
 Water Transportation

VI. ANIMALS
The Aquarium
Farm Animals
Pet Animals
Animals of the Woods
Zoo Animals
Insects and Spiders

VII. THE WORLD I LIVE IN
Day and Night
Food in My World
Plants in My World
Water Around Me
Matching Nature's Colors
Tools & Machines to Use in My
     World
Mathematics in My Everyday
     World
Safety in My World
The Sky is the Limit
Classifying Litter
Rock Collections
Caring for our Environment

VIII. CHILDREN'S LITERATURE
The Little Red Hen
The Three Pigs
City Mouse & Country Mouse
The Gingerbread Man
Little Red Riding Hood
The Three Billy Goats Gruff

IX. USING GOOD MANNERS
Manners on the School Bus
Manners in the Classroom
Manners on the Playground
Manners in the Cafeteria

References: Hamilton et al., 1990;
Krogh, 1995.

Chapter 4

ORAL EXPRESSION CURRICULA

It is now known that a significant portion of the problems faced by students with LD are language-based and that receptive and expressive oral language (listening and speaking) are foundational to the higher level language skills of reading and writing. (Smith et al., 1997, 201–202)

Linguistic Competence
Language Form: Phonology, Morphology, Syntax
Language Content: Semantics
    Figurative Language
Language Use: Pragmatics
    Communicative Competence
    Narrative Discourse
Summary
Scope and Sequence Charts: Oral Expression
    Tables 19-26

Spoken language, also called oral communication or oral language or oral expression, allows humans to communicate with each other using a series of oral-motor movements–speech–to express an abstract and rule-governed set of symbols–language (Polloway, Patton, & Serna, 2008). Communication, language, and speech are three highly interrelated areas. *Communication* is the exchange of information and ideas, while speech and language comprise the message system most often used in human communication (Heward, 2006).

Speech concerns producing the sounds properly (articulation), maintaining an appropriate flow and rhythm in speech (fluency), and using the appropriate volume, pitch, phonation, and resonance (voice). Even though many students with mild disabilities experience speech disorders or disabilities, speech will not be discussed in this book because the speech pathologist has the major responsibility for remediation of speech disorders. Teachers of students with mild disabilities have a primary role in the language development of their students. Although the prevalence has not been determined definitively, a large proportion, if not all, of the students with mild disabilities experience problems with language in varying degrees. Spoken language is one of the basic underpinnings of school-based learning and predicts children's success with reading, spelling, written language, and literacy in general (Polloway, Miller & Smith, 2004, 185).

LINGUISTIC COMPETENCE

Language development and cognitive development are highly interrelated and interdependent areas that significantly impact the academic progress of children and youth. Educators are primarily concerned with three tracks of language development: linguistic competence, communicative competence, and academic competence. *Linguistic competence* is the term for the inner knowledge one has of language and all of its linguistic rules and structures (Gleason, 2005). Linguistic competence includes the knowledge of the five linguistic domains (phonology, morphology, syntax, semantics, and pragmatics); and numerous metalinguistic skills that assist children and youth in acquiring the linguistic domains.

Additionally, linguistic competence forms the foundation for the acquisition of communicative competence and academic competence. *Communicative competence* is linguistic competence plus knowledge of the social rules for using language appropriately in social situations (Gleason, 2005). *Academic competence* refers to using linguistic competence in acquiring language-based academic skills. The *linguistic domains* (phonology, morphology, syntax, semantics, pragmatics); and *metalinguistic skills* (phonological awareness, phonological synthesis, morphological analysis, metasyntactic awareness, metasemantic awareness, metapragmatic awareness, etc.) will be discussed together with language form, language content, and language use.

LANGUAGE FORM: PHONOLOGY, MORPHOLOGY, SYNTAX

Language is a symbol system or code through which ideas about the world are communicated through a conventional set of arbitrary signals (Bartel, 1997, 30). The major elements of language include *inner language* (the language of thought), *receptive language* (understanding spoken and written symbols), and *expressive language* (oral or written thoughts and ideas) (Polloway & Smith, 1992). Inner language is the conversation or "self-talk" that begins during the preschool years as talking out loud during isolated play; and described by a 4-year-old as "I was talking to mine self." Later, the self-talk becomes internal and facilitates cognitive processes. Receptive language includes listening comprehension and gaining information from reading. Expressive language refers to spoken and written expression.

Language form refers to the structure of language—the rules governing the sounds, meanings, words, and sentences (Polloway, Miller & Smith, 2004, 5). The form of language is composed of three linguistic systems: phonology, morphology, and syntax. Phonology is the rule-governed system of speech sounds in a language; morphology is the rule-governed system of meaning units in a language (see TABLE 19); and syntax is the rule-governed grammar system of a language (Lerner, 1997).

Phonology

Phonology includes the sound system of a language, the linguistic rules that govern the sound combinations to make words, and the stress and intonation patterns that accompany them (Polloway et al., 2004). At the receptive level, phonology involves discriminating the various speech sounds, while the expressive level of phonology involves articulation of speech sounds (Mercer, 1997). Before children can engage in flexible uses of words, they must have an implicit understanding that words are separate from their referents. Once children understand that a word and its referent are separable, they can reflect on the properties of words and objects separately (Gleason, 2005, 133).

Phonological awareness is the awareness of the phonological structure of words, and the ability to consciously recognize and manipulate units of the speech stream (Gleason, 2005, 134). Children's awareness that words in language are composed of a variety of units of sound including syllables, the sub-syllabic units of onset (initial consonant or consonant cluster) and rhyme (vowel and final consonant or consonant cluster), and phonemes is referred to as phonological awareness (van Kleech, 1994). Phonological awareness is an aspect of metalinguistic awareness that develops in the late preschool and early school years (Gleason, 2005, 134). *Metalinguistic awareness*, the ability to reflect on the nature of language, is called upon when words are used in unique or unexpected ways such as sarcasm (Nippold, 2006, 253).

The awareness of the phonological structure of words is closely related to *phonemic awareness*, the awareness of the speech sounds in words (Polloway et al., 2004). Children have to learn to recognize and produce the phonemes of their own language and to combine those phonemes into words and sentences with the correct intonational pattern (Polloway et al., 2004). Each separate sound in our language is a phoneme, the smallest unit of language, however, a phoneme by itself has no meaning. The English language consists of about 40 phonemes classified as vowels or consonants (Polloway et al., 2004).

Phonological awareness and phonology rules (see TABLE 19) are prerequisites to understanding and mastering phonics, a reading decoding system based on sound-symbol correspondence (Nippold, 2006). In order to become successful in reading, children must learn the decoding process which involves breaking words down into their individual phonemes or sounds (sound-letter correspondence): and using phonological synthesis to reconstruct words (Polloway et al., 2004). Many students with reading problems experience difficulty with sound-symbol correspondence, phonemic awareness and phonological awareness. Additionally, most spelling rules are primarily rules of phonology and phonics (see TABLE 28).

In addition to phonemes and phonological rules, phonology also includes the study of prosodic features of speech which include stress, juncture, and intonation. *Stress* refers to the emphasis placed on syllables; *juncture* indicates the location of pauses within a sentence; and *intonation* is the rise and fall of pitch of voice which indicate the type of sentence one is speaking (James, 1990). Many of the prosodic features of language are obvious from a child's vocalizations long before the first "true" words are uttered.

Morphology

Morphology is the linguistic rule system that governs the structure of words and the construction of word forms from the basic elements of meaning (Mercer, 1997). A morpheme is the smallest unit of meaning in a language. Two different types of morphemes exist: free (root words) and bound (affixes and endings). Several types of bound morphemes include suffixes, prefixes, and endings that indicate possessives and verb tenses. The reading word recognition skills area, structural analysis, is a decoding application of morphology (see TABLE 29).

Morphology, also, includes grammatical morphemes such as noun forms (plurals, possessives, prepositions, articles); verb forms (tenses, auxiliary, copula); adjective forms (comparative and superlative); and adverb forms (comparative and superlative) (Polloway & Smith, 1992). The most significant morphological advances to occur during the elementary school years includes how to produce *gerunds, agentive forms* of common verbs, and adverb forms of common adjectives by adding the bound morpheme - ly (Polloway, Miller & Smith, 2004). A *gerund* is a noun made from a verb by adding *-ing*, such as *paint–painting. Agentive forms* involve adding *-er* to common verbs to identify the person performing the actions of the verb, as in *sing–singer. Adverb forms* of common adjectives are made by adding -ly to the verb, as in careful–carefully. By the time most children are age 11 years, they understand the exceptions to these rules (see TABLE 19). In written expression many of the skills included in the category of composition skills are applications of morphological skills of word grammar.

Derivational morphology is a complex system in which a single root form can result in a large number of derived forms (Nippold, 2006, 53). In English, the process of combining two or more morphemes to create a new word occurs through two general processes: Compounding (compound words) and morphologic construction. Morphologic construction (inflectional morphemes) creates new words using affixes or inflectional morphemes including: past tense -*ed*; the present progressive -*ing*; the possessive -*s*; the plural -*s*; and third person singular -*s*. Inflectional morphemes do not change the part of speech of the original root word or its basic meaning (Nippold, 2006). Inflectional morphology is generally mastered by the age of 6 or 7 years, whereas derivational morphology continues to develop throughout the school-age years and adolescence, and into adulthood (Nippold, 2006). The greatest and most rapid growth in derivational morphology occurs between grades 4 and 8 (ages 9–14 years). This is also a period of increased exposure to written language, which contains a greater number of morphologically complex words in comparison to spoken language (Nippold, 2006).

Older children demonstrate metalexical development which is the ability to consciously reflect on the structure of words (Nippold, 2006). Research has indicated that morphological analysis combined with the use of context clues is an important strategy for learning the meanings of unfamiliar words, particularly after fourth grade (Wysocki & Jenkins, 1987).

Syntax

Syntax is the linguistic rule system governing the order and combination of words to form sentences, and the relationship among the elements within a sentence (Mercer, 1997). Syntax concerns the use of grammar in phrases and sentences, noun-verb agreement, pronoun case or gender, use of plurals, and forming grammatically correct sentences (Brown, 1994) (see TABLE 20).

During the elementary school years, children use more elaborate noun and verb phrases, adding more adjectives and adverbs including prepositional phrases and subordinate clauses (Polloway, Miller & Smith, 2005). They finally figure out the exceptions to the rules for making tense and plurality, and they begin to include the articles (a, an, the). They also learn the rules for ordering adjectives (e.g., "big, white house" not "white, big house."

Passive sentences using reversible passives (sentence order makes sense any way the words are ordered) and nonreversible passives (sentences that only make sense if the words are in a specific order) are difficult for children until about the end of elementary school years (Polloway et al., 2004). With knowledge of syntax, a child can understand and verbalize an infinite number of sentence types (see TABLE 20). Understanding syntax also allows a child to transform statements from declarative to interrogative or exclamatory expressions, and from active to passive forms (Polloway & Smith, 1992).

Syntax is concerned with clause structures, noun phrases, verb phrases, complex sentences (compound and imbedded), the formulation of the wh-questions, rearranging words to form grammatically correct sentences, and using negatives and negation in sentences (Fressola et al., 1990). By the end of elementary school (age 11 or 12 years), most children acquire mastery over using conjunctions to join two sentences (e.g., if, and, because, therefore, but, or, before, after, when–then). Many of the written expression rules of grammar and word usage are based on the linguistic rules of syntactic structure (see TABLE 20). Metasyntactic awareness also includes an understanding of syntactic structure (Gleason, 2005, 409). In general, schooling may be the single most important source of explicit knowledge about syntax, since talks about the terms "subject and verb" is extremely rare.

LANGUAGE CONTENT: SEMANTICS

The content of language, semantics, concerns the meaning of words and sentences. Semantics involves the understanding (receptive language) and the use (expressive language) of word meanings and word relationships. Semantics encompasses three major categories of skills including word meaning (concrete and relational words) (see TABLE 21), sentence meaning (simple and complex) (see TABLE 22), and nonliteral meaning or figurative language (idioms, metaphors, proverbs) (see TABLE 23).

The development of the ability to classify words into categories and hierarchial subcategories is one of the most important skills children learn by the end of elementary school years (Polloway, et al., 2004). Another ability they develop is the skill to define words by providing details and explanations rather than counting on their personal experiences to define words.

Acquiring age-appropriate vocabulary and word meaning includes acquisition of vocabularies in content subjects (e.g., math, science, social studies) as well as in basal reading programs. Vocabulary and meaning for the relationship concepts of size, shape, quantity, directionality, time and space are critical concepts upon which the foundation of mathematics is based. By the end of their elementary school years, children are able to sort the English pronoun system: Subjective pronouns, objective pronouns, reflexive pronouns, and learn to recognize pronoun antecedents (see TABLE 21). The acquisition of word meaning includes multiple meanings of words, synonyms, antonyms, homonyms, and other categories of words.

Figurative Language

Language users employ language on different levels of abstraction, ranging from the literal and concrete to the abstract and figurative (Miller, 2008).

Figurative language is language that is different from the literal interpretation; it uses exaggerations or alterations to make a particular linguistic point (Nippold, 2006). In order to understand and use figurative language, children and youth must develop the ability to reflect on language, analyze it, talk about it, and manipulate it. This ability is called metalinguistic ability or metalinguistic competence (Nippold, 2006).

There are many different types of figurative language. Idioms are the first component of figurative language that is understood and used by children as they mature (Vicker, 2000). Idioms usually have fixed or common meanings across a variety of situations, for example "horsing around." Metaphors and similies are figurative expressions that draw comparisons between entities that are normally viewed as distinct (Nippold, 2006). A metaphor makes comparisons between things which are essentially not alike; for example, "Her hair is silk." A similie makes comparisons that often use the words "like" or "as"; for example "Jamie runs as fast as the wind." The use of slang terms are popular with adolescents and often used to discriminate cliques or groups, for example, "jocks."

Developmental Levels

The acquisition of figurative language is developmental. Most children in the 2–4 year age group are unable to understand that words are anything different from things they refer to, nor can they understand that language can be talked about, or analyzed. Four-year-olds function on the literal, concrete level (Polloway, Patton & Serna, 2008).

Children's knowledge of and ability to use figurative language develops primarily during the elementary school years (5–11 years old), and continues to develop throughout the lifespan (Nippold, 2006). Elementary school children develop considerable ability with figurative language and metalinguistic skills. Although, there are a large number of figurative language elements or "figures of speech," the major types they use include idioms, similes, metaphors, and proverbs (Nippold, 2006).

Significant development in figurative language occurs during adolescence (Nippold, 2006). Teenagers mark their group membership through the use of the adolescent register. Adolescents use slang expressions that are typical to their peer group. They may use nonstandard discourse markers such as "like" or "you know" (Ely, 2005). They may use regional dialect or immigrant language. Many types of humor rely on figurative expressions or words or phrases with double meanings, such as puns. Adolescents frequently use sarcasm.

Figurative language comprehension and production not only are important in social situations but also become increasingly necessary for academic success as children progress in school (Milosky, 1994). For example, "A page from a recent issue of *Teen* magazine revealed thirty-eight figurative uses on one page" (Milosky, 1994, 275). Also, nonliteral language is used frequently in the stories and videotapes of preschool children through adolescence and adulthood.

LANGUAGE USE: PRAGMATICS

Pragmatics is the socio-linguistic system of rules that patterns the way language (communication) is used to accomplish social ends (Gleason, 2005). Pragmatics is concerned with a student's communicative competence including communicative intentions (see TABLE 24), and conversational abilities (see TABLE 25). Pragmatics encompasses a variety of discourse genres' and metalinguistic awareness skills (Nippold, 2006).

Communicative Competence

The effective use of language requires both a competency with language form and content, and a knowledge of communicative variations. Conversation must be situationally and culturally appropriate. It includes the rules a culture has developed for what people choose to say, to whom, how, and under which circumstances (Polloway, Miller & Smith, 2005). Pragmatic language use requires an understanding and appropriate use of the implied rules of conversation such as how and when to enter a conversation, initiating a new topic, maintaining a conversation, communicative turn-taking, and exiting a conversation (Polloway et al., 2005). Individuals must also have a command of the functional use of language such as greetings and farewells, requesting assistance, expressing and responding to affection, and asking directions.

In addition to the conversational abilities (verbal and nonverbal rules) (see TABLE 25), children and youth must learn the rules of communicative intentions (also called discourse functions) (see TABLE 24). Discourse is defined as a linguistic unit (as a conversation or a story) larger than a sentence (Polloway, Miller & Smith, 2008). There are a variety of discourse functions: Conversation, classroom, narrative, poetic (including songs), dramatic, and expository discourse. *Conversation* discourse provides the child with the role model for conversation in the family's social context. *Classroom* discourse provides the rules for appropriate behaviors and conversation in the classroom. Narrative discourse concerns telling or writing stories. *Dramatic* discourse and poetic discourse concern fine arts productions. *Expository* discourse includes the non-narrative discourses found in textbooks such as descriptive, explanatory, and argumentative or persuasive (Polloway, Miller & Smith, 2004).

Conversation Discourse

Conversation and narration are discourse genres' used to obtain or share information: to entertain, humor, and comfort others; to boast, compete, and dominate; and to establish, build, and maintain friendships and other key relationships (Nippold, 2006, 285). Conversation is essentially a dialogue between people, whereas narration is a monologue in which a particular event, condition, or experience is described. In natural communication, conversations are often interspersed with narratives, as when people tell stories about what happened to themselves or to others, seeking sympathetic or empathetic responses from their listeners (Nippold, 2006).

Upon entering kindergarten, most children can converse easily with others. Growth in conversation throughout the elementary and junior high school years is characterized by gradual refinements in the following: Ability to stay on topic; engage in extended dialogues; make relevant and factually-based comments; shift from one topic to another; adjust the content and style of one's own speech in relation to the thoughts and feelings of others; and support the conversational partner by asking questions of clarification (Nippold, 2006, 286).

Narrative Discourse

Narrative development is an extremely important language aspect for children to acquire (see TABLE 26). It is considered one of the major precursors to reading and writing and is fundamental to a child's ability to interact with the various discourse genres' he or she encounters in school (Polloway, Miller & Smith, 2004). Children who enter school without narrative abilities are at high risk for academic failure because they fail to discover the critical links between spoken language and literacy (reading and writing) (Miller, 2008).

The production of a narrative involves the building up of layers of information about characters, places, and events. It involves the coordination of three cognitive domains: Linguistic devices, pragmatic abilities, and general cognitive abilities (Rathmann, Mann & Margan, 2007, 189). *Linguistic devices* (structures) are used within and across sentences and bigger discourse units including episodes, scenes, plots, and subplots (Peterson & McCabe, 1991). *Pragmatic abilities* are central in narrative production and comprehension including the awareness of a conversation partner or situation that addresses information needs (Hudson & Shapiro, 1991). *General cognitive abilities* are involved in narrative production and comprehension, such as working memory, information processing for the sequencing of large amounts of information (Eisenberg & Berkowitz, 1990).

About age three or four-years, children begin using narration or storytelling to communicate a variety of experiences. Their narrative skills develop over time, and by the time they are ten-years-old they produce "true narratives" (Polloway, Miller & Smith, 2004). *True narratives* emerge when children's stories contain a central theme, character, and plot, as well as a setting and complete episode (Miller, 2008). The full mastery of spoken language narrative devices occurs between 11–13 years old.

Narrative ability is also critical in social settings, as when children and adolescents describe what happened to themselves or to others or when they exchange jokes or humorous anecdotes to gain peer-group acceptance. Narration is thought to be a more challenging and sophisticated discourse genre' than conversation as it uses complex syntax, offers less discourse support, poses more organization problems than conversation, and story telling is guided by sets of internal organization rules called story grammar (Polloway, Patton & Serna, 2008).

SUMMARY

Language is a symbol system through which ideas are communicated. The major elements of language include inner language (the language of thought), receptive language (listening and reading), and expressive language (talking and writing). The form of language includes phonology (individual sounds of language and the prosodic features of language), morphology (smallest meaning units used in the structure of words), and syntax (grammar and the structure of sentences). Semantics or the content of language includes the meanings of words and sentences. Pragmatics or the social use of language is concerned with communicative competence (communicative intention and conversation skills), the functional usage of language, and a variety of discourse genre' including narration.

TABLE 19

ORAL EXPRESSION: SCOPE AND SEQUENCE CHARTS

PHONOLOGY / MORPHOLOGY

PRIMARY GRADES (K-3)

PHONOLOGY

(See Chapter 5, Phonics;
Chapter 3, Phonemic Awareness)

(By age 5 years, Kindergarten)
Produces intelligible conversational
  speech.

Shows mastery of all vowels and
  consonants.

May have articulation problems
  with (l, r, t, z, tr, sl, kr).

May have articulation problems
  with some polysyllabic words.

MORPHOLOGY

Acquisition of word formation rules:

Use regular noun plurals.

Use present progressive tense,
  (i.e., running).

Use adjective forms:
  1. Comparative (-er)
  2. Superlative (-est)

Use noun derivation:
  1. -er (i.e., hitter, farmer)
  2. -man (i.e., fisherman)
  3. -ist (i.e., bicyclist)

INTERMEDIATE GRADES (4-6)

PHONOLOGY

(See Chapter 5, Phonics)

MORPHOLOGY

Use noun forms (plurals,
  possessives, prepositions, and
  articles.

Knows meaning of common
  prefixes and suffixes.

Uses morphological analysis with
  context clues to learn the
  meaning of unfamiliar words
  encountered in reading.

Uses noun forms (plurals,
  possessives, prepositions,
  and articles).

Uses verb forms (progressive
  past, third person singular,
  auxiliary, copula).

Uses adjective forms:
  comparative & superlative.

Use adverb forms.

Use structural analysis
  generalizations:
  - Prefix generalizations
  - Suffix generalizations
  - Syllabication generalizations.

TABLE 19 (cont.)

ORAL EXPRESSION: SCOPE AND SEQUENCE CHARTS

PHONOLOGY / MORPHOLOGY

PRIMARY GRADES (K-3)	INTERMEDIATE GRADES (4-6)
<u>MORPHOLOGY</u> (cont.)	<u>MORPHOLOGY</u> (cont.)
Use adverb derivation (-ly) (i.e., easily).	(See Chapter 5, Structural Analysis; Chapter 6, Grammar)
Comprehend and use prefixes and suffixes.	**ADOLESCENTS**
(See Chapter 5, Structural Analysis; Chapter 6, Grammar)	Continue to gain knowledge of prefixes and suffixes.
	Gain proficiency in using morphological analysis and context clues to learn the meanings of unfamiliar words encountered in reading.

TABLE 20

SCOPE AND SEQUENCE CHARTS: ORAL EXPRESSION

SYNTAX

PRIMARY GRADES (K-3)

Comprehend & use simple imperative sentences (i.e., Go!).

Comprehend & use negative imperative sentences (i.e., Don't go!).

Comprehend & use active declarative sentences with a regular noun & present progressive verb (i.e., The boy is laughing.).

Comprehend & use active declarative sentences with an irregular noun and present progressive verb (i.e., The sheep is eating).

Comprehend & use active declarative sentences: past tense, past participle, future, reversible, perfect.

Comprehend & use interrogative sentences (i.e., who, what, when).

Comprehend negative (explicit & implicit) in sentences.

Comprehend and use reversible passive sentences.

Comprehend and use the conjunctions "if. . . then" and "neither. . . nor" in sentences.

INTERMEDIATE GRADES (4-6)

Use appropriate subject/verb agreement in sentences.

Use grammatically complete sentences.

Formulate "wh" (who, what, when, where, why, how) questions.

Formulate "yes/no" questions.

Rearrange words to form grammatically correct sentences.

Utilize subject, object, and possessive pronouns in sentences.

Utilize verb tenses (present, past, future) in sentences.

Utilize present progressive verbs in sentences.

Use complex sentences with compound sentence embedded.

Use complete thoughts in sentences.

Use negative/negation in sentences.

Use auxiliary verbs including "be" in sentences.

TABLE 20 (cont).

SCOPE AND SEQUENCE CHARTS: ORAL LANGUAGE

SYNTAX

PRIMARY GRADES (K-3)

Use the correct noun/verb plural in sentences.

Use expected average number of words in oral sentences (MLU):
- 5-6 years   = 6.8 words
- 7-8 years   = 7.5 words
- 8-10 years   = 9.0 words
- 10-12 years = 9.5 words

Produces compound sentences with coordinate conjunctions "and."

Produces complex sentences with subordinate conjunctions "because."

Use gerunds, "I like talking on the phone".

Produces sentences with adverbial clauses, "If it rains, let's make cookies".

(See Chapter 6 Word Usage and Grammar).

INTERMEDICATE GRADES (4-6)

Use articles "a", "an", "the", "some" with appropriate nouns in phrases.

Mean T-unit length   words
- conversation discourse = 7+
- expository discourse   = 9+
MLU. . . . . . .10-12 years   = 9.5+
- persuasive writing   = 11+

Use clause structures (equative, transitive, intransitive) in sentences.

Use noun phrase constituent in sentences.

Use easier subordinate conjunctions (e.g., because, before).

Uses easier adverbial conjunctions (e.g., also, then, so, besides).

ADOLESCENTS

MEAN T-unit length words
- conversational discourse = 8+
- expository discourse   = 10+
Persuasive Writing MLU   = 12

Uses moderately difficult
- conjunctions (e.g., even though, so that).
- adverbial conjuncts (e.g., furthermore, nevertheless).

TABLE 21

SCOPE AND SEQUENCE CHARTS: ORAL EXPRESSION

SEMANTICS: WORD MEANING

PRIMARY GRADES (K-3)

Increase vocabulary by adding new nouns, adjectives, verbs, adverbs, prepositions to vocabulary.

Add synonyms, antonyms, & homonyms to vocabulary.

Read & use multiple meaning words.

Use sensory words.

USE CATEGORIES OF VOCABULARY:

I. Concrete Vocabulary

   Observable Objects:

   Classification of objects (shapes, animals, food, clothing).

   Pair-Association Objects (shoe/ sock, cup/saucer/ bread/butter).

   Attributes:

   Physical Attributes (size, color, shape, composition).

   Functional Attributes (i.e., ball can be thrown, bounced, kicked, caught, etc.

Actions (run, jump, play, hop)

II. RELATIONAL VOCABULARY

Temporal Concepts (now, later yesterday).

Temporal Sequencing (days of week, months, seasons).

Temporal Relationships (first, last, before, after, next).

Spatial Relationships (on, in, over, below, under, right, left).

III. Quantitative Concepts:

Cardinal Numbers (one, two, three, four, etc.)

Ordinal Numbers (1st, 2nd, 3rd)

Comparative Concepts (more, less, some, equal).

Polar Concepts (big/little, soft/hard, high/low)

IV. Subcategories of Nouns:
Common nouns, proper nouns, abstract nouns, collective nouns.

Knows meanings of at least 10,000 different words.

TABLE 21 (cont.)

SCOPE AND SEQUENCE CHARTS: ORAL EXPRESSION

SEMANTIC: WORD MEANING

INTERMEDIATE GRADES (4-6)

Increase vocabulary: Add new
  nouns, adjectives, verbs,
  adverbs, prepositions weekly.

Increase vocabulary: Add
  synonyms, antonyms,
  homonyms; sensory words.

Demonstrate word finding ability:
  List items in given categories.

Choose antonym of words with
  prefixes: un, im, in, dis, ir.

Use multiple meaning words.

<u>Categories of Words Acquired:</u>

I. <u>Existence/Nouns</u>
   Science, mathematics, history

II. <u>Actions/Verbs</u>
   Draw, write, check

III. <u>Attributes/Adjectives</u>
   Size, shape

IV. <u>Attributes/Adverbs</u>
   Easily

V. <u>Comparative Relationships</u>
   Taller than

VI. <u>Prepositions</u>
   Locative (on, in, under)
   Directional (off, toward)
   Temporal (before, after)

VII. <u>Conditional Relationships</u>
   "if. . . . then"

VIII. <u>Causal Relationships</u>
   Since, because, therefore

IX. <u>Conjunctive Relationships</u>
   and

X. <u>Disjunctive Relationships</u>
   Either. . . .or

XI. <u>Contrastive Relationships</u>
   But, although

XII. <u>Enabling Relationships</u>
   "so that"

XIII. <u>Personal Pronouns</u>
   Subjective: I, you, she, he, we
   Objective: me, you, him her
   Possessive: my, mine

XIV. <u>Demonstrative Pronouns</u>
   This, that

XV. <u>Indefinite & Negative Pronouns</u>
   Someone, no one, nobody

XVI. <u>Reflexive Pronouns</u>
   myself, herself, himself,
   themselves

XVII. <u>Pronoun Antecedents</u>

TABLE 21 (cont).

SCOPE AND SEQUENCE CHARTS: ORAL EXPRESSION

SEMANTICS: WORD MEANING

INTERMEDIATE GRADES (cont.)	ADOLESCENTS
Knows meanings of at least 20,000 different words.	Knows meanings of at least 30,000 different words.
Knows psychological meanings of some double-function words (e.g., sweet, hard, cold, bright).	Understands how the physical and psychological meanings of double-function terms are interrelated (e.g., bright, sharp).
Defines common concrete nouns.	Uses literate vocabulary in formal speaking and writing.
Can solve some analogy problems with common, concrete, vocabulary.	Defines abstract nouns by mentioning key features or functions.
	Can solve some analogy problems with difficult, abstract, vocabulary.
	Can provide clear and precise explanations of analogy solutions.

TABLE 22

SCOPE AND SEQUENCE CHARTS: ORAL EXPRESSION

SEMANTICS: SENTENCE MEANING

PRIMARY/INTERMEDIATE GRADES K-6)

I. **Follow verbal directions.**

II. **Use sequential vocabulary:
    (size, item, degree, value)**

   - sequence everyday situations.
   - sequence classroom events.
   - sequence by retelling the plot
     of a movie or TV program.
   - sequence events in a book.
   - sequence events by planning
     a logical series of steps in a
     class field trip.

III. **Complete previously incomplete
     thought/sentence.**

IV. **Demonstrate grade appropriate
     understanding of language in
     math word problems.**

   - State key vocabulary and
     irrelevant information.
   - State inferred information.
   - Restate math word problems
     in own words.

V. **Choose appropriate synonym,
    antonym, or homonym to
    complete given sentences.**

VI. **Differentiate between reality
     and fantasy in stories, movies,
     and everyday situations.**

VII. **Answer "wh" questions:**

   - person response to "who."
   - noun or verb response to
     "what."
   - place response to "where."
   - time response to "when."
   - because response to "why."

VIII. **Describe objects or events
      across several dimensions.**

   - Name members of a category
     which contains at least two
     attributes.
   - Describe object by comparing
     similarities and differences.
   - Describe unseen object by
     at least 4 attributes.
   - Categorize objects, pictures,
     events by function.
   - Demonstrate binary
     classification skills.

IX. **Demonstrate grade appropriate
     comprehension of vocabulary
     in reading:**
   - State main idea in sentence/
     paragraph/story.
   - State cause and effect from
   - Comprehend words which
     denote causality by completing
     dependent clauses beginning
     with "because," "when,"
     "therefore."
   - Match newspaper headlines
     to paragraph.

TABLE 23

SCOPE AND SEQUENCE CHARTS: ORAL EXPRESSION

SEMANTICS: FIGURATIVE LANGUAGE

PRIMARY GRADES (K-3)

Explain absurdities in pictured and verbal material.

State relationships of analogies.

Differentiate between literal and nonliteral meanings of idioms, proverbs, similes.

Paraphrase concrete proverbs.

Use sound devices (onomatopoeia, alliteration, rhyme, repetition).

Produces humor by intentionally misnaming objects or people during play.

Produces humor by creating nonsense words during repetitive rhyming activity.

Comprehend figurative language.

Kindergarten

The early bird gets the worm.
Look before you leap.
Practice makes perfect.
A dog is man's best friend.
April showers bring May flowers.

First Grade

Hit the nail on the head.
Wolf in sheep's clothing.
If at first you don't succeed try, try again.
There's no place like home.
Fish out of water.
Golden rule.

Second Grade

Better late than never.
Don't judge a book by its cover.
Don't cry over spilled milk.
Get up on the wrong side of the bed.
Back to the drawing board.
In hot water.

Third Grade

His bark is worse than his bite.
Beat around the bush.
Cold shoulder.
A feather in your cap.
Actions speak louder than words.
The show must go on.

TABLE 23 (cont.)

SCOPE AND SEQUENCE CHARTS: ORAL EXPRESSION

SEMANTICS: FIGURATIVE LANGUAGE

INTERMEDIATE GRADES (4-6)

Explain absurdities in pictured & verbal materials.

Differentiate between literal and nonliteral meanings of idioms, proverbs, similes.

Differentiate between similes and metaphors.

Create a metaphor by changing a simile into a metaphor.

Paraphrase proverbs.

State relationships of analogies.

Use sound devices (alliteration, onomatopoeia, rhyme, repetition.

Can explain the meanings of predictive metaphors that contain concrete nouns (e.g. The butterfly is a flying rainbow.)

Understands proportional metaphors that contain concrete nouns (e.g., "This house was a box with no lid).

Uses context clues to interpret some opaque idioms (e.g. "skating on thin ice"); and sarcasm.

Enjoys jokes and riddles based on different types of ambiguity.

Comprehend Figurative Language:

Fourth Grade

Beauty is only skin deep.
Birds of a feather flock together.
Bury the hatchet.
Don't put all of your eggs in one basket.
Haste makes waste.
Two wrongs don't make a right.
On the warpath.

Fifth Grade

Chip on your shoulder.
Eat crow.
Every cloud has a silver lining.
Sit on the fence.
Don't bite the hand that feeds you.
Read between the lines.
Forty winks.

Sixth Grade

Bite the dust.
Leopard doesn't change its spots.
Rome wasn't built in a day.
Necessity is the mother of invention.
Hitch your wagon to a star.
Nothing will come of nothing.
Nose out of joint.
It's not over, 'till, it's over.

TABLE 23 (cont.)

SCOPE AND SEQUENCE CHARTS: ORAL EXPRESSION

SEMANTICS: FIGURATIVE LANGUAGE

ADOLESCENTS

Explains the meanings of predictive
  metaphors that express abstract
  concepts (e.g., "Jealousy is a
  green-eyed monster.)

Understands and produces slang
  terms during peer interactions.

Uses sarcasm with peers, parents, and
  siblings.

Exchanges humorous anecdotes with
  peers.

Understands difficult opaque idioms
  (e.g., Expectation is better than
  realization).

Explains the humor in jokes and
  riddles is based on linguistic
  ambiguity.

Explains the ambiguity contained
  in some commercial advertisements.

TABLE 24

SCOPE AND SEQUENCE CHARTS: ORAL EXPRESSION

PRAGMATICS: PRIMARY GRADES (K-3)

COMMUNICATIVE INTENTIONS

I. <u>Request Information</u>:

- Ask questions.
- Seek information and/or
  directions.
- Ask someone to play.
- Ask for help.
- Ask for wants and needs

II. <u>Convey Information</u>:

- Answer questions.
- Give information & directions.
- Inform about wants & needs.
- Make promises.
- Make & respond to complaint.
- Participate in class discussions.
- Give opinions.

III. <u>Express Attitudes/Emotions</u>:

- Express feelings, attitudes,
   and opinions.
- Entertain and give pleasure.
- Deal with fear.
- Deal with feeling mad; teasing.
- Express feelings of approval.

IV. <u>Regulate Social Interactions</u>:

- Displays courtesy; conforms
   to social customs.
- Use nice talk (i.e., Thank you).
- Ask a favor.
- Ignore others' inappropriate
   behavior.

- Say "No."
- Respond to compliments.
- Apologize.
- Adapt a given message to the
   listener.
- Express/respond to agreements
   and disagreements.
- Make greetings & farewells.
- Use telephone appropriately.

TABLE 24 (cont.)

SCOPE AND SEQUENCE CHARTS: ORAL EXPRESSION

PRAGMATICS: INTERMEDIATE GRADES (4-6)

COMMUNICATIVE INTENTIONS

I. Request Information/Action:

- Ask for help or permission.
- Ask a question; or for a favor.
- Ask for information, directions, preferences, school assignments.

II. Convey Information:

- Justify actions appropriately.
- Make/respond to complaint.
- Communicate a decision.
- Suggest & respond to warnings.
- Give oral reports.
- Make/respond to promises.
- Give opinions.
- Respond to requests, reminders.
- Express/respond to agreements and disagreements.
- Participate in class discussions.
- Give a variety of directions.
- Explains rules of game or sport
- In accurate way.

III. Express Attitudes/Emotions:

- Express own feelings.
- Show concern for other's feelings.
- Deal with anger: own & others.
- Express affections.
- Deal with fear; accusations.
- Deal with embarrassment.
- React appropriately to failure.
- Apologize when appropriate.

IV. Regulate Social Interactions:

- Introduce self to peers & adults.
- Use tactful interactions.
- Consider listener's needs.
- Use socially appropriate words; please, thank you, excuse me.
- Give/receive compliments.
- Negotiate with peers & adults.
- Respond to teasing.
- Express congratulations.

TABLE 24

SCOPE AND SEQUENCE CHARTS: ORAL EXPRESSION

PRAGMATICS FOR ADOLESCENTS

COMMUNICATIVE INTENTIONS

I. Request Information/Action:

- Ask for help or assistance.
- Ask a question.
- Ask for permission.
- Ask for generic information: directions, school assignments, projects, work related activities.
- Asking and responding to requests to discontinue, change actions, or states.
- Asking for and telling about intentions.
- Asking for & telling wants & needs.

II. Conveying Information:

- Sharing something & helping others.
- Giving instructions.
- Standing up for your rights.
- Standing up for a friend.
- Responding to persuasion.
- Dealing with accusations.
- Dealing with contradictory messages.
- Gives a variety of directions.
- Expressing and responding to expressions of appreciation.
- Gives opinions & persuasive talks.
- Gives oral reports & talks.
- Demonstrate ability to justify actions appropriately.
- Offering favors.
- Engage in task-related problem solving group discussions.
- Using speculation.

III. Express Attitudes/Emotions:

- Knowing and expressing own feelings.
- Express affection & responding to affection.
- Dealing with fears.
- Responding to teasing.
- Dealing with embarrassment.
- Responding to failure.
- Asking for, and talking about feeling states or conditions.
- Asking for, telling about, and responding to expressions of attitudes and reactions.

IV. Regulating Social Interactions:

- Giving & receiving apologies.
- Convincing others.
- Use of humor to defuse anger.
- Understanding others' feelings.
- Dealing with someone else's anger.
- Negotiating with adults; peers.
- Making & answering complaints.
- Getting ready for a difficult conversation.
- Dealing with group pressure.
- Interacting in social situations such as dating.
- Understanding and telling jokes.
- Using telephone appropriately.
- Making & responding to promises.
- Expressing & responding to approval, congratulations.

TABLE 25

SCOPE AND SEQUENCE CHARTS: ORAL EXPRESSION

PRAGMATICS: PRIMARY GRADES (K-3)

CONVERSATIONAL ABILTIES

I. <u>Verbal Abilities:</u>

- Use clear, vivid, exact language appropriate to audience.

- Use appropriate statements to begin, maintain, or finish a conversation.

- Adapt a given message to the listener.

- Use communicative turn-taking.

- Select appropriate topics of conversation.

- Make relevant contributions to the conversations.

- Maintains topic of conversation.

- Actively participates in conversation with children and with adults.

II. <u>Nonverbal Abilities:</u>

- Maintain appropriate eye contact during verbal interaction.

- Use appropriate body language during greetings and closings.

- Interpret others' emotions by noticing facial expressions and body language.

- Demonstrate effective voice control.

- Show sensitivity to listener's perspective.

TABLE 25 (cont.)

SCOPE AND SEQUENCE CHARTS: ORAL EXPRESSION

PRAGMATICS: INTERMEDIATE GRADES (4-6)

CONVERSATIONAL ABILITIES

I. Verbal Abilities:

- Use clear, vivid, exact language appropriate to audience.

- Use appropriate statements to begin, maintain, or finish conversations.

- Sustain topics of conversation.

- Use elaborated and restricted codes.

- Adapt message to listener.

- Use communicative turn-taking.

- Select appropriate topics of communication.

- Use skill in joining-in a conversation in progress.

I. Nonverbal Abilities:

- Use effective voice control.

- Maintain appropriate eye contact during verbal instructions.

- Use effective body movements, facial expressions, & gestures.

- Use appropriate body language during greetings & closings.

- Match verbal and nonverbal messages.

- Interpret others emotions by noticing facial expressions, body language, vocal intonation.

- Maintain socially appropriate distance.

- Be sensitive responsive to listener's perspective.

TABLE 25 (cont.)

SCOPE AND SEQUENCE CHARTS: ORAL EXPRESSION

PRAGMATICS FOR ADOLESCENTS

CONVERSATIONAL ABILITIES

I. Verbal Abilities:

Uses clear, vivid, exact language
  appropriate to audience.
Utilizes appropriate statements to
  begin, maintain, or finish
  conversation.
Sustains topics of conversation.
Uses elaborated & restricted codes.
Adapts a given message to listener.
Uses communicative turn-taking.
Selects appropriate topics of
  conversation.
Uses skill in joining-in a
  conversation in progress.
Uses the teasing, flirting types of
  conversation with opposite sex
  peers.

II. Survival Communication Skills:

Dealing with emergencies (call
  911).
Uses telephone appropriately to
  conduct business.
Conducting banking & financial
  transactions.
Communication in job interviews.
Making doctor's appointments.
Ordering in restaurants.
Asking store clerks for assistance
  in finding needed items.

III. Nonverbal Abilities:

Demonstrates effective voice
  control.
Maintains appropriate eye
  contact during verbal
  interactions.
Use effective body movements,
  facial expressions, & gestures.
Uses appropriate body language
  during greetings & closings.
Matches verbal and nonverbal
  messages.
Interprets others emotions by
  noticing facial expressions,
  body language, and general
  manner.
Maintains socially appropriate
  distances.
Being sensitive to the listener's
  perspective and being
  responsive to cues and
  other forms of feedback
  from the listener.
Using teasing and flirting
  behaviors, facial expressions,
  and vocal intonation that
  convey personal interest.
Matching verbal and nonverbal
  messages in dating situations
  to deliver messages intended.

TABLE 26

SCOPE AND SEQUENCE CHARTS: ORAL LANGUAGE

NARRATIVE LANGUAGE DEVELOPMENT

PRIMARY GRADES (K-3) (Ages 5-7 Years)	INTERMEDIATE GRADES (4-6) (Ages 7-11 Years)
<u>Narrative Production:</u>	<u>Narrative Production:</u>
- Add thoughts & feelings about the actions to take (plan) and make some of the thoughts or actions (reaction or ending).	- Begins to use 4 types of true narratives: recounts (reports past experiences); eventcasts (try to manipulate others' behavior); accounts (tell about experiences, "you know what"); fictionalized narratives describe event using story form).
- Does not produce <u>true narratives</u> because stories do not include a complete episode. (5 years old).	- Begins marking references in stories across long stretches of discourse.
- Narratives include *when* and *who*.	- Experiences problems with where more than one character is involved.
- Children understand basic emotions and intentions; and use in stories.	- Describes each character's actions sequentially rather than switching between overlapping events.
- Begins to use structures around a goal; uses logical progression of events with inclusion of subplots; and uses time frames.	- Begins to correctly use structural components (e.g., setting, events, complications, and outcomes).
- Uses same location for many characters; shows lack of clarity when changing characters.	- Demonstrates how to tell a story to another person.
- Children focus on one character even when there are several in the story.	- Stories indicate use of more complex emotions of characters.
- Experience difficulty introducing subplot complications with their own time frames into the main plot.	
- Begins to use classifiers in sentences.	

TABLE 26 (cont.)

SCOPE AND SEQUENCE CHARTS: ORAL EXPRESSION

NARRATIVE LANGUAGE DEVELOPMENT

INTERMEDIATE GRADES (Ages 5-11 years)	ADOLESCENT LANGUAGE STAGE (Ages 11+)
Narrative Production:	**Narrative Production:**
10 years old:	Produces stories with complete episodes and elaborate details.
Demonstrates more effort to engage the listener's attention, and adapt to different audiences.	Engages in collaborative narratives with peers.
Tells interesting & original stories.	Full mastery of spoken language narrative devices should occur about age 13 years.
Tells stories with multiple plots and subplots.	
Talks about characters' inner thoughts, feelings, goals, and motives.	
Uses all story grammar elements in narratives.	
Uses conjunctions across episodes to create cohesive discourse.	

REFERENCES FOR TABLES 19-26: Bernstein & Tiegerman, 1993; Bos & Vaughn, 1998; Brown, 1994; Core Knowledge Foundation 1995; Fressola et al., 1990; Larson & McKinley, 1995; North Carolina Dept. of Educaton Standards, 1979; Norton, 1985; Nowacek, 1997; Simon, 1979; Wiig & Semel, 1984; Nippold, 2006.

Chapter 5

READING AND LISTENING CURRICULA

Reading is part of the integrated language system, closely linked to oral and written forms of language. (Lerner 1997, 402)

LANGUAGE ARTS AND LITERACY: TERMINOLOGY

There are a number of terms used in education that are often confused and/or used interchangeably with "reading" including language arts, literacy, functional reading and/or literacy, and balanced reading and/or literacy. Traditionally, *Language Arts* is the general academic subject area dealing with comprehension (literature skills) and the capacity for use of written and oral language (language skills). Language Arts is composed of the following academic subject areas: Writing, reading, listening, speaking, viewing and media (McREL, 2008). The National Education Standards and the State Education Standards use the language arts subject areas as the Mid-Continent Research for Education and Learning (Education World, 1996–2008).

There are a number of literacy related terms including emergent literacy, balanced literacy, functional literacy. *Literacy* refers to reading and writing at a level adequate for communication, or at a level that lets one understand and communicate ideas within a literate society. Literacy and language arts have a number of overlapping areas: Reading, writing, spelling, listening, and speaking. However, literacy also focuses on the learner's functioning level. *Emergent literacy* refers to the beginning or preschool level literacy skills including phonological awareness, pre-reading skills, writing development skills, comprehension of stories (listening comprehension) (see Chapter 3,

TABLE 16). Emergent literacy often also includes beginning or preschool math calculation and math processing skills. *Functional literacy* or functional reading has been defined as the ability to employ reading and writing to understand and use printed materials one normally encounters in work, leisure, personal relationships, and home lives. Functional approaches are usually alternative adult programs or adolescent transition programs for individuals with moderate to severe disabilities. *Balanced literacy* and/or reading programs concern instruction more than curricula differences. Balanced reading programs use a model for teaching known as "Reading To, With, and By" (Mooney, 1990) which focuses on skill instruction in decoding, comprehension, language/vocabulary, reading/study strategies, in appropriately leveled reading materials and using a variety of teaching methods.

Language Arts (K-12 Inc., 2007)	
Language Skills	Literature Skills
• Composition	• Comprehension Strategies
• Grammar, Usage & Mechanics	• Comprehension Skills
• Vocabulary	• Informational Materials
• Primary Analysis	• Literary Response
• Spelling	• Poetry
• Handwriting	• Listening & Speaking Strategies
• Public Speaking	• Analysis of Oral and Media Communication

This text focuses on each of the Language Arts components in significant detail in separate chapters: Emergent literacy (Chapter 3), Oral Expression (Chapter 4), Reading and Listening (Chapter 5), and Written Expression (Chapter 6).

READING

Reading is generally viewed as a very complex process involving word recognition (basic reading skills) and reading comprehension. Word recognition has been used interchangeably with the terms word identification and word perception (Gray, 1960). Reading comprehension includes word comprehension and a number of higher-order-thinking levels of passage comprehension. "Reading is the area of language that most frequently troubles school-age children" (Polloway, Miller & Smith, 2004, 254). Reading requires students to break down linguistic codes and translate them into meaningful thought as the basis for appropriate response (Polloway et al., 2004, 256).

The National Reading Panel (NRP, 2000) identified five essential areas of reading instruction: (1) Phonemic Awareness; (2) Phonics; (3) Vocabulary; (4) Fluency, and (5) Comprehension. From the perspective of teachers of students with learning disabilities, reading is viewed as a very complex process involving Basic Reading Skills (Word Recognition and Word Attack) and Reading Comprehension.

Basic Reading Skills

Word recognition skills involve strategies that enable readers to decode or figure out unknown words. The major word recognition strategies used to decode unknown words include configuration, sight words, vocabulary, and word analysis skills (also known as word attack skills). Automaticity in using word recognition strategies allows readers to concentrate on comprehending the meaning of the passage or story they are reading. "Readers who must exert a great deal of effort to recognize words have little processing capacity remaining for comprehension" (Lerner, 1997, 408).

Word Recognition Skills

CONFIGURATION. Using configuration to decode words involves using the outline or general shape of a word for clues to figuring out the word. The configuration can be determined by drawing around the word to establish its form or by using visual imagery to detect form. Clues such as word length and height and placement of consonants can help an inexperienced reader to discriminate between [dog] and [elephant]. "In efficient, rapid word perception, the reader relies almost wholly on context clues and word-form clues" (Gray, 1960, 14).

SIGHT WORDS. Sight words are learned as whole words to be recognized instantly without using any decoding strategies to identify the word. Sight words include high frequency words sometimes called instant words which are the most common words in English written materials ranked in frequency order (see TABLE 27). Numerous sight word lists exist including the following: Dolch Word List (Dolch, 1955), and a number of revisions of the Dolch list including Kucera-Francis List of Basic Sight Words (Johnson, 1971); 1000 Instant Words (Fry et al., 1985), and 3000 Instant Words (Sakiey & Fry,

1984). Other important lists of words for students with mild disabilities are survival words including road signs, safety words, environment words.

VOCABULARY DEVELOPMENT. Vocabulary development refers to the words taught in reading, literature, and other content areas (science, social studies, etc.) that require the use of decoding skills (i.e., phonics, context clues) and the focus is on meaning. One of the benefits of reading basals with controlled vocabulary is the planned, sequential patterning of introducing and maintaining vocabulary (Gray, 1960, 18).

Words are used to represent concepts, therefore, building vocabulary is synonymous with building concepts (O'Donnell & Wood, 1999). Developing students' vocabulary is a good way to enhance their reading fluency and comprehension (Coyne et al., 2006). An effective program for fostering vocabulary development includes: (1) Provision of opportunities for self-selected reading and sharing; (2) Teacher-directed reading of high quality, age-appropriate literature; and (3) Systematic guidance in reading and study of informational texts in the content areas (O'Donnell & Wood, 1999).

An additional source of words for vocabulary development, 1st-5th grades, is the National Reading Vocabulary developed by TampaReads and accessed through Scholastic Word Wizard Dictionary with ample supporting materials (2008). Students are expected to learn a large number of vocabulary words: 1st Grade = 340 words; 2nd Grade = 856 new words; 3rd Grade = 800+ new words; 4th Grade = 900 new words; 5th Grade = 700+ new words. The Grade 5 vocabulary list words were selected from the Houghton Mifflin 5th Grade Literature book along with the most frequently used vocabulary from Houghton Mifflin's 5th Grade Social Studies program; and additional key vocabulary used in the Stanford Achievement Test (Word Wizard Dictionary, 2008). Approximately, 3600 vocabulary words from first through fifth grades, and over 4000 by the end of sixth grade; added to the 1000–3000 high-frequency sight words falls within the range of sight and meaning words estimated by Spache approximately 50 years ago. By the end of sixth grade the average student has sight and meaning vocabularies of 6000–8500 words (Spache, 1964).

Word Analysis Skills

Word analysis skills or word attack skills are a set of strategies or skills for decoding or figuring out unknown words. Word analysis strategies include the following: (1) Phonics analysis, (2) Syllabication, (3) Structural analysis, (4) Context analysis, and (5) Dictionary analysis. Skills in the various word analyses areas develop simultaneously as well as sequentially. Thus, a student does not have to master all phonics skills before beginning to learn structural analysis skills. Efficient readers learn to select which strategies to use, when to use strategies, and to use word analyses strategies together.

PHONICS ANALYSIS. Phonics analysis is based on phonology, the language system of rules that governs sounds and sound combinations. A phoneme (a unit of sound) is the smallest unit of language that combines with other sounds to form words but in isolation has no meaning. The English language consists of about 40 phonemes, classified as either vowels or consonants. Phonics involves learning the various phonemes and usage rules concerning consonants, consonant blends, short and long vowels, vowel digraphs and vowel diphthongs (see TABLE 28). Phonics analysis, then, involves decoding words using sound-symbol associations to derive the pronunciation of words.

STRUCTURAL ANALYSIS. Based on morphology, the language system that is concerned with morphemes or the smallest unit of language that conveys meanings, structural analysis is concerned with root words, prefixes, suffixes, possessives, inflectional endings, plurals, word families, compound words, and contractions. There are also a number of structural analysis generalizations that must be learned to aid students in decoding words and combining meaningful word parts (see TABLE 29). Structural analysis allows students to decode words at a much more rapid rate than phonics analysis, therefore, encourages a faster rate of reading. Syllabication can be taught with phonics or with structural analysis. Syllabication is the process of dividing a word into its component parts according to a number of syllabication generalizations.

CONTEXT ANALYSIS. Context analysis involves using the surrounding text to assist in decoding a word. Language systems of semantics and syntax (grammar) are involved in application of context analysis. The rules of syntax specify word order, sentence organization, and relationships between words and sentence types ("wh" questions, interrogatives, negative sentences) (see TABLE 30 & 33). Thus, the ability to use contextual analysis in decoding is based on the child's facility with language systems and rules. The major types of context clues include the following: direct explanation, experience, comparison and contrast, synonym and restatement, familiar expression, summary, and reflection of a mood or situation (Strang et al., 1967).

DICTIONARY ANALYSIS. Dictionary analysis involves the use of a dictionary to provide assistance in decoding. "The dictionary is an indispensable aid to word perception as soon as children begin to encounter numbers of words whose pronunciations, meanings, and printed forms are unfamiliar" (Gray, 1960, 29). Gaining facility with the organization of dictionaries (alphabetical order) and various dictionary skills includes using the pronunciation key, accents, guide words, phonetic spellings, and selecting the most appropriate meaning (see TABLE 30).

FLUENCY. Fluency is the ability to read a text with speed, accuracy and proper expression with understanding. The ability to identify words quickly and accurately in context is a prerequisite for skilled reading. Reading fluency also includes prosody, a student's ability to read smoothly with proper levels of stress, pauses, volume, and intonation (Dudney, 2005). Skilled readers are fluent–they are able to read quickly and accurately without conscious attention to the individual words (O'Donnell & Wood, 1999). When the printed form of words become so familiar that they are recognized instantly, the reader is free to concentrate fully on constructing meaning from the text.

Research indicates that students who experience reading comprehension difficulties have problems with reading fluency, which refers to the speed and accuracy with which they read orally (Salend, 2008). In addition to reading in a slow and halting way, students may also exhibit difficulties in the areas of phonemic awareness, vocabulary development, memory, decoding, word recognition, reading comprehension, and using clues to help them read (Coyne et al., 2006). Lack of fluency detracts from comprehension since readers are using their cognitive energy to identify words rather than to construct meanings from larger units of text (O'Donnell & Wood, 1999).

Reading Comprehension

For mature readers, reading is a process that involves the transfer of ideas and information from the page directly into the thoughts of the reader facilitated by the automaticity of word recognition and comprehension strategies. Reading comprehension skills are usually presented on four levels of thinking: literal, inferential, evaluation, and appreciation (Barrett, 1972). *Literal comprehension* requires the recognition or recall of ideas, information, and events that are explicitly stated in the selection. *Inferential comprehension* requires the reader to make conjectures about ideas, information, and events not explicitly stated by using prediction, personal knowledge, and imagination. *Evaluation comprehension* also called *critical reading* (Lerner, 1989) requires the reader to make judgments about reality or fantasy, facts or opinions, adequacy or validity, appropriateness or worth using external or internal criteria. *Appreciation comprehension* also called *creative comprehension* (Lerner, 1985) requires the reader to become aware of the literary techniques, forms, styles, and uses of language employed by the author to stimulate emotional responses, and gain new insights and thoughts through identification with the characters and incidents. Specific reading comprehension skills at each of the four levels are indicated on TABLE 32.

LISTENING COMPREHENSION

Most teachers take students' listening abilities for granted. Schools seldom have a specific listening curriculum with sequenced listening skills, regularly scheduled listening lessons, and specific commercial materials to use in teaching listening competencies. Teachers often expect their students with mild disabilities to compensate for poor reading and writing skills by listening to tapes, filmstrips, films, and lectures (Robinson & Smith, 1983).

Listening comprehension is a complex process that is part of the integrated language system. As such, there are many prerequisites to adequate listening comprehension including the following: (1) average cognitive functioning ability; (2) adequate hearing acuity; (3) adequate information processing–attention, perception, memory, metacognition; (4) adequate language competence–phonology, morphology, syntax, semantics, pragmatics; (5) ability to interpret nonlinguistic communication–vocal intonation, facial expressions, body language, gestures (Jones, 1996; Robinson & Smith, 1983).

Students with average and above-average cognitive abilities generally function at a higher level by 1–2 years in listening comprehension than in reading comprehension. Listening comprehension is frequently assessed using informal reading inventories. Generally, listening comprehension should be taught formally with reading comprehension to facilitate listening in academics, and taught with language development to facilitate listening in semantics and pragmatics.

Listening comprehension includes a hierarchical sequence of skills very similar to the reading comprehension sequence with literal, critical listening (evaluative and inferential), and appreciative listening (Alley & Deshler, 1979). Thus, in the scope and sequence charts that follow (see TABLE 32), reading comprehension and listening comprehension skills have been listed together. When writing goals and objectives, teachers need to remember that the input mode for reading comprehension is visual and the input mode for listening comprehension is auditory.

SUMMARY

Learning to read and reading to learn are two of the major tasks of students in school today. Reading is a very complex area composed of two major areas of skills: Basic Reading Skills and Reading Comprehension. Basic reading skills include strategies for decoding unknown words including sight words and the word analysis skills of phonics analysis, structural analysis, contextual analysis, and dictionary analysis. Reading comprehension and listening comprehension focus on skills at the literal, inferential, evaluation, and appreciation levels. A complete reading program should include Phonemic Awareness, Phonics, Vocabulary Development, Fluency, and Reading Comprehension.

TABLE 27

SCOPE AND SEQUENCE CHARTS: BASIC READING SKILLS

SIGHT WORDS AND BASAL VOCABULARY

FIRST GRADE

Read words with
  initial upper/lower
  case letters.
Recite names of ABC
  letters in sequence.
Read rhyming words.
Read words in
  primers and
  preprimers (i.e.,
  200 words).
Read 100 high
  frequency words
  (i.e., Fry).

SECOND GRADE

Use word form clues.

Read rhyming words.
Read 2nd grade basal
  vocabulary words
  (i.e., 300 words).
Read 100 new high
  frequency words
  (i.e., Fry).
Read word families.
Read content area words.

THIRD GRADE

Read 100 new high
  frequency words
  (i.e., Fry).
Read 3rd grade
  basal vocabulary
  (i.e., 500 words).
Read rhyming words.
Read new words in
  content areas.

FOURTH GRADE

Read 300 new high
  frequency words
  (i.e., Fry).
Read 4th grade
  basal vocabulary
  (i.e., 600 words).
Read new words in
  Content areas.
Recognize similarities
  of known words.
Understand and apply
  definitions of words.
Make connections
  between words &
  ideas.
Identify synonyms &
  antonyms.

FIFTH GRADE

Read new high
  frequency words
  (i.e., Fry).
Read 5th grade
  basal vocabulary
  (i.e., 600 words).
Read new words in
  content areas.
Recognize similarities
  of known words.
Understand and apply
  definitions of words.
Make connections
  between words &
  ideas.
Identify synonyms &
  antonyms.

SIXTH GRADE

Read 6th grade basal
  vocabulary words
  (i.e., 600+ words).
Read new words in
  content fields.
Read vocabulary
  (sight & basal) =
  6000-8500 words.
Use word origins &
  derivations to
  determine meanings
  of words.
Learn Latin words
  that form roots of
  many English words.

TABLE 28

SCOPE AND SEQUENCE CHARTS: BASIC READING SKILLS

WORD ANALYSIS SKILLS: PHONICS

KINDERGARTEN	FIRST GRADE
I. Perceptual Skills: Auditory	**Phonics Analysis:**
Repeat words: With 2-3 syllables; with minimal differences.	Name initial consonant letters: (b, c, d, f, g, h, j, k, l, m, n, p, r, s, t, c, w, y)
Contrast beginning/ending sounds.	Match sounds with initial digraphs (sh, wh, ch, kn, th).
Segment a sentence.	
Segment & blend sounds.	Name letters in words to represent final consonants (d, k, l, m, n, p, r, t, x).
Repeat rhyming words.	
Relate spoken sounds to written symbols.	Substitute initial consonants to form new words.
Hear differences in word lengths.	Match sounds with final blends (-st, -ng, -ck, -ch).
II. Perceptual Skills: Visual	Pronounce short vowels in one syllable words.
See likenesses & differences in colors, shapes, designs, size, directionality, letters, words.	Substitute different short vowels to form new one syllable words.
Visualize part to whole by assembling a 7-piece puzzle.	Decode long vowels in words ending with silent /e/.
Aware of left-to-right text progression & top to bottom.	Identify word families.
See word boundaries.	Identify all sounds in short words.
	Blend separate sounds to form words.

TABLE 28

SCOPE AND SEQUENCE CHARTS: BASIC READING SKILLS

WORD ANALYSIS SKILLS: PHONICS (cont.)

SECOND GRADE

Phonics Analysis

Apply consonant sounds in initial, medial, and final positions.

Recall initial two letter consonant blends in isolation.

Recall initial three letter consonant blends in isolation.

Recall final consonant blends in isolation.

Decode words with initial & final consonant blends.

Substitute initial consonant blends to form other words.

Identify (oral) forms & sounds of consonant digraphs in initial, medial, and final positions.

State that initial consonant sound includes all letters up to 1st vowel.

State sounds of /g/ (hard & soft).

Decode words with short vowels.

Decode words with long vowels.

Identify all sounds in short words.

Blend separate sounds to form words.

SECOND GRADE

Phonics Analysis

Decode words ending in vowel-consonant + silent e (make).

Decode consonant variants (s-has, see; g--garden, large).

Decode long /e/, /i/ sound: /y/.

Decode vowel diphthongs: oi, ou, oy, ow, ew.

Decode words with r controlled vowel: ar, er, ir, ur, or.

Decode vowel digraph teams: oa, ai, ay; ee, ea, ie, ei.

Decode sounds of /a/ followed by /l/, /w/, /u/.

Decode multiple sounds of long /a/: ei--weigh; ai--straight; ay--day; ey--they.

Decode words with vowel digraph or vowel team irregularities (bread, heart).

Sound out words when reading.

TABLE 28

SCOPE AND SEQUENCE CHARTS: BASIC READING SKILLS

WORD ANALYSIS SKILLS: PHONICS (cont.)

THIRD GRADE	4TH, 5TH, 6TH GRADES

Phonics Analysis

Use phonetic clues to decode words.

State the initial, middle, & ending sounds of words given orally.

Underline silent vowels in words.

Use consonant digraphs in decoding.

Decode digraph /ph/ in initial, medial, and final positions.

Read words containing diphthongs: ou, ow, oi, oy.

Use vowel digraphs.

Decode new words with r-controlled vowels.

Decode silent /k/ (known); silent /gh/ (through; /wr/; /gn/.

Decode words containing phonetic parts "igh", "ight", "ear."

Decode words containing a schwa.

Recognize similarities of sounds /x/ and /cks/.

Demonstrate full mastery of basic phonics skills.

Use word analysis when reading.

Phonics Analysis

State and apply consonant rules:

1. When /c/ is followed by /e/, /i/, or /y/, it has the sound of /s/ as in "race, city, fancy."

2. When /c/ is followed by /a/ or /o/, it has the sound of /k/ in "cat, cot."

3. /g/ followed by /e/, /i/, or /y/ sounds like /j/ in "gem."

4. /g/ followed by /a/ or /y/ sounds hard as in "gone."

5. When /c/ and /h/ are next to each other, they make only one sound.

6. /ch/ is usually pronounced as it is in "kitchen", not like /sh/ in "machine."

7. A word ending in /ck/ sounds like /k/ in "check."

8. When two same consonants occur together, only one is heard as in "butter."

9. Sometimes /s/ has the sound of /z/ as in "music, raisin."

10. The letter /x/ has sounds of /ks/ and /s/ as in "box, taxi."

TABLE 28

SCOPE AND SEQUENCE CHARTS: BASIC READING SKILLS

WORD ANALYSIS SKILLS: PHONICS (cont.)

4TH, 5TH, 6TH GRADES

<u>Phonics Analysis Rules</u>

<u>State and apply vowel rules:</u>

1. Vowel is short when one-vowel word ends in a consonant (cat).

2. Words that end in /e/ preceded by a single consonant has a long sound for the first vowel (cake).

3. Vowel sound is long when vowel is the final letter in a word (go).

4. Word with 2 consecutive vowels, first vowel is long and second vowel is silent unless vowels are variant vowel digraph/diphthong.

5. When a consonant and /y/ are the last letters in a one-syllable word, the /y/has long /i/ sound, as in "cry, by"; in longer words the /y/ has the long /e/ sound, as in "baby."

6. The /r/ gives the preceding vowel a sound that is neither long nor short, but r-controlled, as in "car, far, fur, fir."

7. The letters/l/ and /w/ give the preceding vowel a sound that is neither long nor short.

<u>Phonics Analysis Rules.</u>

<u>State vowel digraph and vowel diphthong rules:</u>

1. The first vowel is usually long and the second silent in /oa/, /ay/, /ai/, /ee/ as in "boat, say, gain, feed."

2. In /ea/ the first letter may be long and the second silent, or it may have the short/e/ sound, as in "bread."

3. /ow/ has two sounds: one is the sound of /o/ as in "own"; the other is the /ou/ sound as in "cow."

4. Double vowels /au/, /aw/, /oi/, /oy/ blend into a single sound, as in "auto, awful, coin, boy."

Apply phonetic principles in combination with context clues to read unfamiliar words.

TABLE 29

SCOPE AND SEQUENCE CHARTS: BASIC READING SKILLS

WORD ANALYSIS SKILLS: STRUCTURAL ANALYSIS

FIRST GRADE	SECOND GRADE
<u>Structural Analysis</u>	<u>Structural Analysis</u>
Use endings: s, es, ed, ing.	Form compound words with two known words.
Make compound words.	State root/base words in inflected forms of known words.
Pronounce rhyming words.	Decode words in which the final silent /e/ is dropped before adding endings such as /ing/ in "smoking."
Pronounce word families or phonograms: -ail, -ain, -all, - ate, -ay, -eat, -eep, -ell, -en, -ent, -ick, -ight, -ill, -in, -ing, -ock, -at, -ind, -old, -eed.	Decode suffixes: less, full, ness er, est, ly, th, y.
Use adverbial suffix /ly/.	Decode prefixes: un, re, dis, pre, pro, en, ex.
Use noun suffix /er/.	State meanings of contractions with one letter omission.
Use the possessive /s'/.	Use plural endings, irregular plurals, and /'s/ possessives.
Use the adjective forms /er, est/.	Divide words into syllables.

TABLE 29

SCOPE AND SEQUENCE CHARTS: BASIC READING SKILLS

WORD ANALYSIS SKILLS: STRUCTURAL ANALYSIS (cont.)

THIRD GRADE

Structural Analysis

Read root words & recognize prefixes and suffixes.

Decode words ending in /ed/ as in "cooked, looked."

Divide two syllable words.

Decode contractions.

Decode apostrophes to show ownership.

Hyphenate words using syllable rules.

Form noun plurals: changing /y/ to /i/, and adding /es/.

Apply rules to form plurals.

Decode words with suffixes: -tion, -ward, -ment, -ous, -ern, -teen, -ship, -some.

4TH, 5TH, 6TH GRADES

Structural Analysis

Use Prefix & Suffix Generalizations:

Prefix Generalization:

When a prefix is added to a word, the spelling of the base word is not usually changed, but the meaning is changed.

Suffix Generalizations:

1. When adding a suffix that begins with a vowel to a base word that ends in /e/, usually drop the /e/ and add the suffix.

2. When adding a suffix that begins with a vowel to a base word that has a CVC pattern for the last three letters, the last consonant of the root word should usually be doubled.

3. When adding a suffix that begins with a vowel to a base word that ends in a consonant but not the CVC pattern, neither the base nor the suffix is changed when they are joined.

4. Change /y/ to /i/ when adding a suffix beginning with a vowel to words that end in a consonant + /y/.

TABLE 29

SCOPE AND SEQUENCE CHARTS: BASIC READING SKILLS

WORD ANALYSIS SKILLS: STRUCTURAL ANALYSIS (cont.)

4TH, 5TH, 6TH GRADES

Use Syllabication Generalizations:

1. The number of vowels in a word is the same as the number of syllables.

2. When there are two vowels in a word but one vowel sound, the second vowel is a pattern marker and is silent (rain, read).

3. When there are two vowels in a single syllable word separated by a consonant and the final vowel is /e/, the final vowel is silent.

4. When a word has the pattern VCCV, usually divide the word between the consonants.

5. Usually divide a word before the consonant when the word pattern is VCV.

6. When the structure VCV appears in a word and the consonant is an /r/, there can be an exception to Generalization #5, and the /r/ may go with the preceding vowel in the syllable.

7. When dividing words into syllables, consonant blends and digraphs are generally not divided.

8. When dividing compound words into syllables, each of the words is a separate syllable.

9. Prefixes and suffixes are usually separate syllables.

10. When a word ends in /le/ preceded by a consonant, the last syllable usually begins with the consonant preceding the /le/.

Apply rules and use Greek and Latin prefixes, roots, and suffixes.

TABLE 30

SCOPE AND SEQUENCE CHARTS: BASIC READING SKILLS

WORD ANALYSIS SKILLS: CONTEXT ANALYSIS

AND DICTIONARY SKILLS (cont.)

FIRST GRADE	SECOND GRADE	THIRD GRADE
Context Analysis	**Context Analysis**	**Context Analysis**
Use context clues to read words within child's experience.	Use context clues to determine meaning of new words.	Discuss the meaning of words in different contexts. Select best meaning for context. Use background experiences to aid in decoding. Decode using context definitions. Use figurative language to decode words.
Dictionary Skills	**Dictionary Skills**	**Dictionary Skills**
Use picture dictionary.	Alphabetize by lst letter. Uses alphabetical sequence. Divides words into Syllables. Uses phonics skills	Alphabetize by lst and 2nd letters. Use guide words to locate entry words. Divides dictionary into 3 parts to locate words. Uses general entry format (entry word, definitions, & pronunciation). Identifying root words as main entries. Uses phonics skills.

TABLE 30

SCOPE AND SEQUENCE CHARTS: BASIC READING SKILLS

WORD ANALYSIS SKILLS: CONTEXT ANALYSIS

AND DICTIONARY SKILLS (cont.)

FOURTH GRADE	FIFTH GRADE	SIXTH GRADE
Context Analysis	**Context Analysis**	**Context Analysis**
Read and use synonyms, antonyms, and homonyms correctly. Read and use words that signal relationships (on, or, except, still, but, furthermore, especially, such as, in this way, on the other hand).	Use context clues to derive meaning from unfamiliar words. Comprehend and derive meaning from sentence structure. Use meaning of familiar clichés to identify words. Use summary clues to identify unknown words.	Use context clues: - direct explanation - experience - comparison or contrast - synonym or restatement - familiar expression - summary - reflection of a mood or situation. Use a repertoire of word attack skills.
Dictionary Skills	**Dictionary Skills**	**Dictionary Skills**
Alphabetize words by 3 letters. Divide the dictionary to find words. Use guide words. State meaning and use of phonetic spelling. Use pronunciation key. Select best meaning according to context. Identify accent clues. Uses primary & secondary accents. Interprets typical dictionary definitions.	Alphabetize words. Uses Guide Words. Uses diacritical markings. Use Pronunciation Key. Comprehends phonetic spellings. Follows cross references. Uses primary and secondary accents. Uses synonyms, antonyms, & homographs. Uses pictures & diagrams to aid meaning. Interprets syllable divisions & accent accent marks.	State and apply all dictionary skills. Understands & uses dictionary symbols. Uses pronunciation symbols. Uses context clues to select appropriate definitions. Uses context clues to select pronunciations. Uses primary and secondary accent marks.

TABLE 31

SCOPE AND SEQUENCE CHARTS: READING COMPREHENSION

WORD MEANING

FIRST GRADE	SECOND GRADE	THIRD GRADE
Decode unknown words through context. Find word meaning through definitions in sentences. Comprehend: antonyms synonyms synonymous phrases. Answer questions: who, what, where, how.	Decode unknown words through context. Find word meaning through definitions in sentences. Select antonyms, synonyms, homonyms. State multiple meanings of words. Answer questions: who, what, where, when, how.	Decode unknown words through definitions in context. Select antonyms, synonyms, homonyms, etc. Comprehend content area words. State multiple meanings of words. Answer questions: who, what, where, when, why, how.

FOURTH GRADE	FIFTH GRADE	SIXTH GRADE
Decode unknown words; get meaning from context. Use new words in sentences to show meaning. Use definitions to derive meaning. Use antonyms, synonyms, synonymous phrases, homonyms, homographs. Answer wh-questions. Explain the meaning of idiomatic and figurative expressions.	Decode unknown words using context. Define words read in context. Use new words in sentences to show meaning. Use definitions to derive meaning. Comprehend and use multiple meanings. Provide synonyms, antonyms, homophones, homographs. Answer wh-questions. Comprehend: similes, metaphor, etc.	Decode unknown words; get meaning from context. Use definitions to derive meaning. Comprehend & use multiple meanings. Comprehend technical terms. Comprehend foreign root words. Answer & write wh-questions. Comprehend formal & informal language. Write metaphors & similes. Provide synonyms, antonyms, etc.

TABLE 32

SCOPE AND SEQUENCE CHARTS: READING

READING AND LISTENING COMPREHENSION

FIRST GRADE	SECOND GRADE	THIRD GRADE
Literal Level	**Literal Level**	**Literal Level**
Read to find information.	State main idea and and details.	State main idea and supporting details.
Follow printed directions.	Rephrase the main idea.	State main idea in several key sentences.
Comprehend main idea and details.	Arrange sentences in sequence.	Sequence sentences and ideas.
Rephrase main idea.	Sequence within sentences.	Answer questions using key words.
Sequence pictures.	Answer questions about key words.	Verify answers, opinions.
Arrange sentences in logical sequence.	Complete riddles and puzzles.	Complete riddles and puzzles.
Relate causes and effects.	State causes and effects.	Describe cause and effect relationships.
Match pictures with text.	Find proof in text.	Read and follow printed directions.
Answer questions using key words.	Follow printed directions.	State setting of story (place & time).
Distinguish likeness and differences.	Tell previously read story.	
Recall names of characters.	Skim to find information.	
Inferential Level	**Inferential Level**	**Inferential Level**
Infer the main idea from pictures.	State main idea by providing a title.	See relationships among characters.
Indicate main idea by telling a story.	Name the speaker.	Interpret words and phrases.
Name the speaker.	Compare/contrast ideas.	Select appropriate title for selections.
Describe feelings of characters.	Comprehend figures of speech.	Detect absurdities.
Compare and contrast ideas.	Predict outcomes.	Predict outcomes.
	Describe feelings, behaviors, motives, reactions to story characters.	Reconstruct story structure and plot.
		Describe character changes during story.

TABLE 32

SCOPE AND SEQUENCE CHARTS: READING

READING AND LISTENING COMPREHENSION (cont.)

FOURTH GRADE	FIFTH GRADE	SIXTH GRADE
Literal Level	**Literal Level**	**Literal Level**
Rephrase main idea. Find main idea in separate story parts. Select facts to support main idea. Identify main idea, key words, and topic sentences. Verify answers. Arrange ideas in sequence. Find specific information.	Rephrase the main idea. State main idea & supporting details. Relate sequence of events. Identify detail through topical guides. Discuss likenesses and differences. Describe character traits. Categorize ideas and concepts. Classify traits of leading characters.	Underline main idea & supporting details. Rephrase main idea. Sequence the events & ideas in story. Identify detail by matching pictures and text. Select transitional paragraphs. Describe character traits. Compare ideas, events, and character traits.
Inferential Level	**Inferential Level**	**Inferential Level**
Indicate main idea by titling story. Predict possible endings to a story. Interpret figurative descriptive words and phrases. Compare and contrast ideas. Recognize absurdities. Interpret story ideas. See relationships. Define words from implied meanings. Verify conclusions by summarizing.	Compose paragraphs when given a main idea. Compare and contrast ideas. Determine cause and effect. Predict outcomes. Detect absurdities. Interpret figures of speech. Infer character's mood, appearance, traits, feelings. Describe influence of setting on events and characters.	Write paragraphs when given a main idea. Summarize main conflict in story. Interpret causes and effects. Interpret colloquial and figurative figures of speech. State structure and plot of story. Interpret ideas. Infer sequence of events and traits of characters. Predict outcomes. Verify conclusions with evidence.

TABLE 32

SCOPE AND SEQUENCE CHARTS: READING

READING AND LISTENING COMPREHENSION (cont.)

FIRST GRADE	SECOND GRADE	THIRD GRADE
Evaluation Level	**Evaluation Level**	**Evaluation Level**
Distinguish among real and imaginary, fact and fantasy. Draw conclusions from given facts.	Draw conclusions. Recognize sterotyping of people in stories. Make judgments.	Compare and contrast ideas. Compare similar events in different stories. Draw logical conclusions. Read for a definite purpose. Discuss true-false, fact-opinion, make believe-real. Form judgment by selecting solutions to a problem.
Appreciation Level	**Appreciation Level**	**Appreciation Level**
Relate story content to own experiences. Explain story tone, feelings, sadness. Illustrate imaginary stories read. Discuss feelings evoked by stories.	Describe tone, feelings, humor. Discuss an emotional reaction to event. Discuss author's opinion/interest. Dramatize/illustrate stories previously read. Interpret feelings of characters in stories.	Describe tone, feelings, mood. Interpret & discuss feelings of characters. Describe shifts in meaning. Analyze author's language style.

TABLE 32

SCOPE AND SEQUENCE CHARTS: READING

READING AND LISTENING COMPREHENSION (cont.)

FOURTH GRADE	FIFTH GRADE	SIXTH GRADE
Evaluation Level	**Evaluation Level**	**Evaluation Level**
Describe fables, myths, and legends.	Distinguish between good and poor summaries.	Evaluate bias and propaganda.
Discriminate reality from fantasy.	Evaluate bias in fables, myths, & legends.	Locate and interpret irony.
Compare/contrast selections.	Discriminate reality from fantasy.	Compare reading selections to determine purpose.
Make generalizations based upon reading words and phrases.	Locate and interpret irony.	Judge reality or fantasy.
	Evaluate character traits.	Judge fact or opinion.
	Investigate facts and opinions.	Determine adequacy or validity.
		Determine worth, appropriateness, desirability.
Appreciation Level	**Appreciation Level**	**Appreciation Level**
Interpret moods, feelings, attitudes.	React to reading through drama or art.	Describe the mood of the selection.
Determine author's intent and theme.	Interpret & discuss feelings and attitudes.	Discuss elements of characterization.
Discuss character traits.	Comprehend vivid language.	Interpret feelings and attitudes.
	Determine author's intent and point-of-view.	Comprehend vivid language.
	Evaluate author's competence.	Analyze and describe author's point-of-view.
	State reactions to story setting, plot, character development.	Respond emotionally to content.
		Empathize with characters and/or incidents

References for Tables 27-32: Barbe, 1961; Dechant, 1981; Fry et al., 1985; Lanier & Davis, 1972; Mercer & Mercer, 1993; N.C. Dept. of Public Instruction, 1979; Spache, 1964; Wilson & Hall, 1979.

TABLE 33

SCOPE AND SEQUENCE CHARTS: READING

CONTENT READING AND STUDY SKILLS

FIRST GRADE	SECOND GRADE
Locating Information	**Locating Information**
Use the Table of Contents of textbooks. Use alphabetical sequence to locate information in primary grade dictionary or pictionary. Use several sources of information. Use the library to locate information.	Use the Table of Contents in science & social studies texts and reference books. Use alphabetical sequence to 2nd letter to locate information in grade level dictionary and reference books. Use several sources of information. Use the library to locate information for reports.
Reading Study Skills	**Reading Study Skills**
Skim or reread to find specific information. Use context to determine appropriate word to fill in a blank. Make generalizations from facts. Follow oral and written directions. Classify words and pictures.	Skim or reread to locate specific information. Use appropriate word for context. Make judgments: fact or fancy, true or false. Follow oral and written directions. Classify items as like and unlike. Classify related ideas and subordinate details. Write a summary sentence. Prepare simple report following simple outline or format.

TABLE 33

SCOPE AND SEQUENCE CHARTS: READING

CONTENT READING AND STUDY SKILLS (cont.)

THIRD GRADE	FOURTH GRADE
Locating Information	**Locating Information**
Use the Table of Contents in a variety of books.	Use the Table of Contents, index, glossary, title page of a book.
Find information on charts, maps, pictures, calendar.	Derive information from charts, figures, maps.
Use alphabetical sequence (2-3 letter) in locating information.	Use timelines, flow charts, diagrams.
Use the encyclopedia, dictionary, glossary.	Read radio and TV schedules.
Use subtitles to locate information.	Locate information in the newspaper & telephone book.
Locate information in TV schedule.	Use dictionary skills including guide words.
Use glossary, title page & index to locate information and answer questions.	Use library card catalog or computer system to locate information and answer questions.
Select specific information in a telephone directory.	Use thesaurus to find synonyms.
Use a thesaurus to find synonyms.	
Reading Study Skills	**Reading Study Skills**
Skim or reread to find specific information.	Skim or reread to find specific information.
Judge sources of information as relevant or irrelevant.	Skim or reread new ideas.
Judge fact or fancy, true or false.	Judge fact or fancy, true or false.
Make generalizations from facts.	Make generalizations from facts.
Use the appropriate word for context.	Determine time and space relationships.
Follow written and oral directions.	Explain phrase meanings: dialect, idioms, colloquial.
Classify items into categories.	Classify stories, poems, words, pictures, related ideas, & subordinate details.
Take notes for preparing report.	Summarize content lessons, story parts & ideas.
Use test-taking strategies including identifying clue words.	Prepare a simple outline.
Summarize science & social studies lesson (orally or written).	Read at various rates (skim, scan, study, normal).
Organize information for preparing a report.	Take notes for preparing report.
	Use test-taking strategies.

TABLE 33

SCOPE AND SEQUENCE CHARTS: READING

CONTENT READING AND STUDY SKILLS (cont.)

FIFTH GRADE	SIXTH GRADE
Locating Information	**Locating Information**
Use graphs & tables to determine comparisons.	Use the Table of Contents to locate information and answer questions.
Use the Table of Contents to locate information.	Read charts, graphs, maps, pictures, tables.
Gain information from charts, graphs, maps, pictures.	Locate information on timelines, flow-charts, and diagrams.
Use timelines, flow-charts, diagrams.	Use card catalog: author, title, subject and/or library computer system to locate information.
Use encyclopedias, dictionary, glossary, thesaurus.	Use internet to locate information for a report.
Find information in radio and TV schedules, and newspapers.	Determine the best source of information for specific purpose.
Locate information in footnotes, bibliography, and title page.	Use dictionary pronunciation key to pronounce unknown words.
Use card catalog or library computer system.	Use indexes to find page numbers, topics & subtopics.
Use Reader's Guide, Almanac, atlas, newspaper.	Use chapter headings & subheadings.
	Use maps to determine direction, distance, land formation, climate, time zones, scales of miles, locations, distances.
	Use atlases, almanacs, pamphlets, picture files, magazines, newspapers, Reader's Guide, thesaurus.

TABLE 33

SCOPE AND SEQUENCE CHARTS: READING

CONTENT READING AND STUDY SKILLS (cont.)

FIFTH GRADE	SIXTH GRADE
Reading Study Skills	**Reading Study Skills**
Vary reading rate depending on purpose (skim, scan, study).	Adjust reading rate for purpose: scan to locate specific details, skim for overview of material.
Skim or reread to find specific information.	Outline 3 or more paragraphs of an expository selection by selecting & ordering main points & details.
Skim or reread new ideas.	
Make judgments: fact or fancy, true or false.	
Explain time and place relationships.	Write concise summaries of science & social studies lessons.
Interpret phrase meanings: idioms, dialect, colloquial language.	Write summaries of stories and expository materials of 5 or more paragraphs.
Classify items into categories.	
Classify related ideas and subordinate details.	Organize information from at least 3 sources as a basis for report writing.
Write summary paragraphs.	
Prepare a topical outline.	Use test-taking strategies including narrowing possible answers.
Take notes from reading and/or lecture.	
Read questions at end of chapter before reading chapter.	Use strategies such as SQ3R in reading science, social studies, health, etc.
Organize information to prepare a report.	Interpret idioms, dialect, colloquial language used in stories and lessons.
Use test-taking strategies including answering difficult questions last.	

References: Hammill & Bartel, 1990; Hoover, 1997; Toth, Ragno, &
          Gray, 1990; Polloway, Miller & Smith, 2004; Gray, 1960;
          Wagner, 2003; Oxford University Press, undated.

Chapter 6

WRITTEN EXPRESSION CURRICULA

The ability to communicate in written form has been called the highest achievement in language for people in modern cultures. (Smith et al., 1995, 68).

Written expression is a very important part of a student's linguistic development. In recent years there has been a focus on both the process and the product of written expression. Although the writing process is often considered methodology rather than curricula, the perspective of this chapter is the written expression process as curricula involving skills required to progress through several writing stages including prewriting, writing, and postwriting. Written expression process and product skills are intricately interwoven. Written expression product prerequisites generally focus on the three major skill areas of handwriting, spelling, and composition skills. Written expression products often referred to as written compositions include both creative and functional written products.

WRITTEN EXPRESSION PREREQUISITES

Written expression prerequisite skills of handwriting, spelling, and composition skills need to be mastered at the automatic level for written composition to be a fluent transfer of thoughts to paper. Handwriting and spelling are taught as separate subjects, while composition skills are usually taught as part of the English or Language Arts curricula.

Handwriting

The primary goal of the handwriting curriculum is legibility of penmanship in order to convey messages and information. Successful performance of handwriting skills is predicated upon automaticity in visual-motor integration skills. Most commercial handwriting programs focus on manuscript handwriting or printing during the first and second grades, the introduction of cursive handwriting during third grade while using manuscript for most assignments, and the use of cursive handwriting for most school work during fourth through sixth grades.

Basic handwriting skills of legibility include letter formation, slant, proportion, alignment, spacing, and line quality. Letter formation of manuscript and cursive handwriting is very different. The letters are generally introduced to students in a sequence reflecting similarities in strokes needed for letter formation (see TABLE 34 for sequence). Manuscript letters are generally composed of a combination of circles and straight lines (horizontal and vertical), and is written without slant. Cursive letters, composed of curved and flowing strokes, reflects a slant to the right partially due to slanting the writing paper on the desk.

Letter size, proportion, alignment, spacing, and line quality are very important to legibility. Correct letter size and proportion are encouraged through the use of standard grade level handwriting paper which for first through third grades includes a broken line half-way between the lines to serve as a guide for the height of many of the lower case letters. This helps to promote proportion in which all similar letters are of similar sizes. Alignment refers to placement of letters in relation to the base line. Spacing between letters within words, between words, and between sentences should be consistent. Line quality refers to firmness of stroke (lines not wavy) and thickness of lines produced by appropriate pressure on the pencil.

Rate is another important factor in handwriting. The rate should be adequate for age or grade level to complete assignments in a reasonable amount of time. Several commercial writing programs have produced guidelines for rate or letters written per minute, however, the most important consideration is that the rate be similar to that of peers.

The general focus of the handwriting curricula during and after the fourth grade level is the improvement of legibility through self-evaluation using overlay sheets, generalizing the skills of handwriting legibility to other subject areas to produce neat papers and reports in all academic areas. The consistent use of cursive handwriting should increase the student's ability to an automatic level, so the focus in completion of assignments is on the content of the assignment and not on the formation of letters. During the fifth grade, handwriting is generally reduced in size to be similar to adult handwriting size.

Spelling

Spelling is a very complex skill area due to the many auditory and visual perception and perceptual-motor integration skills, linguistic skills, reading word recognition skills and reading word attack skills (phonics and structural analysis skills), and capitalization and punctuation skills that are prerequisite skills for correct spelling.

The spelling curricula in commercial spelling programs are generally composed of phonetic and nonphonetic high frequency words used in written expression. Students are expected to be able to spell 3000 words by the end of eighth grade (Graham & Miller, 1983). The spelling curriculum overlaps the basic reading skills curriculum in the areas of word attack skills (phonics, structural analysis, and dictionary skills) (see TABLE 35). Spelling words are usually taught in groupings with other words having a similar structural pattern. In addition to spelling dictated words, students must also be able to proofread to determine accuracy of spelling in their own reports and stories and those of others. Proofreading skills are generally introduced in the second grade and remain a focus throughout high school years. Spelling is another written expression prerequisite skill area that needs to be at an automatic functioning level in order for students to focus on the content of their reports, stories, and other written compositions.

Composition Skills

Composition skills include the mechanics of written expression taught in isolation: Capitalization, punctuation, grammar, vocabulary, word usage, sentence structure and writing, and paragraph structure and writing. These skills are the major content of the English or Language textbooks from first through sixth or eighth grades, and basic English classes in high school (see TABLE 36). The basic composition skills curricula focuses on teaching the skills in these categories in isolation, in proofing, and ultimately in utilization during creative and functional writing assignments. The composition skills, also, need to be at an automatic level for students to be efficient in creative and functional written composition.

WRITTEN EXPRESSION PROCESS AND PRODUCTS

Facility and automaticity with the written expression prerequisites of handwriting, spelling, and composition skills; and the use of higher order thinking abilities and creativity are critical during the writing process. These prerequisite skills and abilities are utilized during the series of steps in the written expression process which begins with planning a story or report and ends with submitting the completed project to the teacher and/or sharing it with the class.

At minimum the writing process includes three stages including the planning and organization stage; the producing a rough draft stage; and the revising, editing, and preparing the final copy stage (see TABLE 37). Numerous authors have proposed five or more stages in the written expression process, Hall (1981) suggests a simplified process with three stages of the writing process as prewriting, writing, and postwriting. The curriculum for the written expression process includes knowledge and use of the process stages during writing, characteristics of the products assigned, and the skills that students need in order to adequately perform during the various stages.

Written expression products or written compositions generally fall into two categories creative or narrative writing products and functional or expository writing products (see TABLE 38). Creative writing generally includes writing stories of various genres and poetry, while functional writing includes reports, essay tests, and completing job application forms. The two different types of writing require different purposes, different approaches, and different thinking and organizational skills.

Prewriting Stage

The prewriting stage is the planning and initial organization stage. During the prewriting stage the student clarifies the purpose for writing, often the result of an assignment by a teacher. The student must determine the parameters of the writing assignment and the style of writing (functional or creative) that will be needed to complete the assignment. The purpose is often highly related to the expected product.

Functional Writing

Preplanning for functional writing initially requires that the student prepare and use some sort of visual outline or graphic organizer for organizing the main topics and their subtopics. Numerous types of schematic outlines or organizational formats have been devised to assist students in brainstorming the main topics to be covered in their reports. A visual outline format helps to structure the search for information by requiring the student to identify at least three major aspects of the main topic to cover in the report, and some supporting details.

Report writing in simple form requires a student to have a report topic and three subtopics about the main topic decided during the prewriting stage. These three subtopics are then developed into three sections of the report. For example, if the report topic is Bears of North America, the three subtopics might be: Where Bears Live, What Bears Eat, and Life Style of Bears. The content of these three subtopics is the body of the report.

The student's next preplanning task is to locate the content information which will be included in the report. Locating this content information requires a library search (books, magazines, journals) and using the computer to locate additional information. Once the information is located the student must take notes with references from the informational sources found in the library or on the computer. Another prewriting task for functional writing includes selecting a preferred format for the report, letters (business or friendly), comparison chart, and other functional writing tasks. This preferred format will be used during the drafting of the functional writing product.

Creative Writing

Preplanning for creative writing, also, requires that the student prepare a visual outline or semantic web to use in planning for story structure (beginning, middle, ending), and in brainstorming the activities of the various characters during each part of the story. The prewriting stage for creative writing often involves reading a story from one of the numerous narrative genres (i.e., tall tales, fairy tales, mysteries, biographies), and studying the specific characteristics of that genre. The students then use the story studied as a model for writing their story which will include the literary story elements (plot, setting, characters) and the specific genre characteristics. The information in the creative writing assignment usually comes from the student's imagination and experiences, however, for historically authentic settings a library search would be needed.

Writing Stage

During the first part of the writing stage the student utilizes the detailed graphic organizer to draft the story or report in complete thought units and sentences, if possible. Facility during this stage requires automaticity in handwriting, spelling, and composition skills in order to focus on the content or ideas included in the story or report.

Functional Writing

During the writing stage, students should rely heavily on the very detailed graphic organizer prepared during the prewriting stage, primarily turning phrases in the outline into complete sentences. The students need to write an introduction to the report or paper, followed by turning their notes on the three subtopics in their graphic organizer into sentences, and concluded with a summary paragraph. Thus, the actual writing stage of the written expression process may take much less time than the prewriting stage of thinking, organizing, and locating data to include in the report.

Creative Writing

During the writing stage of a creative writing project, the visual organizer or semantic web should be used to keep the story structure (beginning, middle, ending) and literary elements (plot, setting, characters) in mind. The content of a story is primarily derived from brainstorming and imagination rather than from actual library research. However, in writing a story from a specific time period the student may need to research factors about life style (i.e., clothing, manners, routines), types of homes, modes of transportation, businesses, jobs, etc. to include in the story for authenticity.

Most creative stories of elementary school children will include the three story parts (beginning, middle, ending), and each story part will include characters with physical and emotional descriptions, setting descriptions (i.e., rural or urban, season of the year, socioeconomic status of characters' homes), and actions and dialogue of the characters that contributes to the preplanned plot of the story.

The use of descriptive and figurative language is important in creative stories. Thus, the requirements for creative and descriptive language usage are much greater than in functional writing which may use technical vocabulary. Creative writing requires the interweaving of many literary factors which contribute to the interest and complexity of the story. The characters must be described enough to be viable as real people and the dialogue must reflect the way real people talk during interactions of various types.

The story events and developing problem reach a critical point by the end of the middle story section, and the problem or mystery is solved in the final story section. During the various sections of the story, the writer must keep in mind the key events listed on the semantic web, and the actions necessary by the characters to move toward solving the problem and ending the story.

Postwriting Stage

The major activities of the postwriting stage of the written expression process include revising, editing, and preparing the final report or story to submit for a grade. This stage is extremely important because it usually involves using self-evaluation and buddy evaluations to analyze the rough draft and determine what to do to complete the postwriting stage.

Revising

The revising activities require analysis of the report or story with consideration to the content and/or structure. Further analysis of the report, for example, may reveal a need for more information about one aspect of the report which may require an additional library search. The student needs to consider, again, the factors on the semantic web or graphic organizer used during the writing stage to determine if the subtopics are logically sequenced and adequately described.

The revising process is used to evaluate the creative story to determine if the characters, plot, and settings have been logically sequenced and adequately described. The actions and dialogue of the characters are analyzed to determine if they have been adequately described and move the story line smoothly toward the conclusion. Revising may involve adding extra details here and there, and rewriting various sections of the story. Sometimes several drafts of the story must be prepared before the story is completed with all factors integrated.

Editing

A major task of the postwriting stage is to use self-evaluation and buddy evaluation to examine performance on all of the written expression prerequisites of handwriting, spelling, composition skills (capitalization, punctuation, word usage, vocabulary, grammar, sentence structure, and paragraph structure). This process is usually more effective if the self-evaluation is followed by corrections, then the buddy evaluation determines if any additional corrections need to be made. The major purpose of editing is to make sure that the report or story is easily readable and easy to understand.

SUMMARY

The written expression prerequisite skills of handwriting, spelling, and composition skills must be mastered to an automatic level in order for students to be fluent writers able to concentrate on the content of their stories and reports. These written expression prerequisites are composed of a huge number of skills which are generally taught first in isolation, in proofing reports and stories, and used in original compositions.

At minimum the writing process includes three stages including prewriting (the planning and organizational stage), the writing stage (preparing the first draft), and postwriting (revising, editing, and preparing the final copy). Written expression products can generally be divided into two categories: creative or narrative writing (i.e., stories and poetry) and functional or expository writing (i.e., reports and letters). It is important for students to learn the expressive writing process in order to produce written expression products independently.

TABLE 34

SCOPE AND SEQUENCE CHARTS: WRITTEN EXPRESSION

HANDWRITING: FIRST GRADE

Write upper and lower case manuscript letters in similar <u>formation</u> groupings:
Manuscript Lower Case Letters:
(l, i, t), (o, c, a, e), (r, m, n, u, s), (d, f, h, b), (v, w, k, x, z), (g, y, p, j, q).
Manuscript Upper Case Letters:
(L, I, T, E, F, H), (O, C, G, Q), (R, V, S, D, B, P, J), (A, K, N, M, V, W, X, Y, Z)

Write on standard 1st grade paper using appropriate letter <u>size</u>, <u>proportion</u>, and <u>alignment</u>.

Write with consistent <u>spacing</u> between letters within words; between words; between sentences.

Write with confident strokes and consistent <u>line quality</u>.

Write manuscript letters perpendicular to base line without <u>slant</u>.

Write with appropriate <u>rate</u> for 1st grade, less than 20 letters per minute.

Copy manuscript letters and words from book or chalkboard.

Write manuscript letters from memory.

Complete paper in neat and legible manner.

Write using correct writing posture and pencil grip.

Write using correct paper position for manuscript writing and hand preference.

TABLE 34

SCOPE AND SEQUENCE CHARTS: WRITTEN EXPRESSION

HANDWRITING: SECOND GRADE

Write using correct writing
   posture and pencil grip.

Write using correct paper position
   for manuscript writing and for
   hand preference.

Write words, sentences,
   paragraphs using manuscript
   writing.

Write lower and upper case
   manuscript letters with
   appropriate letter formation.

Write on standard 2nd grade
   writing paper using appropriate
   letter size, proportion, and
   alignment.

Write in manuscript with
   consistent spacing between
   letters within words; between
   words; and between sentences.

Write in manuscript with
   confident strokes and consistent
   line quality.

Write manuscript letters
   perpendicular to base line
   without slant.

Write with appropriate rate for
   2nd grade, approximately
   20-25 letters per minute.

Copy manuscript letters and
   words from book or chalkboard.

Write all manuscript letters
   from memory.

Complete paper in neat and
   legible manner.

Evaluate own handwriting
   using an overlay sheet.

Match some manuscript letters
   to cursive letters (lower and
   upper case.

Read simple sentences written
   in cursive handwriting.

TABLE 34

SCOPE AND SEQUENCE CHARTS: WRITTEN EXPRESSION

HANDWRITING: THIRD GRADE

MANUSCRIPT

Write using appropriate writing posture, pencil grip, paper position for manuscript and hand preference.

Write words, sentences, and paragraphs in manuscript handwriting on standard 3rd grade writing paper.

Write in manuscript using appropriate letter formation, letter size and proportion, alignment, spacing, line quality, slant, and rate for 3rd grade (25-35 letters per minute).

CURSIVE

Match manuscript to cursive letters (lower and upper case).

Read paragraphs in cursive writing from chalkboard or paper.

Write lower and upper case cursive letters in groupings reflecting similar letter formation:
Cursive Lower Case:
(i, v, w, t, r, s)
(n, m, v, x)   (e, l, b, h, k, f)
(c, a, g, d, q) (o, p, j) (y, z)
Cursive Upper Case:
(C, A, E)
(N, M, P, R, B, D, U, V, W, K, H, X)
(T, F, Q, Z, L) (S, G) (O, I, J, Y)

Write upper & lower case cursive letters on standard 3rd grade writing paper using appropriate letter formation.

Write cursive letters using appropriate letter size, proportion, and alignment.

Write in cursive with consistent spacing between letters within words, between words, and sentences.

Write in cursive with confident strokes and consistent line quality.

Write in cursive letters and words using uniform slant.

Write all cursive letters from memory.

Maintain overall neat paper appearance and legibility.

Evaluate cursive letters and words using overlay sheets.

TABLE 34

SCOPE AND SEQUENCE CHARTS: WRITTEN EXPRESSION

HANDWRITING: 4TH-6TH GRADES

MANUSCRIPT

Same as third grade.

Write manuscript words and sentences at 35 to 55 letters per minute.

Write in manuscript on maps, charts, labels on science drawings, posters, applications.

CURSIVE

Write in cursive using appropriate writing posture, pencil grip, correct paper position for cursive writing and hand preference.

Write daily assignments in cursive on grade appropriate lined paper.

Write in pen when appropriate.

Write in cursive using appropriate letter formation, letter size and proportion, alignment, spacing, line quality, and rate.

Maintain overall neatness in paper appearance, and legibility in cursive writing.

Grade 5: Reduce overall size of writing by about 1/4th.

References: Graham & Miller, 1983; Larsen & Hammill, 1989; Mercer, 1997; Mercer & Mercer, 1993; Polloway & Patton, 1997.

TABLE 35

SCOPE AND SEQUENCE CHARTS: WRITTEN EXPRESSION

SPELLING

FIRST GRADE	SECOND GRADE
SPELLING VOCABULARY	**SPELLING VOCABULARY**
Spell about 25 words. Spell own first and last name.	Spell 275 new spelling words (total 300 words). Spell number words. Spell color words. Spell high frequency words (nonphonetic). Spell homophones.
SPELLING SKILLS	**SPELLING SKILLS**
Phonics: Consonant Phonemes:	Phonics: Consonant Phonemes:
Write initial consonant sounds in isolation: f, h, k, s, w, c, j, v, y, z. Write final consonant sounds in isolation: d, l, n, p, t, b, g, m, r, x. Write initial consonant blends: gr, sp, sk, fr, pl, sl, st. Write final consonant blends: -ck, -st. Spell words with digraphs: sh, th. Spell rhyming words.	Spell words with regular consonants. Spell words with consonant digraphs: sh, ch, ng, wh, th. Spell words with initial and final consonant blends. Spell words with /x/ spelling of /ks/ (i.e., box). Spell words with consonant /k/ spelled /c/, /k/, and /ck/. Spell words with /s/ spelling of /s/ and /z/ (i.e., sun, as). Spell words with silent consonants (i.e., doll, know).
Phonics: Vowel Phonemes:	Phonics: Vowel Phonemes:
Spell one syllable words with short vowel sounds. Spell words with long vowel sounds.	Spell words with short vowels. Spell words with schwa sound. Spell words with long /a/ sound spelled a-C-e; /ai/ or /ay/. Spell words with long /e/ sound spelled /ea/ or /ee/.

TABLE 35

SCOPE AND SEQUENCE CHARTS: WRITTEN EXPRESSION

SPELLING

FIRST GRADE	SECOND GRADE
SPELLING SKILLS (cont.)	**SPELLING SKILLS** (cont.)
	Phonics: Vowel Phonemes Spell words with long /o/ sound spelled /o/, /oa/, or /ow/. Spell words with vowel digraphs: ew, ow. Spell words with /oy/ spelling of the /oi/ sound (i.e., boy). Spell words with r-controlled vowels.
Structural Analysis: Spell words by adding /s/ ending. Spell words by adding /ing/ ending.	**Structural Analysis** Spell words with /ed/, /ing/, /er/, and /est/ endings. Spell plural words made by adding /s/ or /es/. Spell compound words.
SPELLING RULES Capitalize proper nouns in spelling.	**SPELLING RULES** Capitalize proper nouns in spelling.
DICTIONARY SKILLS Use a picture dictionary. State letters in alphabetical order.	**DICTIONARY SKILLS** Use a picture dictionary. Alphabetize spelling words.

TABLE 35

SCOPE AND SEQUENCE CHARTS: WRITTEN EXPRESSION

SPELLING

THIRD GRADE	FOURTH GRADE

SPELLING VOCABULARY

THIRD GRADE:
Spell 400 new spelling words.
  (total 700 words).
Spell content area words.
Spell high frequency words.
Spell frequently misspelled
  words (irregular spellings).
Spell homophones.

FOURTH GRADE:
Spell 460 new spelling words
  (total 1160 words).
Spell content area words.
Spell high frequency words.
Spell calendar words.
Spell continents & nationalities.
Spell homophones.

SPELLING SKILLS

THIRD GRADE:

Phonics: Consonant Phonemes
Spell words with consonant
  digraphs (th, sh, ch, tch, wr)
  and blends: br, st, sw, fl, cl,
  fr, sp, cl, spr, str, scr.
Spell words with silent
  consonants.
Spell words with /f/ sound
  spelled /gh/.
Spell words with both sounds
  of /s/, /c/, /j/.
Spell words with double
  consonants (bb, tt, dd, pp,
  ss, nn, mm/.

Phonics: Vowel Phonemes:
Spell words with short vowels
  in initial or medial position.
Spell words with vowel
  diphthongs /oi/, /ou/, /oo/.
Spell words with long vowels
  in open syllables.
Spell words with long vowels
  in V-C-e pattern.
Spell words with long /a/ sound
  /ai/ or /ay/.

FOURTH GRADE:

Phonics: Consonant Phonemes
Spell words with consonant
  digraphs and blends.
Spell words with silent letters.
Spell words with /ch/ spelling of
  /k/.
Spell words with /wh/ sound
  spelled/hw/ (i.e., wheel).
Spell words with both sounds of
  /c/, /g/, /j/.
Spell words with /kw/ sound
  spelled /qu/ (i.e., queen).
Spell words with /f/ sound
  spelled /ph/ (i.e., elephant).

Phonics: Vowel Phonemes:
Spell words with short medial
  vowels.
Spell words with long vowels in
  open syllables.
Spell words with long /a/ sound
  spelled /ai/, /ay/, /a/.
Spell words with long /e/ sound
  spelled /ea/, /ei/, /e/.
Spell words with long /i/ sound
  /igh/, /y/, /i/.

TABLE 35

SCOPE AND SEQUENCE CHARTS: WRITTEN EXPRESSION

SPELLING

THIRD GRADE	FOURTH GRADE
<u>SPELLING SKILLS</u> (cont.)	<u>SPELLING SKILLS</u> (cont.)
<u>Phonics: Vowel Phonemes</u>	<u>Phonics: Vowel Phonemes</u>
Spell words with long /e/ sound spelled /ea/ or /ee/.	Spell words with long /i/ sound spelled /igh/, /y/, /i/.
Spell words with long /i/ sound spelled /igh/ or /i/.	Spell words with long /o/ sound spelled /oa/, /ow/, /o/.
Spell words with long /o/ sound spelled /ow/, /oa/, /o/.	Spell word with 2 sounds /oo/.
Spell words with schwa sound.	Spell words with diphthongs /oi/, /ou/, /oy/, /au/.
Spell words with r-controlled vowels /or/, /ur/, /ar/.	Spell words with schwa sound.
Spell words with 2 sounds of /oo/.	Spell words with r-controlled vowels /ar/, /or/, /ir/, /er/, /ur/
Spell words with final /y/ as long /e/, /i/, /a/.	Spell short /o/ sound words /al/, /au/, /aw/ (ie., tall)
Spell words with /le/ spelling of /el/ sound.	Spell r-controlled schwa vowel (schwa-r).
Spell words with long /a/ sound /ai/ or /ay/.	Spell words with /y/ spelling of long /e/.
<u>Structural Analysis</u>	<u>Structural Analysis:</u>
Spell plural words by adding /s/ or /es/.	Spell words with endings: s, ed, d, ing, er, est, ing, ly, en).
Spell words with endings: s, ed, d, ing, er, est.	Spell words with prefixes: un, re, pre, ex, pro.
Spell words with /er/ or /est/ comparative endings.	Spell words with suffixes: ful, ness, ment.
Spell compound words.	Spell regular and irregular plural words.
Spell contractions.	Spell words with comparative endings /er/, /est/.
Spell irregular plural words.	Spell compound words.
	Spell contractions.
	Spell words with number suffixes (i.e., fifteen, fifty).
	Spell words with possessive nouns.

TABLE 35

SCOPE AND SEQUENCE CHARTS: WRITTEN EXPRESSION

SPELLING

THIRD GRADE	FOURTH GRADE
SPELLING RULES (cont.)	**SPELLING RULES** (cont.)
Spell plural words formed by changing /y/ to /i/ and adding /es/.	Spell plural words formed by changing /y/ to /i/ and adding /es/.
Spell words formed by doubling the final consonant before adding /ing/ or /ed/.	Spell words formed by doubling the final consonant before adding /ing/ or /ed/.
Spell words formed by dropping final silent /e/ before adding /ing/.	Spell words formed by dropping final silent /e/ before adding /ing/.
Spell abbreviations.	Spell abbreviations.
Spell words with apostrophes.	Spell words with apostrophes.
State spelling rule that words do not end in /v/.	State spelling rule that words do not end in /v/.
State that /q/ is followed by /u/.	State that /q/ is followed by /u/.
DICTIONARY SKILLS	**DICTIONARY SKILLS**
Sequence words in alphabetical order.	Alphabetize words.
Use dictionary independently.	Use guide words.
	Complete dictionary work independently.

TABLE 35

SCOPE AND SEQUENCE CHARTS: WRITTEN EXPRESSION

SPELLING

FIFTH GRADE	SIXTH GRADE
SPELLING VOCABULARY	**SPELLING VOCABULARY**
Spell 460 new words (total 1620 words).	Spell 460 new words annually: (Total: 6th grade, 2090 words; 7th grade, 2540 words; 8th grade, 3000 words).
Spell high frequency words.	Spell Greek root words.
Spell words from other Languages.	Spell homographs.
Spell synonyms & antonyms.	Spell commonly misspelled words.
Spell state names and abbreviations.	Spell high frequency words.
Spell homophones.	Spell media words.
Spell commonly misspelled words.	Spell Spanish & French words.
	Spell names and places.
	Spell commonly confused words (i.e., advice, advise).
SPELLING SKILLS	**SPELLING SKILLS**
Phonics: Consonant Phonemes	**Phonics: Consonant Phonemes:**
Spell words with digraph sound /sh/ spelled /sh/, /ci/, /ti/.	Spell words with /z/ spelled /s/, /ss/, /z/.
Spell words with digraph sound /ch/ spelled /ch/, /tu/, /tch/.	Spell words with /zh/ sound spelled with /s/ followed by /ion/ or /ual/.
Spell words with consonants /s/ or /k/ spelled /c/.	Spell words with silent consonants: b, h, m, g, p.
Spell words with both sounds of /j/.	Spell words with double consonants.
Spell words with /gh/ spelling of /f/.	Spell words with different spellings of /f/.
Spell words with silent consonants.	
Spell words with both sounds of /s/.	
Spell words with hard /c/.	

TABLE 35

SCOPE AND SEQUENCE CHARTS: WRITTEN EXPRESSING

SPELLING

FIFTH GRADE	SIXTH GRADE
SPELLING SKILLS (cont.)	**SPELLING SKILLS** (cont.)
Phonics: Vowel Phonemes	**Phonics: Vowel Phonemes**
Spell words with short medial vowels.	Spell words with vowel digraphs /ie/, /ei/.
Spell words with long vowel sounds, including two long sounds of /oo/.	Spell words with long /a/ sounds spelled /a/, /a-C-e/, /ai/, /vowel + y/.
Spell words with schwa sound.	Spell words with short /e/ sounds spelled /e/ or /ea/.
Spell final /schwa + l/ spelled /le/, /el/, /il/, /al/.	Spell words with long /e/ sounds spelled /e/, /ee/, /e-C-e/, /y/.
Spell words with final /schwa + n/ spelled /en/ or /on/.	Spell words with long /i/ sound spelled /i/ or /y/.
Spell words with final /schwa + r/ spelled /er/ or /or/.	Spell words with long /o/ sound spelled /o/, /oa/, /o-C-e/.
Spell r-controlled vowel /ur/ spelled /er/, /ear/, /ir/, /ur/, /or/.	Spell words with long /u/ sound spelled /u/ or /ue/.
Spell r-controlled vowel /ar/ spelled /ar/, /are/, /air/.	Spell words with long /oo/ sound spelled /oo/, /ou/, /u/, /u-C-e/.
Spell r-controlled vowel /or/ spelled /or/, /ar/.	Spell words with short /oo/ sound spelled /oo/, /u/, /ou/.
Spell r-controlled vowel /ir/ spelled /er/, /eer/, /ear/, /ier/.	Spell r-controlled vowels /ar/, /ur/, /or/, /ir/, /er/.
Spell words with long diphthongs /ou/, /ow/, /oi/, /oy/.	Spell words with the schwa sound in the unstressed syllable.
Spell words with long /o/ spelled /ow/ (i.e., crow).	Spell words with /o/ sound /o/, /al/, /au/, /aw/.
Structural Analysis:	**Structural Analysis:**
Spell words with endings: en, ize.	Spell words with prefixes: ir, anti, il, non, mis, mid, under, super, sub, inter, intra, uni, mono, duo, bi.
Spell words with prefixes: pre, re, post, co, dis, in, im, non, un, bi, mid, semi, tri.	Spell words with suffixes: ion, tion, ation.
Spell words with suffixes: er, est, ed, ing, or, er, ist, ty, ity, ness, ment, ive, ous, ish, ant, ic.	Spell words with suffixes: ance, ence.

TABLE 35

SCOPE AND SEQUENCE CHARTS: WRITTEN EXPRESSION

SPELLING

FIFTH GRADE	SIXTH GRADE
<u>Structural Analysis</u> (cont.)	<u>Structural Analysis</u> (cont.)
Spell words with regular and irregular plurals. Spell abbreviations Spell compound words. Spell words with number suffixes (i.e., thirteen, sixty).	Spell words with suffixes: ward, ly, ed, ing, able, ible, ful, ness, some, ate, ary, eer, ian, ant, ent. Spell compound words. Spell plurals of nouns which end in /o/. Spell abbreviations and acronyms.
SPELLING RULES	**SPELLING RULES**
Spell words that require doubling the final consonant before adding /ing/. Spell words that require dropping final silent /e/ before adding /ing/.	Spell words that require changing /y/ to /i/ and adding /er/ or /est/. Spell words with short vowels in syllabication patterns: V-CC-V and V-C-V. Spell words with long vowels in syllabication patterns: C-VV-C and V-C-V. Spell words that require attaching suffixes to base words that retain the final silent /e/. Spell words that require attaching suffixes to base words that drop the final silent /e/.
DICTIONARY SKILLS	**DICTIONARY SKILLS**
Use guide words. Find words of uncertain spelling in dictionary.	Spell words which use stress or shifts in stress to spell words with suffixes.

References: Graham & Miller, 1983; Heilman, 1989; Mercer, 1993; Toth et al., 1990; K-12, Inc. Curricula, 2007).

TABLE 36

SCOPE AND SEQUENCE CHARTS: WRITTEN EXPRESSION

COMPOSITION SKILLS

FIRST GRADE	SECOND GRADE
Capitalization	**Capitalization**
Capitalize the following: The child's first and last names. The name of the teacher, school, town, street. The word "I". Names of people. Names of pets. The first word of sentences.	Capitalize the following: First and important words of titles of books, stories, poems. Proper names used in children's writings. Titles: Mr., Mrs., Miss. Initials. Days of the week, and the date. Months of the year. Holidays. Places and Things: Countries, cities, states, landmarks.
Punctuation	**Punctuation**
Punctuate the following: Period after declarative sentence. Period after numbers in a list. Question mark at end of question.	Punctuate the following: Period after imperative sentence. Exclamation mark at end of exclamatory sentence. Comma after greeting and closing of friendly letter or note. Comma between day of month and year. Comma between names of city and state.
Vocabulary	**Vocabulary**
Use new words learned during experiences. Choose words that describe accurately. Choose words that make you see, hear, feel.	Use words with similar meanings. Use words with opposite meanings.

TABLE 36

SCOPE AND SEQUENCE CHARTS: WRITTEN EXPRESSION

COMPOSITION SKILLS

FIRST GRADE (cont.)	SECOND GRADE (cont.)
Word Usage	**Word Usage**

Eliminate unnecessary words (i.e., My father he. . .)
 Use well and good.
 Use verb forms in sentences:
  is, are
  did, done
  was, were
  see, saw, seen
  ate, eaten
  went, gone
  came, come
  gave, given
	Avoid double negatives.
	 Use a and an, may and learn.
	 Eliminate unnecessary words (i.e., this here).
	 Use verb forms in sentences:
	  rode, ridden
	  took, taken
	  grow, grew, grown
	  know, knew, known
	  bring, brought
	  drew, drawn
	  began, begun
	  ran, run

Grammar	**Grammar**
Not applicable.	Use nouns: people, places, things. Use verbs: action words
Sentences	**Sentences**

Write simple sentences:
  Telling
  Asking
	State kinds of sentences:
	  Statement
	  Questions
	 Compose correct and interesting sentences.
	 Avoid running sentences together with and.
	 Show simple sentence combining and expanding.

Paragraphs	**Paragraphs**
Not applicable.	Write a paragraph using a topic sentence and supporting detail sentences. Write paragraph: informative, descriptive, narrative, definition.

TABLE 36

SCOPE AND SEQUENCE CHARTS: WRITTEN EXPRESSION

COMPOSITION SKILLS

THIRD GRADE	FOURTH GRADE
Capitalization	**Capitalization**
Capitalize the following: Proper names. First word in a line of verse. First & important words in titles of books. First word of salutation of letter (i.e., Dear). First word of closing (i.e., Yours). Initials with names. Titles of respect: Mr., Mrs., Ms., Dr., Miss). Places and Things: country, street, state, park, city, school. Months, days, common holidays.	Capitalize the following: Names of organizations: Boy Scouts Names of cities and states. Mother and Father, when used in place of name. Local geographical names. Titles of respect: President, Governor, Captain. Sacred names (God, Jesus, Our Father) Places and Things: clubs, oceans, library, river. Words formed from place names: French, American. First word of direct quotation.
Punctuation	**Punctuation**
Punctuate the following: Period after initials. Period after abbreviation. Commas in a list. Commas in dates. Commas in greetings and closings of letters. Commas to separate city, state, and country. Comma between day and month of year. Exclamation mark after exclamatory sentence. Apostrophe in contractions.	Punctuate the following: Period after abbreviation of days, months, directions, states, streets, avenue, boulevard. Period after command; quotation. Quotation mark around title in a sentence. Quotation mark around quotation. Hyphen separating parts of a word. Exclamation mark at end of exclamatory word or sentence. Comma following date in sentence. Comma after names used in direct address. Comma after yes or no at beginning of sentence. Comma to separate 3 words naming something.

TABLE 36

SCOPE AND SEQUENCE CHARTS: WRITTEN EXPRESSION

COMPOSITION SKILLS

THIRD GRADE (cont.)	FOURTH GRADE (cont.)
	Comma around interpolations (i.e., however).
	Comma with nouns of address.
	Comma with introductory phrases.
	Comma in compound sentences.
	Comma after 'if" phrase.
	Colon after greeting in business letter.
	Apostrophe to form possessive of singular word; plural word.
Vocabulary	**Vocabulary**
Select words for precise meanings.	Divide words into syllables.
Use synonyms.	Use the accent mark.
Distinguish meanings and spellings of homonyms.	Use exact words that appeal to senses.
Use prefixes and suffixes.	Use exact words in explanations.
	Keep individual lists of new words and meanings.
Word Usage	**Word Usage**
Use there is and there are; any and no.	Use subject & verb agreement.
Use let and leave; don't, doesn't; would have not would of.	Use she, he, I , we, they as subjects.
Use verb forms in sentences:	Use bring and take.
throw, threw, thrown	Use verb forms in sentences:
drive, drove, driven	blow, blew, blown
wrote, written	drink, drank, drunk
tore, torn	lie, lay, lain
chose, chosen	take, took, taken
climbed	rise, rose, risen
broke, broken	teach, taught
wore, worn	raise, raised
spoke, spoken	lay, laid
sang, sung	fly, flew, flown
rang, rung	swim, swam, swum
catch, caught	freeze, froze, frozen
	steal, stole, stolen

TABLE 36

SCOPE AND SEQUENCE CHARTS: WRITTEN EXPRESSION

COMPOSITION SKILLS

THIRD GRADE (cont.)

Grammar

Use the following grammar forms:
Nouns: singular, plural, possessive.
Verbs: recognition of action, helping.
Adjectives: recognition; and articles.
Conjunctions: recognition

Sentences

Use a variety of sentences including declarative, interrogative, imperative, exclamatory.
Use interesting beginning and ending sentences.
Avoid run-on sentences (no punctuation).
Proof-read one's own sentences.
Combine short, choppy sentences into longer ones.

Paragraphs

Keep to one idea.
Keep sentences in order, sequences of ideas.
Find and delete sentences that do not belong.
Indent new paragraphs.
Write persuasive paragraphs.
Write comparison/contrast paragraphs.

FOURTH GRADE (cont.)

Grammar

Use the following grammar forms:
Nouns: common & proper in complete subject.
Verbs: in complete predicate
Adjectives: recognition
Adverbs: recognition (telling how, when, where), modifying verbs.
Pronouns: recognition of singular and plural.
Prepositions and prepositional phrases.

Sentences

Use command sentences.
Use complete and simple subject.
Use complete and simple predicate.
Label adjectives, adverbs, and pronouns in sentences.
Avoid fragments of sentences (incomplete) and the comma fault (a comma in place of a period).
Improve sentences in a paragraph.

Paragraphs

Select main topic.
Choose title to express main idea.
Make simple outline with main idea.
Develop interesting paragraphs.

TABLE 36

SCOPE AND SEQUENCE CHARTS: WRITTEN EXPRESSION

COMPOSITIONS SKILLS

FIFTH GRADE	SIXTH GRADE
Capitalization	**Capitalization**
Capitalize the following: Capitalization used in outlining. Commercial trade names. Places and Things: stores, wars, and ships.	Capitalize the following: Names of Deities and the Bible. Proper adjectives showing race, nationality. Abbreviations: proper nouns & titles.
Punctuation	**Punctuation**
Punctuate the following: Colon in writing time. Quotation marks around the title of a booklet, pamphlet, the chapter of a book, and the title of a poem or story. Underline the title of a book. Period after outline Roman numeral.	Punctuate the following: Commas to set off nouns in direct address. Hyphen in some compound words. Colon to set off a list. Comma when writing last name first. Comma after introductory clauses. Comma to clarify meaning.
Vocabulary	**Vocabulary**
Use antonyms. Use prefixes, suffixes, compound words. Focus on choice of words. Use rhyme & rhythm, & words with sensory images. Use adjectives, nouns, verbs to contrast general & specific vocabulary.	Extend meanings, writing with care in choice of words & phrases. Use antonyms, synonyms, etc. Select words for effectiveness, and appropriateness. Select words for courtesy. Editing a paragraph to improve choice of words.
Word Usage	**Word Usage**
Avoid unnecessary pronouns (i.e., the boy he). Use linking verbs and predicate nominative. Conjugate verbs for changes in tense, person & number.	Use parallel structure for parallel ideas, as in outlines. Use transitive & intransitive verbs. Use verb forms in sentences: beat, beaten; learn, learned.

TABLE 36

SCOPE AND SEQUENCE CHARTS: WRITTEN EXPRESSION

COMPOSITION SKILLS

FIFTH GRADE (cont.)	SIXTH GRADE (cont.)
Word Usage	**Word Usage**
Use verb forms in sentences am, was, been say, said fall, fell, fallen dive, dived burst buy, bought	forgot, forgotten swing, swung spring, sprang, sprung shrink, shrank, shrunk slide, slid
Grammar	**Grammar**
Use the following grammar forms: Noun: possessive, object of preposition, predicate noun Verb: tense, agreement with subject, verbs of action, state of being. Adjective: comparison, predicate adjective, proper adjective. Adverb: comparison; words telling how, when, where, how much; modifying verbs. Pronoun: possessive, object of preposition, direct and indirect, personal pronoun case. Pronoun: agreement between pronoun & antecedents. Preposition: recognition, prepositional phrases. Conjunction: recognition. Interjection: recognition.	Use the following grammar forms: Noun: clauses, common and proper, indirect object. Verb: conjugating to note changes in person, number, tense, linking verbs with predicate nominative. Adjective: chart of uses, clauses, demonstrative, descriptive, numerals, phrases. Adverb: chart of uses, clauses, comparison, descriptive, numerals, phrases. Pronoun: antecedents; declension chart- -person, gender, case, demonstrative, interrogative, personal, relative. Preposition: phrases Conjunction: in compound subjects and predicates, in subordinate and coordinate clauses. Interjection: placement of in quotations.

TABLE 36

SCOPE AND SEQUENCE CHARTS: WRITTEN EXPRESSION

COMPOSITION SKILLS

FIFTH GRADE (cont.)	SIXTH GRADE (cont.)
<u>Sentences</u>	<u>Sentences</u>
Write compound subjects and compound predicates. Use a variety of interesting sentences: declarative, interrogative, exclamatory, and imperative (you, the subject). Use agreement of subject & verb. Write sentences reflecting changes in pronoun forms.	Write complex & compound-complex sentences. Develop concise statements (avoiding wordiness or unnecessary repetition). Use indirect object and predicate nominative. Write using clear thinking & expression to avoid vagueness and omissions. Write sentences with dependent & independent clauses. Correct sentence fragments and run-ons.
<u>Paragraphs</u>	<u>Paragraphs</u>
Compose paragraphs of clearly stated ideas. Underline topic sentences. Keep to the topic as expressed in title and topic sentences. Select subheads as well as main topic for an outline. Develop a four-point outline. Write paragraphs from outline. Use new paragraphs for new speakers in written conversation.	Analyze a paragraph to note method of development. Develop a paragraph in different ways: details, reasons, examples, comparisons. Check for accurate statements. Use a fresh or original approach in expressing ideas. Use transition words to connect ideas. Use topic sentences to develop paragraphs. Improve skill in compositions: Introduction, development, conclusion.

References: Core Knowledge Foundation, 1995; Hammill & Bartel, 1997; Mann, Suiter, & McClung, 1987; Toth et al., 1990.

TABLE 37

SCOPE AND SEQUENCE CHARTS: WRITTEN EXPRESSION

THE WRITING PROCESS

1st - 3rd GRADES	4th - 6th GRADES
Describe the writing process as being composed of at least three stages of writing activities: prewriting, writing, postwriting.	Describe the writing process as being composed of at least three stages of writing activities. prewriting, writing, postwriting.
Describe the basic differences between functional and creative writing processes.	Define functional and creative writing, and the differences between the two writing processes.
Describe functional writing products as including letters, book reports, how-to and directions, science reports.	Describe functional writing products as including business & friendly letters, content area reports, news stories, how-to directions, biographies.
Describe creative writing products as including stories of various genres, poetry, personal narratives, personal journals.	Describe creative writing products as including stories of various genres, various types of poetry, character sketches, personnel narratives & journals.

Prewriting Stage Activities:
Functional Writing

1. Clarify the purpose for writing and the basic requirements.

2. Use simple prepared graphic organizers or visual outline formats (i.e., letter format, report format).

Prewriting Stage Activities:
Functional Writing

1. Clarify the purpose for writing and the basic requirements.

2. Use a variety of graphic organizers or creates one to meet need for the specific writing purpose (i.e., Venn Diagrams, semantic maps).

TABLE 37

SCOPE AND SEQUENCE CHARTS: WRITTEN EXPRESSION

THE WRITING PROCESS

1st - 3rd GRADES (cont.)	4th - 6th GRADES (cont.)
3. Use graphic organizer to help structure brainstorming main ideas on assigned report topic with 3 subtopic areas.	3. Use graphic organizer to aid decision-making on report content.
4. Plan methods & means to get information for content of report (i.e., library, computer).	4. Use a variety of sources from which to gain information for report (i.e. books, articles, computer search).
5. Take simple notes from books and information sources to use in report (may write notes on the graphic organizer).	5. Take notes from library sources about topics indicated on graphic organizer.
6. Complete graphic organizer as simple outline to use in writing report.	6. Use notes to complete graphic organizer to use during the writing stage.
7. Select prepared format for report, book report, letter, etc. to use during drafting of the report.	7. Locate examples or formats of the required parts of the report (i.e., title page, body of report, reference page).
Prewriting Stage Activities: **Creative Writing**	**Prewriting Stage Activities:** **Creative Writing**
1. Determine the purpose for writing and the basic requirements of assignment.	1. Determine the purpose for writing and the basic requirements of assignment.
2. Study or reads a story from the specific genre of the writing assignment (i.e., fairy tale) and prepares a short list of genre characteristics (i.e., Fairy Tale Characteristics).	2. List the characteristics of specific genre (i.e., fairy tale, tall tale, mystery, science fiction, myth, short story) or specific type of poetry assigned.

TABLE 37

SCOPE AND SEQUENCE CHARTS: WRITTEN EXPRESSION

THE WRITING PROCESS

1st - 3rd GRADES (cont.)	4th - 6th GRADES (cont.)
3. Use a prepared graphic organizer with 3 sections of story (beginning, middle, ending).	3. Select a graphic organizer or create one for specific assignment with at minimum three story sections (beginning, middle, ending).
4. Brainstorm characters, plot, setting for each section of story and writes notes on graphic organizer.	4. Use graphic organizer and brainstorms plot, setting, characters for each story section.
5. Engage in library search if historically or scientifically accurate information is needed.	5. Engage in library search if historically or scientifically accurate information is needed.
6. Complete the graphic organizer that outlines the creative writing product.	6. Complete the graphic organizer to serve as an outline during the drafting of the creative product.
7. Select prepared format for creative story (i.e., story frames).	7. Select or prepare a format or story frame to use while drafting the creative writing product.

<table>
<tr><td colspan="2" align="center"><u>Writing Stage Activities:</u>
<u>Functional Writing</u></td></tr>
<tr>
<td>1. Use graphic organizer as visual outline to draft report, changing outline points into sentences or at least complete thoughts.</td>
<td>1. Use graphic organizer as visual outline to draft report, changing outline points into sentences or at least complete thoughts.</td>
</tr>
<tr>
<td>2. Write introduction to report that previews contents of the report.</td>
<td>2. Write introduction to report, previewing the contents of the report.</td>
</tr>
<tr>
<td>3. Use the completed graphic organizer to draft each section of the body of the report.</td>
<td>3. Use the graphic organizer and the notes from the information search to draft each section of the body of the report.</td>
</tr>
</table>

TABLE 37

SCOPE AND SEQUENCE CHARTS: WRITTEN EXPRESSION

THE WRITING PROCESS

1st - 3rd GRADES (cont.)	4th - 6th GRADES (cont.)
4. Write summary paragraph.	4. Write summary of report restating a major point from each of the main topics.

Writing Stage Activities: Creative Writing	Writing Stage Activities: Creative Writing
1. Write the introduction of the story based on specific genre characteristics (i.e., Fairy Tale: Once upon a time. . .).	1. Write the introduction of the story based on specific genre characteristics (i.e., Fairy Tale: Once upon a time. . . .).
2. Use the graphic organizer to draft the beginning section of the story including plot, setting, characters' actions that follow preplanned story plot.	2. Use the graphic organizer or semantic web to draft the beginning section of the story interweaving plot, setting, character descriptions, dialogue, and actions that follow the preplanned plot.
3. Use descriptive and figurative language to make story more interesting.	3. Use descriptive and figurative language (genre specific) to enhance story.
4. Use graphic organizer to draft the middle part of the story including plot, setting, characters' actions that lead up to the most exciting part of the story.	4. Use graphic organizer to draft the middle part of the story including plot, setting, dialogue, characters' actions that lead up to the story climax or problem peak by the end of the middle story section.
5. Use realistic dialogue that enhances the story and gives clues to the problem.	5. Use realistic dialogue that enhances the story and gives clues to the emotions of the characters and insight into the problem.

TABLE 37

SCOPE AND SEQUENCE CHARTS: WRITTEN EXPRESSION

THE WRITING PROCESS

1st - 3rd GRADES (cont.)	4th - 6th GRADES (cont.)
6. Use graphic organizer to draft the ending of the story including plot, setting, and characters' actions to solve the problem.	6. Use graphic organizer to draft the ending of the story including plot, setting, and characters' actions that reveal the hidden details and solve the problem.
7. Write very brief ending of story depending on genre (i.e., Fairy Tale: They all lived happily ever after.)	7. Write very brief ending of story depending on genre (i.e., Fairy Tale: They all lived happily ever after.
Postwriting Stage Activities: **Revising** **Functional Writing**	**Postwriting Stage Activities:** **Revising** **Functional Writing**
1. Compare report to graphic organizer to make sure all major ideas were included and logically sequenced.	1. Compare report to graphic organizer to make sure all main ideas and three facts about each were included and logically sequenced.
2. Make corrections after writing buddy considers content for any omissions or additional needed information.	2. Make corrections after writing buddy considers content for any omissions or additional needed information.
Postwriting Stage Activities: **Revising** **Creative Writing**	**Postwriting Stage Activities:** **Revising** **Creative Writing**
1. Use self-evaluation to compare story to semantic web to determine if all preplanned factors have been included in each story section.	1. Use self-evaluation to compare creative writing to semantic web to determine if all major preplanned literary elements were included in appropriate story sections.
2. Make corrections after story is read by writing buddy to (cont.)	2. Make corrections after story is read by writing buddy to (cont.)

TABLE 37

SCOPE AND SEQUENCE CHARTS: WRITTEN EXPRESSION

THE WRITING PROCESS

1st - 3rd GRADES (cont.)	4th - 6th GRADES (cont.)
determine if characters, plot, setting have been adequately described in story.	determine if characters, plot, setting, characters' actions have been adequately described.
3. Use self-evaluation to analyze story plot to determine if it is logically sequenced and complete.	3. Use self-evaluation to analyze story plot to determine if it is logically sequenced and complete.
4. Use self-evaluation to analyze character dialogue for realism.	4. Use self-evaluation to analyze characters' actions and dialogue for realism and contribution to moving the story toward its conclusion.
5. Redraft or make changes in report or story.	5. Redraft or make changes in report or story.
<u>Postwriting Activities: Editing Functional/Creative</u>	<u>Postwriting Activities: Editing Functional/Creative</u>
1. Self-evaluate using prepared outline conducted on story or report examining: capitalization, punctuation, word usage, spelling.	1. Self-evaluate using prepared outline conducted on story or report examining: capitalization, punctuation, word usage, spelling, grammar, vocabulary.
2. Make corrections based on results of self-evaluation.	2. Make corrections based on results of self-evaluation.
3. Use self-evaluation to examine sentences and paragraphs for structure, and any necessary changes are made.	3. Use self-evaluation to examine sentences and paragraphs for structure, and any necessary changes are made.

TABLE 37

SCOPE AND SEQUENCE CHARTS: WRITTEN EXPRESSION

THE WRITING PROCESS

1st - 3rd GRADES (cont.)	4th - 6th GRADES (cont.)
4. Make changes after writing buddy edits story or report to determine if any additional changes need to be made.	4. Make changes after writing buddy edits story or report to determine if any additional changes or corrections are necessary.
<u>Postwriting Activities:</u> <u>Preparing Final Copy</u> <u>Functional Writing</u>	<u>Postwriting Activities:</u> <u>Preparing Final Copy</u> <u>Functional Writing</u>
1. Write final copy in best handwriting.	1. Write final copy in best handwriting or type on computer.
2. Prepare final copy of report to include title page, copy of graphic organizer, & reference page.	2. Prepare final copy of report to include title page, copy of graphic organizer, & reference page.
3. Prepare visuals, pictures, etc. to enhance report.	3. Prepare visuals, pictures as Tables to enhance report.
<u>Postwriting Activities:</u> <u>Preparing Final Copy</u> <u>Creative Writing</u>	<u>Postwriting Activities:</u> <u>Preparing Final Copy</u> <u>Creative Writing</u>
1. Prepare final copy of story in best handwriting.	1. Prepare final copy of story in best handwriting or on computer.
2. Prepare final copy of story with title page, neat copy of semantic map (if required).	2. Prepare final copy of story with title page, and neat copy of semantic map (if required).
3. Prepare artwork to enhance story.	3. Prepare artwork to enhance and illustrate story.
4. Submit report or story to teacher and/or share with class.	4. Submit report or story to teacher and/or share with class.

References: Hall, 1981; Lerner, 1997; Mercer & Mercer, 1993; Polloway & Patton, 1997; Toth et al., 1990.

TABLE 38

SCOPE AND SEQUENCE CHARTS: WRITTEN EXPRESSION

WRITTEN EXPRESSION PRODUCTS

(Written Composition)

FIRST GRADE	SECOND GRADE
CREATIVE WRITING **(Narrative)**	**CREATIVE WRITING** **(Narrative)**
Write daily in a journal.	Write daily in a journal.
	Write a poster message.
Stories:	Stories:
Write sentences for a picture story.	Write a story ending.
Write picture captions.	Write imaginative stories in which ideas and feelings are expressed.
Write a description.	Use a variety of descriptive words and phrases in stories.
Write a very short story that includes structure (beginning, middle, ending); & a character.	Use sensory descriptive words and phrases in stories.
Create make-believe stories.	Write stories that include literary story elements: plot, setting, characters.
	Write fairy tales and tall tales.
Poetry	Poetry
Write riddles, songs, & poems.	Write riddles, songs, & poems.
Write poetry with rhyme.	Write poetry: rhyme, rhythm, onomatopoeia, imagery, alliteration.
FUNCTIONAL WRITING **(Expository)**	**FUNCTIONAL WRITING** **(Expository)**
Write a Thank You letter.	Write persuasive paragraphs.
Write a friendly letter & envelope.	Write friendly letters & envelopes.
Write a book report.	Write invitations, thank you letters, postcards.
Write a pictionary page.	Write book reports.
Write simple reports (i.e., how we go places).	Write short science and content area reports.
Write invitations.	Write directions & instructions.
Write directions.	

TABLE 38

SCOPE AND SEQUENCE CHARTS: WRITTEN EXPRESSION

WRITTEN EXPRESSION PRODUCTS

(Written Composition)

THIRD GRADE	FOURTH GRADE
CREATIVE WRITING **(Narrative)**	**CREATIVE WRITING** **(Narrative)**
Write daily in journals. Write a personal narrative.	Write daily in journals. Write a personal narrative (autobiography).
<u>Stories</u>	<u>Stories</u>
Write imaginative stories about how others feel in various situations. Write interesting dialogue in stories. Write imaginative stories in which ideas and feelings are expressed. Write stories that include the literary story elements: plot, setting, characters. Use a variety of words to express action, mood, sound, feeling in stories. Write fairy tales and tall tales.	Write descriptions of people, places, and events. Write narrative paragraphs with chronologically sequenced events. Write stories which include the literary elements: plot, setting, characters. Write a story from a picture or a story starter. Write different kinds of stories: mystery, adventure, science, fiction, myth, fable, fairy tales. Write and illustrate fiction books.
<u>Poetry</u>	<u>Poetry</u>
Write riddles, songs, and poems. Write poetry: rhyme, rhythm, onomatopoeia, imagery, alliteration. Write couplets & tercets.	Write poetry: rhyme, rhythm, onomatopoeia, imagery, personification, alliteration, Write metaphors and similes. Write lyrics and limericks. Write haiku, cinquain, quatrain.

TABLE 38

SCOPE AND SEQUENCE CHARTS: WRITTEN EXPRESSION

WRITTEN EXPRESSION PRODUCTS

(Written Composition)

THIRD GRADE (cont.)	FOURTH GRADE (cont.)
FUNCTIONAL WRITING (Expository)	**FUNCTIONAL WRITING (Expository)**
Write persuasive paragraphs. Write friendly letters and envelopes, invitations & thank you notes. Write a "How-to" article. Write a description. Write math problems. Write a biography. Write summaries: Compare and contrast. Write short research reports. Write an advertisement. Write instructions and directions. Write book reports.	Write a persuasive argument. Write friendly letters, business letters, invitations, and thank you notes. Write "How-to" articles. Write descriptions of science experiments. Write biographies. Write an article that contrasts. Write bumper stickers. Write science or social studies reports: 2-4 pages. Write a content journal. Write debates: Written arguments on issues such as environment and space.

TABLE 38

SCOPE AND SEQUENCE CHARTS: WRITTEN EXPRESSION

WRITTEN EXPRESSION PRODUCTS

(Written Composition)

FIFTH GRADE	SIXTH GRADE
CREATIVE WRITING (Narrative)	**CREATIVE WRITING** (Narrative)
Write in journals. Write autobiography.	Write in journals. Write autobiography.
<u>Stories</u>	<u>Stories</u>
Write stories including literary elements: plot, setting, characters, dialogue. Write a character sketch. Develop a plot from predictable events. Write character development including the character's mood, feelings, appearance, traits, motives. Write short scripts (play) based on stories read to the group. Write different kinds of stories: mystery, adventure, science fiction, myth, fable, fairy tale, tall tales.	Write stories with well developed beginning, middle, ending in terms of plot, setting, mood, tone, characters, dialogue. Write character sketches. Write article about a character's point of view. Write character development including the character's mood, feelings, appearance, traits, motives. Use figurative language in stories (similes, metaphors). Write a variety of prose based on personal experiences. Write a variety of short fiction: tall tales, folk tales, fairy tales, mysteries, adventure, science fiction. Write original scripts to be produced by the class. Write exaggeration and point of view.

TABLE 38

SCOPE AND SEQUENCE CHARTS: WRITTEN EXPRESSION

WRITTEN EXPRESSION PRODUCTS

(Written Composition)

FIFTH GRADE	SIXTH GRADE
CREATIVE WRITING (cont.)	**CREATIVE WRITING (cont.)**
<u>Poetry</u> Write a variety of poetry: rhyme, rhythm, imagery, onomatopoeia, alliteration, personification, metaphor, simile, lyric, limerick, haiku, cinquain, couplets, tercets, quatrain.	<u>Poetry</u> Write a variety of poetry: rhyme, rhythm, imagery, onomatopoeia, alliteration, personification, metaphor, simile, lyric, limerick, haiku, cinquain, couplets, tercets, quatrain.
FUNCTIONAL WRITING (Expository)	**FUNCTIONAL WRITING (Expository)**
Write a "How-to" article. Write a persuasive article. Write an article that compares. Write a content journal. Write descriptions of science experiments. Write advertisements. Write letters and envelopes: friendly, business, persuasive. Write science and social studies reports of 2-5 pages. Write debates: Written arguments on issues such as the environment.	Write "How-to" article. Write article supporting an opinion. Write a content journal. Write news stories, letters to the editor, and advertisements. Write letters and envelopes: friendly, business, persuasive. Complete forms and job applications. Write 5-10 page content reports. Write debates: Written arguments on controversial issues. Take notes & paraphrase information. Prepare outlines & book reports. Write a travel brochure. Write a daily diary, etc.

References: Mercer & Mercer, 1993; North Carolina Department of Public Instruction, 1979; Polloway & Patton, 1997; Polloway, Patton, & Cohen, 1983; Toth et al., 1990.

Chapter 7

MATHEMATICS CURRICULA:
ELEMENTARY GRADES

Any amount of mathematics instruction is of little use unless students can use knowledge of contents, facts, and procedures to solve problems. (Mastropieri & Scruggs, 1994, 224)

Elementary school curricula no longer include just arithmetic or the basic computational skills composed of addition, subtraction, multiplication, and division operations and algorithms (procedures). Beginning in the primary grades elementary school curricula focus on mathematics which includes arithmetic as well as numeration, number systems, fractions, decimals, problem-solving, geometry, measurement, time, time, money, algebra, and interpretation of charts, tables, and graphs (Mastropieri & Scruggs, 1994). Mathematics content can be classified in a variety of ways. For purposes of diagnosis and program eligibility in learning disabilities, mathematics is viewed from two perspectives: mathematics calculation (arithmetic skills) and mathematics reasoning (numeration, measurement, geometry, algebra, etc.). The focus of this chapter is the National Council of Teachers of Mathematics (NCTM) perspective; and the traditional mathematics calculation and mathematics reasoning skills perspective which are the diagnostic categories for students experiencing learning disabilities in mathematics.

MATHEMATICS CURRICULA OVERVIEW

There has been considerable concern regarding the mathematics curriculum, not only for those who function below or above the norm, but also, regarding the curriculum for average general education students.

NCTM Standards (1989)

The National Council of Teachers of Mathematics (NCTM) has taken a leadership role in modifying the mathematics curricula by publishing the *Curriculum and Evaluation Standards for School Mathematics* (NCTM, 1989). Although different content or standards categories were proposed at three levels (Grades K–4, 5–8, 9–12), there were significant similarities among the content categories. The similar mathematics content or standards categories at the K–4th and 5th–8th grade levels included the following: (1) Mathematics as Problem Solving, (2) Mathematics as Communication, (3) Mathematics as Reasoning, (4) Mathematical Connections, (5) Estimation, (6) Number Sense, Numeration, and Number Relationships, (7) Whole Number Computation, (8) Geometry, (9) Measurement, (10) Statistics and Probability, (11) Patterns, Relationships and Functions (NCTM, 1989). In addition, K–4th grade students studied "Contents of Whole Number Operations," and "Fractions and Decimals"; while 5th–8th grade students also studied "Number Systems and Number Theory," and "Algebra" (NCTM, 1989). Numerous mathematics textbooks for elementary and middle school students have used these standards categories as content strands running through the K–8th grade textbook series.

NCTM Standards (2000)

Principles and Standards for School Mathematics (NCTM, 2000) was released adding underlying principles for school mathematics, elaborating on the 1989 Standards for prekindergarten–2nd grade, grades 3–5, grades 6–8, and grades 9–12. Principles and Standards for School Mathematics remains the comprehensive reference on developing mathematical knowledge across the grades. The Council (NCTM) continues to produce numerous related publications and services to support, expand, and illuminate this work (NCTM, 2006). Three items provide significant information regarding creating mathematics curricula include the following:

1. Mathematics Standards and Benchmarks (NCTM, 2000)
2. Curriculum Focal Points (NCTM 2006)
3. Related Expectations (NCTM, 2006).

Standards

The Standards for school mathematics describe the mathematics under-standings, knowledge, and skills that students should acquire from prekinder-garten through grade 12. There are five Content Standards at each grade level, and five underlying Process Standards (NCTM, 2006) including the fol-lowing:

Content Standards	**Process Standards**
1. Number and Operations	1. Communication
2. Geometry and Spatial Sense	2. Reasoning
3. Data Analysis, Statistics, Probability	3. Representation
4. Measurement	4. Connections
5. Algebra, Functions & Patterns	5. Problem-Solving

Curriculum Focal Points

A subsequent publication, Curriculum Focal Points for Preschool Through Grade 8 Mathematics (NCTM, 2006) identifies 2-to-4 Curriculum Focal Points for each Content Standard (see TABLE 39). The Curriculum Focal Points are the most important mathematical topics for each grade level. They comprise related ideas, concepts, skills, and procedures that for the founda-tion for understanding and learning across the four grade bands: PreKindergarten – Grade 2, Grades 3–5, Grades 6–8, 9–12 (NCTM, 2006).

Related Expectations

Each Curriculum Focal Point for each standard at each grade level/band, has 1–8 Related Expectations which are the most significant concepts and skills at each grade band (see TABLE 39). Therefore, each of the Content Standards (5), has three Curriculum Focal Points (15); and each of the Curriculum Focal Points have 1–8 Related Expectations (15 x 1–8) that pro-vide the mathematics foundation knowledge at each grade level/band (see TABLE 39). These Content Standards, Curriculum Focal Points, and Related Expectations have been created by the NCTM to assist states in developing the mathematics curricula upon which the required state assessment (NCLB, 2007) will be based. Although, States have variability among their State Standards, this content structure ensures that there will be comparability and accountability across the schools, the states, and the nation. It is easy to see how Content Standards and Curriculum Focal Points could become Individual Education Program Goals, and the Related Expectations could become the learning objectives.

Process Standards

The curricula of mathematics includes the language of mathematics, cognitive factors (i.e., concrete-to-abstract concepts, automaticity in prerequisite skills at each level, strategy selection), the structure of mathematics including logical organization of mathematics concepts, and principles, and the developmental sequence in arithmetic as well as mathematics reasoning and problem-solving which includes functional mathematics. The **Process Standards** (see TABLE 40) provide the framework for teaching, learning, and assessing the students acquisition of the Content Standards in mathematics at all grade levels/bands.

Although, NCTM divides the general education mathematics curriculum into five Content Standards and five Process Standards, there are times that teachers of children with disabilities need to know which mathematics skills are mathematics calculation and which are mathematics reasoning for purpose of diagnosis of learning disabilities. Therefore, an outline has been created to align the traditional math organized into two groups (calculation and reasoning) with the NCTM Content Standards.

Alignment of Standards

NCTM Content Standards	Math Calculation/Reasoning
1. Number and Operations ⟷	* Numbers/Numeration/Properties grades 1–6 (see TABLE 42) * Calculation (all areas)(see TABLE 41) * Ratios & Percents (see TABLE 42)
2. Geometry & Spatial Sense ⟷	* Geometry grades 1–6 (see TABLE 42)
3. Data Analysis, Statistics, Probability ⟷	* Probability & Statistics, grades 5–6; (see TABLE 42)
4. Measurement ⟷	* Linear measurement,weight, capacity, temperature, etc. (see TABLE 42)
5. Algebra ⟷	* Algebra (see TABLE 42)

MATHEMATICS CALCULATION

Mathematics calculation or arithmetic involves learning the operations and common algorithms of addition, subtraction, multiplication, and division; and beginning with intermediate grade levels includes calculation of fractions and decimals. Primary grade mathematics calculation curricula focuses on addition content: addition facts, multidigit addition without regrouping, column addition: subtraction content: subtraction facts, multidigit subtraction without regrouping (see TABLE 41). Once students have mastered these beginning calculation skills at the acquisition learning level (90-100% accuracy) and are functioning at fluency (high rate and high accuracy), application, or generalization levels, the students are ready to progress to intermediate mathematics calculation skills. Primary grade level mathematics reasoning skills are taught after students have mastered these beginning mathematics calculation skills (see TABLE 42).

Intermediate level mathematics calculation skills include place value, regrouping in addition and subtraction, multiplication and division basic facts and algorithms (see TABLE 41). Each mathematics calculation level requires teaching basic content and vocabulary prior to teaching computational procedures (Mastropieri & Scruggs, 1994).

MATHEMATICS REASONING

Mathematics reasoning includes numeration, measurement, time, geometry, money, graphs and charts, story or word problems, probability and statistics, ratio, estimation, and algebra (see TABLE 42). The NCTM's 1989 report indicates that the major reason for studying mathematics is to solve problems, not to manage algorithms. In other words, accurate calculation in addition, subtraction, multiplication, and division is not an end in itself but a means or prerequisite for problem-solving and achieving other mathematics reasoning tasks.

Problem-solving requires higher order thinking and should lead to critical thinking and improved reasoning abilities. Mathematics reasoning depends upon a good grasp of math vocabulary, the medium through which math content and principles are described. Decoding mathematics vocabulary is crucial to understanding and solving math word and story problems. Thus, a major mathematics curricular focus is mastery of mathematics vocabulary in isolation and in context. Graphics (figures, diagrams, tables, charts) are as much a part of the language of math as the specialized terminology. Graphics need to be taught as an intrinsic part of the language because most math textbooks use them as visual explanations of verbal material. Math reasoning is the integration of arithmetic skills, cognitive skills, language skills during problem-solving in real-life situations, and improving cognitive abilities.

CONCERNS OF SPECIAL EDUCATION PROFESSIONALS

A number of professionals in the field of special education have expressed a variety of concerns regarding using the NCTM Standards as the mathematics curricula for students with mild disabilities. Those professionals supporting the NCTM Standards focus on the need for students with disabilities especially those with learning disabilities or behavior disorders to acquire the same basic math content as other elementary and middle school students, through modifying the pace of presentation of skills and/or teaching approach. The opposing group focuses on the need for students with disabilities to have a different mathematics curriculum than same-grade peers in general educational settings, a more functional math curriculum "driven by essential mathematical competencies and life skills" (McGuire, 1993, 244). The professionals opposed to using the NCTM's Standards have focused on the lack of research supporting the use of the Standards with students with mild disabilities (Hutchinson, 1993). Many special education professionals also object to the "constructivist only" approach to teaching mathematics promoted by the NCTM Standards.

However, the decision regarding whether students with disabilities would benefit more from mathematics according to NCTM Standards or functional mathematics became a moot topic with the reauthorization of several major Education laws. In the Individuals with Disabilities Education Act of 1997 (IDEA '97), Congress mandated that school districts must document that students with disabilities have access to the general education curriculum, and they must, also, document their involvement with and their progress in the general education curriculum. Additionally, IDEA 2004 required students with disabilities to participate in the state-wide and district-wide testing programs.

The reauthorizations of No Child Left Behind Act of 2001 and 2007, (NCLB) became the major force in general education driving not only the curriculum being taught, but also, determining the methods used in teaching, and sometimes even specifying the specific programs or commercial books and materials used in the classrooms. Mathematics programs for general education have been based on NCTM's Standards. Additionally, IDEA 2004 was aligned with NCLB 2001/2007 to reinforce the mandates of IDEA 1997. All students with disabilities must have access to the general education curriculum with modifications as needed, however, that does not mean that they can not also have applications in functional mathematics.

SUMMARY

Traditionally in special education, mathematics curricula for students with mild disabilities has included both mathematics calculation and mathematics reasoning skills. Mathematics calculation includes the basic arithmetic operations of addition, subtraction, multiplication, division, decimals and fractions. Mathematics reasoning includes the application of math knowledge and skills: Number and numeration, geometry, measurement, time, money, mathematics language, ratio and proportion, estimation, story or word problems, and functional mathematics.

The National Council for Teachers of Mathematics (2000) has provided leadership in preparing the standards for general education mathematics. These standards have been divided into 5 Content Standards and 5 Process Standards that span prekindergarten through grade 12. These Standards, Curricular Focus Points, and Related Expectations provide the knowledge and skills for mathematics curricula across the grade levels/bands. These skills have been integrated into the content of many math textbook series, thus, provide the cognitive structure for many math programs. As a result of IDEA 1997 and 2004; and NCLB 2001 and 2007, the mathematics curriculum for students with disabilities is the general education curriculum as specified by NCTM (1989, 2000). The general education math curricula adapted is the special education program for most students with mild disabilities.

TABLE 39

MATHEMATICS CONTENT STANDARDS

STANDARD 1: NUMBER AND OPERATIONS

CURRICULUM FOCAL POINTS:
* Understand numbers, ways of representing numbers relationships among numbers, and number systems.
* Understand meanings of operations and how they relate to one another.
* Compute fluently and make reasonable estimates.

RELATED EXPECTATIONS:
<u>PreK - 2 Grades</u>   <u>3 - 5 Grades</u>   <u>6 - 8 Grades</u>   <u>9-12 Grades</u>

STANDARD 2: ALGEBRA

CURRICULUM FOCAL POINTS:
* Understand patterns, relations, and functions.
* Represent and analyze mathematical situations and structures using algebraic symbols.
* Use mathematical models to represent and understand quantitative relationships.
* Analyze change in various contexts.

RELATED EXPECTATIONS:
<u>PreK - 2 Grades</u>   <u>3 - 5 Grades</u>   <u>6 - 8 Grades</u>   <u>9 - 12 Grades</u>

STANDARD 3: GEOMETRY
CURRICULUM FOCAL POINTS:

* Analyze characteristics and properties of two- and three-dimensional geometric shapes and develop mathematical arguments about geometric relationships.
* Specify locations and describe spatial relationships using coordinate geometry and other representational systems.
* Apply transformations and use symmetry to analyze mathematical situations.
* Use visualization, spatial reasoning, and geometric modeling to solve problems.

RELATED EXPECTATIONS:
<u>PreK - 2 Grades</u>   <u>3 -5 Grades</u>   <u>6 - 8 Grades</u>   <u>9 - 12 Grades</u>

TABLE 39

MATHEMATICS CONTENT STANDARDS (cont.)

STANDARD 4: MEASUREMENT

   CURRICULUM FOCAL POINTS:
* Understanding measurable attributes of objects and the units, systems, and processes of measurement.
* Apply appropriate techniques, tools, and formulas to determine measurements.

   RELATED EXPECTATIONS:
    Pre-K - 2 Grades   3 - 5 Grades   6 - 8 Grades   9 - 12 Grades

STANDARD 5: DATA ANALYSIS AND PROBABILITY

   CURRICULUM FOCAL POINTS:
* Formulate questions that can be addressed with data and collect, organize, and display relevant data to answer.
* Select and use appropriate statistical methods to analyze data.
* Apply transformations and use symmetry to analyze mathematical situations.
* Develop and evaluate inferences and predictions that are based on data.
* Understand and apply basic concepts of probability.

   RELATED EXPECTATIONS:
    PreK - 2 Grades   3 - 5 Grades   6 - 8 Grades   9 - 12 Grades

Directions: Access grade level/bands of RELATED EXPECTATIONS online from Education World, National Mathematics Standards at the selected grade/level band.

(From National Mathematics Standards, NCTM, 2000)

TABLE 40

MATHEMATICS PROCESS STANDARDS

**Students should have an understanding of the following
  mathematical processes:**

I. **PROBLEM SOLVING:**
   * Build new mathematical knowledge through problem solving.
   * Solve problems that arise in mathematics and in other contexts.
   * Apply and adapt a variety of appropriate strategies to solve problems.
   * Monitor and reflect on the process of mathematical problem solving.

II. **REASONING AND PROOF:**
   * Recognize reasoning and proof as fundamental aspects of mathematics.
   * Make and investigate mathematical conjectures.
   * Develop and evaluate mathematical arguments and proofs.
   * Select and use various types of reasoning and methods of proof.

III. **COMMUNICATION:**
   * Organize and consolidate their mathematical thinking through
     communication.
   * Communicate their mathematical thinking coherently and clearly to
     peers, teachers, and others.
   * Analyze and evaluate the mathematical thinking and strategies
     of others.
   * Use the language of mathematics to express mathematical ideas
     precisely.

IV. **CONNECTIONS:**
   * Recognize and use connections among mathematical ideas.
   * Understand how mathematical ideas interconnect and build on one
     another to produce a coherent whole.
   * Recognize and apply mathematics in contexts outside of
     mathematics.

V. **REPRESENTATION:**
   * Create and use representations to organize, record, and
     communicate mathematical ideas.
   * Select, apply, and translate among mathematical representations
     to solve problems.
   * Use representations to model and interpret physical, social, and
     mathematical phenomena.

(From: Principles and Standards for School Mathematics, NCTM 2000)

TABLE 41

SCOPE AND SEQUENCE CHARTS: MATHEMATICS

CALCULATION

FIRST GRADE	SECOND GRADE
ADDITION	**ADDITION**
State facts (whole number combinations) sums less than 12.	State facts 11 to 20.
Add facts sums less than 12 horizontally & vertically.	Complete number sentences with missing digits.
Add 2-digits with no regrouping.	Add 2-digit and 3-digit numbers with and without regrouping, sums (up to 999) of any two whole numbers.
Define mathematics vocabulary: addend, sum.	Define math vocabulary: addends.
Discuss reversing order of addends does not change sum.	Add horizontally & vertically.
Memorize addition facts with sums to twelve.	Check sums by changing order of addends.
State what happens when you add zero.	Estimate sums by rounding.
Add three one digit numbers.	Add three 2-digit numbers.
	Add by doubling (adding a number to itself).
SUBTRACTION	**SUBTRACTION**
State subtraction fact differences to 12.	State facts 11-20.
Subtract horizontally and vertically.	Use number sentences with missing digits.
Subtract 2-digits, no regrouping.	Subtract 2-digit & 3-digit numbers with & without regrouping.
Define mathematics vocabulary: minuend, subtrahend, difference, take away.	Find the difference of two whole numbers of 999 or less.
Describe what happens when you subtract "0".	Discuss inverse relation between addition and subtraction; uses addition to check subtraction.
Explain the relationship between addition & subtraction.	Memorize addition and subtraction "fact families".
Subtract 10 from a 2-digit number.	Subtract horizontally & vertically.
	Explain meaning of "0" in subtraction number sentences.
	Estimate differences.

TABLE 41

SCOPE AND SEQUENCE CHARTS: MATHEMATICS

CALCULATION

THIRD GRADE	FOURTH GRADE
ADDITION	**ADDITION**
Add 2, 3, and 4 digit numbers with & without regrouping.	Define addition vocabulary.
Master basic addition facts with sums through 18.	Add 1- to 6-digits and 5 addends with regrouping.
Use mental computation strategies to add 2, 3, & 4 digits with regrouping.	Discuss commutative and associative properties of addition.
Mentally estimate sums to 3-digits.	Add whole numbers including all regrouping and zero difficulties. Estimate sums by rounding.
Find the sum of two whole numbers up to 10,000.	Use addition properties and strategies.
Explain addition & subtraction as opposite operations.	
Explain regrouping in addition of numbers with up to 4 digits.	
Add "0" properly.	
Use addition to check subtraction.	
SUBTRACTION	**SUBTRACTION**
Write subtraction facts related to known addition facts.	Define subtraction vocabulary.
Underline minuends which must be regrouped before subtracting & explain regrouping orally.	Subtract 2 to 4 digits with regrouping.
Use addition to check subtraction.	Name minuends which require regrouping and give their regrouped value.
Subtract 2, 3, & 4 digit numbers with and without regrouping.	Subtract whole numbers including all regrouping and zero difficulties.
Master basic subtraction facts.	Subtraction with regrouping twice.
Mentally estimate differences.	Use zeroes in subtraction.
Use mental computation strategies.	
Estimate differences to 1000s.	
Subtract 2 whole numbers of 10,000 or less to find difference.	
Subtraction with regrouping more than once and with zero in minuend.	

TABLE 41

SCOPE AND SEQUENCE CHARTS: MATHEMATICS

CALCULATION

FIFTH GRADE	SIXTH GRADE
ADDITION	**ADDITION**
State names and describe the properties of commutative & associative properties of addition. Add 2 addends with 5 columns. Add 3 addends with 4 columns. Add 4 addends with 4 columns. Add equations. Calculate averages.	State the names & describe the commutative & associative properties of addition. Add Base 2; Base 5. Estimate sums. Calculate 2-digit, 3-digit, 4-digit, and larger numbers. Add equations. Calculate averages. Use properties of addition.
SUBTRACTION	**SUBTRACTION**
Subtract 4 & 5 digits with regrouping. Explain concept of "0". Estimate differences.	Subtract Base 2; Base 5. Estimate differences. Subtract 2-digit, 3-digit, 4-digit, and larger numbers.

TABLE 41

SCOPE AND SEQUENCE CHARTS: MATHEMATICS

CALCULATION

FIRST GRADE	SECOND GRADE
MULTIPLICATION	**MULTIPLICATION**
Demonstrate the multiplication concept using concrete and pictorial models.	Demonstrate the multiplication concept using concrete and pictorial models. Multiply products through 25. Relate multiplication to repeated addition. Explains the "times" sign: x Define multiplication vocabulary: factor, product. Multiply groups of 2, 3, 4, 5. Recognize multiplication and division as inverse operations.
DIVISION	**DIVISION**
Demonstrate the division concept using concrete and pictorial models.	Demonstrate the division concept using concrete and pictorial models.

TABLE 41

SCOPE AND SEQUENCE CHARTS: MATHEMATICS

CALCULATION

THIRD GRADE	FOURTH GRADE
MULTIPLICATION	**MULTIPLICATION**
Master multiplication facts to 10 x 10.	State basic multiplication facts to 10 x 10.
Multiply by 10, 100, 1000.	State multiples of a given number; common multiples of two given numbers.
Multiply 2 whole numbers with and without regrouping in which one factor is 9 or less & the other is a multi-digit number up to 3 digits.	Multiply by 10, 100, 1000.
	Multiply by 2 and 3 digit numbers.
Write numbers in expanded form using multiplication (i.e., 9,728= (9 x 1000) + (7 x 100) + (2 x 10) + 8).	Write numbers in expanded form using multiplication.
Estimate the product.	Estimate a product.
Explain multiplication and division as opposite operations.	Use mental computation strategies for multiplication, such as breaking a problem into partial products, for example: 3 x 27= (3 x 20) + (3 x 7) = 60 + 21 = 81.
Explain that multiplication is repeated addition.	Check multiplication by changing the order of the factors.
Use known multiplication facts to determine unknown facts (i.e., 2 x 6=12, so 4 x 6= 24).	Explain multiplication & division as opposite operations.
Demonstrate that changing the order of factors does not change the product.	Multiply with regrouping.
Define multiplication vocabulary.	Multiply 2, 3, 4 digit numbers.
Explain the product when zero is one factor.	
Multiply 2-digits by 1-digit; 3-digits by 1-digit; 10-digits by 1 digit with products through 1000.	

TABLE 41

SCOPE AND SEQUENCE CHARTS: MATHEMATICS

CALCULATION

FIFTH GRADE	SIXTH GRADE
MULTIPLICATION	**MULTIPLICATION**
Multiply 3 digits x 3 digits.	State the names & describe the commutative, associative, & distributive properties of multiplication.
Multiply 4 digits x 3 digits.	
Name prime numbers.	
State names & describe commutative, associative, and distributive properties.	Multiply multi-digit factors with and without a calculator.
Multiply 2 factors of up to 4 digits each.	Estimate products.
Write numbers in expanded form using multiplication.	Multiply by a decimal.
Estimate products.	Explains multiplication and division as opposite operations.
Estimate a product of two 2-digit whole numbers by rounding both and multiplying mentally.	Show modular and lattice methods of multiplication.
Review mental computation strategies for multiplication, such as breaking a problem into partial products.	Multiply by 4-digit numbers.
Explain that tens times tens produces hundreds; tens times hundreds produces thousands.	
Demonstrate mastery of the steps in multiplying by a 2-digit number (algorithm).	
Solve any realistic problem dealing with multiplication of whole numbers.	
Using zeroes in multiplicand.	
Multiplication with money.	

TABLE 41

SCOPE AND SEQUENCE CHARTS: MATHEMATICS

CALCULATION

THIRD GRADE	FOURTH GRADE
DIVISION	**DIVISION**

THIRD GRADE	FOURTH GRADE
Explain multiplication & division as opposite operations.	Define division vocabulary: dividend, divisor, quotient.
Define division vocabulary: dividend, divisor, quotient.	Master basic division facts to 100 divided by 10.
Master basic division facts to 100 divided by 10.	Demonstrate different ways of writing division problems: horizontal, vertical, fractional.
Explain rules: Cannot divide by zero. Any number divided by 1 = that number.	State factors of a given number; common factors of two given numbers.
Divide 2 and 3 digit dividends by 1-digit divisors, no remainders.	Explain rules: Cannot divide by zero. Any number divided by 1 = that number.
Solve division problems with remainders.	Estimate quotients.
Check division problems with multiplication (and adding the remainder).	Divide dividends up to 4 digits by 1 digit and 2 digit divisors.
Solve equations in horizontal & vertical form.	Solve division problems with remainders.
Show division facts related to known multiplication facts.	State division facts related to multiplication facts.
Demonstrate division as a process of repeated subtraction.	Check division by multiplication.
Explain division process with remainder.	Solve equations in horizontal & vertical form.
Divide using multiples of 10.	Divide using multiples of 10.
	Divide with 2 or 3-digit quotients.
	Use zero in quotient and greater dividends.

TABLE 41

SCOPE AND SEQUENCE CHARTS: MATHEMATICS

CALCULATION

FIFTH GRADE	SIXTH GRADE
DIVISION	**DIVISION**
Divide by 2 digit divisor with quotient remainder.	Explain division and multiplication as opposite operations.
Divide by 3 digit divisor.	Divide multi-digit dividends by up to 3-digit divisors with & without calculators.
Define vocabulary: divisibility.	Estimate quotients.
Explain rules for divisibility.	Divide by a decimal.
Estimate quotients.	Solve problems requiring division of a dividend expressed in dollars and cents.
Move the decimal point when dividing by 10, 100, 1000.	Demonstrate that multiplying or dividing both the divisor & the dividend by the same number does not change the quotient.
Divide dividends up to 4 digits by 1, 2, and 3 digit divisors.	Divide with zero in the quotient.
Solve division problems with remainders; rounding a decimal quotient.	
Check division by multiplying (and adding remainder).	
Determine divisibility of whole numbers by 2, 3, 5, 9, 10.	
Explain the steps involved in dividing a 3-digit number by a 2-digit number (algorithm).	
Use short division.	

TABLE 41

SCOPE AND SEQUENCE CHARTS: MATHEMATICS

CALCULATION

THIRD GRADE	FOURTH GRADE
FRACTIONS	**FRACTIONS**
Name fractions to 1/12.	Name fractions to 1/12.
Label numerator and denominator.	Define vocabulary: numerator, denominator.
Write mixed numbers.	Add & subtract fractions with like and unlike denominators.
Write equivalent fractions (1/2 = 3/6).	Write mixed numbers; changes improper fractions to mixed numbers.
Compare fractions with like denominators using signs for greater than, less than, = .	Write equivalent fractions.
Write equivalent fractions through twelfths.	Reduce fractions to lowest terms.
Estimate & write fractional parts of a whole or parts of a set.	Rename fractions with unlike denominators to fractions with common denominators.
Write mixed numbers in standard & word name forms.	Compare fractions with like and unlike denominators using signs for greater than, less than, = .
Add & subtract fractions with like denominators through twelfths.	Solve problems in the form of 2/3 = ?/12.
	Add and subtract word problems of like fractions with no regrouping.

DECIMALS	DECIMALS
Read and write decimals to hundredths.	Read, write, round decimals to nearest thousandths.
Recognize and write decimals as tenths and hundredths.	Read and write decimals as fractions (i.e., 0.39 = 39/100).
Compare and order decimals through hundredths.	Write decimals in expanded form.
Add & subtract decimals and money amounts with & without regrouping.	Understanding decimal place value.
Identify and use numerical patterns to solve problems.	Add & subtract mixed numbers.
	Compare decimals using signs for greater than, less than, = .
	Read & writes decimals on a number line.
	Dividing with money.

TABLE 41

SCOPE AND SEQUENCE CHARTS: MATHEMATICS

CALCULATION

FIFTH GRADE	SIXTH GRADE
FRACTIONS	**FRACTIONS**

Multiply whole numbers by a fraction.	Add & subtract fractions.
Multiply a fraction by a fraction.	Determine greatest common factor; least common multiple.
Multiply a mixed number by a whole number.	Add & subtract mixed numbers & fractions with like and unlike denominators.
Multiply a mixed number by a mixed number.	Round fractions to the nearest whole number.
Arrange fractional numbers in sequence on a number line.	Multiply a fractional number by a whole number; a fractional number by a fractional number.
Read, record, & order commonly used mixed numbers such as 1 3/4; 1 2/3; 11/2.	Divide fractions with like and unlike denominators.
Demonstrate equalities of mixed numbers & improper fractions.	Divide improper fractions.
Explain subtraction of like fractions requiring regrouping.	Divide mixed numbers.
Explain addition and subtraction of unlike but related fractions.	Compare mixed numbers and fractions with like and unlike denominators, using the signs for greater than, less than, = .
Add & subtract mixed numbers.	Explain the reciprocal of a given fraction (the product of a given number and its reciprocal = 1).
Create realistic problems using fractional numbers, and explain the solutions.	Write fractions as decimals.
Determine the least common denominator (LCD) of fractions with unlike denominators.	Write fractions as percents.
Recognize equivalent fractions.	
Reduce fractions to lowest terms.	
Compare fractions of like and unlike denominators using the signs for greater than, less than & equal to.	
Explain the reciprocal of a given fraction; know that the product of a given number and its reciprocal = 1.	
Round fractions to nearest whole number.	
Write fractions as decimals.	

TABLE 41

SCOPE AND SEQUENCE CHARTS: MATHEMATICS

CALCULATION

FIFTH GRADE	SIXTH GRADE
FRACTIONS (cont.)	
Dividing fractions by fractions.	
Dividing fractions by whole numbers.	
Dividing mixed numbers by fractions.	
Dividing fractions by mixed numbers.	
Renaming fractions sums, mixed number sums, and differences with like denominators.	
DECIMALS	**DECIMALS**
Read, write, order decimals to the nearest ten-thousandth.	Read, interpret, & record mixed numbers expressed in decimal form (i.e., 2.75).
Write decimals in expanded form.	Write decimal equations for proper & improper fractions.
Read and write decimals on a number line.	Add & subtract decimals through hundred-thousandths.
Add, subtract, read, write decimals to tenths and hundredths.	Multiply decimals by 10; 100; 1000; or by another decimal.
Round decimals (and decimal quotients) to the nearest tenth; to the nearest hundredth; to the nearest thousandth.	Divide decimals by whole numbers and by decimals.
Estimate decimal sums, differences, and products by rounding.	Round decimal addends and estimate the sum.
Estimating decimal quotients.	Add & subtract measures expressed in decimal form.
Add & subtract decimals through ten-thousandths.	Read, write, & order decimals to nearest hundred-thousandths.
Multiply decimals: by 10, 100, 1000; by another decimal.	Round decimals & decimal quotients to the nearest tenth; hundredth; thousandth.
Divide decimals by whole numbers.	Write decimals in expanded form.
Using zeroes in division.	Write decimals as fractions.
	Write decimals as percents.

TABLE 41

SCOPE AND SEQUENCE CHARTS: MATHEMATICS

CALCULATION

FIFTH GRADE	SIXTH GRADE
INTEGERS, RATIONAL NUMBERS, AND REAL NUMBERS	**INTEGERS, RATIONAL NUMBERS, AND REAL NUMBERS**
Exploring prime and composite numbers.	Define integers, rational numbers, and real numbers.
	Compare & order integers.
	Explain properties of integers.
	Add, subtract, multiply, divide integers.
	Explain that the sum of an integer and its opposite is "0."
	Compute with rational numbers.
	Use scientific notation.

References: Core Knowledge Foundation, 1995; Fernandez & Vandegrift, 1991; Mann, Suiter, & McClung, 1987; Mercer & Mercer, 1993; North Carolina Department of Public Instruction, 1979/2008; South Carolina Department of Public Instruction, 1998/2007; K-12 Curriculum, 2007.

TABLE 42

SCOPE AND SEQUENCE CHARTS: MATHEMATICS

REASONING

FIRST GRADE	SECOND GRADE
NUMBERS, NUMERATION, NUMBER PROPERTIES	**NUMBERS, NUMERATION, NUMBER PROPERTIES**
Recognize and write numerals 0-50.	Write numbers to 200.
Explain "0" as the numeral meaning "none."	Order & compare numbers to 1000 (100 less or 100 more).
Count orally 0-100.	Count & write by 2's to 100; 3's to 36; 4's to 48; 5's to 100; 10's to 200; 50's to 1000; 100's to 1000.
Count and write by 10's to 100; 5's to 50.	Explain place value: ones, tens, hundreds.
Explain place value 0-100.	Explain odd and even numbers.
Rename 1's and 10's through 100.	Match numerals up to 20 with printed names.
Name odd and even numbers.	Count forward and backward.
Match numerals 1-10 with printed names.	Arrange numerical cards in any sequence between 100 and 200 in ascending or descending order.
Count forward and backward.	Use a number line.
State more and less; counting how many more or less.	Round to the nearest ten.
Arrange given set of numerals from smallest to largest.	Use tallies.
Compare quantities using signs for more than, less than, = .	State ordinals through twelfth.
State ordinal position, 1st to 10th.	Name equivalent subsets.
Sort and classify objects. according to likeness and differences of attributes: size, shape, color, amount, function.	Write numbers in expanded form (i.e., 64-60+4).
Define a set by the common property of its elements.	
Count sets 0-5.	
Comprehends language of sets.	
Mark sets with "more" or "less."	
State which item does not belong.	
Understand & describe skip counting to 100 by 2s, 5s, & 10s.	

TABLE 42

SCOPE AND SEQUENCE CHARTS: MATHEMATICS

REASONING

THIRD GRADE	FOURTH GRADE
NUMBERS, NUMERATION, NUMBER PROPERTIES	**NUMBERS, NUMERATION, NUMBER PROPERTIES**
Write numerals in sequence 1-999.	Count & write by 6's to 72; 7's to 84; 8's to 96; 9's to 108.
Write from dictation 1-999.	Write from dictation 1-100,000.
Read & write numbers (digits & words) up to 5 digits.	Read & write numbers (digits & words) up to 6 digits.
Order & compare numbers to 99,999 using signs for greater than, less than, = .	Explain place value to hundred millions.
Demonstrate place value up to one hundred thousand.	Demonstrate rounding of numbers to nearest 10; hundred; thousand.
Use place value to explain 3, 4, & 5 digit numbers.	State place value of any digit in a whole number up to 6 digits.
Rename 10's to 100's.	Rename 10's, 100's, 1000's.
Interpret Roman numerals I to XX.	Interpret Roman numerals XI to C.
Count by 2's, 3's, 5's, 10's; counts by 10's to any given number.	Order & compare numbers to 999,999 using the signs for greater than, less than, = .
Write numbers in expanded form.	Write numbers in expanded form.
Use a number line.	Use a number line; locate positive and negative whole numbers on a number line.
Name ordinal positions, 1st to 20th.	Round to nearest 10; 100; 1000.
Round to nearest 10; 100.	State perfect squares and square roots to 144; recognize square root sign.
State perfect squares and square roots to 100; recognizes the square root sign.	State universal sets.
Explain concept of negative numbers: locate positive and negative whole numbers on a number line.	State intersection of sets.
Place Value: read & write numbers through 999,999 in standard, expanded, and word name forms.	Read ordinals through thirtieth.

TABLE 42

SCOPE AND SEQUENCE CHARTS: MATHEMATICS

REASONING

FIFTH GRADE	SIXTH GRADE
NUMBERS, NUMERATION, NUMBER PROPERTIES	**NUMBERS, NUMERATION, NUMBER PROPERTIES**
Read and write whole numbers to 8 or 9 digits.	Read & write numbers to the trillions.
Order & compare numbers to 999,999,999 using greater than, less than, and = signs.	Round numbers to nearest 10; 100; 1000; 100,000; 1,000,000.
Round numbers to nearest 10; 100; 1000; 100,000.	Comprehend place value to hundred-billions.
Use a diagram to explain place value of numbers up to 8 or 9 digits.	Use a number line to describe a set of integers.
Demonstrate place value to one billion.	Explain the function of "0" on a number line showing positive and negative integers.
Write numbers in expanded form.	Interpret Roman numeral years.
Using a number line, locate positive and negative whole numbers.	Determine if a number is a prime or a composite number.
Sequence fractional numbers on a number line.	Calculate using integers, negative numbers, rational numbers, place value to billions place.
Interpret Roman numerals C to M.	Name and record finite and infinite sets of whole numbers.
Demonstrate unions of sets, disjoint sets, finite, and infinite sets, empty sets.	Demonstrate solution sets; sets of ordered pairs.
Label a set and the members of a set as indicated by { }.	Write in expanded notation using exponents.
Name & define prime & composite numbers.	Use scientific notation.
State prime numbers less than 50.	Use exponential notation.
Define common factors, and Greatest Common Factor.	Use symbols for greater than or equal to; less than or equal to.
Name multiples of numbers & Least Common Factor.	Evaluate numerical expressions with exponents.
Estimate if sum of two whole numbers will be even or odd.	Use the terms "squared", "cubed" & "to nth power".
Estimate if difference between two whole numbers is even or odd.	

TABLE 42

SCOPE AND SEQUENCE CHARTS: MATHEMATICS

REASONING

FIRST GRADE	SECOND GRADE
MEASUREMENT	**MEASUREMENT**
<u>LINEAR MEASURE:</u> Measure length in inches and feet; and in centimeters. Determine longer and shorter. Measure length in nonstandard units.	<u>LINEAR MEASURE:</u> Measure in feet & inches or in centimeters. State that one foot = 12 inches. State abbreviations: ft., in., cm. Estimate linear measurements; then check by measuring. Measure lengths using nonstandard units (i.e., straws, clothes pins). Define meter as a standard unit for measuring length.
<u>WEIGHT (MASS):</u> Compare weight of objects using a balance scale in pounds; compares for heavier or lighter. Measure weight in nonstandard units.	<u>WEIGHT (MASS):</u> Compare weights of objects using a balance scale. Estimate and measure weight in pounds and ounces. Use abbreviation for pound (lb.); ounce (oz.).
<u>CAPACITY (VOLUME):</u> Measure capacity in cup, pint, quart.	<u>CAPACITY (VOLUME):</u> Estimate and measure capacity in cups. Measure liquid volumes: cups, pints, quarts, gallons. Compare US Customary & metric liquid volumes: quart & liter.
<u>TEMPERATURE:</u> Associate temperatures in degrees Fahrenheit with weather. Read thermometer to find temperature in Fahrenheit.	<u>TEMPERATURE:</u> Measure and record temperature in degrees Fahrenheit (to nearest 2 degrees). Use the degree sign: $^\circ$

TABLE 42

SCOPE AND SEQUENCE CHARTS: MATHEMATICS

REASONING

THIRD GRADE	FOURTH GRADE
MEASUREMENT	**MEASUREMENT**

THIRD GRADE

LINEAR MEASURE:
Make linear measurements in feet & inches; centimeters & meters.
State: 1 foot = 12 inches
      1 yard= 36 inches
      3 feet = 1 yard
      1 meter=100 centimeters
      1 meter is a little larger than 1 yard.
Convert inches, feet, yards.
Measure & draw line segments to 1/4 inch; centimeters.
Estimate linear measures, check by measuring.
State the properties (thickness, length, circumference) of selected objects for which the centimeter & meter are appropriate units of measure.
Measure distances in immediate environment.
Use a map to estimate and find differences.

WEIGHT (MASS):
Compare weights of objects using a balance scale.
Estimate and measure weight in pounds and ounces; in grams & kilograms.
1 kilogram = 1000 grams
State abbreviation for grams is g. and kilograms is kg.

FOURTH GRADE

LINEAR MEASURE:
Convert one unit of measure to another.
Find perimeter of shapes.
Estimate and make linear measurements in yards, in feet and inches; and in meters, centimeters, and millimeters.
Estimate and measure designated properties (length, width, girth) of familiar objects to the nearest centimeter.
Use models to demonstrate understanding of perimeter, area, circumference.
Use term "square centimeter."
State following equivalences & solve problems involving changing units of measure:
1 foot = 12 inches
1 yard = 3 feet= 36 inches
1 mile =5,280 feet=1,760 yards
1 centimeter =10 millimeters
1 meter = 1000 millimeters
1 meter= 100 centimeters

WEIGHT (MASS):
Estimate & measure weight in pounds & ounces; grams and kilograms.
State equivalences and solve problems in changing units:
1 pound = 16 ounces
1 ton = 2000 pounds
1 centigram = 10 milligrams (mg.)
1 gram = 1000 milligrams
1 gram = 100 centigrams (cg.)

TABLE 42

SCOPE AND SEQUENCE CHARTS: MATHEMATICS

REASONING

THIRD GRADE	FOURTH GRADE
MEASUREMENT (cont.)	MEASUREMENT (cont.)

CAPACITY (VOLUME):
Convert half pint, quart.
Label liter, quart, gallon as
  units for measuring capacity
  of containers.
Use appropriate materials to
  demonstrate invariance of
  quantity (changing to a different
  size & shape container does not
  change quantity being measured)
Estimate & measure liquid
  capacity in cups, pints, quarts,
  gallons, liters.
State: 1 quart = 2 pints
  1 gallon = 4 quarts
Compare US Customary and
  metric liquid volumes: quart
  vs. liter (liter is a little bigger).
Explain relationship of grams &
  kilograms; liter & milliliter.
	CAPACITY (VOLUME):
	Estimate & measure liquid capacity
	  in teaspoons, tablespoons, cups,
	  pints, quarts, gallons; liters,
	  milliliters.
	Use scale to read killograms.
	State equivalences & solves
	  problems changing units:
	  1 cup = 8 fluid ounces
	  1 pint = 2 cups
	  1 quart= 2 pints
	  1 gallon = 4 quarts
	  1 centiliter = 10 milliliters
	  1 liter = 1000 milliliters
	  1 liter = 100 centiliters
	Explain dry measures.

TEMPERATURE:
Measure & record temperature
  in degrees Fahrenheit & Celsius.
Use the degree sign.
State the freezing point of
  water as 32^0 F= 0^0 C.
Read room temperature on a
  Celsius scale thermometer.
	TEMPERATURE:
	State freezing & boiling points
	  on a Celsius thermometer.
	Explain that weather reports
	  are sometimes given in
	  US Customary measure or
	  Fahrenheit degrees and in metric
	  or Celsius degrees.

* Use English & metric units to
  estimate weight, length, and
  capacity.	

TABLE 42

SCOPE AND SEQUENCE CHARTS: MATHEMATICS

REASONING

FIFTH GRADE	SIXTH GRADE
MEASUREMENT	**MEASUREMENT**
LINEAR MEASURE:	LINEAR MEASURE:
Estimate & make linear measurements in yards, in feet & inches (to 1/16th); and in meters, centimeters & millimeters.	Use US Customary & metric units to determine length.
Use appropriate measuring device to determine & record height in centimeters.	Find perimeter, area, surface area.
Explain & use a formula to find the perimeter of a triangle.	Use a protractor & compass to measure points on a circle.
Determine distances on a map using scale provided.	Measure line segments; & polygons.
WEIGHT (MASS):	WEIGHT (MASS):
Use solid measurements.	Select metric measure to use in determining weight of common things.
Find areas of squares and rectangles.	Read to nearest tenth kilogram, the weight of common objects on a scale.
Use appropriate measuring device to determine personal weight in kilograms.	Read the measure of liquid in a graduated container to the nearest 10 milliliters.
CAPACITY (VOLUME):	CAPACITY (VOLUME):
Use concrete materials to explain volume & identify standard units for measuring it.	Use equations to determine volume.
Explain interrelations of the units of length and volume in the metric system.	Find volumes of rectangular prisms & cubes.
	Use cubic units to measure volume.
	Find volume of composite solids.
TEMPERATURE:	TEMPERATURE:
Measure temperature of water in acquarium in Celsius.	Use numbers less than 0 on Celsius & Fahrenheit thermometers.
Compare temperatures on Celsius & Fahrenheit thermometers.	Add temperatures with - and + signs.
Graph temperatures Celsius and Fahrenheit from an experiment.	Subtract 2 positive numbers on a thermometer.

TABLE 42

SCOPE AND SEQUENCE CHARTS: MATHEMATICS

REASONING

FIRST GRADE	SECOND GRADE:
TIME Tell time on the clock on the hour and half hour. State days of week and months of year. Discuss time vocabulary: today, yesterday, tomorrow, morning, afternoon, evening, night. Use calendar to identify "today" and other days.	**TIME** Read a clock face and tell time to 5 minute intervals. Use a.m. and p.m.; noon and midnight. Solve problems involving how much time has passed. Use calendar and identify the date, day of week, month, & year. Write the date using words and numbers; and only numbers.
MONEY State relative value of penny, nickel, dime, quarter. Compare value of penny, nickel, dime, quarter. Name and use dollar ($) and cent signs. Show how different combinations of coins equal the same amounts of money. Adding & subtracting with money to make change with small coins (5 to 20 cents).	**MONEY** State relative value of penny nickel, dime, quarter, dollar. Explain change after purchase. Substitute money values: penny, nickel, dime, quarter. Write amounts of money using $ and cent signs, and the decimal point. Show how different combinations of coins equal the same value. Label the half dollar, and the paper dollar; and give their value in cents.
GRAPHS AND CHARTS Create & interprets simple pictorial graphs and bar graphs. Interpret picture graphs showing comparisons.	**GRAPHS AND CHARTS** Create & interpret simple bar graphs. Create & interpret simple pictographs.

TABLE 42

SCOPE AND SEQUENCE CHARTS: MATHEMATICS

REASONING

THIRD GRADE	FOURTH GRADE
TIME	**TIME**
Tell time in 5 minute intervals; quarter hours, minute.	Make-up story problems that can be solved by using the clock and the calendar.
Tell time in terms of "minutes before" and "minutes after".	Use clock and calendar to solve problems involving time.
Use a.m. and p.m.	Tell time to nearest minute on conventional clock.
Solve problems on elapsed time.	
Use calendar: Identify date, day of week, month, & year.	
Write the date using words and numbers, and only numbers.	
Read a digital clock.	
Determine approximate time on a conventional clock.	
MONEY	**MONEY**
Compare money value $0.50 and $1.00.	Add purchases and count out change.
Add and subtract money problems.	Solve problems involving making change in amounts up to $100.00.
Estimate sums/differences by rounding to nearest dollar.	Estimate differences by rounding.
Read & write dollars and cents using decimal notation.	Solve multiplication & division problems with money.
Make change using as few coins as possible.	Round money amounts through $99.99 to nearest dollar.
Demonstrate the equivalence of a dollar with a variety of coins: pennies, nickels, dimes, quarters.	Add money amounts with sums $99.99 without regrouping.
GRAPHS AND CHARTS	**GRAPHS AND CHARTS**
Create and interpret bar and line graphs.	Create and interpret bar and line graphs.
Collect information & present it in a pictograph.	Plot points on a coordinate plane (grid), using ordered pairs of positive whole numbers.
Interpret a pictograph.	Interpret pictograph when a single symbol represents many.
Solve problems using information presented on a bar graph.	

TABLE 42

SCOPE AND SEQUENCE CHARTS: MATHEMATICS

REASONING

FIFTH GRADE	SIXTH GRADE
TIME	**TIME**
Solve problems on elapsed time; regroup when multiplying and dividing amounts of time. Explain time zones, belts, and standard time. Locate latitude and longitude.	Determine elapsed time. Use different time zones to determine time. Express parts of an hour in fraction or decimal form. Solve problems regarding time.
MONEY	**MONEY**
Count change after purchase. Use symbols for dollars and cents. Substitute money values; penny, nickel, dime, quarter, half dollar, paper bills.	Add, subtract, multiply, divide money amounts. Estimate money. Relate money to decimals. Make change with a wide variety of money amounts including large bills. Solve problems regarding money.
GRAPHS AND CHARTS	**GRAPHS AND CHARTS**
Read graphs: bar graph, line graph, pictograph. Read road maps. Determine distances on a road map using the scale provided. Interpret a broken line graph. Find and interpret information presented in bar and broken line graphs in newspapers, textbooks, etc.	Construct a graph using selected numerical data. Read & interpret data from a circle graph. Collect relevant information on some topic and organize it into bar and/or circle graph form (see probability and statistics). Prepare/interpret graphs: bar, line, circle, double bar. Graph ordered pairs, linear equations, & inequalities. Interpret frequency tables & histograms.

TABLE 42

SCOPE AND SEQUENCE CHARTS: MATHEMATICS

REASONING

FIRST GRADE	SECOND GRADE
GEOMETRY	**GEOMETRY**

FIRST GRADE — GEOMETRY

Name & reproduce circles, squares, rectangles, triangles, & diamonds.

Describe squares, rectangles, triangles, diamonds according to number of sides.

Label and reproduce straight and curved lines.

Explain line segments are not closed curves.

Label basic solid figures: cone cube, sphere.

Name shapes in common objects.

Use math language for spatial orientation: left, right, top, bottom, above, below, between, inside, outside, etc.

Recognize line symmetry as equal parts of plane figures.

SECOND GRADE — GEOMETRY

Name and draw basic plane figures: square, rectangle, triangle, circle.

Describe squares, rectangles, triangles, diamonds according to number of sides.

Name things in immediate environment shaped like circle, square, rectangle, triangle.

Distinguish between square and rectangle as regards length of sides.

Measure perimeter of squares and rectangles in inches.

Use a model to identify a square corner.

Label solid figures: sphere, cube, pyramid, cone, cylinder.

Associate solid figures with plane shapes: sphere (circle). cube (square), pyramid (triangle).

Make congruent shapes & designs.

Label lines as horizontal, vertical; perpendicular; parallel.

Name line and line segment (i.e., line AB).

Draw a line of symmetry, and create simple symmetric figures.

TABLE 42

SCOPE AND SEQUENCE CHARTS: MATHEMATICS

REASONING

THIRD GRADE	FOURTH GRADE
GEOMETRY	**GEOMETRY**

THIRD GRADE GEOMETRY	FOURTH GRADE GEOMETRY
Name spheres, cylinders, rays, planes, right angles, parallel lines.	Label prism, pyramid, cube, triangular & rectangular prisms, tetrahedron, perpendicular intersecting lines, line segments, planes, rays, angles.
Calculate diameter & radius.	Use "n" for missing number.
Determine if a figure is symmetric by finding lines of symmetry.	Label the intersection of sets symbol.
Create symmetric figures.	Use concrete materials to produce examples of parallel lines and intersecting lines.
Determine if figures are congruent.	Label examples of parallel and intersecting lines in the immediate environment.
Compare characteristics of cubes, spheres, cylinders.	Determine whether two figures are congruent.
Label lines as horizontal, vertical, perpendicular, parallel.	Label and draw points, segments, rays, lines.
Name lines and line segments.	Draw lines & label: horizontal, vertical, parallel, perpendicular, intersecting.
Label polygons: vertex.	Label angles as right, acute, obtuse.
Label the sides of polygons as line segments.	Label polygons:
Label polygons: pentagon, hexagon, octagon (regular).	1. Triangle, quadrilateral, pentagon, hexagon, octagon.
Draw a right angle.	2. Parallelogram, trapezoid, rectangle, square
Show there are four right angles in a square or rectangle.	Draw and label diagonals of quadrilaterals.
Compute area in square inches and in square centimeters.	Draw circles: Label radius & diameter.
Label solid figures: sphere, cube, rectangular solid, pyramid, cone, cylinder.	State & use formula for area of Rectangle; perimeter.
	Compute volume of rectangular prism in cubic units (cm^3, in^3).

TABLE 42

SCOPE AND SEQUENCE CHARTS: MATHEMATICS

REASONING

FIFTH GRADE	SIXTH GRADE
GEOMETRY	GEOMETRY

FIFTH GRADE

GEOMETRY

LINES & POINTS:
Draw & name points, line
 segments, rays, angles, and
 intersecting lines.
Draw lines & label: horizontal,
 vertical, perpendicular, parallel,
 intersecting.

ANGLES:
Label right angles; angles greater
 than and less than right angles.
Define a degree as a unit for
 measuring angles.
Measure the degrees in angles:
 right angle (90^0),
 acute angle (less than 90^0),
 obtuse angle (greater than 90^0)
 straight angle (180^0)

TRIANGLES:
Construct & label different
 kinds of triangles: right,
 equilateral, isosceles.
Define what it means for triangles
 to be congruent.

POLYGONS:
Label polygons:
 1. triangle, quadrilateral,
  pentagon, hexagon, octagon.
 2. parallelogram, trapezoid,
  rhombus, rectangle, square.
State regular polygons have sides
 of equal length and angles of
 equal measure.
Draw & label diagonals of polygons.

SIXTH GRADE

GEOMETRY

Name and use signs that mean
 "is congruent to," "is similar to,"
 "is parallel to."

PARALLEL & PERPENDICULAR:
Construct parallel lines; and a
 parallelogram.
Reconstruct a parallelogram to
 make a rectangle & explain how
 to find the area.
Construct a perpendicular bisector.
Explain rules:
 1. If two lines are parallel, any
  line perpendicular to one is
  perpendicular to the other.
 2. Two lines perpendicular to
  the same line are parallel.

ANGLES:
Label & measure the degrees in
 (right, acute, obtuse, straight,
 central).
Bisect an angle.
Classify angles.

CONGRUENT:
Construct an angle congruent to
 a given angle.
Construct a figure congruent to a
 given figure using reflection over
 a line of symmetry, and identify
 corresponding parts.
Show how congruent plane figures
 can be made to correspond
 through reflection, rotation, &
 translation.

TABLE 42

SCOPE AND SEQUENCE CHARTS: MATHEMATICS

REASONING

FIFTH GRADE	SIXTH GRADE
GEOMETRY	**GEOMETRY**

FIFTH GRADE — GEOMETRY

CIRCLES:
Define arc, chord, radius, diameter.
Using a compass, draw circles with given diameter or radius.
Find the circumference of a circle using formulas.

AREA:
Review formula for a rectangle (area = length x width) and solve problems involving finding area in a variety of square units (such as mi^2, yd^2, ft^2, km^2, cm^2, mm^2).
Find the area of a parallelogram using the formula: A= b x h.
Find the area of an irregular figure (such as a trapezoid) by dividing into regular figures for which you know how to find the area.
Compute volume of rectangular prisms in cubic units (cm^3, in^3) using the formula V= l x w x h.
Find the surface area of a rectangular prism.

SIXTH GRADE — GEOMETRY

Label congruent angles & sides.
Label axes of symmetry in squares, parallelograms, rhombuses, rectangles.

TRIANGLES:
State that the sum of the measures of the angles of a triangle is 180^0.
Construct different kinds of triangles: equilateral, isosceles, scalene, right, acute, obtuse.
Use manipulatives to explain the derivation of a formula for finding the area of a triangular region.

AREA & PERIMETER:
Find the area (A) and perimeter (P) of plane figures (i.e., rectangle, square, triangle, parallelogram). Given the area or perimeter of plane figures, find the missing dimension using formulas.

CIRCLES:
Use formulas to find the circumference & area of a circle.

RECTANGULAR SOLIDS:
Find the volume of rectangular solids.
Draw geometric solids & cross-sections.
Given the volume of a rectangular solid, find a missing dimension using formulas.

TABLE 42

SCOPE AND SEQUENCE CHARTS: MATHEMATICS

REASONING

FIRST GRADE	SECOND GRADE
STORY PROBLEMS	**STORY PROBLEMS**
Solve oral problems using "more" and "less". Solve written addition and subtraction problems. Solve one-step story problems, 0-10. Estimate the answer to story problems and determine if it is reasonable. Solve problems using logical reasoning, drawings, & models.	Solve written addition and subtraction problems through 20. Solve one-step problems. Use 3-digit numbers and solve simple 2-step problems. Use pictures and drawings to demonstrate addition or subtraction situations.
FRACTIONS	**FRACTIONS**
Explain fractions: concrete and pictorial models. Divide shapes and sets in half; quarters. Recognize, name, and write 1/2, 1/3, 1/4 as part of a whole or part of a set.	Divide shapes and sets in halves, fourths, thirds. Draw & label fractional parts. Recognize, name, compare, and write fractions to twelfths.

TABLE 42

SCOPE AND SEQUENCE CHARTS: MATHEMATICS

REASONING

THIRD GRADE	FOURTH GRADE
STORY PROBLEMS	**STORY PROBLEMS**
Solve written two-step story problems involving addition, subtraction, multiplication, division.	Solve multiple-step word problems using addition, subtraction, multiplication, division.
State the question in a word problem as well as the facts necessary to solve it.	Write number sentences.
Select and use familiar operations (algorithms) to solve word problems.	Solve problems with averages.
Compose simple story problems which require using familiar facts and operations.	Demonstrate verbal ability to identify the question and facts needed to answer it.
Make reasonable estimates of answers to easy "story" problems.	Write word problems which require the use of multiplication; the use of division.
Solve story problems using manipulatives, then write mathematical algorithm.	Separate extraneous facts from facts necessary to solve "word" problems.
	Solve problems involving finding the area of a rectangle in a variety of square units.
	Use problem-solving strategy: Multistep problem.
FRACTIONS	**FRACTIONS**
(see Math Calculation)	(see Math Calculation)

TABLE 42

SCOPE AND SEQUENCE CHARTS: MATHEMATICS

REASONING

FIFTH GRADE	SIXTH GRADE
STORY PROBLEMS	**STORY PROBLEMS**
Solve multiple-step problems using fractions, decimals, ratio, measurement, graphs (bar, circle). Solve problems with more than one operation (addition, subtraction, multiplication, division).	Solve problems dealing with time, work, rate, distance, speed, averages, percent. Solve multiple-step word problems requiring addition, subtraction, multiplication, division, decimals, fractions. Solve problems with more than one operation (with and without calculator). Solve consumer math problems involving purchasing (i.e., unit pricing, better buys); interpreting maps and schedules; sales tax; checking account balances; discounts.
FRACTIONS (see Math Calculation)	**FRACTIONS** (see Math Calculation)

TABLE 42

SCOPE AND SEQUENCE CHARTS: MATHEMATICS

REASONING

FIRST GRADE	SECOND GRADE
PROBABILITY & STATISTICS	**PROBABILITY AND STATISTICS**
	Identify and predict outcomes in probability.
THIRD GRADE	**FOURTH GRADE**
PROBABILITY & STATISTICS	**PROBABILITY & STATISTICS**
Read, interpret, and make tally charts, pictographs, and bar graphs with up to six groups. Make organized lists and tree diagrams to count arrangements up to 6 objects. Predict outcomes based on probability.	Graphing--create pictographs bar graphs, line graphs, circle graphs. Predicting probability. Find the probability of a single event with probabilities expressed as fractions with denominators through eight.

TABLE 42

SCOPE AND SEQUENCE CHARTS: MATHEMATICS

REASONING

FIFTH GRADE	SIXTH GRADE
PROBABILITY & STATISTICS	PROBABILITY & STATISTICS
Explain probability as a measure of the likelihood that an event will happen; using simple models, express probability of a given event as a fraction.	Explain probability as a measure of the likelihood that an event will happen, expressed as a fraction or a ratio.
Collect and organize data in graphic form (bar, line, & circle graphs).	Collect & organize data into graphic form (bar, line, circle).
Solve problems requiring interpretation and application of graphically displayed data.	Solve problems requiring interpretation & application of graphically displayed data.
Find the average (mean) of a given set of numbers.	Calculate the mean, median, & mode when given a set of data.
Plot points on a coordinate plane, using ordered pairs of positive and negative whole numbers.	Construct a histogram; a tree diagram.
Graph simple functions.	Plot points on a coordinate plane, using ordered pairs of positive & negative whole numbers.
Complete tree diagrams.	Graph simple functions and solve problems involving use of a coordinate plane.
Predicting probability based on independent and dependent events.	Finding averages.

TABLE 42

SCOPE AND SEQUENCE CHARTS: MATHEMATICS

REASONING

FIFTH GRADE	SIXTH GRADE
RATIO	**RATIO, PROPORTION, PERCENT**
Determine and express simple ratios.	Use ratios and proportions to interpret map scales and scale drawings.
Use ratio to create a simple scale drawing.	Solve proportions including word problems involving proportions with one unknown.
Solve problems on speed as a ratio, using the formula $S = d/t$ or $D = r \times t$	Express equivalences between fractions, decimals, & percents.
Using ratios as fractions.	Find the given percent of a number; and find what percent a given number is of another number.
Using scales on maps.	Solve problems involving percent increase and decrease.
PERCENT	Find an unknown number when a percent of the number is known.
Label percent sign (%).	Use expressions with percents greater than 100%.
Express equivalences between fractions, decimals, and percents.	Explain percent as a ratio (1/100 or one out of one hundred) or as a decimal (0.01).
State common equivalences:	
1/10 = 10%	
1/4 = 25%	
1/2 = 50%	
3/4 = 75%	
Find the given percent of a number.	
Relate fractions to percents.	
Relate percents to decimals.	

TABLE 42

SCOPE AND SEQUENCE CHARTS: MATHEMATICS

REASONING

FIRST GRADE	SECOND GRADE
ESTIMATION	ESTIMATION
	Estimate the duration of an event (time).
	Use rounding to estimate sums & differences.
	Measure, compare, and estimate length, capacity, and weight (mass) in English and metric units.
	Estimate by rounding to the nearest hundred or dollar to find sums of differences.

THIRD GRADE	FOURTH GRADE
ESTIMATION	ESTIMATION
Estimate differences using front-end estimation with numbers through 9,999.	Estimate quotients with 2- and 3-digit dividends and 1-digit divisors by rounding dividends to the nearest ten.
Estimate differences of money using rounding to the nearest ten cents, dollar, or ten dollars with money amounts through $99.99.	Estimate money quotients with 3- and 4-digit dividends and 1-digit divisors by rounding to the nearest dollar through $99.99.
Estimate multiplication products through $999 using front-end estimation.	Estimate multiplication products through $999 by rounding 2- and 3-digit factors to the nearest 10 cents or dollar.

TABLE 42

SCOPE AND SEQUENCE CHARTS: MATHEMATICS

REASONING

FIFTH GRADE	SIXTH GRADE
ESTIMATION	**ESTIMATION**
Estimate sums & differences. Estimate products. Estimate quotient with 2-digit divisors. Estimate length & area. Estimate money amounts. Estimate fractions; & finding a fraction of a number. Estimate with percents.	Estimate by rounding whole numbers. Adjusting estimates (underestimates and overestimates). Estimate by rounding decimals. Use estimation in problem-solving. Estimate in measurement, geometry, fractions, percents, algebra. Determine reasonable answers by estimating. Estimate decimal sums, differences, products, quotients. Estimate using percentages. Estimate with money.

TABLE 42

SCOPE AND SEQUENCE CHARTS: MATHEMATICS

REASONING

FIRST GRADE

ALGEBRA
Sort, classify, and order by one
    attribute (size, number, shape
    color, thickness).
Recognize and extend simple
    repeating patterns.
Use concrete, pictorial, and verbal
    representations to develop an
    understanding of invented and
    conventional symbolic notations.
Describe qualitative change.
Find unknowns in problems
    Involving addition & subtraction.

SECOND GRADE

ALGEBRA
Create, identify, describe, and
    extend patterns.
Find unknowns in simple
    arithmetic problems.
Understand basic properties of
    odd and even numbers.
Model situations that involve
    the addition and subtraction of
    whole numbers, using objects,
    pictures and symbols.
Use concrete, pictorial, and verbal
    representations to develop an
    understanding of invented and
    conventional symbolic notations.
Sequence random numerals between
    1 and 1000.
Analyze change in various contexts.

THIRD GRADE

ALGEBRA
Explore and understand arithmetic
    relationships among positive
    whole numbers.
Create, describe, explain and extend
    patterns based on numbers,
    operations, geometric objects, &
    relationships.
Find the unknown in simple
    equations that involve one or
    more of the four arithmetic
    operations.
Represent and analyze patterns &
    functions, using words, tables,
    graphs, & equations to draw
    conclusions.
Express mathematical relationships
    among equations.

FOURTH GRADE

ALGEBRA
Use properties of arithmetic to
    solve simple problems.
Find the unknown in simple
    linear equations.
Evaluate simple expressions such
    as $na+b$, and $na-b$, where a, b, n
    are whole numbers or fractions.
Describe, extend, and make
    generalizations about geometric
    and number patterns.
Represent and analyze patterns
    and functions, using words,
    tables and graphs, and equations
    to draw conclusions.

TABLE 42

SCOPE AND SEQUENCE CHARTS: MATHEMATICS

REASONING

FIFTH GRADE	SIXTH GRADE
ALGEBRA	ALGEBRA
Locate variables and solve equations using variables.	Determine missing numbers in number sentences.
Write and solve equations for word problems.	Use variables and equations.
Identify such properties as commutativity, associativity, & distributivity, & use them to compute with whole numbers.	Comprehend algebraic patterns, unctions & relations.
Express mathematical situations with objects & representations, such as graphs, tables, and equations to draw conclusions.	Use algebraic expressions, formulas, & inequalities.
Find the unknown in simple linear Equations (i.e., 96 + 67= b + 67)	Write and solve equations for word problems.
	Understand that the system of negative and positive numbers obeys and extends the laws governing positive numbers.
	Understand why the product or quotient of two negative numbers must be positive.
	Represent and use algebraic relationships in a variety of ways.
	Solve problems involving translation among & between verbal, tabular, numerical, algebraic, and graphical expressions.
	Use symbolic algebra to represent situations and to solve problems especially those that involve linear relationships.

References: Core Knowledge Foundation, 1995; Fernandez & Vandegrift, 1991; Mann, Suiter, & McClung, 1987; Mercer & Mercer, 1993; North Carolina Department of Public Instruction, 1979/2008; South Carolina Department of Public Instruction, 1998/2007; K-12 Curriculum, 2007.

Chapter 8

EDUCATIONAL TECHNOLOGY CURRICULA

TANDRA TYLER-WOOD

Technology supports instruction, learning, and inquiry and has the potential to enhance the independence, integration, and well-being of students with learning and behavior problems. (Brett, 1998, 443)

"Technology has proven to be an excellent tool in education" (Goldstein, 1998, 16). The requirements for use of technology in the classroom are quickly changing to meet the technology demands of society. Technological advances including new software and hardware devices are developed daily. Several professional organizations have developed standards for the use of technology in K-12 classrooms. Resources are becoming increasingly available for school districts to systematically integrate effective technology into the curriculum with the 2004 amendments to the Assistive Technology Act. Each state submitted a grant application in the form of a three-year plan for Assistive Technology programming that spanned October 1, 2005 through September 30, 2008. The focus of this chapter is to review recent changes in technology, to assist teachers in developing effective technology plans for their students, especially those students with special needs.

TECHNOLOGY IN THE CLASSROOM

Education in the classroom must focus on training students for a new age, the age of technology. Our daily lives are inundated with technology. *What is technology?* Technology is simply the use of mechanized tools which can be used to accomplish a task easier, faster, better or more independently. Technology frequently used by special educators includes video disks, television, computers, augmentative communication devices, assistive technology devices, and adaptive computer devices. Many students with disabilities must use these technological devices to effectively compete in the new technology arena.

Assistive Technology

The concept of assistive technology has been available in areas such as speech pathology for some time. Assistive technology pedagogy is relatively new to the field of special education. In 1997, The Individuals with Disabilities Education Act Amendments mandated that Individualized Educational Program (IEP) teams consider assistive technology services for all students receiving special education services. However, federal law does not stipulate what constitutes consideration or which components of assistive technology are to be included in the consideration process (Watts, O'Brian, & Wojcik, 2004). As new forms of technology become available, new opportunities arise for the use of technology with students with disabilities. Blackhurst (2001) defines assistive technology as a cognitive prosthesis that can replace an ability that is impaired or as a cognitive scaffold that provides support needed to accomplish a task more effectively, efficiently, and independently that otherwise would not be possible.

Technology as a Tool for Teachers

Technology in the classroom benefits teachers by facilitating the tasks required for classroom management, such as paperwork and curriculum planning. As more and more students with disabilities move into the inclusion classroom, the paperwork load for teachers has increased. Technology offers strong classroom management options with computer-based IEP development software. According to Serfass & Peterson (2007), the ability of SEAPs (special education assistance programs) to ensure compliance with both timeframes and mandated requirements of special education processes provides educators more time to focus on the needs of students by reducing preparation time.

Prerequisite Skills

To maximize the potential of technology use, it is necessary for students to master certain prerequisite skills. At the most fundamental level, it is important that students learn that personal actions can result in a change in the environment. Students need to learn that they are the locus of control for a particular technology. Even students with limited skills can learn to operate simple switches. Thus, an initial objective in any technology program is assisting students to understand locus of control. Because technology allows the student with a disability control over the learning environment, an effective technology program can increase achievement as well as increase self-esteem.

Technology Assessment

Recent legislation has placed greater emphasis on technology assessment (Watts, O'Brien & Wojcik, 2004). A primary purpose of the educational assessment process is the collection of data for the provision of individualized supports in order to achieve success for learners with special needs.

STUDENT FUNCTIONING LEVEL. The first step in implementing an effective technology plan for an individual student is to ascertain the student's current level of functioning in the use of technology. An effective technology plan should compliment a special education student's Individual Education Program goals and objectives. It is important to determine any weaknesses a student might have that would limit the use of technology.

Initially, it is important to determine if the student has the capability of mastering keyboarding skills by assessing and teaching keyboarding skills. For example, a student with poor visual-motor coordination might have difficulty mastering the typing skills necessary for inputting information into the computer. Additional time and practice may be all that are necessary to acquire the proper skills. However, some students because of physical or intellectual limitations might not be capable of using a keyboard to input information into the computer, thus, alternative input devices may be required such as a stylus held in the mouth to strike keys or a voice recognition system. Adaptive devices selected must suit the needs, skill level, and personality of the individual with disabilities. Many school systems, rehabilitation centers, and some universities specialize in matching appropriate input devices to the individual with special needs. A checkout system where an individual with a disability is allowed to use the assistive device for a period of time before purchasing the device is quite helpful when matching needs to devices.

A student's functioning level must be determined in all categories of technology standards adopted for the general education curriculum (see TABLE 44). Although, there are few commercial assessments to determine student performance in technology, most states are involved in creating curriculum-based technology assessments that are based on the general education technology standards adopted. For example, North Carolina has a required computer test for high school graduation, **The North Carolina Computer/ Technology Skills Assessment** and an alternative test for students with disabilities who need assistive provisions, **The North Carolina Computer Skills Alternate Assessment** (Standard Course of Study, 2004).

Assessment and Review of Software

In addition to assessing the student's ability, it is also necessary for the teacher to assess and review all software before using it. Student needs should drive the purchase and implementation of any piece of software. Every piece of software should be reviewed by the teacher. In reviewing software, it is important to note the skills that are addressed by the software as well as all of the prerequisite skills. Software that provides skills at different levels is very helpful. Many software packages also provide a record keeping system. If a record system is not provided with the software, the teacher has the additional responsibility of observing and recording the student's progress with the software. It is important for the teacher to monitor progress to determine if the student's computer time is effectively used.

Types of Tool Software

"Using the computer as a tool is the most versatile and productive use of computers in schools" (Brett, 1998, 420). There are many types of tool software including word processing, desktop publishing, keyboarding, database management, spreadsheets, graphics, and drawing and painting programs.

Word Processing and Desktop Publishing

Across the curriculum, word processing and desktop publishing are very useful tools in the writing process. Word processing has proved to be very helpful for students with learning and behavior problems who experience great difficulty with any assignment involving writing and producing a written product (i.e., report, story, essay test). Many students with disabilities experience difficulty with coordinating handwriting, spelling, and composition skills (i.e., capitalization, punctuation, grammar, word usage) with the organization and preparation of a written product, and with editing and producing a final draft. Word processing and desktop publishing provide the student with assistance with the mechanics in order to produce a written assignment that is neat and legible.

Keyboarding and Other Input Modes

KEYBOARDING. Although, there are many input devices available, the keyboard is by far the most common device. In the past, most curricula did not address keyboarding until middle school or high school. Clearly, the availability of preschool and elementary school software has made it necessary to readdress when keyboarding skills are taught. It is important to introduce appropriate keyboarding skills before students develop inappropriate "hunt and peck" skills which are difficult to "unlearn." Computers have made it necessary to introduce keyboarding skills as early as the second grade.

THE MOUSE. Another common input device is the mouse. Using the mouse requires eye-hand coordination, thus, some students with special needs may need extended practice to obtain mastery of using the mouse. In some cases it might be necessary to use an adaptive mouse. Different mice require different levels of manual dexterity. Some mice are operated through the use of the thumb alone, while some mice resemble large baseballs and can be manipulated by running a palm over the baseball. It is important to match the motor skill level of the student to the mouse.

ADAPTIVE COMMUNICATION. Computers can help students communicate their needs and ideas. Voice synthesizers can read for students with vision impairments or limited reading ability. Computers can transfer Braille into print or print into Braille reducing the need for a special teacher or paraprofessional to transfer assignments for students who are visually impaired and to transcribe Braille assignments into written English. Touch screens allow students with limited developmental skills to interact with the computer. Adaptive communication devices have opened fantastic learning opportunities for students with disabilities.

Databases, Spreadsheets, and Other Tool Software

"A database is a collection of information or data stored in digital form on a computer. Database management software provides the ability to enter, store, update, organize, and retrieve information" (Brett, 1998, 423). Large amounts of information are stored in databases and available to students using computers including encyclopedias, atlas and maps, and online databases which can support education across the curriculum. Students can also create their own databases of information.

"A spreadsheet, like a database, is a tool for gathering information, manipulating it, and presenting it. A spreadsheet is primarily for numerical data, while databases focus on text" (Brett, 1998, 425). Spreadsheet software presents information in a grid of rows and columns, calculates desired information, and creates graphs and charts of the cumulative information. This software allows students to present mathematical data in a visual form for comparisons and drawing conclusions.

Graphics, drawing and painting programs are very popular with students. Graphics software allows students to make banners, signs, stationery, greeting cards, calendars; and illustrate stories, poems, newsletters with clip art in color. Drawing programs facilitate the production of straight lines, curves, circles, ovals, polygons, and freehand drawings, while paint programs allow for creation of expressive paintings with electronic brushes, pencils, and paints (Brett, 1998).

Instructional Software

"Instructional software is traditionally categorized as drill and practice, tutorial, simulation, problem-solving, and exploratory" (Brett, 1998, 428) (See TABLE 45 for Instructional Software.)

Remedial Programs

Students with disabilities often need additional time to master skills. Computer programs offer an excellent opportunity for drill and practice as the computer is a tireless tutor. Drill and practice represents the most common classroom use of the computer, however, these activities do not utilize the maximum capabilities of the computer.

There are several important considerations in selecting effective drill and practice software. Programs that take too much time loading or lock-up frequently, contain too many activities unrelated to the skill being learned. These programs take away from academic learning time. To maximize academic learning time, it is important for programs to provide high rates of responding relevant to the skill being learned. The use of graphics and animation makes an attractive package for many software programs, however, animation or graphics that are unrelated to the program's instructional objectives may distract the student and reduce academic learning time and skill mastery. Occasionally, the graphics associated with an incorrect response are more reinforcing than the graphics associated with a correct response. All software used for drill and practice should be analyzed carefully.

Programmed Instruction

During recent years integrated learning systems (ILS) have been developed that provide a large networked instructional, management, and assessment system. These commercial software systems provide school districts a comprehensive curriculum for reading, mathematics, and almost every other subject area across grade levels as an alternative to purchasing individual instructional software.

Caution should be used when implementing an integrated learning system with special needs learners since mastery of certain prerequisite skills is assumed. Students with disabilities often have significant gaps in achievement. Many programmed learning packages assume that a student's mathematics and reading abilities are on similar levels. A student with learning disabilities who has a reading problem might be able to calculate mathematics problems at the sixth grade level, but read only on a third grade level. A program that requires substantial reading at the sixth grade level in order to complete mathematics problems would be inappropriate. Therefore, the teacher must be very familiar with the requirements of the programmed instructional package and may need to skip some components of the system.

SIMULATION. "Simulation software imitates a situation or models the underlying characteristics of a real phenomenon without the limitations of time, distance, cost, or danger associated with the actual situation" (Brett, 1998, 431). Computer simulations offer a unique opportunity to master and generalize skills. Simulated real life situations are most useful for teaching decision-making and problem-solving skills.

PROBLEM-SOLVING. Students with disabilities often experience difficulty with critical thinking and problem-solving skills. The volume of knowledge that can be accessed with the computer requires the ability to evaluate and select materials and information relevant to the student's needs. Students with disabilities must be directly taught to use the computer effectively for problem solving, while many students in the regular education classroom develop strategies for accessing information on the computer without realizing that they are using a problem-solving process. Eisenburg (1990) proposed the "Big Six" process to teaching an information problem-solving process to students with disabilities including the following: (1) Task definition; (2) Information seeking strategies; (3) Location and access of information; (4) Information use; (5) Synthesis (organizing and presenting information); and (6) Self-evaluation.

EXPLORATORY. Exploratory software promotes discovery learning, gives the student a high degree of control over their learning, and the sound and graphics may bypass the reading barrier (Brett, 1998). "Multimedia software refers to the use of computers to present information in the form of text, images, graphics, sound, animation, and motion video linked together in a nonlinear format" (Brett, 1998, 433). Multimedia software, such as electronic books, are interactive and exploratory. Multimedia stories can lead children with language and reading disabilities to read print augmented with graphics, animation, and movies (Andrews & Jordan, 1998). Multimedia applications are especially useful for deaf children because video dictionaries of sign language can be built right into the stories (Andrews & Jordon, 1998).

The Internet

The Internet is a network of computers connected together around the world in a World Wide Web. Students can use the Internet to send and receive electronic mail, browse data bases of information, access public resources such as universities and libraries, join special interest discussion groups, and send and receive programs (Brett, 1998). The World Wide Web facilitates differentiating curriculum for gifted students by providing for independent research on current classroom topics (Lewis, 1998). There are World Wide Web sites designed for K–12 students in art, languages, literature, math, science, social studies, and numerous gifted education listservs that expand the parameters of the classroom textbooks.

The Internet provides numerous benefits for students by enhancing their understanding of research, increasing their organization skills, and facilitating skills in critical thinking (i.e., analyzing, evaluating, ordering). The Internet provides numerous avenues to find information and provides field trips to virtual museums. Using the Internet to complete assignments (i.e., writing reports, writing stories, etc.) allows students to focus on the writing process and content without getting bogged down in mechanics, thus, increasing student productivity and learning.

Simulations and Games

Simulations and games offer unique training opportunities for individuals with disabilities. The Individuals with Disabilities Education Improvement Act (IDEA, 2004) encouraged preparation for post-secondary employment of students with disabilities by mandating transition services for students beginning at age 16 or before. Trying out various jobs can help prepare young people with disabilities to become productive adults, by providing a chance to develop and demonstrate skills and competencies that school and home do not provide.

Additional Technology Pedagogy/Concerns

Universal Design for Learning

Recently, advocates have become more vocal concerning the need to provide universal learning opportunities for all children. Universal Design for Learning (UDL) helps meet the challenge of diversity by suggesting flexible instructional materials, techniques, and strategies that empower educators to meet divergent learners needs (CAST, 2008). Three primary principles guide UDL: (1) Provide multiple means of representation; (2) Provide multiple means of action and expression; and (3) Provide multiple means of engagement (CAST, 2008).

UDL seeks to provide equal access to learning opportunities for all learners. In the past, inflexible, one-dimensional curriculum raised barriers for learning. Often students without disabilities find that curriculum is too poorly designed to meet their learning needs. Learners with disabilities are even more vulnerable to poorly designed curriculum that limits access. As educators adopt Universal Design Principles, all learners and particularly learners with special needs will benefit.

Advocating for Assistive Technology

There are a number of factors that teachers and parents should remember when advocating for assistive technology for students with special needs. These include the following:

- Assistive technology needs must be considered along with a student's other educational needs.
- Assistive technology needs should be determined for each student on an individual basis.
- Identification of technology needs must involve parents, the student when appropriate, and a multidisciplinary team.
- A member of the IEP team can ask for additional evaluation or an independent evaluation to determine assistive technology needs.
- When an evaluation is being conducted, consider mobility, fine-motor skills, communication, and alternatives to traditional learning approaches.

- Lack of availability of equipment or cost alone cannot be used as an excuse for denying assistive technology services.
- If included in the IEP, assistive technology services and devices must be provided at no cost to the family (Kelker, 1998).

One Laptop Per Child (OLPC) Initiative

Visionaries such as Seymour Papert (2002) recognized the importance that technology could play in the education of children. The mission statement of OLPC is to create educational opportunities for the world's poorest children by providing each child with a rugged, low-cost, low-power, connected laptop with content and software designed for collaborative, joyful, self-empowered learning (Negroponte, 2002).

Clearly, as the educational value of technology is beginning to be recognized globally, it is critical for those of us who work with special needs learners to provide these children and adolescents access to critical learning resources through technology. As children of the world begin to receive laptops, we must increase our efforts to provide an opportunity for learners with special needs to have access to the wide range of opportunities that technology offers.

TECHNOLOGY CURRICULA

The technology curricula for K–12 students will focus on teaching students to use the various types of tool software, instructional software, and the Internet. Acquisition of these computer skills and developing precision in their usage is spread across K–12 years and integrated with the curriculum in all subject areas. Several professional organizations have developed standards for the use of technology in K–12 classrooms. These sets of technology standards were developed by the following:

(1) International Society for Technology in Education (ISTE, 2007) prepared **National Educational Technology Standards** (NETS-S) and **Performance Indicators for Students** composed of 6 standards and 4 performance indicators per standard.
(2) Mid-Continent Research for Education and Learning (McREL, 2008) includes 6 standards and 39 topics; also organizes standards and benchmarks into four grade ranges.

(3) International Technology Education Association (ITEA, 2008) prepared **Standards for Technology Literacy** (STL) which includes 20 standards divided into 5 topical areas, and detailed benchmarks across four grade ranges, K–2, 3–5, 6–8, and 9–12.

(4) International Education Technology Association (IETA, 2008) prepared the Technology Education Standards includes 6 standards and 14 benchmarks.

These sets of standards have many similarities and overlapping benchmarks. Additionally, many states have prepared their own technology standards using some combination of standards from the above lists of standards.

This chapter and the Technology Scope and Sequence Chart TABLES 43 and 44 will use the International Education Technology Association Standards and Benchmarks. The Technology Scope and Sequence Chart: Technology K-12 (see TABLE 44) presents suggested technology curricula under the following six standards or goals areas: (1) Basic Operations and Concepts; (2) Social, Ethical and Human Issues; (3) Technology Productivity Tools; (4) Technology Communication Tools; (5) Technology Research Tools; (6) Technology Problem-Solving and Decision-Making (Education World, 2007). These generic regular education technology goals (standards) and objectives (benchmarks) should assist teachers in preparing IEPs for students with disabilities. Use the information in Chapter 2 for the process in preparing an IEP, and use the technology skills in TABLE 44 to write the specific curricular skills to be taught in the classroom.

SUMMARY

Computers offer both challenge and opportunity to the special educator. To enable students to maximize learning potential through computer usage, special educators will need to keep abreast of the developments in the field of technology, select appropriate hardware and software to accommodate student needs and implement effective technology plans which maximize student learning potential. Technology is opening a new era in education, especially in special education. The opportunity for using technology to assist the special needs learner is increasing on a daily basis.

TABLE 43

TECHNOLOGY EDUCATION STANDARDS

STANDARD 1: BASIC OPERATIONS AND CONCEPTS

Students understand the operations and function of technology systems and are proficient in the use of technology.

STANDARD 2: SOCIAL, ETHICAL AND HUMAN ISSUES

Students understand the social, ethical and human issues related to using technology in their daily lives and demonstrate responsible use of technology systems, information and software.

STANDARD 3: TECHNOLOGY PRODUCTIVITY TOOLS

Students use technology tools to enhance learning, to increase productivity and creativity and to construct technology-enhanced models, prepare publications and produce other creative works.

STANDARD 4: TECHNOLOGY COMMUNICATION TOOLS

Building on productivity tools, students will collaborate, publish, and interact with peers, experts and other audiences using telecommunications and media.

STANDARD 5: TECHNOLOGY RESEARCH TOOLS

Students utilize technology-based research tools to locate and collect information pertinent to the task, as well as evaluate and analyze information from a variety of sources.

STANDARD 6: TECHNOLOGY AS A TOOL FOR PROBLEM SOLVING AND DECISION MAKING

Students use technology to make and support decisions in the process of solving real-world problems.

(Education World, National Technology Standards, 2008)

TABLE 44

SCOPE AND SEQUENCE CHARTS: TECHNOLOGY K-12

I. BASIC OPERATIONS AND CONCEPTS

K--2nd Grades	3rd--5th Grades
Identify the computer as a machine that helps people work and play.	Identify role of technology in a variety of careers.
Describe ways technology is used at home, school, and work.	Recognize that technologies have costs and benefits.
Recognize that new tools affect all aspects of life.	Identify areas where technology improves life.
Identify role of technology in a variety of careers.	Recognize that new inventions lead to more new inventions.
Identify uses of technology in the community.	Identifies ways technology has changed the lives of people in communities.
	Identifies computers as tools for accessing information.
	Describe the influence of technology on life in the USA.
	Identify computers as tools for accessing current information.

TABLE 44

SCOPE AND SEQUENCE CHARTS: TECHNOLOGY K-12

I. BASIC OPERATIONS AND CONCEPTS (cont.)

<u>6th--8th Grades</u>	<u>9th--12th Grades</u>
Recognize that technology uses scientific discovery. Identify influences of technology and society on each other (i.e., new products). Identify technological skills required for various careers. Knows that technology and science are reciprocal (e.g., technology drives science, as it provides new technology). Knows ways in which technology has influenced the course of history. Knows that science cannot answer all questions and technology cannot solve all problems.	Identify career paths and role of technology in them. Understand impact of introducing new technologies. Know examples of advanced and emerging technologies. Knows that science & technology are pursued for different purposes. Knows examples of advanced & emerging technologies (e.g., virtual environment, personal digital assistant, voice activated programs). Knows that technological knowledge is often not made public because of patents & financial concerns. Knows ways in which social & economic forces influence which technologies will be developed and marketed.

TABLE 44

SCOPE AND SEQUENCE CHARTS: TECHNOLOGY K-12

II. SOCIAL, ETHICAL, AND HUMAN ISSUES

K--2nd Grades

Demonstrate respect for the computer work of others.
Describe the right of an individual to ownership of his/her created computer work.

3rd--5th Grades

Explain that the copyright law protects what a person or company has created.
State that violation of copyright law is a crime.
Describe the need for protection of software and hardware from vandalism.
Understands the concept of software piracy, and that piracy is illegal.
List resources used in creating print and multimedia products.

6th--8th Grades

Identify, as intellectual property, work created using a computer.
Distinguish between public & private data.
Identify examples of copyright law violations and possible penalties.
State the need for protection of software and hardware from computer viruses.
Follow procedures for using electronic materials/images.
Cite sources of copyrighted materials in assignments.

9th--12th Grades

Identify examples of copyright violations and possible penalties.
Discriminate between ethical & unethical access to information stored on computers.
Understand concept of software piracy and violations.
State the need for protection of software and hardware from computer viruses.
Follow procedures for using electronic materials/images.
Cite sources of copyrighted materials in assignments.

TABLE 44

SCOPE AND SEQUENCE CHARTS: TECHNOLOGY K-12

III. TECHNOLOGY PRODUCTIVITY SKILLS

Hardware

K--2nd Grades

Identify the physical components of a computer system.
Identify fundamental computer terms.
Identify the function of physical components of a computer system.
Identify physical components of a computer system as either input, output, or processing.
Power-up computer and monitor and adjust speakers.
Handle diskettes and computer equipment with care.

3rd--5th Grades

Identify basic functions of hardware.
Demonstrate correct use of hardware and software.
Recognize potential hazards to computer equipment.
Identify additional peripherals.
Know basic functions of hardware (input, output, processing).
Power-up computer and monitor, and adjust speakers.
Handle diskettes and computer equipment with care.

6--8 Grades

Power-down computer, printer and monitor.
Perform basic troubleshooting techniques.
Minimize potential hazards to equipment.
Utilize peripherals.
Know capacities and advantages for storage devices.
Recognize use of new projection devices.

9--12 Grades

Identify malfunctions and problems in hardware.
Avoid potential hazards to equipment.
Use a variety of peripherals.
Know limitations and advantages of hardware.
Choose and utilize appropriate storage devices.
Know features of current and emergent technology.
Use a variety of input devices (i.e., keyboard, mouse, scanner, voice/sound recorder, touch screen, etc.).

TABLE 44

SCOPE AND SEQUENCE CHARTS: TECHNOLOGY K-12

III. TECHNOLOGY PRODUCTIVITY TOOLS (cont.)

Keyboarding

K--2 Grades

Identify parts of a keyboard
   (letters, numbers, & commonly
   used keys).
Know proper finger placement on
   home row keys.
Locate and use symbol keys and
   special function keys.
Demonstrate correct keyboarding
   posture.

3--5 Grades

Demonstrate proper keyboarding
   techniques for keying all
   letters, numbers, and special
   keys.
Use proper fingering for all keys
   while maintaining posture.
Develop mouse and keyboard
   skills while monitoring speed
   and accuracy.

6--8th Grades

Type a minimum of 25 words
   per minute with acceptable
   accuracy.
Types with some facility,
   demonstrating memorization
   of keys.

9--12 Grades

Type a minimum of 30 words
   per minute with acceptable
   accuracy.

TABLE 44

SCOPE AND SEQUENCE CHARTS: TECHNOLOGY K-12

IV. TECHNOLOGY COMMUNICATION TOOLS

K--2nd Grades

Identify operating software by
name.
Understand proper way to shut
down a computer.
Understand proper way to open
and close a program.

3rd--5th Grades

Understand the purpose of an
operating system.
Shut down a computer properly.
Understand relationship between
operating system, application,
software, hardware, and
peripherals.
Navigate between drives to save
and retrieve information.
Open/close a program.
Reboot a computer.
Explain difference between a
networked and stand-alone
computer.

6th--8th Grades

Understand relationship between
operating system, application
software, hardware, and
peripherals.
Navigate between drives to save
and retrieve information.
Demonstrate basic functions of
an operating system.
Understand concept of file
management.
Login, log off, and access
network programs.
Access programs on the hard
drive.
Explain difference between LAN
and WAN.
Select appropriate troubleshooting techniques.

9th--12th Grades

Select appropriate troubleshooting techniques.
Demonstrate advanced functions
of an operating system.
Understand features of the
control panel.
Understand different operating
systems.

TABLE 44

SCOPE AND SEQUENCE CHARTS: TECHNOLOGY K-12

V. TECHNOLOGY RESEARCH TOOLS

<u>**Word Processing**</u>

<u>K--2nd Grades</u>	<u>3rd--5th Grades</u>
Identify word processing terms. Demonstrate beginning word processing techniques: entering, saving, printing, retrieving. Create, edit, save, open, close, and print document. Recognize formats. Create or insert simple graphics. Knows basic distinctions among computer software programs. Use menu options & commands, and tool bar functions.	Use a word processing program to load, enter, save & print text. Use a word processing program to edit a paragraph & save changes. Use a word processing program to enter a paragraph & print it. Use a word processing program to publish a report with centering, tabs, etc. Apply formats. Use spellcheck & thesaurus. Create tables, columns, & borders. Import graphics from other files. Adjust page set up. Use bullets and numbering. Troubleshoot simple problems in software. Know how formats differ among software applications. Knows common features and uses of databases.

TABLE 44

SCOPE AND SEQUENCE CHARTS: TECHNOLOGY K-12

V. TECHNOLOGY RESEARCH TOOLS (cont.)

Word Processing

6th--8th Grades	9th--12th Grades
Identify the function of word processing utilities.	Apply formats.
Identify terms related to computer generated productions.	Use spellcheck & thesaurus.
Describe the advantages of using computers to generate production.	Insert objects and files from application software/Internet.
Revise word processed text to be a simple desktop published document.	Set margins, tabs, page setup.
Apply formats.	Format & use bullets & numbering.
Use spellcheck & thesaurus.	Complete complex functions (i.e., headers, footers, pagination).
Create tables, columns, & borders.	Use tool bars.
Insert objects & files from application software/Internet.	Knows the common features and uses of desktop publishing.
Set margins, tabs, & page setup.	Apply complex formats (i.e., styles, paragraphs, indentation).
Format & use bullets and numbering.	Create and manipulate complex columns, tables, & borders.
Complete complex functions (headers, footers, pagination).	Customize tool bars.
Use tool bars.	Recognize advanced applications (i.e., labels, mail merge, macros).
Knows the common features and uses of desktop publishing.	Knows how to import, export, and merge data stored in different formats.
Uses advanced features and utilities of word processors (i.e., uses clip art, spelling).	Knows how to import & export text, data, and graphics between software programs.
	Identifies some advanced features of software products (i.e., galleries, templates, macros, mail merge).
	Use desktop publishing software to create a variety of publications.

TABLE 44

SCOPE AND SEQUENCE CHARTS: TECHNOLOGY K-12

V. TECHNOLOGY RESEARCH TOOLS (cont.)

Spreadsheet Software

K--2nd Grades

No skills.

3rd--5th Grades

Create, edit, save, save as, open, close, and print simple spreadsheets.
Select and move between cells.
Use spreadsheet terminology.
Add text and numbers.
Select appropriate graph to display data.
Create simple formulas.

6th--8th Grades

Identify spreadsheet terms.
Create and add formulas to calculate.
Format cells (currency, decimals).
Edit spreadsheets with tools.
Create & modify graphs to display data.
Import/export information to/from a spreadsheet.
Identify the differences between paper spreadsheets and computer spreadsheets.
Use a prepared spreadsheet to enter & edit data & explain results of changes.

9th--12th Grades

Create & modify graphs to display data.
Import/export information to/from a spreadsheet.
Edit spreadsheets with tools.
Create and add advanced formulas to calculate.
Format cells (i.e., decimals).

TABLE 44

SCOPE AND SEQUENCE CHARTS: TECHNOLOGY K-12

V. TECHNOLOGY RESEARCH TOOLS (cont.)

<u>Data Base Software</u>

K--2nd Grades

No skills.

3rd--5th Grades

Recognize use of a simple
 data base.
Describe the differences between
 a print data base and a
 computer data base.
Identify data base management
 terms.
Use a prepared data base to
 enter and edit data.
Makes back-up copies of stored
 data and data bases.
Use data base software to add,
 edit, and delete records,
 and to find information.
Knows the common features
 and uses of data bases.

6th--8th Grades

Use data base to access information.
Use various tools to edit data base.
Manipulate & retrieve information
 based on various parameters.
Use a data base to sort and print
 specific records.
Use a data base to search for
 desired information given 1
 or 2 criteria.
Use commercial software to
 organize & visually display data
 to draw conclusions.
Given a data base, use sorting
 & searching techniques to
 solve a problem.

9th--12th Grades

Manipulate & retrieve
 information based on various
 parameters.
Create & edit a data base.
Search a data base using
 advanced sorting techniques.
Designs & creates web pages and
 simple websites (e.g., incorporates
 text, images, video & audio;
 navigation and linking, publishes
 files on local and remote systems.

TABLE 44

SCOPE AND SEQUENCE CHARTS: TECHNOLOGY K-12

V. TECHNOLOGY RESEARCH TOOLS (cont.)

Multimedia Software

K--2nd Grades

Recognize linear and
non-linear presentations.

3rd--5th Grades

Create & display linear &
non-linear presentations.
Import graphics into a
presentation.
Use painting & drawing tools.
Insert graphics from other
directories.
Display multimedia presentations.

6th--8th Grades

Create & display linear and
non-linear presentations.
Use painting & drawing tools.
Insert graphics from other
directories.
Insert sound & animation.
Display multimedia
presentations.
Insert objects and files from
application software and the
Internet.
Use a variety of advanced
features (looping,
formatting).

9th--12th Grades

Create & display effective
multimedia presentations
which link various media.

TABLE 44

SCOPE AND SEQUENCE CHARTS: TECHNOLOGY K-12

VI. TECHNOLOGY PROBLEM-SOLVING AND DECISION-MAKING TOOLS

<u>Information Gathering</u>

<u>K--2nd Grades</u>	<u>3rd--5th Grades</u>
Access electronic encyclopedias. Access on-line catalogs. Access the Internet through bookmarks or search strategies. Recognize Web site on Internet. Work in a Web site using links. Use the Netscape menu for "back, forward, home".	Access electronic encyclopedias. Identify telecomputing terms. Compare the process of sending & receiving messages electronically & nonelectronically. Access the Internet through bookmarks or search strategies. Use data bases to search for information. Use LAN to locate information. Evaluate electronic information for appropriateness, content, and usefulness. Recognize and participate in interactive communication. Recognize what makes up a URL (Web site address). Access a Web site by using its URL. Perform a simple search using Yahooligans! or other kidsafe search engines. Send and receive e-mail.

TABLE 44

SCOPE AND SEQUENCE CHARTS: TECHNOLOGY K-12

VI. TECHNOLOGY PROBLEM-SOLVING AND DECISION-MAKING TOOLS

Information Gathering (cont.)

6th--8th Grades	9th--12th Grades
Use search engines to locate & retrieve information. Create and manage bookmarks. Select/use resources to collect, analyze, and display data. Use techniques to copy and save data and graphics. Modify and use information relevant to assignments. Evaluate/critique information for validity, content, use. Recognize & participate in interactive communication. Identify ways telecomputing promotes a global community. Use telecomputing to communicate with a distant computer or on-line service. Become familiar with & apply proper Netiquette. Print off the Internet. Cut and paste off the Net into documents. Understand how information is processed on the Internet.	Select/use resources to collect, analyze, and display data. Use techniques to copy & save data & graphics. Modify and use information relevant to assignments. Evaluate/critique information validity, content, use. Recognize & participate in interactive communication. Use search strategies to locate electronic information. Use networks to collect information. Collect & share original research. Create a home page & Web site. Use features of e-mail (i.e., flagging, filing, attachments). Do extensive research. Set preferences.

References: Goldstein, 1998; Richland, 1998; McRel, 1997; NC DPI, 1995-96; NC DPI, 2008); Education World, 2008; McREL, 2009.

TABLE 45

INSTRUCTIONAL SOFTWARE

Part A: Early Childhood Programs
Toddler Programs

Pre-Academic Programs	Skills Covered	Publisher	Age/Grade
Sesame Street Toddler Learning Basics	Colors, Shapes, Numbers, Counting Letters, Sounds	Encore Software	2-4 yrs.
Reader Rabbit's Toddler	Mouse Control, Matching	The Learning Company	18 mo. - 3 yrs.
Fisher-Price Ready for School Toddler Edition	Numbers, Letters Mazes, Coloring	Davidson	18 mo.- 3 yrs.
Sesame Street Toddler Delux	Drawing, Numbers, Letters	Creative Wonders	2-4 yrs.
JumpStart Toddlers	Mouse Skills Numbers, Letters	Knowledge Adventure	18 mo.- 4 yrs.

Preschool Programs

Pre-Reading Programs	Skills Covered	Publisher	Ages/Grades
Finding Nemo: Learning with Nemo	Preschool Skills	Disney/Pikar	4-5 yrs.
Beginning Sounds	Pre-Reading Skills	School Zone	3-5 yrs.
Reader Rabbit Preschool Sparkle Star Rescue	Letters, Sounds, Shapes & Patterns	The Learning Company	3-5 yrs.
Does It Belong	Relationships With Sets	School Zone Interactive	3-5 yrs.
Thinking Skills	Problem Solving Directions, Matching	School Zone Interactive	3-5 yrs.
Dr. Seuss Preschool	Dr. Seuss Characters	Broderbund	2-4 yrs.
Reader Rabbit's Preschool	Letters, Sounds, Shapes, Patterns	The Learning Company	3-5 yrs.

TABLE 45

INSTRUCTIONAL SOFTWARE

Part A: Early Childhood Programs (cont.)

Pre-Reading Programs	Skills Covered	Publisher	Ages
JumpStart Preschool	10 Skills-Based Activities	Knowledge Adventure	2-4 yrs.
Sesame Street Elmo's PreSchool	Pre-Reading, Pre-Math	Creative Wonders	2-5 yrs.

Early Childhood Programs: Grades P-2

Early Reading Programs	Skills Covered	Publisher	Age/Grade
Sight Words with Samson	224 Most Common	Knowledge Adventure	4-7 yrs.
The Book of LuLu	Story with a Plot	Oranga	5+ yrs.
Leapster: Scholastic Clifford The Big Red Dog Reading	Educational Adventures	Leapfrog	4-6 yrs.
JumpStart Reading With Karaoke	Phonics-Based, Learning to Read	Knowledge Adventure	4-7 yrs.
Clifford The Big Red Dog Phonics	Letters, Sounds, Word Families	Scholastic	3-6 yrs.
The JumpStart Phonics Learning System	Expands on Basic Phonics	Knowledge Adventure	P-3
Reader Rabbit's Reading 4-6	Phonics-Based Reading Program	The Learning Company	4-6 yrs.
Stories and More Animal Friends	Literature, Reading Comprehension	Edmark	5-7 yrs.
Leap into Language	Early Reading Skills Multimedia	INNOVA	4-7 yrs.

Problem-Solving Programs	Skills Covered	Publisher	Ages/ Grades
Gary Gadget: Building Cars	Classic Search, Solve Puzzles	Viva Media	5-9 yrs.

TABLE 45

INSTRUCTIONAL SOFTWARE

Part A: Early Childhood Programs (cont.)

Problem-Solving Programs	Skills Covered	Publisher	Ages
Learns to Play Chess With Fritz & Chesster	Beginners & Early Learners	Viva Media	6+ yrs.
Freddi Fish 5: The Case of the Creature Of Coral Cove	Solve a Mystery	Humongous/ Infogrames	4-7+ yrs.

Early Childhood Math	Skills Covered	Publisher	Ages/ Grades
Leapster Sonic X	Math Adventures, Math Problems	Leap Frog	5-7 yrs.
Transition Math	Accelerated K-1	School Zone Publishing	4-6 yrs.
Grade 1 Math	Math Reinforcement	School Zone Publishing	6-7 yrs.
Grade 2 Math	Single Digit Subtraction; Double & Triple Addition	School Zone Publishing	6-7 yrs.

Early Childhood Writing	Skills Covered	Publisher	Ages
The Write Connections	Handwriting	Children's Choice	2-8 yrs.

Early Science Programs	Skills Covered	Publisher	Ages/ Grades
What Smart Kids Know About Endangered Species	Causes of Animal Endangerment	Magikids Interactive	4-7 yrs.
True Blue Friend	About Whales	Block Printing	4-9 yrs.
Stanley: Wild For Sharks	Interactive, Animated	Disney Interactive	3-6 yrs.
JumpStart Animal Adventures	Intro. to Animals	Knowledge Adventure	4-7 yrs.

TABLE 45

INSTRUCTIONAL SOFTWARE

Part B: Elementary and Middle School+ Programs

Vocabulary Programs	Skills Covered	Publisher	Ages/Grades
Words Rock!	Vocabulary, Spelling, Grammar	EdAlive	4-14+ yrs
Word Adventure 2K1	Repetitive Learning	Word Smart	7-12 yrs.

Reading Programs	Skills Covered	Publisher	Ages/Grades
Reading for Meaning	Reading Comprehension	Tom Snyder Productions	8-13 yrs.
Clue Finders Reading Adventures	Reading Comprehension	The Learning Company	9-12 yrs.
My Reading Coach	Remedial Reading For Older Students	Mindplay	7- adult

Problem Solving Programs	Skills Covered	Publisher	Ages/Grades
Nancy Drew: The Creature of Kapu Cove	Solves the Mystery	Her Interactive	10+ yrs.
Nancy Drew: Curse of Blackmoor Manor	Solves the Mystery	Her Interactive	10+ yrs.
Puzz 3D: The Orient	3D Jigsaw Puzzle With Mystery	Wrebbit	10+ yrs.
Animal Hospital: Pet Vet 3D	Simulation, Problem-Solving	Viva Media	10+ yrs.

Writing Programs	Skills Covered	Publisher	Ages/Grades
Secret Writer's Society	Topic Sentences, Punctuation	Panasonic Interactive	7-9 yrs.
Inspiration Software Education Edition	Develop Ideas, Use Webs	Inspiration Software	9+ yrs.
Kaplan: Writing & Vocabulary Essential Review	Composition, English, Test Skills	Encore Software	14-18 yrs.

TABLE 45

INSTRUCTIONAL SOFTWARE

Part B: Elementary and Middle School + Programs (cont.)

Spelling Programs	Skills Covered	Publisher	Age/Grades
Curious George Reads, Writes, Spells	Spelling	Houghton Mifflin	6-8 yrs.
JumpStart Spelling	Spelling Drills	Knowledge Adventure	4-9 yrs.
Spelling Blaster	Spelling Development	Knowledge Adventure	6-9 yrs.
Words Rock	Spelling, Grammar, Vocabulary	EdAlive	4-14 yrs.

Typing Software	Skills Covered	Publisher	Age/Grades
Disney's Adventures In Typing with Timon & Pumba	Animated Program, Beginning Typing	Disney Interactive	6+ yrs.
JumpStart Typing	Learn to Type	Talking Fingers	7-10 yrs.
Slam Dunk Typing	Basketball & Video To Teach Typing	The Learning Company	10+ yrs.
Type to Learn	Keyboarding	Sunburst	8-14 yrs.
Typing Instructor Delux	Complete Typing Instruction	Individual Software	10+ yrs.
Mavis Beacon	Improves Keyboarding	The Learning Company	12-adult

Mathematics Programs	Skills Covered	Publisher	Ages/Grades
Robob's Cubetronic Quizimajig	Match Shapes Replicate Patterns	Ohio Distinctive Software	3- adult
Professor Finkle's Basic Division	Introductory Division	MME Multi-media Educators	8+ yrs.
Timez Attack	Times Tables	Big Brainz	7-10 yrs.

TABLE 45

INSTRUCTIONAL SOFTWARE

Part B: Elementary and Middle School + Programs (cont.)

Mathematics Programs	Skills Covered	Publisher	Age/Grades
The Number Devil: A Mathematical Adventure	Number Concepts: Prime Number, Square Roots	Viva Kids	8+ yrs.
Math Missions: The Amazing Arcade Adventure	Dozen Math Activties--Range of Skills 3-5 grades	Scholastic	8-11yrs.,
Mia's Math Adventure: Just in Time	Reinforce Variety of Math Skills	Kutoka & Topics Entertainment	6-10 yrs.
Decimal & Fraction Maze	Sequence & Problem Solving	Great Wave Software	8 - adult
Nothin' But. . . . The Fractions I	Fraction Tutorials, Practice Problems	IEP Math	8-14 yrs.
Study Works Mathematical Delux	Practice & Homework	Mathsoft	14+ yrs.
Math Advantage (2002)	6-12th Grade Math	Encore Software	11+ yrs.

Algebra Programs	Skills Covered	Publisher	Age/Grades
Pre-Algebra	Practice Basic Algebra Concepts & Solve problems	Bagatrix	12+ yrs.
Astro Algebra	Basic Concepts, Skills Practice	Edmark	12-14+
Grade Builders Algebra I	Focus on Problem Areas & Extra Practice	The Learning Company	12-14+
Math Blaster Algebra	Beginning Algebra Problem Solving	Davidson	12-14+
Mathpert Algebra Assistant	Step-by-Step Problem-Solving	Mathpert	12-adult

TABLE 45

INSTRUCTIONAL SOFTWARE

Part B: Elementary and Middle School + Programs (cont.)

Science Programs	Skills Covered	Publisher	Age/Grades
Rock Sim-Model Rocket Design & Simulation	Aerodynamics in Designing rockets.	Apogee Rockets	10+ yrs.
Virtual Labs: Electricity	Simulations using Electricity	Edmark	12-18yrs.
Future Lab: Circuits for Physical Science	Design Electrical Circuits on Computer & Make a Model	Simulations Plus	9-18 yrs.
Telling Our Stories: Women in Science	8 Contemporary Female Scientists	McLean Media	10+ yrs.
Wild Life Tycoon: Venture Africa	Simulation to Balance Ecosystem	Pocketwatch Games	6-12 yrs.

Social Studies Programs	Skills Covered	Publisher	Ages/Grades
The Ellis Island Experience	Oral Histories, Factual	South Peak Interactive	11-adult
Lionel Trains Presents: Trans-Con!	American History, Building Railroad, Problem Solving	Knowledge Adventure	7-12 yrs.
The Advanced Scholar's US Capitals	US Geography & State Capitals	Software Guidance Corp.	7-12 yrs.
World Disney Delux	World Geography	Great Wave Software	7-14 yrs.
Talking Walls	Cultures Around the World	Edmark	8-14 yrs.
Virtual Safari	Authentic Safari	Fujitsu Interactive	10-14 yrs.
Oregon Trail Classic	Decision-Making in Guiding Covered Wagons to Oregon	The Learning Company	5th+ Grade

TABLE 45

INSTRUCTIONAL SOFTWARE

Part B: Elementary and Middle School + Programs (cont.)

Social Studies Programs	Skills Covered	Publisher	Ages/ Grades
Breaking the Code	Using Hierglyphics In Stories about Egypt	Learner Education Software	10+ yrs.
The Civil War Experience	Factual Information	South Peak Interactive	11-Adult
Mission Possible World Geography	Basic World Geography Facts	EdVenture Software	12-adult
The Advanced Scholar's US Capitals	US Geography & State Capitals	Software Guidance Corp.	7-12

Part C: Special Needs Software and Tools

Special Software/Tools	Skills, etc.	Publisher	Ages
KidzMouse	Special Mouse	KidzMouse	2+
Take A Stand	Conflict Resolution	Leo Media	12+
Touch Free Switch	Combines Digital, Video Camera with Switch Software to Control a Mouse	Edmark	5+
Touch Windows	Input Device That Can be Used as a Touch Screen, Graphic Tablet or Keyboard Substitute	Edmark	All Ages

SuperKids Educational Software Review (nd). Retrieved March 8, 2009 from http://www.superkids.com

Note: This is only a sample of the Instructional Software found on the World Wide Web.

Chapter 9

SOCIAL AND SELF COMPETENCE CURRICULA

The social and emotional growth and development of a child does not occur in isolation. . . . Social and emotional growth and development are closely linked with all aspects of child development into a synergistic relationship. (Jones, 1988, 241)

Normal Social and Emotional Development
 Middle Childhood: Primary Grades
 Middle Childhood: Intermediate Grades
Social/Emotional Problems of Students with Mild
 Disabilities
  Cognitive and Language Deficits
  Social/Skills Deficits
Cognitive Deficits Impact on Social Deficits
Social Competence Curricula
 Social Competence Skills
Self Competence Curricula
Summary
Scope and Sequence Charts: Social and Self
 Competence Tables 46–49

Various aspects of social, adaptive, and behavioral skills have long been routinely included in the Individual Educational Programs (IEPs) of students with mental retardation and/or behavior disorders. Many educators now indicate that problems in social skills are as debilitating as academic problems to students with learning disabilities (Mercer, 1997). The prognosis for children and youth who lack social-emotional competence is not encouraging because social problems become more debilitating over time and exert a powerful negative, influence on adult adjustment (Elksnin & Elksnin, 2006).

Kids Count (2007) indicated that 1,428,000 teens were not attending school, and 13,097,000 live in poverty. During school year 2006–2007, IDEA provided special education services to 6.7 million children and youth ages 3–21 (USDE, 2008). The Institute of Education Services (IES, 2008) reported that more than half a million young people dropped out of high school, and the rate at which they dropped out has remained about the same for the past 30 years. However, this is not an all inclusive list of children and youth who probably experience difficulty with social and emotional development. IES (2008) in a **Dropout Prevention Guide** provided six recommendations to reduce the dropout rate; and the 4th recommendation was "Implement programs to improve students' classroom behavior and social skills." Huge numbers of students are at-risk or experiencing school and life problems due to a lack of appropriate social and behavioral skills.

NORMAL, SOCIAL AND EMOTIONAL DEVELOPMENT

Social and emotional growth and development are intricately linked with all aspects of child development. Personality development is closely intertwined with socialization (Cole & Cole, 1989). In normal development there is a close relationship among cognitive, social, and emotional development. As children develop cognitively, they mature in social skills such as social perspective taking, social regulation, moral development, social problem solving, and social relationships (see TABLE 46). Children and youth mature emotionally in areas of self-competence including self-knowledge, self-evaluation, and sense of personal control as they develop cognitively (see TABLE 46). These complex social and emotional skills depend on abstract thinking, metacognition, the use of logic, and automaticity in self-monitoring.

Middle Childhood: Primary Grades

The development of social competence, self competence, and self-concept begin in infancy and continue throughout one's lifetime, constantly undergoing modification in response to interpersonal interactions and life experiences. The social skills of preschoolers are immature, but by five years of age, children are able to cooperate, share, and take turns; use social problem-solving (see TABLE 7); and display sensitivity to social problems and social consequences. It is through play that these social interactions and skills are practiced. Preschool emotional skills include developing trust and autonomy, maintaining self-control, facing reality, and exhibiting empathy and sympathy (see TABLE 7).

During the early middle childhood, ages six to eight years, the child makes significant changes and growth in cognition, communication, physical, social, and emotional abilities. The major theorists of child development agree that there is an important shift in mental functioning around ages five to seven years which includes the internalization of language (Skolnick, 1986). Socially the primary grade child, first grade through third grade, learns to function in three separate worlds: the family, the school, and the peer group–each with its own rules and behavioral expectations. Important social developments during the primary grade years involve emerging understandings of social relationships and moral feelings, insights in perspective-taking (understanding the view point of others), and self-control (managing one's temper). The ability to assume increased responsibility stems from cognitive advances that result in "a greatly increased ability to think more deeply and logically, to follow through on a problem once it is undertaken, and to keep track of more than one aspect of a situation at a time" (Cole & Cole, 1989, 407).

Regardless of the theory used to explain it, a good deal of evidence suggests that by the time children are about six or seven years old, they have formed a stable concept of their own identity as male or female (Cole & Cole, 1989). Another feature of self-description at this stage is the use of social comparison as a means of determining the competence or adequacy of the self (Harter, 1988, 52).

At about eight years of age, children begin to incorporate the observations of others into their own self-perceptions and directly evaluate themselves by internalizing these observations and expectations into self-standards, thus, developing the capacity for self-criticism (Harter, 1988). Emotionally, then, the primary grade child is developing a new personal identity which incorporates the opinions of valued others. Prior to age eight years, children are not capable of constructing a global concept of themselves as a person that can be evaluated in terms of overall worth (Harter, 1985). Therefore, a major achievement during the primary grade years is to begin to develop a global self-worth or a global self-concept.

Middle Childhood: Intermediate Grades

By the end of the late middle childhood years, ages 9–12 years, the intermediate or 4th–6th grade child is significantly more mature than the primary grade child. Late middle childhood is characterized by an increased understanding of the self, and development of a self-theory or self definition. Increasingly sophisticated social cognitive and metacognitive skills allow the intermediate grade youth to make social inferences about the personality characteristics of others and to understand others through social perspective-taking (see TABLE 47). Intermediate grade children understand society's moral rules, social conventions, and various peer group norms. Advances in cognitive processes facilitate using social problem-solving techniques. Upper intermediate grade students must become sensitive not only to social problems, but to social consequences usually gained through social comparison and perspective-taking.

During the intermediate grades, children make strides in understanding their personal emotional characteristics which leads naturally to an ability to control one's emotions and related behaviors, particularly anger. The emergence of self control as an evaluation criteria indicates higher level cognitive functioning. By the end of middle childhood, intermediate grade youth have evaluated their competence in several areas–social, cognitive, and physical; and have created a global concept of self-worth.

SOCIAL/EMOTIONAL PROBLEMS OF STUDENTS WITH MILD DISABILITIES

Most children and youth with mild disabilities (LD, MMR, BD, etc.) experience problems in almost all aspects of social and emotional development.

Cognitive and Language Deficits

Cognitive and language deficits interfere with or significantly delay maturation in social and emotional skills. Social and emotional skills are dependent on adequate cognition. Many students with disabilities experience difficulty processing information and selecting and using appropriate social responses (see TABLE 48). Typical information processing problems include problems with perception of the situation correctly. Students with disabilities may misread the emotions and intent of others including facial expression, body language, and vocal intonation.

Students with disabilities often experience difficulty with at least one aspect of attention, *disinhibition,* which refers to the inability to think something but not say it. This deficit frequently causes individuals to make inappropriate comments. Students with disabilities, even those with average range intellectual functioning, often experience deficits in memory skills. The lack of ability to effectively use executive processes results in problems with self-regulation of one's behavior in specific social settings.

Many children and youth with disabilities not only experience difficulty using strategies automatically in acquiring academics, but also in acquiring and automatically using appropriate social skills. Children and youth who experience difficulty using higher level thinking skills can not analyze social situations or use problem-solving in life problems.

Language acquisition and use are so closely intertwined with acquisition of cognitive skills that a deficit in one area results in a deficit in the other. Almost all students receiving special education services experience difficulty in language use (pragmatics) and find themselves in social situations trying to use their literal level language skills. Students, especially, adolescents with mild disabilities experience significant difficulty understanding figurative language, sarcasm (see TABLE 48). If everyone in the group is laughing except the student with disabilities, they may feel that others are making fun of them and get very angry. It is difficult to behave appropriately if language deficits have rendered them unable to determine exactly what is going on.

Most students gain clues to what behavior is expected through interpreting nonlinguistics; the facial expressions, body language, and vocal intonation of others. However, students with disabilities experience severe deficits in non-linguistic as well as linguistic skills. Cognitive skills in information processing, higher level thinking skills, and language skills form the foundation for acquiring social-emotional skills. Therefore, students with mild disabilities function on a significantly less mature level than same age/grade peers in social competence areas such as social perspective-taking, social regulation, moral development, social problem-solving, and social relationships. Additionally, these deficits interfere with maturation emotionally in areas of self-competence such as self-knowledge, self-evaluation, and developing a sense of personal control.

Students with mild disabilities generally function cognitively on a literal level and are, therefore, unable to understand the complex thinking required for social and self-competence. Language deficits in linguistic and nonlinguistic aspects of language interfere with understanding the parameters of the social situation. Nonlinguistic language deficits include inability to read facial expressions and body language, and inability to interpret vocal intonation. These nonlinguistic language deficits reduce the many clues to the dynamics of a social situation. Linguistically functioning on a literal level compromises the student's ability to understand humor, sarcasm, figurative language, flirting, and teasing. Since students with mild disabilities frequently cannot understand higher level usage of language, their literal interpretation makes them angry and defensive, feeling that others are making fun of them.

Thus, the lack of age-appropriate cognitive and language skills acquisition interferes with the development of positive social interactions of students with mild disabilities (social competence). Cognitive and language deficits also interfere with the development of self-competence, therefore, students with mild disabilities are unable to determine how they can modify their inappropriate social behaviors to be more acceptable.

Social Skills Deficits

The primary social skills that children and youth need to acquire in order to function within the normal range for their age and grade, and be accepted by peers of many ages can be outlines as three major categories of skills: Social

Competence, Social Interactions, and Self Competence (see TABLE 46). Underneath each category is a list of specific skills or objectives for each category of Social Skills. Social Competence is described as the overall ability to engage in all expected social skills and to leave the impression of a successful social interaction. *Social Competence* includes at least four important categories of social skills: (1) Social Perspective-Taking (showing sensitivity to the feelings of others); (2) Moral Development (demonstrating understanding expectations to conform to at least three sets of rules–family, school, peer group); (3) Social Regulation (controlling ones temper in a variety of conflict situations); and (4) Social Problem-Solving (using a logical procedure to solve personal social problems and reduce dangerous risk-taking) (see TABLE 46).

Social Interactions

Social Interactions require knowledge of the rules for appropriate behavior and in general involve four categories of skills: (1) Social Conventions (appropriate polite behavior in greetings, appropriate table manners, using appropriate behavior to gain teacher's attention); (2) Social Communication (knowledge and use of appropriate communication a variety of social settings); (3) Cooperation (taking turns, appropriate interactions with peers); and (4) Social Effectiveness (understanding and using politeness according to specific group norms, friendship making skills, and overall success in the social area) (see TABLES 46 and 47).

Self Competence

Self Competence concerns the emotional skills and inner feelings regarding the self (see TABLES 46 & 47). *Self Competence* concerns three categories of skills including the following: (1) Self Knowledge (concerns the ego and self-concept, self perceptions, one's private subjective self, accepting one's strengths and weaknesses); (2) Self Evaluation (involves comparing one's performances and behaviors to their internalized self standard); and (3) Sense of Personal Control (involves using social metacognition to monitor one's behavior). Sense of Personal Control also involves using self-evaluation and self-reinforcement to change inappropriate behaviors; using motivation to stay on task and to achieve goals; and using causal attributions to make decisions that result in higher levels of success.

COGNITIVE DEFICITS IMPACT ON SOCIAL DEFICITS

Cognitive skills (previously discussed) form a foundation for the development of social skills. The majority of students receiving special education services, and many others in a variety of circumstances experience significant cognitive and language deficits; thus, it is quite predictable that this inadequate foundation results in inadequate social skills (see TABLE 48).

Refer to TABLE 49, **Relationship Between Cognitive and Social Deficits**. Lines have been drawn between some of the cognitive deficits to indicate the resulting social skills deficits. For example, Cognitive Deficits: Information Processing Problems in Perception Problems causes Social Skills Deficits: Social Competence in Social Perspective Taking. Cognitive deficits in problem-solving cause deficits in social problem-solving. Therefore, if a child or youth experiences deficits in cognitive skills, they will experience a similar deficit in social skills because social skill knowledge and use depends upon adequate cognition. TABLE 49 was left incomplete because due to the many overlapping lines, it would be difficult to determine cognitive deficit causes and social skills deficit results.

SOCIAL COMPETENCE CURRICULA

Social Competence has been defined as "a person's overall ability to achieve his or her goals and desires in the personal aspects of life" (Serna, 1997, 460) and "the ultimate goal of social skills training programs" (Rivera & Smith, 1997, 222). Although a verified taxonomy for social skills training does not exist, there has been considerable research about a variety of skills that fall within the realm of social skills training (Rivera & Smith, 1997).

A number of models of social skills or social competence have been prepared, many of which have been developed into commercial training programs. Vaughn & Haagar's (1994) model of social competence is composed of four components including both personality variables and social competence variables: (1) Positive peer relationships (social acceptance), (2) Social cognition (self-concept), (3) Absence of maladaptive behaviors, and (4) Effective social skills. Rivera and Smith (1997, 226) have proposed a similar schema for social competence which includes four categories: (1) Social Cognition (role-taking, perception, comprehension, interpretation); (2) Social Interaction (cooperation, communication, social conventions); and (3) Social Effectiveness (peer and adult acceptance, appearance, assertiveness, compliance, nondisruption); and (4) Decision Making (predicting consequences, social reasoning, problem solving).

An invaluable resource in determining a specific curricular program can be found in Elksnin and Elksnin, (2006) *Teaching Social-Emotional Skills at School and Home.* This book includes numerous lists of assessments as well as specific curricular programs (commercial and informal) including the following: Programs that teach about feelings; Programs that teach anger control; Programs that teach problem solving; Programs that teach peer-pleasing skills; Programs that teach teacher pleasing skills.

Commercial Curriculums

A number of social skills curriculums have been developed for use with students with mild disabilities. The "Skillstreaming" curriculums are frequently used with students with mild-moderate disabilities and include several levels: *Skillstreaming in Early Childhood* (McGinnis & Goldstein, 2003); *Skillstreaming the Elementary School Child* (McGinnis & Goldstein, 1997); *Skillstreaming the Adolescent* (Goldstein, Sprafkin, Gershaw and Klein, 1997). The early childhood social tasks included in this commercial program include the following: Beginning social skills, school-related skills, friendship-making skills, dealing with feelings, alternatives to aggression, and dealing with stress (McGinnis & Goldstein, 1997). The elementary school social skills include the following: Classroom survival skills, friendship-making skills, skills for dealing with feelings, skill alternatives to aggression, and skills for dealing with stress (McGinnis & Goldstein, 1997). A benefit of these programs to teachers is that the skills are well task-analyzed, and presented on a grid format for monitoring success.

A popular commercial program used with students with mild mental retardation is *Social Skills for School and Community* (Sargent, 1991). The focus of this program is to teach social behaviors that will improve the social affect, social skills, and social thinking of students. Social affect includes appearances that the individual presents to others (i.e., posture, attitude, etc.). Social skills are the overt behaviors used in a variety of social contexts involving both initiating and responding appropriately in personal interactions. Social cognition is the thinking component of social competencies. The text presents social skills lessons for appropriate behavior in the classroom and school building, personal skills, initiation and response skills for interactions for four age-grade levels of students: Primary grades, intermediate grades, Junior High, and Senior High School.

Social Competence Skills

The **Scope and Sequence Charts: Social Competence and Self Competence: Primary Grades** and **Scope and Sequence Charts: Social Competence and Self Competence: Intermediate Grades** are an attempt to combine factors from normal social growth and development in middle childhood with the factors in the numerous models proposed including commercial programs, research findings, and teachers' experiences. The skills or tasks organized under these various headings are interrelated and overlapping and are intended as a resource to assist teachers in developing the social competence or social skills section of an Individual Education Program.

The Social Competence skills on the **Scope and Sequence Charts: Social Competence and Self Competence** (see TABLES 46 and 47) are organized into five major categories:

1. *Social Perspective-Taking* or understanding the thinking and emotions of others involves empathy and sympathy, making social inferences about how other people affect your behavior, making social comparisons between yourself and others, and understanding the reciprocal nature of social interactions.
2. *Moral Development* concerns understanding codes of conduct and behavioral expectations in a variety of situations and settings, and societal responsibilities and expectations.
3. *Social Regulation* concerns knowledge of societal behavior expectations and the ability of a person to regulate their own behavior in socially appropriate ways.
4. *Social Problem-Solving* requires complex cognitive abilities to understand social problems using social reasoning and to determine potential solutions, the ability to predict social consequences of various behaviors, and to determine appropriate social behaviors.
5. *Social Interactions* is a complex category composed of social communication, cooperation, knowledge of social conventions, and global social effectiveness.

SELF COMPETENCE CURRICULA

Self Competence has been referred to as emotional and personality factors or the self-concept which includes self-knowledge, self-evaluation, and sense of personal control. A number of commercial self competence curricula have also been developed for use with students of a variety of ages. The *Metacognitive Approach to Social Skills Training* (MASST) (Sheinker, et al., 1988) is actually a self competence curriculum to teach students how to self-direct, self-monitor, self-evaluate, and self-correct to produce appropriate social behaviors. The program is based on the premise that internal control is necessary to responsible, productive behavior and problem-solving, and that self-knowledge is essential to self-control. The program includes five curriculum segments addressing aspects of metacognition including: (1) self-concept; (2) goal setting; (3) taking responsibility for achieving those goals; (4) getting friendship, love, and respect; (5) locus of control of feeling, behavior, and success (Sheinker et al., 1988).

The Self Competence Skills on the **Scope and Sequence Charts: Social Competence and Self Competence** (see TABLES 46 and 47) are organized into three major categories:

1. **Self Knowledge** requires one to possess an understanding of himself or herself, their personal and emotional characteristics, and the effects others have on them.
2. **Self Evaluation** is the actual act of determining self-knowledge; the feelings of self worth, ability for self-control, determining one's anxiety level and implementing stress reduction when needed, forming a self-concept based on competence and enhancing the self-concept through self-pride.
3. **Sense of Personal Control** is generally viewed as including metacognition skills, motivation, and causal attributions. Metacognition involves the self strategies that allow one to complete activities and tasks and determine the quality of the job completed. Motivation refers to one's ability to maintain interest and perseverance until a task is completed. Causal attributions are personal assessments for the reasons for our successes and failures.

SUMMARY

Students with mild disabilities frequently do not give evidence of the cognitive growth that provides them the use of higher order thinking skills, metacognition, and logical thinking needed during adolescence and adulthood. This lack of cognitive abilities effects all aspects of their lives including social and self competence, and interferes with acquiring self determination. Research indicates that students' abilities in social and self competence can improve with specific programming and generalization training. Social

Competence involves social perspective-taking, social interactions, moral development, social regulation, social problem-solving, and social interactions. Self-Competence development includes the areas of self-knowledge, self-evaluation, and sense of personal control, and are very important in the development of self determination.

TABLE 46

SCOPE AND SEQUENCE CHART: SOCIAL AND SELF COMPETENCE

Primary Grades, 1st -- 3rd, Ages 6 - 8 Years

Social Competence

Social Perspective Taking

Understand his/her roles as a
student, friend, etc.
Show sensitivity to friends'
attitudes.
Show sensitivity to feelings of
others.
Demonstrate ability to observe
self and others simultaneously
and engage in comparison
(social comparison).
Show development of insights in
perspective-taking.
Exhibit empathy and sympathy.

Moral Development

State desire to do things right.
State that fairness is important.
Show eagerness to please teacher,
parents, and other role models.
Show desire to help and pride in
increased responsibility.
Demonstrate understanding of
expectations to conform to
several sets of rules regarding
moral codes & behaviors
(family, school, peer group).
Show emerging understanding of
social relationships and moral
feelings.
Tell the truth and accept
consequences.

Social Regulation

Control his/her temper in conflict
situations with peers.
Follow classroom rules regarding
entering the classroom without
disruption.
Follow rules and procedures for
boarding & riding a school bus.
Follow school building rules:
- Walk through hallway (a) at a
moderate pace, (b) without
obstructing the path of others,
(c) quietly, and (d) directly to
destination.
- Wait in line without losing place
or disrupting others in school
setting.
- Use restroom appropriately.
- Drink from water fountain
properly.
- Follow lunchroom rules and
standard procedures.

Social Problem-Solving

Accept consequences for wrong
doing.
Show increasing reasonableness.
Use problem-solving to reduce
dangerous risk-taking.
Decide what to do to deal with
stress of making a mistake.
Face reality of a situation.

TABLE 46

SCOPE AND SEQUENCE CHART: SOCIAL AND SELF COMPETENCE

Primary Grades 1st-3rd, Ages 6 - 8 Years

Social Competence (cont.)

Social Interactions

I. **Social Conventions:**

Smile when encountering friends
   and acquaintances.
Attend to teacher during
   instruction.
Gain teacher attention
   appropriately.
Use appropriate table manners in
   cafeteria and in public.
Accept "No" in response to a
   request of an adult.
Show increased sensitivity to
   feelings of others.

II. **Social Communication:**

Say "please" and "thank you."
Speak in appropriate tone of
   voice.
Greet peers & others appropriately.
Ask another child to play.
Ask for assistance or information.
Listen while another talks.
Use "nice talk" when asking for a
   favor, meeting persons, etc.
Ignore inappropriate teasing and
   name calling by others.

III. **Cooperation:**

Take turns in games & activities.
Borrow from peers and return
   items when finished in good
   condition.
Engage in appropriate behavior
   to be accepted by others.
Cooperate and take turns when
   playing a game.
Take turns being first.

IV. **Social Effectiveness:**

Understand peer group norms.
Use friendship-making skills:
   - Greeting others nicely.
   - Reading others purpose or
     mood.
   - Joining in conversations or
     play at appropriate time.
   - Waiting properly for turn.
   - Offer to help another peer
     or adult.
Deal with winning and losing.
Show increased control of temper.

TABLE 46

SCOPE AND SEQUENCE CHARTS: SOCIAL AND SELF COMPETENCE

Primary Grades 1st-3rd, Ages 6 - 8 Years

Self- Competence

Self-Knowledge:
Deal with own feelings in many
    situations such as feeling left
    out.
Deal with feelings of fear
Deal with being teased and feeling
    angry.
Deal with making personal
    mistake and feeling ashamed
    or embarrassed.
Know when to tell the truth.
Know that each person has a
    private subjective self.

Self-Evaluation:
Use social comparisons as a means
    to determine competence of self
    or performance.
Begin to develop capacity for
    self-criticism.
Begin to develop a global self-
    concept including character
    traits.

Sense of Personal Control:
I. Social Metacognition:

Use simple self-planning and
    self-organization strategies.
Begin to use self-monitoring
    in social situations (given a
    cue) and modify behavior
    accordingly.
Use self-evaluation to control
    inappropriate behaviors.
Use self-reinforcement to
    reward self for achieving goals.

II. Motivation:
Use self-motivation to finish
    social or academic tasks.
Show increased ability to
    stay on task & complete
    disliked or boring task.
Use self-talk to encourage
    staying on task.

III. Causal Attributions:
Attribute success to effort.
Evaluate own achievements
    realistically.
Demonstrate self-confidence
    in completing desired task.
Develop positive self-concept.

References: Biehler & Hudson, 1986; Berger, 1986; Cole & Cole, 1989;
          Dweck & Elliot, 1983; Greenwald, 1980; Goldstein, 1996;
          Harter, 1988; Kohlberg, 1976; Rivera & Smith, 1997;
          Rose-Krasnor, 1988; Serna, 1997; Sargent, 1991.

TABLE 47

SCOPE AND SEQUENCE CHART: SOCIAL AND SELF COMPETENCE

Intermediate Grades, 4th - 6th, 9 - 12 Years

Social Competence

Social Perspective-Taking (role-taking)

Demonstrate care & concern about how others feel (empathy and sympathy).

Make inferences about characteristics of people.

Recognize others' personality characteristics & anticipate how these characteristics will affect the person's behavior (social inferences).

Demonstrate ability to observe self and others simultaneously and engage in comparison.

Develop a more mature self-portrait using social comparison.

Moral Development

Understand expectations to conform to several sets of rules regarding moral codes and behaviors (family, school, peers).

Assume certain roles based on unrestrained responses of others.

Aware of nuances of written and unwritten duties to society and own conscience (self).

Social Regulation

Demonstrate understanding of the social world.

Learn through indirect socialization techniques such as discussion & explanation.

Shows increased ability to get along with people.

Demonstrate ability to regulate own behavior according to agreed upon social rules and rule governed play.

Demonstrate growing understanding of self and others in social interactions.

Understand appropriate behavior differs in various social settings (behavioral repertoire).

Sensitive to negative reactions by others.

Understand self-shame as a reaction to antisocial conduct or lack of moral behavior.

Demonstrate knowledge of social conventions of behavior.

Control own emotions especially anger.

Follow classroom rules when teacher is in/out of room.

TABLE 47

SCOPE AND SEQUENCE CHART: SOCIAL AND SELF COMPETENCE

Intermediate Grades, 4th - 6th, 9 - 12 Years

Social Competence (cont.)

<u>**Social Problem-Solving**</u>

Sensitive to social problem-solving and social consequences.
Use the social strategy repertoire:
* **Use social problem solving skills.**
* **Comprehend social situations and determines direction for positive action (social cognition).**
* **Understand the importance of goal setting in the problem-solving strategy.**
* **Understand causal thinking, determining cause-effect relationships in social problems.**
* **Use social reasoning skills and predicts consequences of behaviors.**
* **Understand own role in the consequences of behavior.**

<u>**Social Interactions:**</u>

I. <u>Social Conventions:</u>
Treat parents, teachers, and other authority figures with proper respect.
Use appropriate manners in variety of situations & settings.
Negotiate with parents regarding clothing style, chores, social activities.
Demonstrate appropriate independence in decision-making.
Demonstrate appropriate manners in several situations.
Participate politely in a classroom discussion initiated by teacher

(i.e., make relevant remarks, refrain from using negative Comments.)
Follow verbal/written directions by teacher or school staff.
Respond politely when adults or peers are introduced in the Classroom.

II. <u>Social Communication:</u>
Interpret vocal intonation and body language.
Use vocal intonation and body language to convey meaning.
Adapt messages to listeners.
Use polite conversation.
Interpret verbal & nonverbal communication.
Make appropriate eye contact during conversation.
Display proper manners when introduced to adults (ie., respond with a greeting).
Produce the types of open-ended conversation that allows a conversation to continue.
Demonstrate communicative interaction skills including initiating, reciprocal turn-taking, remaining on topic, terminating interaction.
Speaks positively about school work refraining from making negative statements about academic work.
Listen appropriately when peers speak in class & play situations.

TABLE 47

SCOPE AND SEQUENCE CHART: SOCIAL AND SELF COMPETENCE

Intermediate Grades, 4th - 6th, 9 - 12 Years

Social Competence (cont.)

III. Cooperation:

Interact cooperatively with peers in supervised and unsupervised situations.

"Co-regulate" own behavior with parents and teachers.

Cooperate with family members (siblings, grandparents, parents) in a variety of situations and settings.

Actively belongs to and interacts in clubs and groups.

Learn sex role parameters through socialization in sexually segregated clubs.

Willingly share & interact with other class members as requested.

Work cooperatively & appropriately with partners during class activities.

IV. Social Effectiveness:

Make & maintain friendships with peers & adults.

Show assertiveness in expressing own needs & desires, advocating for self, avoiding submission to an inappropriate behavior.

Dress appropriately for various situations and peer groups.

Maintain clean, neat, and well-groomed appearance.

Demonstrate appropriate compliance with parents, teachers, and other authority figures.

Avoid classroom & home disruptions & inappropriate behaviors.

Show understanding of the ritualized routines & conventions of self-presentation and self-disclosure.

Develop a sense of humor.

Avoid making inappropriate physical contact with peers and adults.

Deal with another's anger and/or accusations by ignoring or avoiding hostile confrontation.

Exhibit hygienic & appropriate behavior at school & in public places (i.e., avoid spitting, scratching privates, etc.)

Express anger in nonaggressive terms & refrain from physical aggression including yelling & name calling.

TABLE 47

SCOPE AND SEQUENCE CHARTS: SOCIAL AND SELF COMPETENCE

Intermediate Grades, 4th - 6th, 9 - 12 years

Self Competence

Self-Knowledge:

Demonstrate increased understanding of self.

Show increased understanding of own personal and emotional characteristics.

Show increased knowledge of how own behavior affects another's actions & reactions to self.

Take responsibility for own beliefs commitments, and attitudes.

Develop a personal moral belief system.

Identify own feelings and deal appropriately with feelings of anger, fear, & affection.

Self-Evaluation:

Make global evaluations of self-worth.

Control own emotions & related behaviors (self control).

Form a self-concept based on competence (i.e., athletics, intelligence, artistic abilities).

Understand self pride as an emotional response to an evaluation of competence.

Evaluates own level of stress & implements stress reduction techniques as needed.

Understand trait stability or consistency of attributes that define the self.

Make positive statements about self without bragging.

Sense of Personal Control:

I. Social Metacognition:

Use metacognition in self-planning & self-organization.

Use self-monitoring in social situations & modify behavior when appropriate.

Use self-evaluation to control inappropriate behaviors.

Use self-reinforcement to reward self for achieving goals.

II. Motivation:

Use self-motivation to complete social & academic responsibilities.

Increase ability to persevere on boring or difficult assignments.

Use self-talk to encourage self to persevere, as needed.

III. Causal Attributions:

Attribute success & failure to own effort & actions (social & academic).

Evaluate own intellectual competence & achievements realistically.

Demonstrate self-confidence, responsibility, independence.

Improve any negative perceptions of ability.

See References on TABLE 46.

TABLE 48

COGNITIVE DEFICITS AND SOCIAL DEFICITS

SOCIAL DEFICITS

SOCIAL COMPETENCE

-- Social Perspective-Taking
-- Moral Development
-- Social Regulation
-- Social Problem-Solving

SOCIAL INTERACTIONS

-- Social Conventions
-- Social Communication
-- Cooperation
-- Social Effectiveness

SELF-COMPETENCE

-- Self-Knowledge
-- Self-Evaluation
-- Sense of Personal Control
   -- Social Metacognition
   -- Motivation
   -- Causal Attributions

COGNITIVE DEFICITS

LOW AVERAGE IQ 75-90

INFORMATION PROCESSING PROBLEMS

-- Perception Problems
-- Attention Problems: Disinhibition
-- Memory: STM, LTM, Working
-- No/Little Use of Executive Processes
   -- Metacognition: Self-Regulation Skills
   -- Lack of Automatic Use of Learning Skills

LACK HIGHER LEVEL THINKING SKILLS

-- Analysis, Synthesis, Evaluation
-- Cause-Effect Reasoning: Problem-Solving

LANGUAGE DEFICITS

-- Receptive and/or Expressive Language Deficits
-- Functions on Literal Level
   -- Problems with Figurative Language,
   -- Complex Language, Innuendos, Humor,
   -- Teasing, Sarcasm, Flirting, etc.
-- Nonlinguistic Deficits
   -- Facial Expressions, Body Language,
      Vocal Intonation

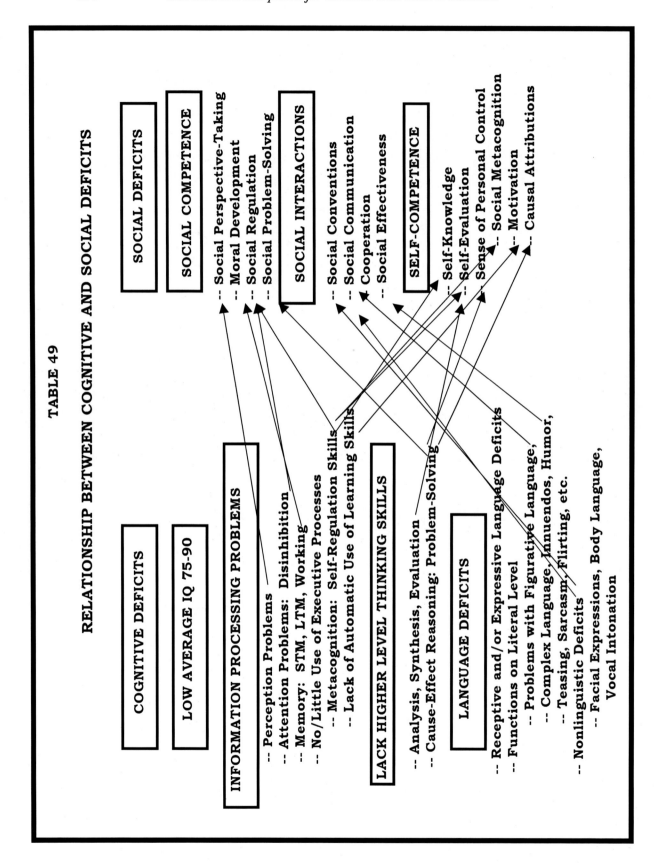

TABLE 49

RELATIONSHIP BETWEEN COGNITIVE AND SOCIAL DEFICITS

COGNITIVE DEFICITS

LOW AVERAGE IQ 75-90

INFORMATION PROCESSING PROBLEMS

-- Perception Problems
-- Attention Problems: Disinhibition
-- Memory: STM, LTM, Working
-- No/Little Use of Executive Processes
   -- Metacognition: Self-Regulation Skills
   -- Lack of Automatic Use of Learning Skills

LACK HIGHER LEVEL THINKING SKILLS

-- Analysis, Synthesis, Evaluation
-- Cause-Effect Reasoning: Problem-Solving

LANGUAGE DEFICITS

-- Receptive and/or Expressive Language Deficits
-- Functions on Literal Level
   -- Problems with Figurative Language,
   -- Complex Language, Innuendos, Humor,
   -- Teasing, Sarcasm, Flirting, etc.
-- Nonlinguistic Deficits
   -- Facial Expressions, Body Language,
      Vocal Intonation

SOCIAL DEFICITS

SOCIAL COMPETENCE

-- Social Perspective-Taking
-- Moral Development
-- Social Regulation
-- Social Problem-Solving

SOCIAL INTERACTIONS

-- Social Conventions
-- Social Communication
-- Cooperation
-- Social Effectiveness

SELF-COMPETENCE

-- Self-Knowledge
-- Self-Evaluation
-- Sense of Personal Control
-- Social Metacognition
-- Motivation
-- Causal Attributions

Chapter 10

SCIENCE CURRICULA

The teaching of science and social studies is often given a low priority in special education.
(Mastropieri & Scruggs, 1994, 243)

Science Curricula Standards
    Science Education Standards
Science Pedagogy
    Performance of Students with Mild Disabilities
    Pedagogy for Students with Mild Disabilities
    Promising Practices for Students with Mild
        Disabilities
Summary
National Science Education Standards: Table 50

Traditionally, elementary grade students with mild disabilities have missed much of the content of science and social studies while they were in the special education resource classroom receiving remediation primarily for reading or mathematics. This lack of foundational knowledge in science and social studies has proven to be an enormous disadvantage when students reach middle school grades. The content of science includes critical life skills and knowledge for students with mild disabilities to make successful transitions to life and work demands of adulthood.

In 1997, with the reauthorization of the Individuals with Disabilities Education Act, and subsequent reauthorization in 2004, Congress mandated changes that have had significant effect on the curriculum of students with disabilities. Congress mandated that students with disabilities not only have access to the general education curriculum, but must show progress in the general education curriculum. By aligning IDEA 2004 with No Child Left Behind Act of 2002 (NCLB), students with disabilities were included in the general education curriculum and were required to be tested in the general education curriculum on the same schedule and grade level as children without disabilities. The NCLB accountability schedule has been phased in over several years with science standards developed by each state in 2005–2006; science assessments administered for one grade at each of three grade levels

(3–5, 6–9, 10–12) during the 2007–2008 academic year with the scores disaggregated; and 2008-2009 academic year, the science assessment data will be disaggregated and used in state accountability calculations (ED.gov) Thus, all public schools in all states are currently involved with science standards, curriculum, assessments, and monitoring student progress of approximately 98 percent of the students attending public schools.

SCIENCE CURRICULA STANDARDS

Science programs generally include four science curricular areas: (1) Life Science: the study of living things including biology, zoology, botany, ecology; (2) Physical Science: the study of nonliving things including chemistry and physics; (3) Earth Science: the study of the earth including astronomy, meterology, and geology; and (4) Science Process Skills: the thinking process in science including observing, classifying, measuring (Mallinson et al., 1993; Mastropieri & Scruggs, 1994; Polloway & Patton, 1997). These content strands spiral throughout the elementary school science textbooks and provide foundational knowledge for separate science courses in high school.

Science Education Standards

The National Science Education Standards developed by the National Research Council (1996) recommended the following eight categories of science content standards for grade levels kindergarten through twelfth grade: (1) Unifying Concepts and Processes; (2) Science as Inquiry; (3) Physical Science; (4) Life Science; (5) Earth and Space Science; (6) Science and Technology; (7) Science in Personal and Social Perspective; and (8) History and Nature of Science (see TABLE 50). These standards have been adapted and adopted by a number of professional organizations as well as the various State Departments of Education. These National Science Education Standards are the basis for the required NCLB state standards and state accountability assessments.

Each state has created their own benchmarks at four academic levels, and science assessments. Standards I and II (see TABLE 50) are presented in one list for K-12 grades because the understanding and abilities transcend disciplinary boundaries and will be developed over an entire education (The National Academic Press, 1996, 104). In Science for All Americans Prospect 2016, the American Association for the Advancement of Science recommended six science themes: Systems, Models, Constancy, Patterns of Change, Evolution, and Scale (The Wright Group, 1995). These themes (Standard I) (see TABLE 50) have been integrated across the science curricular areas of life science, physical science, earth science, and technology in the *Innovations in Science* textbook series (The Wright Group, 1995).

The Science as Inquiry (Standard II, see TABLE 50) content skills reflect the scientific thinking that is important not only for science but for life. These science process skills include observation, measurement, experimentation, data collection, classification, interpretation, inference, prediction, formulating hypotheses, model construction, and problem solving (Mallinson et al., 1993). For students with mild disabilities these higher order cognitive skills are not learned automatically and must be taught directly. Each grade level's knowledge and skills content is based on the knowledge and skills learned in the previous grade level.

An additional important source for national academic standards content including science is the Mid-Continent Research for Education and Learning (McREL) which not only focuses on standards but provides benchmarks (scope and sequence charts at four grade ranges) and topics which are units with teaching materials for each major theme indicated in the benchmarks. For example, there are 57 Topics for Science—units with lesson plans, activities, background teaching information, and related materials. A scope and sequence chart, therefore, is not provided in science as the benchmarks (objectives) are readily accessible on the McREL website.

SCIENCE PEDAGOGY

Recently, there has been a resurgence in the interest of effective practices for teaching science in schools. Issues with the environment, global warming, concerns about the costs of gas and energy have increased the need for providing a strong science background for all students including students with disabilities (Scruggs & Mastropieri, 2007). The National Science Education Standards support the importance of inclusion for those who traditionally have not received encouragement and opportunity to pursue science including students with disabilities (National Research Council, 1996).

The National Science Foundation provides funding under the Research in Disabilities Initiative to promote promising practices for including more students with disabilities in science education. An emphasis on teaching science was stated in the *America 2000 Goals* (U.S. Department of Education, 1990). Several professional organizations including the National Science Teachers Association and the National Science Foundation have agreed upon several important concepts for teaching science including: (1) Science should be organized by the world around us; (2) Common science themes should be studied: and (3) Science should emphasize a general understanding of the "big picture" (Scruggs & Mastropieri, 2007).

The Organization for Economic Cooperation and Development (2007) reported that only 9 percent of U.S. students demonstrate a well-developed capacity for scientific inquiry on the 2006 Program for International Student Assessment. Moreover, only 37 percent of U.S. students indicated that they would like to work in a career involving science.

Performance of Students with Mild Disabilities

Although the need for improving science education is widely accepted, the specific science education needs of students with disabilities are seldom addressed. Evidence suggests students with disabilities are at a greater disadvantage than their nondisabled peers when it comes to science education. Donahoe and Zigmond (1990), for example, found that students with disabilities in mainstreamed science classes were most likely to receive D's and F's. Carlisle and Chang (1996) followed two cohorts of students over three years and found that science teachers consistently rated students with learning disabilities as having lower learning capabilities than their general education students.

In part, the lower performance of students with disabilities in science can be attributed to differences in the number of courses taken and the amount of time spent engaged in active learning in science (Scruggs & Mastropieri, 2007; McCarthy, 2005; Raizen, 1988). Raisin (1988) found that middle school students with disabilities receive on average 29 minutes per week of science instruction in general education classrooms. Moreover, in a survey of special education teachers, Patton, Polloway, and Cronin (1990) discovered that 38 percent of students with disabilities received no science instruction in self-contained settings, and almost half of students with disabilities received less than 60 minutes of science instruction per week. Now that science testing is mandated by NCLB, three times for students from third through twelfth grade, the school districts will be forced to include science in the curriculum of all students.

The lower performance of students with disabilities may also be attributed to curricula focused on the quality of science instruction that they are receiving in general and special education settings. Both general education and special education science teachers rely heavily on the use of science textbooks (McCarthy, 2005). Patton et al., (1990) reported that nearly 60 percent of special education teachers surveyed depend on textbooks for science instruction. The use of science textbooks as the primary mode of instruction in mainstreamed classrooms is problematic given the increased efforts to mainstream students with disabilities into general education classrooms. Science texts are typically written at higher readability levels than the recommended grade usage (Chankin, 1997; Yarborough, 2007). Given that many students with disabilities have language and reading deficits (Fletcher, Lyons, Fuchs, & Barnes, 2007; Cawley, Miller, & Carr, 1990; Parmar, DeLuca, & Janczak, 1994), the use of science textbooks puts them at further disadvantage than their general education peers.

Pedagogy for Students with Mild Disabilities

Two highly researched instructional methods for teaching science range from **direct instruction**, a model that promotes highly structured lessons in which teachers present material to students in an explicit way; and **discovery learning**, a model where students learn through experiments, lab work with only periodic guidance from teachers (Cavanagh, 2004). A model of teaching that lies between the two extremes, often called **"inquiry based learning"** emphasizes both knowledge and skills (direct instruction and discovery learning); and is preferred by the National Research Council, 1996).

Gurganus, Janas, & Schmitt (1995) emphasized the importance of using science materials rather than textbooks in order to provide students with more impactful learning experiences. There is evidence to suggest that hands-on thematic instruction in science results in significantly better performance for students with disabilities than textbook-driven instruction. McCarthy (2005), for example, studied 18 middle school students with serious emotional disturbances who were instructed on the topic of "matter" using a traditional textbook approach or a hands-on thematic approach. McCarthy found that students in the hands-on program performed significantly better than those in the textbook program. Similarly, Mastropieri et al. (2006) report that collaborative hands-on activities statistically facilitate learning of middle school science content as measured by state high-stakes tests for all students, those with and without disabilities, in inclusive classrooms. Also, supplemental peer mediated hands-on activities may provide necessary review and practice for students with disabilities.

According to renowned psychologist Clark Moustakas (1969), too often, learning for students is disconnected from their lives because the focus is on passively absorbing facts that are unrelated to their day-to-day experiences. It is important to provide real-world, problem-based learning for students with disabilities. Grumbine and Alden (2006) have identified six critical principles for assisting students with mastering science curriculum. These principles include the following:

1. Content learning is supported by explicit instruction in skills and strategies.
2. Learning is enhanced when teachers recognize and teach to diverse learning styles and strengths.
3. Learning is facilitated when instruction and assessment are clearly organized.
4. Learning is maximized when instruction and assessment are based on explicit objectives.
5. Learning is improved when teachers provide consistent feedback.
6. Learning is sustained when students develop self-knowledge.

Promising Practices for Students with Mild Disabilities

There are several promising practices which could be implemented to increase the mastery of science curriculum. These practices include: (1) After-School Programs; (2) Project-Based Service Learning; (3) Technology-Based Scientific Inquiry; and (4) Peer-Mentoring.

After-School Programs

Interest in academic learning time can be traced to Carroll's (1963) model of school learning which hypothesized that learning is a function of time-engaged relative to time-needed for learning. For some time, educators have been interested in methodologies that might provide the extra learning time that students with special needs must have in order to master critical curriculum. After-school programs represent an opportunity to increase academic learning time. Hock, Pulvers, Deshler, and Schumaker (2001) found that after-school programs offer a successful platform for increasing at-risk students' achievement. Through an after-school program, students successfully completed classroom assignments and mastered learning strategies that led to increased long-term achievement. Also, Gardner (2001) found that when specific academic skills were targeted in an after-school program, at-risk students made significant academic gains. There is substantial support for after-school learning programs providing increased academic learning opportunities for students with disabilities.

Project-Based Service Learning

Starting with concrete, hands-on, real-world problems is a great motivator for students, as Seymour Papert (2002) and many others have noted. In project-based learning in particular, students try to answer a question that has relevance for them and is greater than the immediate task at hand. That is, the work students do is productive work valued by a community outside of the classroom.

Through service-based learning, students can learn that the scientific knowledge they gain can have an important impact on their own lives. For example, students can learn that collecting and organizing information helps people see the impact of simple decisions in areas such as local energy use, and that reducing energy consumption is a powerful way to make an impact on patterns of behavior that impact climate change.

SERVICE-BASED LEARNING SCENARIO. The following is an example of a service-based learning scenario.

1. Maria attends a safety lesson and signs out an energy monitoring device on Wednesday after school.

2. On Wednesday night, Maria plugs in several devices for easy tests and finds out her brother's power bar (with his video games connected) uses almost as much power, even when not in use, as the lamp in the family room that her mother will never let them leave burning all night. She mentions this to her Mom, who implements a new "power bar off" rule for the games in their house.

3. On Thursday, Maria tests the two refrigerators in their house. She finds the older refrigerator, used mainly for overflow groceries and drinks, uses double the energy of their new one—even though the older refrigerator stays closed and almost empty most of the time. Her family resolves to begin looking at weekend garage sales for an Energy Star replacement, since the spreadsheet template Maria brought home shows them they could recover the cost of a $50.00 garage sale refrigerator (and start saving money) in just a few months.

4. Over the weekend, Maria pulls out a list that was developed by her group and includes standard household appliances. Maria begins to measure the consumption of many of these household devices on her list; this information is also being gathered by other members of her group. Maria records her collected data in a spreadsheet. Over the coming months Maria's data will be combined with those gathered by others and used to project where the greatest gain might occur in appliance energy efficiency for her community.

Researchers such as Gallagher (1994) have shown that student involvement in inquiry-based science instruction at the middle school level is a strong indicator of students' later placement in high-level science courses, while other researchers such as Gibson & Chase (2002) have shown that participation in science-related activities at a two-week summer inquiry-based science camp at the sixth grade level stimulated interest in science and science-related careers. One can infer from these findings that middle school involvement in inquiry-based science activities will lead to a greater likelihood of students selecting a science-based future career.

Peer-Mentoring

Britner & Pajares (2006) reviewed the literature on the effectiveness of mentoring programs for students with special needs. In general, mentoring programs are well received as support services; however, very little empirical research has been conducted to assess the effectiveness of these programs in meeting the diverse needs of the special populations of youth. Mentoring can be an effective tool for encouraging successful interaction with complex curriculum for students with disabilities (Tyler-Wood & Mortensen, 2006). Careful planning of the mentoring process, including recruitment and training of mentors, is required to increase the probability of success. Students with disabilities certainly can benefit from mentoring relationships, but because of their vulnerability, the process has to be implemented and monitored with care.

SUMMARY

Science standards and benchmarks have been developed for grades K–12 by the National Association of Science Teachers. McREL (2009) has developed benchmarks (scope and sequence charts of science skills) for the science standards as well as topics or units of lesson plans, activities, and additional information for teaching. Thus, science benchmarks (objectives) have not been included in this chapter as they are readily available on the McREL website. These standards and benchmarks will be very helpful as special education teachers plan specifically for IEP science education needs of students with disabilities. The standards include knowledge and skills which will help students with special needs compete in the twenty-first century job market. It is important to recognize the critical role that science will play in the future workforce. To make certain that students with disabilities are prepared for the future, the strategies discussed in this chapter should be implemented to assist students with mastering science content (knowledge and skills).

TABLE 50

NATIONAL SCIENCE EDUCATION STANDARDS

I. UNIFYING CONCEPTS AND PROCESSES OF SCIENCE K-12
    a. Systems, order, organization
    b. Evidence, models, explanation
    c. Change, constancy, measurement
    d. Evolution, equilibrium
    e. Form and function

II. SCIENCE AS INQUIRY K-12
    a. Abilities Necessary to do Scientific Inquiry
    b. Understanding Scientific Inquiry

KINDERGARTEN - FOURTH GRADE	FIFTH GRADE - EIGHTH GRADE
III. PHYSICAL SCIENCE a. Properties of objects & materials b. Position and motion of objects c. Light, heat, electricity, magnetism	**III. PHYSICAL SCIENCE** a. Properties and changes of properties in matter b. Motions and forces c. Transfer of energy
IV. LIFE SCIENCE a. Characteristics of organisms b. Life cycles of organisms c. Organisms and environments	**IV. LIFE SCIENCE** a. Structure and function of living systems b. Reproduction and heredity c. Regulation and behavior d. Populations and ecosystems e. Diversity and adaptations of organisms.
V. EARTH AND SPACE SCIENCE a. Properties of earth materials b. Objects in the sky c. Changes in earth and sky	**V. EARTH AND SPACE SCIENCE** a. Structure of the earth system b. Earth's history c. Earth in the solar system
VI. SCIENCE AND TECHNOLOGY a. Abilities of technological design b. Understanding about science and technology c. Abilities to distinguish between natural objects and objects made by humans.	**VI. SCIENCE AND TECHNOLOGY** a. Abilities of technological design b. Understanding about science and technology

TABLE 50

NATIONAL SCIENCE EDUCATION STANDARDS (cont.)

VII. PERSONAL AND SOCIAL PERSPECTIVES
a. Personal health
b. Characteristics and changes in populations
c. Types of resources
d. Changes in environments
e. Science and technology in local challenges

VIII. HISTORY AND NATURE OF SCIENCE
a. Science as a human endeavor

VII. PERSONAL AND SOCIAL PERSPECTIVES
a. Personal health
b. Populations, resources, and environments
c. Natural hazards
d. Risks and benefits
e. Science and technology in society

VIII. HISTORY AND NATURE OF SCIENCE
a. Science as a human endeavor
b. Nature of science
c. History of science

(NCES, 1996)

APPENDICES

Appendix A

EVALUATION REPORT: DIANA

Evaluation Report #1: Diana

Age: 5 Years, 9 Months   Grade: Kindergarten   Date: October, 20__

BACKGROUND AND EDUCATIONAL CONCERNS

REASONS FOR REFERRAL:

Diana is a 5 year, 9-month-old kindergarten student at Adams Street Elementary School. She was referred for evaluation by her kindergarten teacher because of academic failure. She is unable to work independently, and has a very short attention span.

Diana has numerous academic deficits. She does not know her alphabet or recognize letters, does not recognize numerals, cannot listen and comprehend, cannot follow directions, cannot do any of the pre-academic work of her classmates. Diana is easily distracted and attempts to interact with peers while they are working independently or in a group situation. The teacher aide has been assigned to work almost exclusively with Diana in a one-to-one situation to prevent classroom disruptions.

HEALTH:
No medical history or immunization data is available. Diana's mother has 30 days to show proof of immunizations according to state law or Diana will be terminated from school. The school social worker has been contacted.

VISION AND HEARING SCREENING:
School screening indicated normal range visual and auditory acuities.

SPEECH AND LANGUAGE SCREENING:
Diana exhibited maturational articulation deficits. Her performance indicated deficits in language development areas including names for concepts and associative responses. A language evaluation is recommended.

BEHAVIOR HISTORY:

Diana's behavior problems appear to be a result of immaturity and short attention span rather than rebellion and intent to challenge authority figures. She talks or sings almost continuously, and remains in her seat for only minutes at a time. Diana cannot work independently on any school work.

SOCIOECONOMIC AND HOME INFORMATION:

English is the language of the home. Diana, her mother, and two younger sisters live in a small three bedroom house with her aunt (mother's sister) and 3 cousins. All six children range in age from 2–7 years old. Diana indicated that the children fight a lot and must be sent to their rooms. She indicated that they sleep in sleeping ("fleeping") bags on the beds.

Diana misses quite a bit of school, by her report, she must stay home and take care of her younger sisters. She frequently comes to school wearing urine-smelling clothing, apparently Diana and her sisters sleep together and the youngest one wets the bed. Diana often comes to school hungry.

There is no telephone and mother does not respond to notes sent home. The school security officer was sent to the home to deliver a letter regarding the referral for special education testing. Mother indicated an interest, but did not understand the problem. Social Services have been contacted.

CURRENT MULTIDISCIPLINARY EVALUATION

This evaluation includes assessments in the areas of intelligence, perception and memory, academic achievement, communication, and social development.

PSYCHOLOGICAL REPORT

TESTS ADMINISTERED:

Peabody Picture Vocabulary Test   IQ 81

Stanford-Binet Intelligence Scale   (Form L-M) IQ 86

Boehm Test of Basic Concepts   55 %ile using Low SES Norms

Human Figure Drawing   Low Average to Average Range

Test of Visual-Motor Integration   5 years, 7 mo./ 44th %ile

TESTING INTERPRETATION:

On the **Stanford-Binet**, Diana's overall performance fell within the low average range of intelligence. All items were passed (basal) at Level V, partial success was achieved at Level VI, and all items were failed (ceiling) at Level VII. Diana's performance on the **Peabody Picture Vocabulary Test** indicated low average language and cognitive functioning.

Diana successfully completed several visual-motor tasks including completing a partial drawing, and copying a simple geometric figure. She was unable to successfully complete several mazes. Perceptual-motor assessment indicated average development for age expectations in terms of ability to perceive and reproduce geometric designs.

Diana's **Human Figure Drawing** was examined according to the Koppitz criteria. Her drawing consisted of a head, eyes, nose, mouth, ears, hair, arms, and legs. One expected item, a trunk, was not included. This performance suggested intellectual functioning within the low average to average range, and, as such, is commensurate with obtained measured intellectual data.

Diana correctly identified 29 of 55 concepts presented on the **Boehm**. This performance placed her at the 55th %ile (using low socio-economic norms). She correctly identified "top," "second," but could not identify such concepts as "next to," "almost," "least."

In summary, Diana is a 5 year, 9 month old kindergarten student functioning within the low average range of intelligence.

_____

School Psychologist

COMMUNICATION EVALUATION

TESTS ADMINISTERED:
Informal Speech/Language Pathologist Assessment

TEST INTERPRETATION:

Receptively, Diana appears to be functioning at the 3 to 3 1/2 year developmental level. She points to pictures of some common objects when they are named and can identify some objects when told their use. She experiences difficulty answering the "wh-questions" because she wants to tell a story or relate any associative information that comes to mind. She understands negatives "no, not, can't, don't". Due to short attention span, she does not listen to usual children's stories read aloud. She cannot carry out a series of 2-4 related directions. She needs directions specified one direction at a time. Diana has some understanding of comparatives.

Expressively, Diana is functioning on the 3-4 year developmental level. Her expressive language is significantly affected by her deprived environment, lack of basic concepts, and lack of labels for concepts. She uses sentences of three or more words and talks about past experiences. At school she has learned some nursery rhymes and to sing abc's from watching Seseme Street. Her speech is understandable to strangers, though she makes some maturational misarticulations such as "fl" for "sl" (e.g., fleeping for sleeping).

In summary, Diana appears to be functioning receptively and expressively at the 3–4 year developmental level in language.

_____

Speech/Language Pathologist

PSYCHO-EDUCATIONAL REPORT

TESTS ADMINISTERED:

Woodcock-Johnson Psycho-Educational Battery

PreSchool Cluster	GE 1.01	AE 4-0	%ile 3	SS 70
Knowledge	GE 1.02	AE 3-6	%ile 2	SS 69

Slingerland Screening Test: PreReading, Revised

Far Point Copying	88%
Visual Discrimination	38%
Visual Memory to Written (symbols)	70%
Auditory Visual Association- Pictured Object	75%
Letter Knowledge and Sound Symbol	0%

Developmental Tasks for Kindergarten Readiness (DTKR)

Subtests	Norm Rating	Percent Accuracy
Social Interaction	D	70
Name Printing		80 (Dana)
Body Concepts: Awareness	C	63
Body Concepts: Use	D	20
Auditory Sequencing	A	83
Auditory Association	D	38
Visual Discrimination	D	0
Visual Motor	B	81
Visual Memory	C	14
Color Naming	A	100
Relational Concepts	C	60
Number Knowledge: Counting	A	100
Number Knowledge: Use	B	75
Number Knowledge: Naming	D	10
Alphabet Knowledge	D	4

Test of Early Reading (TERA)

Total Raw Score	6
Reading Quotient	73
Percentile	3
Reading Age	3–7

TESTING INTERPRETATION:

Testing Behaviors

Diana is a very verbal five year, nine-month-old kindergarten student. Her continuous talking appeared to interfere with her concentration and task performance. Her attention span appears to be only a few minutes at most even in a one-to-one structured setting. She was very pleasant and eager to make friends with the examiner.

Diana's thinking was very associative. Any stimulus item would remind her of something that she just had to talk about or a song to sing. It was difficult to refocus her attention on task, to stop the singing, or to cease the story before she was finished. She did not remain in her seat longer than a few minutes at a time. She could be encouraged to do a task by offering a Mickey Mouse pencil for proper behavior. She demonstrated no independent work skills.

Learning Modality

Several subtests of the **Slingerland** were administered to assess auditory and visual processing. Diana wrote some letters of her first name (DANA). Her performance on the far-point copying test was adequate, however, she required much reinforcement and redirection to complete the task. She experienced significant difficulties on the visual discrimination of letters task making two transpositions of letters, two inversions, and four letter reversals. Visual discrimination appears to be an area of significant weakness. On the visual memory with written response subtest, Diana performed in the below average range. On two items she forgot one detail each, she indicated to the examiner that she remembered something but could not remember where to put it. Diana's performance on the auditory-visual association task indicated low average functioning. Her attention had to be continually redirected to the task.

Several subtests of the **Developmental Test of Kindergarten Readiness** (DTKR) concerned learning modality processing. No clear learning modality preference emerged. Diana's performance in visual motor skills indicated functioning in the average range for age expectations. Auditory sequencing was an area of strength. Areas of severe deficit included visual discrimination, visual memory, and auditory association. On the visual discrimination subtest, Diana missed all items by reversing, inverting, or substituting letters. On the visual memory subtest, she accurately answered only one item, committing reversals and transpositions. Diana's performance on the auditory association subtest indicated that she talked associatively about the stimulus, but seldom answered the question asked.

Kindergarten Readiness Tests:

Diana demonstrated strength in color naming and rote counting skills. Her performance in number use indicated functioning in the average range for age expectations. However, Diana's performance indicated deficits in body awareness and relational concepts; and severe deficits in knowledge of body use, social interactions, number naming, and alphabet knowledge. Diana appears to have no number-symbol association knowledge. She only recognizes two alphabet letters and has not yet acquired letter-symbol association.

On the Preschool Cluster of the **Woodcock-Johnson**, Diana's performance indicated that knowledge of preschool skills is an area of severe deficiency for age expectations. She performed approximately two years below expectancy. Diana could identify no letters, answered three applied problems (picture clues), and wrote the letter "O." On the Knowledge Cluster, her performance indicated functioning 2 1/2 years below age expectations. Diana could not identify animals or the sounds associated with them, tell why she went to school ("to be quiet"), or relate nursery rhymes.

On the **TERA**, Diana's performance indicated functioning approximately 2 1/2 years deficit for age expectancy. She recognized the McDonald's symbol and that of the 7 Eleven Store. She could point to the top and bottom of a page. She answered a question correctly after being read a short story, and sang her alphabet. She identified no letters or words correctly.

Summary

Diana appears to be severely deficit in the visual memory and visual discrimination processing areas. She, also, experiences difficulties with auditory association. Areas of adequate performance include the following: far-point copying, visual memory to written (symbols), auditory visual association (pictured object), auditory sequencing, and visual motor tasks.

Academically, Diana's performance indicates functioning in the severe deficit range for age expectations in all areas. She recognizes no numbers or letters, though she can count by rote and recite her alphabet. She appears deficit by 2 1/2 years in general knowledge information. She knows her colors and understands one-to-one correspondence to seven.

Educational Examiner

SOCIAL DEVELOPMENT

TEST ADMINISTERED
Informal Teacher Observation

TESTING INTERPRETATION:

Diana is socially immature. She has little idea of the purpose of school. She talks continuously, eager to make friends. She shows affection for her younger siblings and is expected to care for them when mother is gone. She does not appear to be able to interpret adults' emotions from facial expressions and intonation. She is eager to please but because of her short attention span and lack of knowledge of the purpose of school her behaviors are inconsistent.

Diana is unable to play simple table games because she does not possess many of the readiness skills used in the games–colors, numbers, alphabet letters, relational concepts. She does not understand games with rules. Socially, Diana is functioning at approximately the 3 to 3 1/2 year level.

_____

Resource Room Teacher

EVALUATION SUMMARY

Diana is a 5 year, 9-month-old kindergarten student. Her overall cognitive ability falls within the low-average range of intelligence (IQ 86). She lacks understanding of many of the basic cognitive concepts required to perform mathematics tasks (e.g., least, almost). Psychomotor skills of perceiving and reproducing geometric designs are within average expectations, as is auditory sequencing. Diana experienced significant difficulties with visual discrimination, visual memory, and auditory association. Thus, no clear learning modality preference emerges as she experiences problems with both visual and auditory processing skills.

Academically, Diana has not mastered preschool skills. While she can rote count, she has no understanding of one-to-one correspondence above seven and no number-symbol association knowledge. Diana is functioning 2 1/2 years deficit in general preschool knowledge and in reading readiness skills. She possesses no sound-symbol letter knowledge.

Behaviorally, while not severely behavior disordered, her short attention span and continuous talking significantly interfere with acquisition of basic skills. Her inability to monitor her own behavior and to change it to be more appropriate in the school setting causes her to experience difficulty with the teacher. She is frequently punished for misbehavior and has no concept of what she did incorrectly or why the teacher is mean to her. Socially, Diana is functioning at the 3 to 3 1/2 years developmental level.

Diana appears to live in an environmentally deprived home and has not been exposed to relational concepts and language expected for her age. She appears to lack an understanding of the purpose of school and her role as a student. While a child of Diana's measured ability level would be expected to function approximately a year below her chronological age expectations, after nearly one year of kindergarten Diana appears to be functioning 2 1/2 to 3 1/2 years below expected developmental levels.

_____

Case Manager

Diagnosis: _____

Appendix B

EVALUATION REPORT: DEBBIE

Age: 8 Years, 3 Months   Grade: lst grade   Date: May, 20__

BACKGROUND AND EDUCATIONAL CONCERNS

REASONS FOR REFERRAL:

Debbie is an 8 year, 3-month-old first grade student at Mason Elementary School. She was retained in kindergarten and enrolled in a transitional kindergarten program. She was retained in lst grade because she had not mastered lst grade skills. After the second year in lst grade, Debbie continues to function at a preschool level. The classroom teacher has requested this evaluation to assist in planning Debbie's academic program for next year.

HEALTH:

School immunizations are current. Debbie takes dimetapp or sudafed seasonally for allergies. She seems to experience more upper respiratory illness than average. A physical last summer indicated no specific concerns.

VISION AND HEARING SCREENINGS:

School screenings indicated normal range visual and auditory acuities.

SPEECH AND LANGUAGE SCREENING:

Speech screening indicated functioning 2-3 years deficit with misarticulations of /l/, /r/, /sh/, /v/, /t/, /s/. Language screening indicated functioning 2-3 years deficit with problems with noun and adverb derivations, irregular plurals, questions, and negatives.

BEHAVIOR HISTORY:

Although, Debbie has been retained a number of times, she seems to be a happy child. She wants the teacher to like her and gets upset if she thinks the teacher is not pleased with her. She willingly plays with most of the children in class and has learned to turn to peers for assistance.

SOCIO-ECONOMIC AND HOME EVALUATION:

English is the language of the home. Debbie's father is an Army National Guard technician on helicopters and her mother sells cosmetics out of the home. They live in an older settled working-class neighborhood several blocks from both sets of grandparents. Debbie has two younger preschool-aged sisters at home. There appears to be no economic deprivation.

CURRENT MULTIDISCIPLINARY EVALUATION

This evaluation includes assessments in the following areas: intelligence, perception and memory, academic achievement, speech and language, self-help skills, and social development.

PSYCHOLOGICAL EVALUATION

TEST ADMINISTERED:

Wechsler Intelligence Scale for Children-Revised (WISC-R)

Verbal IQ	64	Performance IQ	65	Full Scale IQ 64
Information	6	Picture Completion	4	
Similarities	4	Picture Arrangement	5	
Arithmetic	3	Block Design	4	
Vocabulary	5	Object Assembly	7	
Comprehension	3	Coding	3	
Digit Span	3			

TEST INTERPRETATION:

Debbie is an 8 year, 3-month-old first grade student who was retained in kindergarten and 1st grade. She came eagerly to the testing situation to "play games." Rapport was easily established.

Results of the **WISC-R** indicate overall functioning within the mild retardation range with little variation in verbal expressive and psychomotor skills. No significant strengths or weaknesses were noted. A relative weakness in verbal expressive skills was noted in information gained from experience and education. Relative weaknesses were noted in ability to manipulate number concepts, anticipation and judging consequences of behavioral situations, attention, and auditory memory and sequencing.

Relative strength was noted in psychomotor skills in concentration and simple assembly tasks. Weakness was noted in the ability to learn unfamiliar tasks and speed of visual-motor reaction and association of symbols.

In summary, Debbie's testing behavior was appropriate and she attempted to respond to all "games." Her overall cognitive functioning appears to be within the mild mental retardation range with little variability among verbal expressive and psychomotor abilities.

_____

School Psychologist

PSYCHO-EDUCATIONAL EVALUATION

TESTS ADMINISTERED:

Slingerland Screening Test: PreReading, Revised

Far Point Copying	weak
Near Point Copying	adequate
Visual Memory–Choice Response	63%
Visual Discrimination	75%
Visual Memory/Written Response	50%
Auditory Memory/Written Response (Letters)	25%
Auditory Discrimination	70%
Auditory Visual Association (Pictured Object)	88%
Auditory Visual Association (Comprehension)	63%
Auditory Visual Association (Letter Knowledge)	25%
Auditory Visual Association (Sound Symbol)	25%

Brigance Diagnostic Inventory of Early Development
Skills Within (+), Below (-) Age/Grade Expectancy

Color Recognition	+
Visual Discrimination	-
Gross Motor Coordination	-
Identification of Body Parts	-
Directional/Positional Skills	-
Personal Data Response	-
Visual Motor Skills	+
Body Image-Picture	-

Brigance Diagnostic Inventory of Basic Skills: Reading Readiness
Skills Within (+), Below (-) Age/Grade Expectancy

Recites Alphabet (Slurs "l, m, n")	-
Recognizes Upper & Lower Case Letters (Auditory Cue)	-
Recognizes Upper Case Letters by Naming (Visual Cue)	-
Recognizes Lower Case Letters by Naming (Visual Cue)	-
Writes Lower Case Letters From Dictation (Mixed Order)	-

Sight Word Recognition: Stop, Go, Color Words   -
Initial Consonant Sounds   -
Initial Sound Symbol   -
Oral Reading Comprehension, Primer Level   -
Oral Reading Comprehension, lst Grade Level   -
Writes Alphabet in Order   -
Writes Upper Case Letters From Dictation (Mixed Order) -

Brigance Diagnostic Inventory of Basic Skills: Math Readiness
Skills Within (+), Below (-) Age/Grade Expectancy
Counting to 39   -
Numeral Recognition to 10   -
Writing Numbers in Sequence to 10   -
Counting Objects to 10   -
Joining Sets   -
Ordinal Concepts (first, last, middle)   +

Test of Early Reading (TERA)
Total Raw Score   16
Reading Quotient   <60
Percentile   <1
Reading Age   5-2

TESTING INTERPRETATION:

Learning Modality

Debbie was administered the Slingerland level that is ordinarily administered to kindergarten-aged students. Her performance on near-point copying and visual discrimination were in the adequate range. She experienced significant difficulties on the far-point copying, visual memory and visual memory to written subtests, auditory discrimination and auditory memory to written (letters) subtests. On the auditory visual association subtests, Debbie scored within the adequate range on pictured objects. She experienced significant difficulties on the auditory visual comprehension, sound symbol, and letter knowledge subtests. A clear learning modality is not established, however, auditory and visual memory with a written response is very difficult.

Readiness: General Knowledge

Debbie's areas of strength at the readiness level (early lst grade) include the following: quantitative concepts; sorting by color, shape, and size; naming shapes (circle, square, triangle, diamond); use of objects. Her areas of weakness in General Knowledge included directional and positional concepts, knowledge of body parts, time concepts, knowledge of what to do in certain circumstances, community helpers and services. On the Readiness subtest, Debbie's performance indicated adequate visual discrimination; and matching of shapes, upper and lower case letters, and words. She sang the alphabet slurring the letters together. On the Basic Reading Skills test, Debbie's performance was significantly deficit for age expectations. She could read some color words (red), some number words (one, two), and some signs (stop, go).

Written Expression

Debbie experienced significant difficulties on the Manuscript Writing test. She can print her first name, age, and phone number. She attempted to print her upper case letters sequentially, but could not. Some letters were omitted, others reversed, transposed, rotated and inverted. She said that she could not write the lower case letters either sequentially or dictated. Debbie could not write a sentence because she lacks the concept of "sentence." The quality of her manuscript writing is poor, revealing difficulties with slant, size, shape, spacing, and alignment.

Mathematics

Debbie's performance in mathematics is significantly better than her reading performance. She counted by rote to 20, recognized numerals through 5, matched quantity with symbol through 5, understood ordinal concepts (first, last, middle), wrote numerals in sequence through 5, and wrote numerals dictated through 5. Her performance indicated no knowledge of addition or subtraction combinations, a significant deficit for 1st grade. Though Debbie recognizes money, she knows the value of only the penny and dime. She has very few time concepts.

Reading

On the TERA, Debbie's performance indicated that her reading level is at the 5 year, 2-month level, a significant deficit by 3+ years for age expectations. She experienced difficulties with meaning, alphabet knowledge, and conventions of written language (e.g., right-left orientation).

Summary

Academically, Debbie appears to be functioning at a pre-kindergarten level in all areas. She does not recite her alphabet by rote, recognize or write the alphabet. She can count by rote to 20, but recognizes numerals to 5 and matches quantity with symbol to 5. She has no prereading skills and lacks most math cognitive prerequisites. Debbie is functioning at least three years deficit for age expectations.

_____

Educational Examiner

SPEECH AND LANGUAGE EVALUATION

TESTS ADMINISTERED:

Language Screening Sample (Informal Test)

Informal Receptive and Expressive Language Checklists

Northwest Syntax Screening Test (NSST)

TESTING INTERPRETATION:

Receptive Language

Debbie's performance on the NSST and informal tests indicate receptive language functioning at the 5 1/2 year level. She knows right from left and number concepts to five, understands words of quantity (e.g., more, less, bigger), follows a three-stage command, repeats four digits and remembers a sentence of 10 words in length. She appears to be functioning over 2 1/2 years deficit for age expectancy.

Expressive Language

Debbie's performance on the NSST and informal tests indicate expressive language functioning at the 5 1/2 year level. She asks "when, how, why" questions; can tell a story by pointing to pictures and describing the action in multiword sentences. Debbie's mean sentence length is 5-6 words. She has acquired personal pronouns (I, me, it) and possessive pronouns (my, mine, his, her). She uses present and past tense verbs and prepositions (e.g., after, before, into, down, near, over, under). She is beginning to use conjunctions "if . . . so," and irregularly formed plurals. Debbie experiences difficulty with negative sentences and conjunction sentences (e.g., if-then, neither-nor).

Pragmatics

Debbie is a happy little girl and talks freely much of the time. She understands that communication requires turn-taking; gives and receives information; communicates with family, friends, and strangers. She understands initiating and maintaining a conversation, but not concluding a conversation. Debbie understands basic emotions, body language, and vocal inflection accompanying "happy, sad, angry."

Speech

Informal testing indicates that Debbie is functioning on the 5-6 year level in speech skills. She experiences difficulty articulating /t/, /th/, /v/, /l/, /y/, /z/, /zh/, /s/, /kt/, /tr/, /sp/. She correctly articulates most single consonants and consonant blends. Voice, fluency, and oral peripheral structures are within normal limits.

Summary

Debbie appears to be functioning at the 5 1/2 year level in receptive and expressive language, pragmatics, and speech skills. There is little variability among her speech and language abilities.

_____

Speech/Language Pathologist

SOCIAL DEVELOPMENT

TESTS ADMINISTERED:

Informal Social Skills Development Checklist

Informal Self-Help Skills Checklist

Vineland Social Maturity Scale   CA 8 years, 3 months
                                      AE 5 years, 8 months

TESTING INTERPRETATION:

Self-Help Skills

Debbie appears to be functioning at the 5–6 year level in self-help skills. She is independent in eating: serves herself at the table, spears food with a fork, spreads soft butter on bread with a knife, and knows not to speak with her mouth full of food. Debbie is independent in dressing: buttons (except back), zips zippers, ties shoes, puts on coat and rainboots. She is independent in toileting. Debbie is independent in grooming: bathes independently, washes hands and face, combs and brushes hair but needs help with washing hair, brushes teeth.

Social/Emotional Behavior

Debbie appears to be functioning at the 5–6 year level in social and emotional development. She wants to do what is expected and respects reasonable authority. She is willing to play with most other children in the class, engages with other children in cooperative play, and shares readily. She enjoys role play in housekeeping, in various adult occupations, and on the playground. Debbie plays simple table games and games with rules. She enjoys singing and playing rhythm band instruments. She produces art projects: cutting, coloring, pasting, painting, molding clay.

Emotional Behavior

Debbie is usually happy and will attempt any task given. She cries when she can not do a task that the teacher expects her to do and feels very unhappy if the teacher is angry. Debbie seldom gets angry or has temper tantrums, and has learned to turn to peers for help in completing tasks that she cannot do. Debbie is liked by most children in the class because she is usually happy and chatty. She respects others' property rights. She participates appropriately in group activities.

_____

Resource Teacher

EVALUATION SUMMARY

Debbie is an 8 year, 3-month-old first grade student who has been retained in kindergarten and 1st grade. Her overall cognitive functioning appears to be within the mild mental retardation range with both verbal expressive and psychomotor skills within that range.

Academically, Debbie is functioning at a pre-kindergarten level. She cannot recite or write her alphabet, and does not possess pre-reading skills. She counts to 20, writes and recognizes numbers to 5, but she has no knowledge of addition and subtraction.

Speech and language evaluations indicate functioning at the 5 1/2 year level in receptive and expressive language, pragmatics, and speech. She has not mastered all morphological and syntax conventions, and experiences difficulty articulating the harder consonant sounds. Pragmatics skills with peers are good.

Debbie's **adaptive behaviors**, self-help and social/emotional, appear to be at the 5-6 year level. She is independent in eating, dressing, grooming, and toileting. Socially, she enjoys peers, cooperates and shares. She enjoys most play activities including singing, dancing, role playing, and art work. She is a happy and pleasant child.

_____

Case Manager

Diagnosis: _____

Appendix C

EVALUATION REPORT: BOBBY

Age: 12 years, 6 months   Grade: 6th grade   Date: October , 20___

BACKGROUND AND EDUCATIONAL CONCERNS

REASONS FOR REFERRAL:

Bobby is a 12 year, 6-month-old sixth grade student at Madison Elementary School. Previously, he attended St. Martin's Elementary School from 1st through 5th grades. During 5th grade at St. Martin's, Bobby was placed in a special classroom for students who experience behavior problems. Mother removed him from the private school and enrolled him in public school when St. Martin's initiated special education procedures.

Bobby has been verbally and physically aggressive to the classroom teacher and to other students in his 6th grade classroom. He refuses to obey, refuses to work and tears up school books and peers' belongings when he gets angry. Bobby is failing all academics because he refuses to do any school work. This emergency evaluation was requested for immediate placement to protect other students and teachers.

HEALTH:

Immunizations are current and there appears to be no medical concerns.

VISION AND HEARING SCREENING:

School screening indicates normal visual and auditory acuities.

SPEECH AND LANGUAGE SCREENING:

Screening indicates speech and language skills are within normal limits.

BEHAVIOR:

Bobby exhibits severe behavior problems. He is verbally and physically abusive to his classroom teacher and to other students. He has torn up his books and school supplies, and repeatedly destroyed or tried to destroy school property. Bobby refuses to obey, Mr. Wilson, his classroom teacher, and refuses to do any school work in any class. His teachers including PE, music, art, etc. cannot control him.

Bobby has a history of behavior problems. Last year he was placed in a special classroom at St. Martin's for students who are difficult to control, though not labeled disabled. This was not a successful intervention.

SOCIO-ECONOMIC AND HOME INFORMATION:

English is the language of the home. Bobby comes from a very wealthy family. His mother is a socialite, spending lavishly from an inheritance left by her grandmother. Father is vice-president in grandfather's company and is seldom at home. Neither parent attempts to discipline Bobby, although at times they bribe him with special gifts, activities, or trips.

Bobby is allowed to roam the estate, play in the woods, ride horses, and play with an unlimited number of toys and games. He has little supervision at home. He has committed destructive acts at home when adults attempt to control him—destroyed the flower garden and broke china in the house. It is felt by the family that he will "grow out of " this behavior.

CURRENT MULTIDISCIPLINARY EVALUATION

This evaluation includes assessments in the areas of intelligence, perception and memory, and academic achievement. The file of documented behavior problems will be summarized and added to this report.

PSYCHOLOGICAL REPORT

TEST ADMINISTERED:

Wechsler Intelligence Scale for Children-Revised (WISC-R):

Verbal IQ	109	Performance IQ	123	Full Scale IQ	118
Information	12	Picture Completion	14		
Similarities	15	Picture Arrangement	15		
Arithmetic	6	Block Design	14		
Vocabulary	13	Object Assembly	14		
Comprehension	12	Coding	9		
Digit Span	11				

TESTING INTERPRETATION:

Bobby is a 12 year, 6-month-old sixth grade student who entered the testing session by saying, "I don't have to do anything that I don't want to do". The examiner replied, "Ok" and began to get out the materials for test administration. Bobby became curious and entered into the testing situation, once started he worked diligently.

Results of the **WISC-R** indicate that Bobby's overall cognitive ability is within the superior range. A significant discrepancy exists between his average range verbal expressive abilities and his superior range psychomotor skills. Bobby reveals significant weakness in mental alertness and the ability to manipulate number concepts. His other verbal skills range from high average through superior range. No true weaknesses are noted among psychomotor skills. He demonstrated a relative weakness in the ability to learn symbols and shapes and to recreate them. Other performance abilities fall within the superior range.

In summary, Bobby's overall intellectual ability falls within the superior range. He demonstrated significant weakness in auditory memory and the ability to abstractly manipulate number concepts. Other skills assessed fall within the high average to superior range.

_____

School Psychologist

PSYCHO-EDUCATIONAL REPORT

Wepman Auditory Discrimination   93%

Slingerland Screening Test, Form D
Near Point Copying	90%
Visual Memory	93%
Visual Discrimination	100%
Visual Memory/Written Response	90% items/100% sequencing
Auditory Memory/Written Response	77% items/75% sequencing

Woodcock-Johnson Psycho-Educational Battery: Tests of Cognitive Ability
Visual Perceptual Speed Cluster	GE 4.4 AE 9.9 %ile 10 SS 81
Visual Matching	GE 3.0-5.0 (100%)
Spatial Relations	GE 3.0- 5.0 (87% items, 75% puzzles)
Auditory Memory Cluster	GE 10.0 AE 15-1 %ile 71 SS 108
Memory for Sentences	GE 12.9
Numbers Reversed	GE 5.0-7.0 (58%)

Woodcock Reading Mastery Test
Letter Identification	GE 6.2
Word Identification	GE 8.3
Word Attack	GE 12.9

Word Comprehension GE 12.4
Passage Comprehension GE 9.9
Total Test GE 9.6 AE 15-2 %ile 81 SS 113

Test of Written Spelling: GE 4.4 SA 9-10 SQ 77
Predictable Words GE 5.4 SA 10-9 SS 84
Unpredictable Words GE 3.7 SA 9-0 SS 70

Test of Written Language: Written Language Quotient 113
Vocabulary %ile 50 SS 100
Thematic Maturity %ile 84 SS 115
Word Usage %ile 91 SS 120
Style %ile 63 SS 105

Peabody Individual Achievement Test: Spelling GE 3.9 %ile 12 SS 82

Key Math Diagnostic Arithmetic Test: GE 7.8 AE 13-2 %ile 83 SS 114
Numeration GE 9.6 Mental Computation GE 5.2
Fractions GE 12.0 Numerical Reasoning GE 5.2
Geometry GE 9.1 Word Problems GE 12.0
Addition GE 12.0 Missing Elements GE 12.0
Subtraction GE 9.8 Money GE 10.5
Multiplication GE 7.0 Time GE 8.7
Division GE 7.6 Measurement GE 9.0

TESTING INTERPRETATION:

Learning Modality
Bobby's overall performance in **visual processing** indicates strengths in the areas of visual memory, visual discrimination, visual matching of numbers, visual memory with a written response, and visual sequencing. Bobby experienced significant deficits in the areas of visual perceptual speed discrimination of numbers and spatial relationships for age and grade expectancies.

Bobby's overall performance in **auditory processing** indicates average functioning for age and grade expectations. His strengths include the areas of auditory memory for sentences and auditory discrimination. He experienced significant deficits in the areas of auditory memory with a written response including auditory sequencing, auditory reorganization of numbers, and spelling (letter sequencing).

Both the visual and auditory learning modes appear to be strong for learning with the exception of very specific areas of processing deficits.

Reading

Bobby's overall performance in reading indicates average functioning for cognitive expectations. Primary areas of strength included word attack, word comprehension, and passage comprehension. His oral reading was fluent and he utilized his superior knowledge of phonics and syllabication in decoding unfamiliar words. He utilized context clues effectively in decoding unfamiliar words and in deriving meaning.

Written Expression

Bobby's performance in written language indicated average functioning for cognitive expectations. His primary areas of strength on the Word Usage Subtest included plurals, comparatives, verb tenses, and pronoun antecedents. Bobby's performance on the Style subtest (capitalization and punctuation) indicated average functioning for cognitive expectations. Major strengths included capitalization of proper nouns, punctuation (periods, commas). Weaknesses included the use of apostrophes.

Bobby's overall performance in spelling indicated severely deficit functioning for cognitive expectations in recognition and production of correct spelling words. A significant discrepancy exists between his ability to spell predictable (phonetic) words and unpredictable (non-phonetic) words. Bobby appears to rely heavily on visual memory skills for easier predictable words. Above the 5th grade level attempts to utilize phonics skills reveal vowel substitutions, omissions, and additions of letters. Severely deficit performance on the unpredictable words reflects ineffective reliance on visual configuration and phonics.

On the expressive writing sample, Bobby's use of higher level vocabulary words was in the average range. He utilized fourteen higher level vocabulary words. His performance on the thematic maturity subtest (story content and structure) was in the average range. He utilized 13 of the 20 evaluation items in his story including a title, personal names of main characters, theme of building a new life.

Mathematics

Bobby's overall performance in mathematics indicates functioning in the average range for cognitive expectations. Primary areas of deficit included mental computation and numerical reasoning. He appears to understand the algorithms of addition, subtraction, multiplication, and division. He appears to know basic mathematics facts of addition, subtraction, multiplication, and division.

On the applied problems subtest, Bobby's performance revealed poor abstract mental calculation skills and poor abstract reasoning ability. He demonstrated understanding of computation of two-step problems and good ability to calculate problems dealing with money, time, and measurement. He revealed the ability to sort through extraneous information to isolate basic information required to solve problems. Bobby revealed an understanding of relationship concepts that indicate which mathematical process is required in problem solving.

Summary

In summary, Bobby appears to be experiencing very specific learning modality deficits in the area of auditory memory including sequencing of letters, auditory reorganization and sequencing of numbers. He experiences difficulty with visual perceptual speed discrimination of numbers and spatial relationships.

Bobby appears to be functioning commensurate with his above-average cognitive abilities except in the areas of spelling and some mathematical reasoning areas. Psychological processing deficits appear to be impacting the areas of spelling and mathematical reasoning.

_____

Educational Examiner

BEHAVIOR EVALUATION

Bobby is a 12 year, 6-month-old sixth grade student with a history of behavior problems. At St. Martin Elementary School, Bobby had been in conflict with the teachers (Catholic Sisters) and authority figures since he entered kindergarten. When he was smaller in size teachers could physically restrain him from injuring peers, but as he grew larger this option became more difficult.

Periodically, Bobby would engage in "fun" classroom activities, but most of the time he refused to participate preferring to draw, play with toys, read books or comic books. In primary grades he fought over toys; pushed other children out of swings if he wanted one; hit, kicked, pinched, and bit other children and the teacher when she interfered. Bobby, also, used verbal abuse including swearing and name calling. His attitude was fierce and aggressive. At St. Martin's during primary grades a teacher aide was hired by Bobby's parents to provide one-to-one supervision, entertainment, etc.

During 4th and 5th grades, Bobby was gradually moved from part-time "time out room" accompanied by a teacher aide to full-time behavior management classroom. In the special classroom, Bobby refused to obey, refused to complete any classwork, and was verbally and physically aggressive to peers and authority figures. For short periods during the day, he would become engrossed in art activities such as drawing with markers. When school officials indicated to parents that they were initiating Special Education procedures to have Bobby sent to the Special Day School his parents transferred him to Monroe Elementary School.

Behaviors at Monroe mirrored those at St. Martin's. Bobby spent most of the first six weeks in the time-out room. During an attempt to pull him away from aggressive actions against another student, he broke the teacher's arm. (See file for observation charts and checklists.)

_____
Resource Room Teacher

EVALUATION SUMMARY

Bobby's current intellectual functioning falls within the superior range. He experiences weaknesses in auditory memory and attention, and the ability to abstractly manipulate number concepts. Bobby appears to be experiencing very specific learning modality deficits in the area of auditory memory and sequencing of letters and numbers.

Academically, Bobby appears to be functioning commensurate with his above-average cognitive abilities except in the areas of spelling and some mathematical reasoning areas. Information processing deficits appear to be negatively impacting progress in spelling and math reasoning.

Behaviorally, Bobby is uncontrollable; verbally and physically aggressive to peers and authority figures. This is a long standing pattern of behavior problems. He is a clear and present danger to others in the regular classroom.

_____
Case Manager

Diagnosis: _____

Appendix D

EVALUATION REPORT: DREW

Age: 7 Years, 9 Months   Grade: 2nd grade   Date: December , 20__

BACKGROUND AND EDUCATIONAL CONCERNS

REASONS FOR REFERRAL:
Drew is a 7 year, 9-month-old second grade student attending Washington Elementary School. The primary reasons for the school's request to have Drew evaluated include short attention span, significant problems with any writing task (e.g., copying work from the board and/or textbook), and problems with mathematics. Teachers indicate that he seems bright.

Drew is functioning in the lower third of his class in all academic areas. He received failing grades in mathematics, spelling, and language the second grading period. Behaviorally, Drew gets along well with peers and adults. He appears rather shy, but has a good sense of humor.

HEALTH:
Drew's immunizations are current. An intramural physical examination indicated no medical concerns. He has a history of ear infections and seasonal allergy problems.

VISION AND HEARING SCREENING:
School screenings indicate adequate visual (with glasses) and auditory acuities.

SPEECH AND LANGUAGE SCREENING:
Screening indicates speech and language skills are within normal limits

BEHAVIOR HISTORY:
In the classroom Drew is somewhat shy. His attention span is short and he seems tired after concentrating for a brief period. He has several "buddies" with whom he has been friends since preschool days, and who appreciate his subtle humor. He works well in a small group, particularly with his "buddies."

SOCIO-ECONOMIC AND HOME INFORMATION:

English is the language of the home. Drew is the only child of professional parents, an accountant and a broker. The family lives in a new upper-middle class suburban housing area, just down the block from Drew's "buddies". There are no obvious social or economic environmental concerns.

Drew's parents keep him busy in intramural sports, Boy Scouts, and summer league activities. They enjoy Sunday afternoon "family activities". Drew has an entertainment center in his interconnecting bedroom and play room, and unlimited toys and games which he enjoys playing with his friends. Drew does have several regular chores—emptying the waste baskets into appropriate recycling bins in the garage, making his bed, picking up his toys before he goes to bed, and keeping his room tidy. He is supervised by the housekeeper until his parents get home from work.

CURRENT MULTIDISCIPLINARY EVALUATION

This evaluation includes assessments in the areas of intelligence, perception and memory, academic achievement, and social development.

PSYCHOLOGICAL REPORT

TESTS ADMINISTERED:

Wechsler Intelligence Scale for Children Revised (WISC-R)

Verbal IQ	101	Performance IQ	91	Full Scale IQ	97
Information	10	Picture Completion	10		
Similarities	13	Picture Arrangement	11		
Arithmetic	10	Block Design	7		
Vocabulary	11	Object Assembly	8		
Comprehension	12	Coding	7		
Digit Span	6	Mazes	7		

Peabody Picture Vocabulary Test-Revised (PPVT): AE 8-3   SS   111

Beery Visual Motor Integration Test   AE 6-0

TESTING INTERPRETATION:

Drew is a delightful seven year, nine-month-old second grade student. He is rather shy, but rapport was easily established. Drew conscientiously attempted every task presented, however, he tired easily during the performance subtests. He indicated that his glasses were new and he was not used to them.

Results of the **WISC-R** indicate Drew's overall cognitive functioning is within the average range. Verbal expressive skills were within the average range, while psychomotor skills were within the lower limits of the average range. Relative strengths in verbal expressive skills were noted in verbal concept formation, practical knowledge and social judgment. A significant weakness was noted in auditory sequencing of numbers. Psychomotor skills involving visual-motor perception and coordination of space relationships and symbols, and the ability to learn symbols and recreate them were difficult for Drew. He also experienced difficulty with tasks requiring visual planning and following a visual pattern.

The results of the **PPVT** indicated that Drew functioned above age expectations in receptive language. On the **Beery,** Drew experienced significant difficulties functioning 1 1/2 years deficit for age expectations in observing and reproducing shapes. Difficulties were consistent with his functioning on the psychomotor skills of the WISC-R.

In summary, Drew's overall cognitive functioning is within the average range with weaknesses in visual-motor skills and spatial relationships. Receptive language appears to be an area of strength.

_____

School Psychologist

PSYCHO-EDUCATIONAL REPORT

TESTS ADMINISTERED:

Slingerland Screening Test Form B

Far Point Copying	poor
Near Point Copying	poor
Visual Memory	92%
Visual Discrimination	75%
Visual Memory to Written	33%
Auditory Memory to Written	poor
Auditory Discrimination	94%
Auditory Visual Association	72%

Woodcock-Johnson Psycho-Educational Battery: Tests of Cognitive Ability
Visual Perceptual Speed Cluster CA 7-9 AE 6-10 GE 1.6 %ile 17 SS 86
      Visual Matching   Grade Range 1.0-1.5
      Spatial Relationships   Grade Range 1.5-2.0
Auditory Memory Cluster   CA 7-9 AE 9-0 GE 4.0 %ile 89 SS 118
      Memory for Sentences   Grade Range 12.9
      Numbers Reversed   Grade Range 1.0-2.0

Woodcock-Johnson Psycho-Educational Battery: Tests of Achievement

Reading Cluster	GE 2.5	AE	7-8	%ile	46	SS	98
Mathematics	GE 2.0	AE	7-2	%ile	22	SS	88
Written Expression	GE 2.2	AE	7-8	%ile	43	SS	97

Test of Written Spelling (TWS): GE 1.3   SA 6-7   SQ 84

Test of Written Language (TOWL): Written Language Quotient 90

Vocabulary	%ile 5	SS	75
Thematic Maturity	%ile 25	SS	90
Word Usage	%ile 25	SS	90
Style	%ile 63	SS	105

Silvaroli Informal Reading Inventory Form D

Oral Reading	Word Recognition	Comprehension
1st grade	Independent	80%
2nd grade	Frustration	80%
3rd grade	Frustration	20%

Durrell Analysis of Reading Difficulties: Listening Comprehension 5th grade

TESTING INTERPRETATION:

Learning Modality
    Several instruments were administered to assess Drew's auditory and visual processing skills. On the **Woodcock-Johnson,** his performance on visual speed tasks indicated functioning in the below average range for age expectations. Both visual matching of numbers and spatial relationships were difficult for him.
    Drew's performance on auditory memory tasks indicated above average functioning for age expectations. Auditory memory subtest scores, however, reveal a significant discrepancy among skills. On the memory for sentences task, Drew scored at the 12.9 GE, while on the numbers reversed task he scored at the 1.0-2.0 GE. Drew's performance indicates excellent imme-

diate auditory recall for words, but poor auditory reorganization skills especially with numbers.

On the **Slingerland**, Drew experienced considerable difficulties with both near-point and far-point copying. Drew's performance on the visual memory test was very good, but he drew lines to assist in visual tracking which seemed to be very difficult. Though visual discrimination performance was adequate, he experienced three letter transpositions (self-corrected one). Drew experienced significant difficulty on the visual memory to written task including: following the directions, spatial organization, letter and number reversals, substitutions, omissions, transpositions, additions, and inversions.

Though Drew's auditory discrimination skills are good, he experienced difficulty in organizing his page (following directions), transposing numbers, and reversing letters. Auditory memory to written tasks presented significant difficulties for Drew including all of the previously mentioned problems associated with a written task. Auditory visual association is nearly adequate, however, responses indicate that he is drawing lines to assist with visual tracking and experiences many letter transpositions.

Reading and Listening Comprehension

Drew's overall performance in reading indicated average range functioning for age, grade, and cognitive expectations. On the **Silvaroli**, Drew's performance indicated oral reading word recognition instructional level at the 1st grade level. At the 2nd grade level he mispronounced two words and omitted eight words, and at the 3rd grade level he mispronounced 3 words and omitted 23 of the 105 words in the passage. He read quickly and omitted the words without a pause in reading. Word recognition appears to be an areas of significant weakness.

Comprehension is an area of relative strength. Despite orally reading at frustration level at the 2nd grade level, his comprehension was well within instructional level.

Listening performance on the **Durrell** indicated instructional level at the 5th grade level. On the comprehension check he scored 80% indicating excellent listening skills especially on areas of interest to him.

Written Expression

Deficiency areas in manuscript writing indicated on the Slingerland included sizing, spatial organization, spacing, and letter formation. In writing words he committed the following errors: letter additions, transpositions, substitutions, and letter omissions.

The **TWS** performance indicated functioning in the below-average range for age and grade expectations in spelling. Drew's score was depressed due to reversals. He performed one year below age and grade expectations on the predictable (phonetic) words and could spell none of the unpredictable (non-phonetic) words. Spelling appears to be an area of significant weakness.

Drew's performance in written language (knowledge of rules) on the **Woodcock-Johnson** indicated average range functioning for age and grade expectations, however, a significant discrepancy exists among the subscores. On punctuation, capitalization, and word usage, Drew scored in the 3rd grade range, while in spelling his scores were at the 1.5 grade level.

On the **TOWL** Drew's overall performance indicates average range functioning for age expectations, though significant discrepancies exist among the subtests. Drew demonstrated above average knowledge of punctuation and capitalization rules, but he did not utilize those rules in his expressive writing sample. On word usage knowledge, Drew performed above-average in knowledge of verb tenses, plurals, and comparatives. On the expressive writing sample, Drew's performance was in the low average range in thematic maturity and significantly below average range in use of higher level vocabulary. Informal evaluation reveals that Drew did not write an integrated story, but rather, described the pictures. He did not write in complete sentences, nor utilize proper punctuation and capitalization. Drew's thoughts were connected by the use of conjunctions.

Mathematics

Drew's performance in mathematics indicates below average functioning for age and grade expectations. Calculation scores were at the 1.5-2.0 grade range, while applied problems was at the 2.5 GE. He experienced significant difficulty with calculation in addition and subtraction. He has not mastered the basic math facts, experiences difficulty with alignment of numbers, and experiences difficulty with the algorithms. He cannot regroup in addition or subtraction, and experienced difficulty with money, time, and fractions. Applied problems were a relative strength for Drew in areas of numerical reasoning, mental calculation, and word problems.

Summary

Drew experienced strengths and significant deficits in both the auditory and the visual learning modes. Auditory and visual memory in isolation were areas of strength, but became significant weaknesses when paired with a written response. Visual discrimination deficits among letters and numbers are significantly impacting his academic functioning. He experiences difficulty with following directions, spatial organization, visual tracking, and very simple visual-motor tasks. Drew is experiencing extremely significant perceptual integration deficits.

Academically, Drew's perceptual integration deficits seem to be negatively impacting his skill acquisition in reading word recognition, mathematics calculation, and all expressive writing tasks. Academics that depend on reasoning such as reading and listening comprehension, and mathematics reasoning reveal above grade level functioning.

_____

Educational Examiner

SOCIAL DEVELOPMENT

TEST ADMINISTERED:
Teacher Behavioral Observation

TESTING INTERPRETATION

An informal social development assessment indicated that Drew was functioning at the 8 year old developmental level. He is friendly, selective in his choice of friends, and has several "best buddies." He likes organized games in small groups, but also enjoys team sports. Drew uses language as his medium of interaction. He understands the peer group norms of his social strata. He has a good sense of humor.

Emotionally, Drew is sensitive to the feelings of others especially his buddies. He is sensitive to criticism and ridicule, and is quite concerned about his academic failure. He is happy much of the time and secure in many areas. Drew is, however, beginning to feel insecure about school now that written expression takes precedence over oral language.

_____

Resource Room Teacher

EVALUATION SUMMARY

Drew is a 7 year, 9-month-old second grade student. Current psychological evaluation indicates average range **cognitive functioning** with average verbal skills and low average psychomotor skills. Drew experienced significant difficulty on visual-motor and visual discrimination skills, and spatial relationships. Auditory memory tasks with a written response also presented significant difficulties.

Academic assessment in **reading** indicated significant weakness in word recognition (lst grade level) and strength in reading comprehension

(2nd grade level). **Listening comprehension** is an area of significant strength (5th grade level). On written composition skills of knowledge of capitalization, punctuation, and word usage in isolation, Drew functioned within the average range. On the **written expression** sample, Drew did not use these composition mechanics skills accurately. He experienced significant difficulty with **handwriting** and in story construction. **Spelling** is an area of significant weakness. Drew's **math** performance appears to be an area of weakness with a significant difference between his abilities in calculation and applied problems.

Drew's **perceptual motor** problems especially visual processing problems significantly interfered with his academic functioning in areas that require visual discrimination, visual memory, and visual memory with a written response.

Social development and behavior appear to be areas of strength. Language skills in social communication and humor are areas of strength. Drew is feeling some concerns regarding his academic failure.

Case Manager

Diagnosis: _____

Appendix E

EVALUATION REPORTS:
TESTING INFORMATION

TESTS USED IN EVALUATION REPORTS

I. Evaluation Report: Diana

Intelligence Tests:
Stanford-Binet Intelligence Scale
Boehm Test of Basic Concepts
Human Figure Drawing Test

Language Test:
Peabody Picture Vocabulary Test

Information Processing Tests:
Test of Visual-Motor Integration
Woodcock-Johnson Psycho-Educational Battery: Tests of Cognitive Ability
Slingerland Screening Test: PreReading, Revised

Academic Tests:
Developmental Tasks for Kindergarten Readiness
Test of Early Reading

II. EVALUATION REPORT: DEBBIE

Intelligence Test:
Wechsler Intelligence Scale for Children Revised (WISC-R)

Information Processing Test:
Slingerland Screening Test: PreReading, Revised

Academic Tests:
Brigance Diagnostic Inventory of Early Development
Brigance Diagnostic Inventory of Basic Skills: Reading Readiness
Brigance Diagnostic Inventory of Basic Skills: Math Readiness
Test of Early Reading

Language Test:
*Northwest Syntax Screening Test

Social Skills Test:
*Vineland Social Maturity Scale

III. EVALUATION REPORT: BOBBY

Intelligence Test:
*Wechsler Intelligence Scale

Information Processing Tests:
*Wepman Auditory Discrimination
*Slingerland Screening Test
*Woodcock-Johnson Psycho-Educational Battery: Tests of Cognitive Ability

Academic Tests:
*Woodcock Reading Mastery Test
*Test of Written Spelling
*Test of Written Language
*Peabody Individual Achievement Test
*KeyMath Diagnostic Arithmetic Test

IV. EVALUATION REPORT: DREW

Intelligence Test:
*Wechsler Intelligence Scale for Children-Revised (WISC-R)

Language Test:
*Peabody Picture Vocabulary Test-Revised

Information Processing Test:
*Beery Visual Motor Integration Test
*Slingerland Screening Test
*Woodcock-Johnson Psycho-Educational Battery: Tests of Cognitive Ability

Academic Tests:
*Woodcock-Johnson Psycho-Educational Battery: Tests of Achievement
*Test of Written Language
*Classroom Reading Inventory (Silvaroli)
*Durrell Analysis of Reading Difficulty

SUMMARIES OF TESTS USED IN THE
EVALUATION REPORTS

1. Bender Visual-Motor Gestalt Test, 2nd edition. (BVMGT-2)

The original test was published in 1938 by Bender; and in 1972 by Koppitz; and has been a much used test over the years. The BVMGT-2 version of the test is designed to measure perceptual motor skills. It intends to determine visual-motor gestalt functioning in children, neurological maturation, and organic brain defects. The test consists of a copying test that requires test takers to reproduce designs individually on stimulus cards that remain in view. The test is untimed. The three supplementary tests are a design recall subtest, a motor subtest, and a perception subtest. The BVMGT-2 is norm-referenced to assess ages 4–0 to 85+ years. (Salvia, et al., 2007),

Brannigan, G. & Deckler, S. (2003). *Bender Visual Motor Gestalt Test-Second Edition* (BVMGT-2). New York, NY: The American Orthopsychiatric Assn. Inc.

****

2. Boehm Test of Basic Concepts-Revised. (BTBC-R)

The BTBC-R is an individually administered, norm-referenced test designed to measure children's mastery of verbal instruction and for early school success (grades K-2). The relational concepts measured on the test include size, direction, position in space, quantity, and time–concepts commonly found in preschool and primary instructional materials. Another version of the test, *Boehm Test of Basic Concepts, Preschool-Third Edition* was designed specifically for children ages 3–0 to 5–11 years. The *Boehm-3 Preschool* is normed on a nationally representative sample. (McLean, Wolery, & Bailey, 2004).

Boehm, A. (1986). *Boehm Test of Basic Concepts-Revised.* San Antonio, TX: The Psychological Corp.
Boehm, A. (1986). *Boehm Test of Basic Concepts, Preschool-Third Edition.* San Antonio, TX: The Psychological Corp.

3. Brigance Diagnostic Inventory of Early Development-II (IED-II)

The Brigance Assessment System has been revised to include criterion-referenced tests, norm-referenced diagnostic tests, screening tests, and management systems for monitoring progress. Until its recent revision, the *Brigance Diagnostic Inventory of Early Development* was exclusively a criterion-referenced measure, widely used in assessment of school readiness skills and in developing IEPs.

With the publication of the *Brigance Diagnostic Inventory of Early Development-II (IED-II)* the tests is also norm-referenced and validated for children from birth to seven years of age (to 7–0 years). There are forty-six different assessments within the CRT portion of IED-II clustered into five domains: Motor, language, academic, cognitive, daily living, social-emotional, and adaptive behavior. The NRT version of IED-II does not test all CRT skills in the hierarchies. Thus, to use the IED-II, teachers will use the **IED-II Classroom Implementation Kit** which includes Brigance IED-II Criterion Referenced Skill areas with comprehensive skills ssequences in Developmental skills sections and Early Academic Skills sections (e.g., Readiness, Basic Reading Skills, Manuscript Writing, Basic Math).

(Curriculum Associates, INC: The Brigance System; Assessment Programs; Brigance IED-II Standardized Assessment; Brigance Inventories (ud). Retrieved on April 27, 2009 from www.curriculumassociates.com/ products/Brigance Overview.asp7

Note: Evaluation Report: Debbie used the CRT version of the Brigance in developmental areas, reading readiness, and math readiness.

****

4. Classroom Reading Inventory, 11th Edition (CRI)

The *Classroom Reading Inventory* provides a quick, easy-to-use, and accurate diagnosis of the reading levels of individuals K-12 students and adults. The Informal Reading Inventory identifies students' functioning levels: Independent, Instructional, Frustration, and Listening Comprehension. The informal test is designed to be administered in about 15 minutes. Reading word recognition as well as reading comprehension are assessed. The Classroom Reading Inventory includes the stories/passages for the students to read as well as the comprehension questions for the teacher to ask. The system provides easy-to-use down loadable forms for teachers to use during the test administration. The CRI can be used to assess K-12 grade students and adults.

Wheelock, W., Campbell, C. & Silvaroli, N. (2008). Classroom Reading Inventory, 11th edition. Dubuque, IA: McGraw-Hill. Retrieved 2-27-2009 from www.classroomreadinginventory.com/about.html

****

5. Detroit Tests of Learning Aptitude-4th Edition (DTLA-4)

The DTLA-4* was designed to assess a variety of cognitive abilities or learning aptitudes in children ages 6-0 through 17–11 years. There are ten subtests grouped into three domains: Linguistic, Attentional, and Motoric. The test is an individually administered, norm-referenced test, and standard scores are provided for each subtest. There are two other versions of the DTLA:

Hammill, D. & Bryant, B. (2005). *Detroit Tests of Learning Aptitude-Primary-Third Edition.* (DTLA-P-3) Austin, TX: PRO-ED. (for ages 3-0 through 9-11 years)

Hammill, D. & Bryant, B. (1991). *Detroit Test of Learning Aptitude-Adults.* (DTLA-A). Austin, TX: PRO-ED. (for ages 16-0 to 79-11 years)

*Hammill, D. & Bryant, B. (1998). Detroit Tests of Learning Aptitude-4th Edition. (DTLA-4). Austin, TX: PRO-ED. DTLA-4. Retrieved 4-27-2009 from www.proedinc.com

****

6. Developmental Tasks for Kindergarten Readiness-II (DTKR-II)

The DTKR-II provides objective data on a child's skills and abilities as they relate to successful performance in kindergarten. The test is individually administered to prekindergarten children (ages 4-6 to 6-2) to determine their readiness for kindergarten. The DTKR-II can be used for screening and/or diagnostic prescriptive purposes. The DTKR-II is a re-standardized, updated version of the DTKR.

Lesiak, W. & Lesiak, J. (1994). *Developmental Tasks for Kindergarten Readiness-II. Austin, TX*: PRO-ED. Retrieved 4-27-2000 from www.proedinc.com

7. Developmental Test of Visual Motor Integration-5th Edition (VMI-5)

The VMI-5 is designed to assess the integration of visual and motor skills by asking a child to copy geometric designs. This standardized, norm-referenced test has two forms: The Short Format and the Full Format tests.
The Full Format VMI-5 is intended for use with individuals ages 2 years to 18 years old; while the Short Format is often used with children ages 2-8 years old. The VMI-5 can be used to identify individuals who may be experiencing difficulties in visual-motor integration; to make appropriate referrals for needed services; and to test effectiveness of educational and other interventions. Key Features of the VMI-5 include the following: (1) It is among the few assessments that provide standard scores as low as 2–0 years. (2) The Examiner's Manual provides approximately 600 age-specific norms from birth through age 6 in gross motor, fine motor, visual and visual-motor developmental skills. (3) VMI-5 is a culture-free, non-verbal assessment that can be used with individuals of diverse environmental, educational, and linguistic backgrounds. (4) Screening administration takes about 10-15 minutes.

Beery, K., Buktenica, N. & Beery, N. (2004). The Beery-Buktenica
     Developmental Test of Visual-Motor Integration-Fifth Edition (Beery
     VMI-5). Austin, TX: PRO-ED.
     Retrieved 4-28-2009 from www.proedinc.com

****

8. Developmental Test of Visual Perception, 2nd Edition (DTVP-2)

     The DTVP-2 is the 1993 revision of Marianne Frostig's popular Developmental Test of Visual Perception (DTVP). The new edition includes numerous improvements: (a) is suitable for children ages 4-0 through 10-0 years, (b) measures both visual perception and visual motor integration of skills, (c) has eight subsets; and (d) is based on updated theories of visual perceptual development. The DTVP-2 is reliable, valid, and nationally normed on the U.S. 1990 census data.

Hammill, D., Pearson, N. & Voress, J. (1993). *Developmental Test of Visual
     Perception*, 2nd edition (DTVP-2). Austin, TX: PRO-ED. Retrieved
     on 4-2-2009 from http://www.proedinc.com

9. *Durrell Analysis of Reading Difficulty (DARD)-3rd Edition*

This test was designed to screen for reading problems. The "Durrell" has a long history, since the early 1950s as an Informal Reading Inventory with numerous other subtests designed to help diagnose children's reading difficulties. A continuing strength of the test is its set of behavioral checklists. The test has 12 subtests including the following: Oral reading, silent reading, listening comprehension, sounds in isolation, spelling of words, phonic spelling of words, visual memory of words, identifying sounds in words, pre-reading phonics abilities inventories.

The test was standardized and appropriate for students in grades 1-6, or students functioning at those levels. However, since the most recent edition was published in 1980, the test would best be used as an informal test. There are numerous current tests with current norms that are preferred. (Pierangelo & Giuliani, 1998).

Durrell, D. & Catterson, J. (1980). *Durrell Analysis of Reading Difficulty*, 3rd Edition. New York: The Psychological Corp.

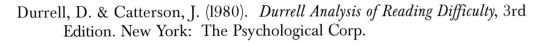

10. *Fisher-Logemann Test of Articulation Competence*

The *Fisher-Logemann Test of Articulation Competence* can be used to determine information about an individual's phonological system in about 45 minutes. For individuals from preschool through adulthood, the test provides both a method for eliciting spontaneous responses that are prestructured for required phonemic occurrence and a framework for analysis of data. All of the English phonemes are examined according to syllabic function—prevocalic, intervocalic, and postvocalic. Analysis recognizes and accounts for regional and ethnic differences.

Fisher, H. & Logemann, J. (2009). Fisher-Logemann Test of Articulation Competence. Academic Communication Associates, Inc. Retrieved 4-26-2009 from www.acadcom.com/scripts/default.asp

11. *Full Range Test of Visual Motor Integration (FRTVMI)*

The FRTVMI assesses the ability to accurately relate visual stimuli to motor responses. The test is a highly reliable measure of visual-motor integration skills that not only covers the full range of school ages, but includes norms appropriate for special education students in the age range of 19-21 years. Its norms use the 2000 U.S. Census data and includes adults as well as children from age 5-0 through 74 years. The FRTVMI requires the person being tested to copy a series of increasingly complicated designs. Key features include the following: (a) completely nonverbal; (b) shows the absence of gender and ethnic bias; (c) is appropriate for group or individual administration; and (d) testing time is about 5 - 15 minutes.

Hammill, D., Pearson, N., Voress, J. and Reynolds, C. (2006). *Full Range Test of Visual Motor Integration (FRTVMI)*. Austin, TX: PRO-ED. Retrieved 4-27-2009 from http://www.proedinc.com

****

12. Human Figure Drawing Test (HFDD)

Figure drawings are projective diagnostic techniques in which an individual is instructed to draw a person, an object or a situation so that cognitive, interpersonal, or psychological functioning can be assessed. There are a number of variations of this projective technique and a number of scoring systems. The Koppitz (1972) scoring system was used to score the *Human Figure Drawing Test* for cognitive maturation (indicated by the school psychologist in Evaluation Report: Diana). *The Bender Gestalt Test with the Human Figure Drawing Test for Young Children: A Manual for Use with the Koppitz Scoring System* (Koppitz, 1972) was used as one of several assessments to determine the child's cognitive functioning. Koppitz Scoring System is also used for screening and diagnostic uses with emotionally disturbed, brain damaged, or perceptually disabled children ages 5 years to 11 years old.

There has been much debate over the reliability and validity of figure drawing tests (and projective tests in general). However, when a structured scoring system is used the HFD/DAP have been found to be a reliable measure, especially for cognitive development in children. There is relatively little support for using figure drawings to examine personality characteristics, self-image issues, or personality dysfunctions (Encyclopedia of Mental Disorders Del-Fi, nd).

Koppitz, E. (1972). *The Bender Gestalt Test with the Human Figure Drawing Test for Young School Children: A Manual for Use with the Koppitz Scoring System*. ERIC # ED074645 Retrieved 4-27-2009 from www.eric.ed.gov:80

Encyclopedia of Mental Disorders Del-FI. (nd). *Figure Drawings.* Retrieved
4-27-2009 from www.minddisorders.com/Del-Fi/Figure-drawings.html

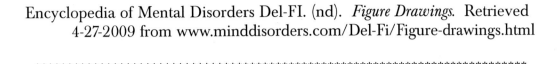

13. *KeyMath Revised/Normative Update (KeyMath-R/NU)*

KeyMath-R/NU is an individually administered, norm-referenced test that also
offers some of the features of a criterion referenced assessment. Test items are
linked to skill domains and instructional objectives. There are two forms of
the test, each contains 13 subtests that are organized into three major areas of
mathematics: Basic Concepts, Operations, and Applications.
The *KeyMath-R/NU* is designed for K–9 grades, and ages 5–0 through 22–11
years. The *KeyMath-R/NU* is a broad-based mathematics test for the identification of strengths and weaknesses in mathematics skill development.
(McLoughlin & Lewis, 2008)

Connolly, A., Nachtman, W. & Pritchett, E. (1998). KeyMath Revised/
Normative Update. Circle pines, MN: American Guidance Service.

14. *Northwestern Syntax Screening Test (NSST)*

The NSST is a norm-referenced test designed to identify problems in either
receptive or expressive syntax. Syntax, as defined in this test includes morphology. It is an individual test that is appropriate for young children ages
3–0 to 7–4 years. Two subtests are included: Receptive and Expressive grammatical form and structure. The NSST is a screening test, thus, its purpose is
to identify children in need of further assessment. It is best used as an informal measure because of lack of information about technical quality.
(McLoughlin & Lewis, 2008).

Lee, L. (1971). Northwestern Syntax Screening Test. Evanston, IL:
Northwestern University Press.

15. *Peabody Individual Achievement Test-Revised/Normative Update* (PIAT-R-NU)

The *PIAT-R-NU* is an individually administered, norm-referenced instrument
designed to provide a wide-ranging screening measure of academic achieve-

ment in six content areas: Math, reading recognition, reading comprehension, spelling, general information, and written expression. The test can be used with students in kindergarten through grade 12. The most recent edition of the PIAT is not a new edition of the test, but a normative update of the 1989 edition of the PIAT-R. (McLoughlin & Lewis, 2008)

Markwardt, F. (1998). *Peabody Individual Achievement Test-Revised-Normative Update.* Circle Pines, MN: American Guidance Service.

****

16. *Peabody Picture Vocabulary Test-III (PPVT-III)*

The PPVT-III is an individually administered, norm-referenced measure of receptive vocabulary. The test assesses a child's understanding of spoken words in standard English, by having the child point to the correct item on a variety of cards. Thus, the test is nonverbal test for the student. The test has been used as a screening test of verbal ability. The PPVT-III is an untimed power test. (Salvia et al., 2007)

Dunn, L. & Dunn, L. with Williams, K. (1997). *Peabody Picture Vocabulary Test-III.* Circle Pines, MN: American Guidance Service.

****

17. *Slingerland Screening Tests for Identifying Children with Specific Language Disability*

The <u>Slingerland Screening Tests</u> for individuals or groups are designed to identify children who may have a specific language disability. There are Forms A, B, C, D which cover grades 1st-6th. There is also a specific form for preschool level and one for middle school. The test primarily assesses information processing skills that underlie academic skills rather than the academic areas. This is an informal test to assess subtests 1–5: visual-motor integration, visual memory, visual discrimination, visual memory linked with motor coordination. Subtests 6–8 assess: auditory-visual discrimination and auditory memory -to-motor coordination. Form D contains a subtest for evaluating orientation in time and space as well as the ability to express oneself in writing. All forms also contain individual auditory tests to identify those children unable to recall or pronounce words correctly or unable to express organized thoughts either spoken or written language. The *Slingerland*

Screening Tests are informal tests on school-like tasks.
(Pierangelo & Giuliani, 1998).

Slingerland, B. (2005). *Slingerland Screening Tests for Identifying Children with Specific Language Disability.* Cambridge, MA: Educator's Publishing Service, Inc.

****

18. Stanford-Binet Intelligence Scale - 5th Edition (SB5)

The *Stanford-Binet Intelligence Scale -5th Edition* (2003) is an individually administered assessment of intelligence and cognitive abilities for individuals from age 2 years to 85+ years. The SB5 assesses five areas of cognitive ability: Fluid Reasoning, Knowledge, Quantitative Reasoning, Visual-Spatial Processing, and Working Memory. There are two domain scales: Nonverbal IQ (combines the 5 nonverbal subtests); Verbal IQ (combines the results of the 5 verbal subtests). The Full Scale IQ combines all ten subtest results.

An additional form, the *Stanford-Binet Intelligence Scales for Early Childhood* (Early SB5) (2003) assesses children ages 2–0 to 7–3 years (2–0 to 5–11 years for full battery; 6–0 to 7–3 years for the abbreviated battery). The Early SB5 addresses the same five areas of cognitive ability as the SB5.

This revised edition of the Early SB5 has improved low end items for better measurement of low functioning children and adults. Enhanced non-verbal/low-verbal content requires no (or minimal) verbal responses from the examinee, so is useful in assessment for LEP/ELL, deaf and hard of hearing, and autism. These assessments are ideal for measuring basic psychological processes in problem-solving models like Response to Intervention (RTI).

Roid, G. (2003). *Stanford-Binet Intelligence Scales-Fifth Edition* (SB5). Itaska, IL: The Riverside Publishing Company. Retrieved 2-27-2009 from www.riverpub.com/products/sb5/scoring.html

****

19. Test of Early Mathematics Ability-Third Edition (TEMA-3)

The TEMA-3 is a norm-referenced standardized test for individual administration designed to identify children between the ages of 3-0 and 8-11 years who are functioning significantly behind or ahead of their peers in development of mathematical thinking. The test results should identify strengths and weaknesses in mathematical thinking, suggest instructional practices, and document children's progress in learning math. (Salvia et al., 2007)

Ginsburg, H. Baroody, A. (2003). *Test of Early Mathematics Ability-Third Edition.* (TEMA-3). Austin, TX: PRO-ED.

****

20. *Test of Early Reading Ability-III* (TERA-3)

The TERA-3 is a norm-referenced standardized test for individual administration to identify those children between the ages of 3-6 and 8-6 who are functioning significantly below their peers in emergent literacy and reading development. The test was designed to identify strengths and weaknesses in three skill areas: (1) alphabet knowledge, (2) knowledge of conventions of print, and (3) reading comprehension. (Salvia et al., 2007)

Reid, D., Hresko, W. & Hammill, D. (2001). *Test of Early Reading Ability-III* (TERA-3). Austin, TX: PRO-ED.

****

21. *Test of Written Language-4th Edition (TOWL-4)*

The TOWL-4 is a norm-referenced, comprehensive diagnostic test of written expression for students ages 9–0 through 17–11 years. It is used to (a) identify students who write poorly, (b) determine students' particular strengths and weaknesses in various writing abilities, (c) document students' progress in special writing programs. The TOWL-4 has two forms (A and B), each of which contains seven subtests. Subtests 1–5 use contrived formats; subtests 6–7 use a spontaneously written story to assess important aspects of language. The subtests include the following: Vocabulary, spelling & punctuation, logical sentences, sentence combining, contextual conventions, and story composition.

The TOWL-4 was normed on demographic characteristics of the U.S. population in 2005; new normative data was collected in 2006–2007. The new edition includes grade-level based norms as well as age-based norms. The test items were evaluated to eliminate bias. (Silvia, et al., 2008)

Hammill, D. & Larsen, S. (2009). *Test of Written Language-Fourth Edition.* (TOWL-4). Austin, TX: PRO-ED. Retrieved 4-28-2009 from http://www.proedinc.com

22. *Test of Written Spelling-Fourth Edition (TWS-4)*

The Revised TWS-4 is a norm-referenced test of spelling administered using a dictated word format. The TWS-4 now has two alternate or equivalent forms (A and B) which make it more useful in teach-test-teach situations. The TWS-4 is appropriate for students in grades 1–12, as well as for students in remedial programs. The TWS-4 was developed after a review of 2000 spelling rules. The words to be spelled were drawn from 10 basal spelling programs and popular graded word lists. The TWS-4 can be administered in about 20 minutes to either groups or individuals and results in standard scores, percentiles, spelling ages, and spelling grade equivalents. Changes to the fourth edition of this test included doing away with having two separate tests: predictable and unpredictable words.

Larsen, S., Hammill, D. & Moats, L. (1999). TWS-4: *Test of Written Spelling-Fourth Edition.* Austin, TX: PRO-ED. Retrieved 4-28-2009 from http://www.proedinc.com

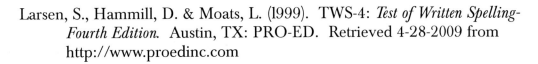

23. *Vineland Adaptive Behavior Scales, Second Edition (Vineland II)*

The Vineland Adaptive Behavior Scales (VABS) (1984) was an extensive revision of the Vineland Social Maturity Scale. The Vineland II is the second edition of the VABS (1984). This instrument is the leading instrument for supporting the diagnosis of intellectual and developmental disabilities. The Expanded Interview Form can be used to evaluate individuals ages 0–90 years. The Teacher Rating Form was designed for individuals ages 3–0 through 21–11 years. The Vineland II is a norm-referenced test to assess four domains of skills: Communication, Daily Living Skills, Socialization, Motor Skills. There is an optional domain scale, Maladaptive Behavior Index. Not only does the Vineland II aid in diagnosis, but it gives valuable information for developing educational and treatment plans.

Sparrows, S., Cicchetti, D. & Balla, D. (2005). *Vineland Adaptive Behavior Scales,* Second Edition (Vineland II). Upper Saddle River, NJ: Pearson/Prentice Hall. Retrieved 4-27-2009 from www.pearsonassessments.com

24. The Wechsler Scales of Intelligence

WISC-IV is the individual test most often used to assess general intellectual performance and specific cognitive abilities of school-aged children ages 6-0 to 16-11 years. In special education assessment, the WISC-IV is often used to gain an overall estimate of the students' current global intellectual performance. This measure may also provide information about strengths and weaknesses in specific areas of aptitude. Previous versions of the WISC-IV classified subtests as belonging either to the Verbal Scale or Performance Scale, the 4th Edition does not. The WISC-IV provides several types of scores: Overall IQ Score (Full Scale IQ); and four composite scores: Verbal Comprehension Index (Verbal IQ), Perceptual Reasoning Index (Performance IQ), Working Memory Index, and Processing Speed Index. The Wechsler tests have consistently over the years demonstrated very high reliability (especially on the Full Scale IQ), high validity, and well-normed assessments.
The Wechsler family of tests spans all age levels.

There are five Wechsler Intelligence Scales, each has been revised a number of times, as follows:

1. *Wechsler Abbreviated Scale of Intelligence* (WASI) (1999)
   for ages 6-0 to 89.
2. *The Wechsler Preschool and Primary Scale of Intelligence-III*
   (WIPPSI-III) (2002) for ages 2-6 to 7-3 years.
3. *The Wechsler Intelligence Scale for Children-IV* (WISC-IV) (2003)
   for ages 6-0 to 16-11.
4. *Wechsler Intelligence Scale for Children-Forth Edition Integrated*
   (WISC-IV-I) (2004) for children ages 6-0 to 16-11 years.
5. *Wechsler Adult Intelligence Scale-III (WAIS-III)* (1997) for ages 16-0
   to 89 years.

Wechsler, D. (2004). *Wechsler Intelligence Scale for Children- Fourth Edition* (WISC-IV). San Antonio, TX: The Psychological Corp. (Harcourt Assessment).

****

25. Wepman's Auditory Discrimination Test, Second Edition (ADT-2)

The ADT-2 is an individually administered norm-referenced screening test that assesses the child's ability to recognize the fine differences between phonemes used in English speech. The examiner reads aloud 40 pairs of words, and the child indicates, verbally or gesturally, whether the words in each pair are the "same" or "different." The entire test can be administered and scored in about 5 minutes. The ADT-2 can be used for preschool and kindergarten screening as well as elementary school assessment. (McLoughlin & Lewis, 2008)

Wepman, J. & Reynolds, N. (1987). *Wepman's Auditory Discrimination Test, second edition* (ADT-2). Los Angeles, CA: Western Psychological Services.

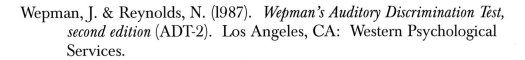

26. Woodcock-Johnson Psycho-Educational Battery-III NU (WJ-III NU)

The *Woodcock-Johnson-III NU Complete* is composed of two distinct, co-normed batteries: Tests of Cognitive Ability and Tests of Academic Achievement. The *WJ-III-NU* provides a comprehensive system for measuring general intellectual ability, specific cognitive abilities, scholastic aptitude, oral language, and academic achievement. There are 20 cognitive tests and 22 achievement tests. The test is validated on individuals from 2 years to 90+ years of age. The *WJ-III-NU* System includes the Woodcock Interpretation and Instructional Interventions Program which is "an expert system for interpreting test results that provides direct links between assessment results and evidence-based interventions." The *WJ-III-NU* Tests of Achievement match all eight areas of IDEA legislation. Additionally, the *WJ-III-NU* System test version is ideal for measuring basic psychological processes and specific skill deficits that will be the focus of intervention curriculum in problem-solving models like Response-to-Intervention (RTI). (Salvia et al., 2007)

Woodcock, R., McGrew, K. and Mather, N. (2005). Woodcock-Johnson Psycho-Educational Battery III NU: Tests of Cognitive Abilities and Tests of Achievement. Chicago, IL: The Riverside Publishing Co.

Woodcock, R. McGrew, K., & Mather, N. (n.d.). Woodcock-Johnson III-NU Complete. Retrieved 2-27-2009 from http://www.riverpub.com/products/wjIIINormativeUpdate/details.html

27. Woodcock Reading Mastery Tests-Revised/Normative Update (WRMT-R/NU)

The *WRMT-R/NU* is a norm-referenced measure that is used to pinpoint students' strengths and weaknesses in reading. The test is designed for individual administration to students in grades K–16.9 (college senior). The major content areas tested include: Reading readiness, basic reading skills (word identification and word attack), and word and passage comprehension. The WRMT-R/NU is a broad-based reading test for the identification of strengths and weaknesses in reading skill development. (McLoughlin & Lewis, 2008)

Woodcock, R. (1998). *Woodcock Reading Mastery Tests–Revised/Normative Update.* Circle Pines, MN: American Guidance Services.

REFERENCES FOR TESTS USED IN
THE EVALUATION REPORTS

Beery, K., Buktenica, N. & Beery, N. (2004). *The Beery-Buktenica Developmental Test of Visual-Motor Integration*-Fifth Edition. Austin, TX: PRO-ED.

Bender, L. (1938). *Bender Visual Motor Gestalt Test* (BVMGT). New York, NY: The American Orthopsychiatric Assn. Inc.

Boehm, A. (1986). *Boehm Test of Basic Concepts-Revised.* San Antonio, TX: The Psychological Corp.

Boehm, A. (1986). *Boehm Test of Basic Concepts, Preschool-*Third Edition. San Antonio, TX: The Psychological Corp.

Brannigan, G. & Deckler, S. (2003). *Bender Visual Motor Gestalt Test-Second Edition.* New York, NY: The American Orthopsychiatric Assn.

Brigance, A. (2004). *Brigance Inventory of Early Development-II.* N. Billerica, MA: Curriculum Associates.

Connolly, A., Nachtman, W. & Pritchett, E. (1998). *KeyMath Revised/ Normative Update.* Circle Pines, MN: American Guidance Service.

Durrell, D. & Catterson, J. (1980). *Durrell Analysis of Reading Difficulty, 3rd Edition.* New York: The Psychological Corp.

Dunn, L. & Dunn, L. with Williams, K. (1997). *Peabody Picture Vocabulary Test-III.* Circle Pines, MN: American Guidance Service.

Fisher, H. & Logemann, J. (2009). *Fisher-Logemann Test of Articulation Competence.* Academic Communication Associates, Inc.

Ginsburg, H. Baroody, A. (2003). *Test of Early Mathematics Ability - Third Edition.* Austin, TX: PRO-ED.

Hammill, D. & Bryant, B. (2005). *Detroit Tests of Learning Aptitude-Primary-Third Edition. Austin*, TX: PRO-ED.

Hammill, D. & Bryant, B. (1991). *Detroit Test of Learning Aptitude-Adults.* Austin, TX: PRO-ED.

Hammill, D. & Bryant, B. (1998). *Detroit Tests of Learning Aptitude-4th Edition.* Austin, TX: PRO-ED.

Hammill, D. & Larsen, S. (2009). *Test of Written Language-Fourth Edition.* Austin, TX: PRO-ED.

Hammill, D., Pearson, N. & Voress, J. (1993). *Developmental Test of Visual Perception, 2nd edition.* Austin, TX: PRO-ED.

Hammill, D., Pearson, N., Voress, J. & Reynolds, C. (2006). *Full Range Test of Visual Motor Integration.* Austin, TX: PRO-ED.

Koppitz, E. (1972). T*he Bender Gestalt Test with the Human Figure Drawing Test for Young School Children: A Manual for Use with the Koppitz Scoring System.* ERIC # ED074645 Retrieved 4-27-2009 from www.eric.ed.gov:80

Larsen, S., Hammill, D. & Moats, L. (1999). TWS-4: *Test of Written Spelling- Fourth Edition.* Austin, TX: PRO-ED.

Lee, L. (1971). *Northwestern Syntax Screening Test.* Evanston, IL: Northwestern University Press.

417

Lesiak, W. & Lesiak, J. (1994). *Developmental Tasks for Kindergarten Readiness-II.* Austin, TX: PRO-ED.

Markwardt, F. (1998). *Peabody Individual Achievement Test-Revised-Normative Update.* Circle Pines, MN: American Guidance Service.

Reid, D., Hresko, W. & Hammill, D. (2001). *Test of Early Reading Ability III.* Austin, TX: PRO-ED.

Roid, G. (2003). *Stanford-Binet Intelligence Scales-Fifth Edition* (SB5). Itaska, IL: The Riverside Publishing Company.

Slingerland, B. (2005). *Slingerland Screening Tests for Identifying Children with Specific Language Disability.* Cambridge, MA: Educator's Publishing Service, Inc.

Sparrows, S., Cicchetti, D. & Balla, D. (2005). *Vineland Adaptive Behavior Scales, Second Edition* (Vineland II). Upper Saddle River, NJ: Pearson/Prentice Hall.

Wechsler, D. (2004). *Wechsler Intelligence Scale for Children- Fourth Edition* (WISC-IV). San Antonio, TX: The Psychological Corp. (Harcourt Assessment).

Wepman, J. & Reynolds, N. (1987). *Wepman's Auditory Discrimination Test, Second Edition* (ADT-2). Los Angeles, CA: Western Psychological Services.

Wheelock, W., Campbell, C. & Silvaroli, N. (2008). *Classroom Reading Inventory, 11th edition.* Dubuque, IA: McGraw-Hill.

Woodcock, R. (1998). *Woodcock Reading Mastery Tests–Revised/Normative Update.* Circle Pines, MN: American Guidance Services.

Woodcock, R., McGrew, K. & Mather, N. (2005). *Woodcock-Johnson Psycho-Educational Battery III NU: Tests of Cognitive Abilities and Tests of Achievement.* Chicago, IL: The Riverside Publishing Co.

BIBLIOGRAPHY

Adelman, H. & Taylor, L. (1993). *Learning problems and learning disabilities: Moving forward.* Pacific Grove, CA: Brooks/Cole.

Alley, G. & Deshler, D. (1979). *Teaching the learning disabled adolescent: Strategies and methods.* Denver: Love.

America 2000 Goals. (1990). Goals 2000 Legislation and Related Items. Archived Information. Retrieved 8-9-2009, from <http://www.ed.gov/G2Kindex.html>

Andrews, J. & Jordan, D. (1998). Multimedia stories for deaf children. *Teaching Exceptional Children, 30* (5): 28–33.

The Annie E. Casey Foundation. (2007). Teens not attending school. *Kids Count Data Center.* Retrieved 2-20-2009, from <http://www.kidscount/org>

Arnold, J. & Dodge, H. (1994). Room for all. *The American School Board Journal, 191* (10): 22–26.

Bailey, D. & Wolery, M. (1992). *Teaching infants and preschoolers with disabilities* (2nd ed.). New York: Merrill.

Bank Street Head Start. (2006). *A tool kit for evaluating initiatives to improve child care quality.* Retrieved 2-20-2009, from < http://www.bankstreet.edu/iccc/toolkit.html>

Bank Street Head Start. (2006): *Curriculum and Assessment.* Retrieved 2-20-2009, from <www.bankstreet.edu/headstart/curriculum.html>

Barbe, W. (1961). *Educator's guide to personalized reading instruction.* Englewood Cliffs, NJ: Prentice-Hall.

Barraga, N. (1983). *Visual handicaps and learning.* Austin, TX: Educational Resources.

Barrett, T. (1972). Taxonomy of reading comprehension. *Reading 360 Monograph.* Lexington, MA: Ginn.

Bartel, N. (1997). Enhancing speaking and listening skills. In D. Hammill & N. Bartel, *Teaching students with learning and behavior problems* (6th ed.). Austin, TX: PRO-ED.

Beirne-Smith, M., Ittenbach, R., & Patton, J. (2002). *Mental retardation,* (6th ed.). Upper Saddle River: Merrill/Prentice Hall.

Bennett, J. (Sept. 26, 2004). *Curriculum in Early Childhood Education and Care.* UNESCO Policy Brief No. 26 on Early Childhood. Retrieved 2-20-2009, from < http://www. unesco.org/education/ecf/briefs.>

Berger, K. (1986). *The developing person through childhood and adolescence.* New York: Worth.

Bernstein, D. & Tiegerman, E. (1993). *Language and communication disorders in children.* New York: Merrill/Prentice Hall.

Biehler, R. & Hudson, L. (1986). *Developmental psychology.* Boston: Houghton Mifflin.

Blackhurst, A. (2001) *A functional approach to the delivery of assistive technology services.* Lexington, KY: University of Kentucky, National Assistive Technology Institute.

Boca, L. & Cervantes, H. (1989). *The bilingual special education interface.* Columbus, OH: Merrill.

Bodrova, E., Leong, D. & Shore, R. (March 2004). Child outcome standards in pre-k programs: What are standards; what is needed to make them work? *National Institute for Early Education Research.* Retrieved 2-20-2009, from <http://nieer.org/>

Boehm, A. (1986). *Boehm Test of Basic Concepts-Revised.* San Antonio, TX: The Psychological Corp.

Boehm, A. (1986). *Boehm Test of Basic Concepts, Preschool*-Third Edition. San Antonio, TX: The Psychological Corp.

Boeree, C. (2003). *Jean Piaget and cognitive development.* Retrieved 2-20-2009, from <http://webspace.ship.edu/cgboer/genpsypiaget.html>

Bos, C.S. & Vaughn, S. (1998). Strategies for teaching students with learning and/or behavior problems (4th ed.). Boston: Allyn & Bacon.

Brannigan, G. & Deckler, S. (2003). *Bender Visual Motor Gestalt Test*-Second Edition (BVMGT-2). New York, NY: The American Orthopsychiatric Assn. Inc.

Brehony, K. (2008). A history of preschool education in Europe. *European Primary School Association.* Retrieved 2-20-2009, from <www.epsaweb.org/preschool/education.htm>

Brett, A. (1998). Educational technology. In C. Bos & S. Vaughn, *Strategies for teaching students with learning and behavior problems* (4th ed.). Boston: Allyn & Bacon.

Britner, S. & Pajares, F. (2001). Self-efficacy, beliefs, motivation, race, and gender in middle school science. *Journal of Women and Minorities in Science and Engineering,* vol. 7, p. 271–285. Retrieved 2-04-2009, from <http://citeseerx.ist.psu.edu/>

Brown, A. (1994). Language deficiencies. In S. Adler & D. King (Eds.) *Oral communication problems in children and adolescents* (2nd ed.). Boston: Allyn & Bacon.

Caplan, F. (1971). *The first twelve months of life.* Princeton: The Princeton Center for Infancy and Early Childhood.

Carlisle, J. & Chang, V. (1996). Evaluation of academic capabilities in science by students with and without learning disabilities and their teachers. *Journal of Special Education, 30,* 18–34.

Carroll, J.B. (1963). A model of school learning. *Teachers College Record, 64,* 723–733.

CAST (2008). The Third Annual Conference of the Association for Software Testing (CAST) July 14–16. Toronto, Ontario, Canada.

Cavanagh, S. (Nov. 10, 2004). NCLB Could Alter Science Teaching. *Education Week, 24* (11): 1, 12-14. Retrieved on 2-08-2009, from <http://www.edweek.org/ew/articles/2004/11/11science.h24.html>

Cawley, J., Miller, J., & Carr, S. (1990). An examination of the reading performance of students with mild educational handicaps or learning disabilities. *Journal of Learning Disabilities, 23,* 284–290.

Cegelka, P. & Berdine, W. (1995). *Effective instruction for students with learning difficulties.* Boston: Allyn & Bacon.

Chankin, L. (1997). Readability and reading ease revisited. State-adopted science textbooks. *Clearing House, 70* (3), 151.

Chard, S. (2008). *Three phases of project development.* Retrieved 2-20-2009, from < http://www.projectapproach.org/index>

Chard, S. (1998). *The project approach: Managing successful projects.* New York: Scholastic. Retrieved 8-7-2009, from <http://ceep.crc.uiuc.edu>

Clark, A.M. (2006). *Changing classroom practice to include the project approach.* Retrieved 2-20-2009, from <ecrp.uiuc.edu/v8n2/clark.html>

Cole, M. & Cole, S. (1989). *The development of children.* New York: W.H. Freeman.

Coleman, M., Budysse, V. & Neitzel, J. (Sept. 11, 2008). *Early intervention for young children at-risk for learning disabilities.* Retrieved 2-20-2009, from <http://www.ncld.org/images/stories/downloads>.

Comenius, Jan Amos. (undated). *Jan Amos Comenius.* Retrieved 2-20-2009, from <http://www.cals.ncsu.edu/agexed/aee 501/comenius.html>

Coppell Montessori Academy. (2008). *Curriculum overview.* Retrieved 2-20-2009, from <http://www.coppellmontessori.com/curriculum/>

Core Knowledge Foundation. (1995). *Core knowledge sequence: Content guideline for grades K-6.* Charlottesville, VA: Core Knowledge Foundation.

Council of Chief State School Officers (CCSSO). (1-2-08). Federal programs: Early Childhood. *Early Childhood Education: The Head Start Program.* Retrieved 2-20-2009, from <http://www.ccsso.org/federal_programs/earlychildhood/index.cf>

Council for Exceptional Children. (1998). *IDEA 1997 Changes to Individual Education Programs.* Retrieved 2-20-09 from <http://www.cec.sped.org>

Council for Exceptional Children. (2002). *CEC's satellite broadcast highlights focus on the IEP and assessment.* Retrieved 2-20-2009, from <www.cec.sped.org/pd/sbsre.htm.>

Council for Exceptional Children (CEC). (10-25-2005). *A Primer on IDEA 1997 and its regulations.* Retrieved 2-20-2009, from <www.cec.sped.org>

Council for Exceptional Children. (12-21-2006). *A primer on the IDEA 2004 regulations.* Retrieved 2-20-2009, from <www.cec.sped.org>

Council for Exceptional Children. (Oct. 18, 2007). *Position on Response-to-Intervention.* Retrieved 2-20-09, from <http://www.cec.sped.org>

Council for Exceptional Children. (Nov. 9, 2007). *Response-to-Intervention.* Retrieved 2-20-09, from <http://www.cec.sped.org>

Coyne, M., Zirpoli, R. & Ruby, M. (2006). Beginning reading instruction for students at-risk for reading disabilities: What, how, when. *Intervention in School and Clinic, 41*: 169–174.

Creative Curriculum System. (2002-2008). Literacy in the creative curriculum for preschool. *Teaching Strategies, Inc.* Retrieved 2-20-2009, from <http://www.creativecurriculum.net>

Cromwell, S. (1997). Whole language and phonics: Can they work together? *Education World.* Retrieved 4-08-2009, from <http://www.education-world.com/a_curr/curr029.shtml>

Curiosity Corner Scope and Sequence. (2004). Language and Literacy. *The Success for All Foundation.* Retrieved 2-20-2009, from <http://www.successforall.net/early/early–curriculum.htm>

Dechant, E. (1981). *Diagnosis and remediation of reading disabilities.* Englewood Cliffs, NJ: Prentice-Hall.

Department of Education, New Jersey. (2006). Division of Early Childhood (DECE HOME). *Bankstreet developmental interaction approach.* Retrieved 2-20-2009, from http://www.nj.gov/education/ece/curriculum/curriculum.htm

Dolch, E. W. (1955). *Methods in reading.* Champaign, IL: Garrard.

Donahoe, K. & Zigmond, N. (1990). Academic grades of ninth-grade urban learning disabled students and low-achieving peers. *Exceptionality - A Research Journal, 1*, 17–27.

Dummer, G., Connor-Kuntz, F. & Goodway, J. (1995). A physical education curriculum for all preschool students. *Teaching Exceptional Children, 27* (3) : 28–34.

Dunn, D.W. (2000). Pre-K3 educators learn from the Reggio Emilia approach. *Education World.* Retrieved 2-20-2009, from <http://education-world.com/a_curr/curr256.shtml>

Dweck, C. & Elliot, E.S. (1983). Achievement motivation. In E.M. Hetherington (Ed). *Handbook of child psychology: Socialization, personality, and social development* (Vol. 4). New York: Wiley.

Educational Technology Network. (on-line serial). *Educational Technology/Instructional Technology.* Retrieved 2-20-2009, from <http://www.edutechnet.com.>

Education for All Handicapped Children Act (P.L.94-142) (1975). U.S. Department of Education. Washington, D.C.

Education World (1996/2008): National Education Standards, and State Education Standards. Retrieved 4-08-2009 from <http://www.educationworld.com/>

Eisenberg, M. & Berkowitz, R. (1990). *Information problem solving: The big six skills approach to library and information skills instruction.* Norwood, NJ: Ablex.

Elksnin, L. & Elksnin, N. (2006). *Teaching social-emotional skills at school and home.* Denver: Love.

Eller, C. & Mulroy, M. (no date). What are the developmental needs of school-aged children? School's Out from *Resource Notebook: School-Age Care, Out-of-School Time*, Child Care Bureau, Department of Health and Human Services Retrieved 2-20-2009, from <http://www.siu.edu/~aftersch/dev_nds.htm>

Ellis, A.K. (1977): *Teaching and Learning Elementary Social Studies.* Boston: Allyn & Bacon.

Ely, R. (2005). Language and literacy in the school years. In J.B. Gleason (Ed.), *The development of language* (6th ed., pp. 395-443). Boston, MA: Allyn & Bacon.

Federal Register (1977). Education for all Handicapped Children Act (PL94-142). (Vol. 42, pp. 42472–42515). Washington, DC: U.S. Government Printing Office, August 23, 1977.

Fernandez, D. & Vandegrift, J. (1991). *Addison-Westley mathematics.* Menlo Park, CA: Addison-Wesley.

Fisher, G. & Harlan, C. (1998). *Roles of Men, Women, and Children in Ancient Rome.* Retrieved 2-20-2009, from <http://oncampus.richmond.edu/academics/education/projects/webunits/greecerome/>

Fletcher, J.M., Lyon, G.R., Fuchs, L.S., & Barnes, M.A. (2007). *Learning Disabilities: From Identification to Intervention.* New York: Guilford.

Fressola, D., Ciponeri-Hoerchler, S., Hagan, J., McDannold, S. & Meyer, J. (1990). *Speech and language classroom intervention manual.* Columbia, MO: Hawthorne Educational Services.

Froebel Foundation. (2002-2007). *Froebel Foundation USA.* Retrieved 2-20-2009, from http://froebel foundation.org/

Froebel. (2002). *Fredrich Froebel.* Retrieved 2-20-2009, from <http://www.friedrichfroebel.com>

Frost, J. L. (1972). *Developmental checklists for 3-, 4-, and 5-year-olds.* Austin, TX: University of Texas.

Fry, E., Fountoukidis, D. & Polk, J. (1985). *The new reading teacher's book of lists.* Englewood Cliffs, NJ: Prentice-Hall.

Gallagher, S.A. (1994). Middle School Classroom Predictors of Science Persistence, *Journal of Research in Science Teaching, 31*(7), 721–735.

Gard, A., Gilman, L. & Gorman, J. (1980). *Speech and language development chart.* Salt Lake City, UT: Word Making Productions.

Gardner, R. (2001). Mt. Olivet After-School Program, *Remedial and Special Education, 22*(1) 22–36.

Georgia Department of Early Care and Learning. (Feb. 2007). *Bright from the Start.* Georgia's Prekindergarten Program Approved Curriculum Models, Quick Reference Sheet/Content Standards. Retrieved 2-20-2009, from < http://decal.ga.gov>

Gibbs, D. & Cooper, E. (1989). Prevalence of communication disorders in students with learning disabilities. *Journal of Learning Disabilities, 22*: 60–63.

Gibson, H. & Chase, C. (2002). Longitudinal impact of an inquiry-based science program on middle school students' attitudes toward science. *Science Education*, Vol. 86, Issue 5, pp. 693–705. Wiley Periodicals, Inc. Retrieved 8-10-2009, from <http:dx.doi.org/10.1002/sce.10089>

Glasser, W. (1965). *Reality therapy: A new approach to psychiatry.* New York: Harper & Row.

Gleason, J.B. (2005). *The development of language* (6th ed.). Boston: Pearson/Allyn & Bacon.

Goffin, S. (Aug. 2000). The role of curriculum models in early childhood education. *ERIC Digest Clearinghouse on Elementary and Early Childhood Education,* #ED443597. Retrieved 2-20-2009, from <http://ericeece.org>

Goldstein, C. (1998). Learning at cybercamp. *Teaching Exceptional Children, 30* (5): 16–21.

Graham, S. & Miller, L. (1983). Handwriting research and practice: A unified Approach. In E. Meyen, G. Vergason, & R. Whelan, *Promising practices for exceptional children curriculum implications.* Denver: Love.

Gray, W. (1960). *On their own in reading* (revised). Glenview, IL: Scott, Foresman.

Greenwald, A.G. (1980). The totalitarian ego: Fabrication and revision of personal history. *American Psychologist, 7*: 603–618.

Grossman, H. (Ed.) (1973). *Manual on terminology and classification in mental retardation.* Washington, DC: American Association on Mental Deficiency, Special Publication No. 2.

Grumbine, R. & Alden, P. (2006). Teaching science to students with learning disabilities: Guiding principles and practices for adapting instruction for students with learning disabilities. *The Science Teacher, 73* (3). Retrieved May 4, 2009, from <http://www.thefreelibrary.com/Science+for+students+with+disabilities-a0159534744>

Gurganus, S., Janas, M. & Schmitt, L. (1995). Science instruction: What special education teachers need to know and what roles they need to play. *Teaching Exceptional Children, 27,* 7–9.

Hall, J. (1981). *Evaluating and improving written expression: A practical guide for teachers.* Boston, MA: Allyn & Bacon.

Hallahan, D. & Kauffman, J. (1994) *Exceptional children: Introduction to special education.* Englewood Cliffs, NJ: Prentice-Hall.

Hammill, D. & Bryant, B. (2005). *Detroit Tests of Learning Aptitude-Primary-Third Edition.* (DTLA-P-3) Austin, TX: PRO-ED. (for ages 3–0 through 9–11 years)

Hamilton, D., Flemming, B., & Hicks, J. (1990). *Resources for creative teaching in earlychildhood education* (2nd ed.). San Diego: Harcourt Brace Jovanovich.

Hammill, D. & Bartel, N. (1997). *Teaching students with learning and behavior problems* (6th ed.). Austin, TX: pro-ed.

Hardman, M., Drew, C., & Egan, M. (1990). *Human exceptionality.* Boston: Allyn & Bacon.

Haring, N., McCormick, L. & Haring, T. (Eds.) (1994). *Exceptional children and youth* (6th ed.). New York: Merrill/Macmillan.

Harter, S. (1985). Competence as a dimension of self-evaluation: Toward a comprehensive model of self-worth. In R. Leahy (Ed.). *The development of the self.* Orlando: Academic Press.

Harter, S. (1988). Developmental processes in the construction of the self. In T. Yawkey & J.E. Johnson (Eds.). *Integrative processes and socialization: Early to middle childhood.* Hillsdale, NJ: Erlbaum.

Hawaiian Transition Project. (1987). *Transitional resources Honolulu.* University of Hawaii, Department of Special Education.

Hendrick, J. (1990). *Total learning developmental curriculum for the young child.* Columbus, OH: Merrill.

Healy, A., McAreavey, P., Von Hippel, C.S. & Jones, S.H. (1978). *Mainstreaming preschoolers: Children with health impairments.* Washington D.C.: U.S. Department of Health, Education, and Welfare.

Heilman, A., Blair, T. & Rupley, W. (1986). *Principles and practices of teaching reading.* Columbus, OH: Merrill.

Henley, M., Ramsey, R. & Algozzine, R. (1993). *Characteristics of and strategies for teaching students with mild disabilities.* Boston: Allyn & Bacon.

Herr, J. & Libby, Y. (1990). *Designing creative materials for young children.* San Diego: Harcourt Brace Jovanovich.

Heward, W. (2006). *Exceptional children: An introduction to special education* (8th ed.). Upper Saddle River, NJ: Pearson/Merrill/Prentice-Hall.

High/Scope Educational Research Foundation. (2008). *High/Scope Preschool Curriculum.* Retrieved 5-20-2009, from <http://.highscope.org>

Hock, M.F., Pulvers, K.A., Deshler, D.D., & Schumaker, J.B. (2001). The effects of an after-school tutoring program on the academic performance of at-risk students and students with LD. *Remedial and Special Education, 22*(10), 172–186.

Hohmann, M., Banet, B. & Weikart, D. (1983). *Young children in action.* Ypsilanti, MI: High/Scope Press.

Howell, K. & Morehead, M. (1987). *Curriculum-based evaluation for special and remedial education.* Columbus, OH: Merrill.

Hudson, J. & Shapiro, L. (Nov. 1991). Tell me a make-believe story: Coherence & cohesion in young children's picture-elicited narratives. *Developmental Psychology,* Vol. 27, Issue 6, pp. 960–974.

Hutchinson, N. (1993). Students with disabilities and mathematics education reform—Let the dialogue begin. *Remedial and Special Education, 14* (6): 20–23.

Illinois Early Learning Project (2002-2008). *Resources for early learning; Illinois early learning standards; benchmark index.* Retrieved 2-20-2009, from <http://illinoisearlylearning.org>

James, S. (1990). *Normal language acquisition.* Austin, TX: PRO-ED.

James, F. (2004). Response-to-Intervention in the Individuals with Disabilities Education Act (IDEA 2004). *International Reading Association.* Retrieved Dec. 5, 2004, from <http://www.reading.org>

Jarolimek, J. & Foster Sr., C. (1989; 2004). *Teaching and learning in the elementary school* (8th ed.). New York: Macmillan.

Johnson, D. (1971). The Dolch list reexamined. *The Reading Teacher, 24*: 449–457.

Jones, C.J. (2008). *Curriculum-Based assessment: The easy way to determine response-to-intervention* (2nd ed). Springfield, IL: Thomas.

Jones, C.J. (2008) *Social and emotional development of exceptional students* (2nd ed.). L'Abeille Publishing USA and UK.

Jones, C. J. (2002). *Evaluation and educational programming of students with deafblindness and severe disabilities: Sensorimotor stage* (2nd ed.). Springfield, IL: Thomas.

Jones, C.J. (1996). *An Introduction to the nature and needs of students with mild disabilities: Mild mental retardation, behavior disorders, and learning disabilities.* Springfield, IL: Thomas.

Jones, M.G. & Brader-Araje, L. (Spring 2002). The impact of constructivism on education: Language, discourse, and meaning. *American Communication Journal, 5*(3).

Kameenui, E. & Simmons, D. (1990). *Designing instructional strategies.* Columbus, OH: Merrill.

Kamii, C. (1991). What is constructivism? In C. Kamii, Manning, M. & Manning, G (Eds). *Early literacy: A constructivist foundation for whole language* (pp. 17–29). Washington D.C.: National Education Association (ERIC Document No. ED335703.

Katz, L. (1994). *The project approach.* ERIC Document No. EDO-PS-94-6.

Katz, L. & Chard, S. (Oct. 1998). Issues in selecting topics for projects. *Clearing House on Early Education and Parenting,* EDO-PS-98-8. Children's Research Center, University of Illinois at Urbana-Champaign. ERIC Document No. ED 424031.

Kelker, K. (1998). *Family guide to assistive technology: Parents, Let's Unite for Kids (PLUK).* Retrieved Nov. 21, 2005, from <http:www.pluk.org/ATI.html#2>

Keith, K. (2008). *Arnold Gesell and your child from five to ten.* Retrieved 2-20-2009, from<http://childparenting.about.com/od/childdevelopment/a/geselletal.htm>

Kohlber, L. (1976). Moral stages and moralization: The cognitive developmental approach. In T. Lickona (Ed.) Moral development and behavior: Theory, research, social issues. New York: Holt, Rinehart, Winston.

Kostelnik, M., Soderman, A., & Whiren, A. (1991). *Developmentally appropriate curriculum: Best practices in early childhood education.* Upper Saddle River, NJ: Prentice Hall.

Krogh, S. (1994). *Educating young children infancy to grade three.* New York: McGraw-Hill.

Krogh, S. (1995). *The integrated early childhood curriculum* (2nd ed.). New York: McGraw-Hill.

Kwon, Young-Ihm (2002). *Changing curriculum for early childhood education.* ECRP, Vol. 4, No. 2. Retrieved 5-15-2009 from <http://ecrp/uiuc.edu/v4n2/kwon.html>

Lanier, R. & Davis, A. (1972). Developing comprehension through teacher-made questions. *Reading Teacher, 26* (2): 153–157.

Larsen, S. & Hammill, D. (1989). *Test of legible handwriting.* Austin, TX: PRO-ED.

Larsen, V. & McKinley, N. (1995). *Language disorders in older students: Preadolescents and adolescents.* Eau Claire, WI: Thinking Publications.

Lascarides, V.C. & Hinitz, B.F. (2000). *History of early childhood education.* New York: Falmer Press.

Lawton, J. (1988). *Introduction to child care & early childhood education.* Glenview, IL: Scott, Foresman.

Lerner, J.: *Learning disabilities theories, diagnosis, and teaching strategies.* Boston: Houghton Mifflin, 1989, 1993, 1997.

Lesiak, W. & Lesiak, J. (1994). *Developmental Tasks for Kindergarten Readiness-II.* Austin, TX: PRO-ED. Retrieved 4-27-2000, from <www.proedinc.com>

Lewis, J. (May/June, 1998). How the internet expands educational options. *Teaching Exceptional Children, 30* (5): 34–41.

Lewis, R. & Doorlag, D. (1999). *Teaching special students in general education classrooms* (5th ed.). Upper Saddle River, NH: Merrill/Prentice Hall.

Louisiana Department of Social Services. (2005). Early childhood curriculum can involve activities specific teaching. *Office of Family Support.* Retrieved 2-20-2009, from <www.dss.state.la.us/index>

Lovitt, T. (1989). *Introduction to learning disabilities.* Boston: Allyn & Bacon.

Luckasson, R. (Ed.) (1992). *Mental retardation: Definition, classification, and systems of supports* (9th ed.). Washington, DC: American Association on Mental Retardation.

Mallinson, G., Mallinson, J., Froschauer, L., Harris, J., Lewis, M. & Valentino, C. (Program Authors). (1993). *Science Horizons (Sterling Edition).* Morristown, NJ: Silver Burdett Ginn.

Mann, P., Suiter, P. & McClung, R. (1987). *Handbook in diagnostic-prescriptive teaching in the elementary schools.* Boston: Allyn & Bacon.

Mastropieri, M & Scruggs, T. (1994). *Effective instruction for special education* (2nd ed.). Austin, TX: PRO-ED.

Mastropieri, M., Scruggs, T., Norland, J. Berkeley, S. McDuffie, K., Tornquist, E. et al. (2006). Differentiated curriculum enhancement in inclusive middle school science: Effects on classroom and high-stakes tests. *Journal of Special Education, 40* (3), 130–137.

McCarthy, C. (2005). Effects of thematic-based, hands-on science teaching versus a textbook approach for students with disabilities. *Journal of Research in Science Teaching, 42*(3), 245–263.

McGinnis, E. & Goldstein, A. (2003). *Skillstreaming in early childhood: Teaching prosocial skills to the preschool and kindergarten child.* Champaign, IL: Research Press.

McGinnis, E. & Goldstein, A. (1997) *Skillstreaming the elementary school child: A guide for teaching prosocial skills.* Champaign, IL: Research Press.

McGinnis, E. & Goldstein, A. (1997). *Skillstreaming the adolescent.* Champaign, IL Research Press.

McGuire, M. (1993). Teaching mathematics to students with mild disabilities. In T. Smith, D. Finn, & C. Dowdy, *Teaching students with mild disabilities.* Ft. Worth, TX: Harcourt Brace Jovanovich.

McKown, R. (1961). *Pioneers in mental health.* New York: Dodd, Mead & Co.

McLoughlin, J. & Lewis, R. (2008). *Assessing students with special needs* (7th ed.). Upper Saddle River, NJ: Pearson/Merrill/Prentice Hall.

McNergney, R. & Herbert, J. (1995). *Foundations of education the challenge of professional practice.* Needham Heights, MA: Allyn & Bacon.

McREL (MidContinent Regional Educational Content Knowledge) (2008). A Compendium of Standards. *Technology Standards & Benchmarks.* Retrieved 2-20-2009, from <http://www.mcrel.org/compendium/SubjectTopics.asp?SubjectID=19>

Meichenbaum, D. (1977). *Cognitive behavior modification: An integrative approach.* New York: Plenum.

Mellard, D. (2003). Understanding responsiveness to intervention in learning disabilities determination. Paper presented at the National Research Center on Learning Disabilities Responsiveness-to-Intervention Symposium, Kansas City, MO. Retrieved on 4-08-2009, from <http://www.nrcld.org/about/publications/papers/mellard.html>

Mercer, C. (1997). *Students with learning disabilities* (5th ed.). Columbus, OH: Merrill/Prentice Hall.

Mercer, C. & Mercer, A. (2000). *Teaching students with learning problems* (5th ed.). Upper Saddle River, NY: Merrill/Prentice Hall.

Michigan Project Great Start. (2005). *Preschool curriculum models.* Retrieved 2-20-2009, from <www.michigan.gov/greatstart.>

Miller, L. (2008). Spoken language. In Polloway, E., Patton, J. & Serna, L. *Strategies for teaching learners with special needs* (9th ed.). Upper Saddle River, NJ: Pearson/Merrill/Prentice Hall.

Milosky, L. (1994). Nonliteral language abilities. In G. Wallach & K. Butler, *Language learning disabilities in school-age children and adolescents some principles and applications.* New York: Merrill/Macmillan.

Monighan-Nourot, P. (1990). The legacy of play in American early childhood education. In E. Klugman & S. Smilansky, *Children's play and learning perspectives and policy implications.* New York: Teacher's College Press.

Mooney, M. (1990). *Reading to, with, and by children.* Katonah, New York: R.C. Owen.

Morrow, L. (1989). *Literacy development in the early years helping children read and write.* Englewood Cliffs, NJ: Prentice Hall.

Moustakas, C. (1969). *Personal growth: The struggle for identity and human values.* Cambridge, MA: H.A. Doyle.

NAMTA (North American Montessori Teacher's Association. (1991). Montessori Research Summary. Retrieved Feb. 18, 2009, from <http://www.montessori-namta.org>

NAEYC. (2009). *Teaching young children: Resources and links.* Retrieved 2-20-2009, from <http://tyc.naeyc.org/links>

NAEYC. (2009). *Developmentally appropriate practice.* Retrieved 2-20-2009, from <http://naeyc.org>

National Association for the Education for Young Children. (1992). *Guidelines for appropriate curriculum content and assessment in programs serving children three through eight years of age.* Washington, DC: Author.

National Early Childhood Technical Assistance Center (Jan. 2007). *History of OSEP: Funded early childhood projects.* Retrieved 2-20-2009, from <http://www.nectar.org/>

National Research Council. (1996). National science education standards. Washington D.C.: National Academy Press.

National Standards. (2009). Language Arts Standards; Mathematics Standards; Science Standards; Social Sciences Standards; Technology Standards. Retrieved 2-20-2009, from <www.educationworld.com/standards/national/Index.html>

(NCTM) National Council for Teachers of Mathematics. (1989). Curriculum and evaluation standards for school mathematics. Retrieved 8-9-2009, from <http: nctm.org>

(NCTM) National Council for Teachers of Mathematics. (2000). Principals and standards for school mathematics. Retrieved 8-9-2009, from <www.nctm.org/standards/

(NCTM) National Council for Teachers of Mathematics. (2006). Curriculum focal points. Retrieved 8-9-2009, from <www.nctm.org/

(NCTM) National Council for Teachers of Mathematics. (2006). Related expectations. Retrieved 8-9-2009, from <www.nctm.org/

Negroponte, N. (2002). *One laptop per child talks.* Retrieved 8-9-2009, from <http://www.olpctalks.com/nicholas_negroponte/negroponte_analyst_meeting.html>

Nippold, M.A. (2006). *Later language development: School-age children, adolescents, and young adults* (3rd ed.). Austin, TX: PRO-ED.

North Carolina Department of Public Instruction (1979). *Competency goals and performance indicators K-12.* Raleigh, NC: Author.

North Carolina Department of Public Instruction. (1995–96): *Standard course of study K-12 computer skills.* Raleigh, NC: Author.

North Carolina Department of Education (2004). *The North Carolina Computer Skills Alternate Assessment.* Retrieved Feb. 18, 2009, from <www.ncpublicschools.org/does/accountability/testing/computerskills/csaltassesswebinfosheet 070712.pdf >

North Carolina Department of Education (2004). *North Carolina Computer/technology skills standard course of study.* Retrieved 2-18-2009, from <http://www.ncpublicschools.org/curriculum/computerskills/scos>

North Carolina Public Schools. (2009). More at four pre-kindergarten program. *Office of School Readiness.* Retrieved 2-20-2009, from <http://www.osr.ne.gov/MoreFour/index.asp>

Norton, D. (1985). *The effective teaching of language arts* (2nd ed.). Upper Saddle River, NJ: Merrill/Prentice Hall

Nowacek, E.J. (1997). Spoken language. In E. Polloway & J. Patton, *Strategies for teaching learners with special needs* (6th ed.). Upper Saddle River, NJ: Merrill/Prentice Hall.

Nursery Schools. (2008). *Nursery schools: The Early Infant Schools and Kindergartens.* Retrieved 5-20-2009 from <http://www.faqs.org/childhood/Me-Pa/Nursery-Schools.html

Olaf, M. (2008). *An introduction to Montessori's philosophy and practice.* Reprinted from: Michael Olaf's, *Child of the World: Essential Montessori for Age Three to Twelve.* Retrieved 2-20-2009, from <www.michaelolaf.net> or <www.Montessori.org>

Olsen, J. & Platt, J. (1996). *Teaching children and adolescents with special needs* (2nd ed.). Columbus, OH: Merrill/Prentice Hall.

OLPC (One Laptop per Child Initiative). (2002). *One laptop per child.* Retrieved Feb.18, 2009, from <http://laptop.org/en/ or http://papert.org/>

Orem, R.C. (1991). *Montessori Today.* New York: Putnam's Sons.

Organization for Economic Cooperation and Development. (2007). *PISA 2006: Science Competencies for Tomorrow's World,* Volume 1, Paris: Author.

Papert, S. (2002). The turtle's long slow trip: Macro-educological perspectives on microworlds. *Journal of Educational Computing Research, 27,* 7–27.

Parmar, R., DeLca, C. & Janczak, T. (1994). Investigations into the relationship between science and language abilities of students with mild disabilities. *Remedial and Special Education, 15,* 117–126.

Patton, J., Bierne-Smith, A. & Payne, J. (1990). *Mental retardation* (3rd ed.). Columbus, OH: Merrill.

Patton, J. & Polloway, E. (1990). Mild mental retardation. In N. Haring & L. McCormick (Eds.) *Exceptional children and youth* (5th ed.). Columbus, OH: Merrill.

Patton, J., Polloway, E., & Cronin, M. (1990). A survey of special education teachers relative to science for the handicapped. Unpublished paper, University of New Orleans.

Paul, J. (1991). Emotional and behavioral disorders in children. In J. Paul & B. Epanchin (Eds.) *Educating emotionally disturbed children and youth: Theories and practices for teachers* (2nd ed.). New York: Merrill.

Peterson, C. (1994). Narrative skills and social class. *Canadian Journal of Education, 19:*3, p. 251–269.

Peterson, C. & McCabe, A. (1991). *Developing narrative structure.* Hillsdale, NJ: Lawrence Erlbaum.

Peterson, N. (1987). *Early intervention for handicapped and at-risk children.* Denver: Love.

Pinnacle Curriculum. (2005). *Pinnacle early childhood curriculum.* ChildCare Education Institute. Retrieved January 15, 2008, from <www.cceionline.com>

Pierangelo, R. & Giuliani, G. (1998). *Special educator's complete guide to 109 diagnostic tests.* West Nyack, NY: The Center for Applied Research in Education.

Plucker, J. (2007). *Human intelligence: Jean Piaget.* Retrieved 5-20-2009, from <http://www.indiana.edu/~intell/piaget.shtml>

Polloway, E. & Patton, J. (1997). *Strategies for teaching learners with special needs* (6th ed.). Columbus, OH: Merrill/Prentice Hall.

Polloway, E., Patton, J. & Cohen, S. (1983). Written language. In E. Meyen, G. Vargason & R. Whelan (eds.), *Promising practices for exceptional children: Curriculum implications.* Denver: Love.

Polloway, E., Patton, J. & Serna, L. (2008), Strategies for teaching learners with special needs (9th ed.) Upper Saddle River, NJ: Pearson, Merrill/Prentice Hall.

Polloway, E. & Smith, T. (1992). Language instruction for students with disabilities. (2nd ed.). Denver: Love.

Polloway, E., Miller, L. and Smith, T.E.C. (2004). *Language instruction of students with disabilities* (3rd ed.). Denver: Love.

Portage Project. (2003). *The New Portage Guide: Birth to Six.* The National Portage Association. Retrieved 2-20-2009, from <www.portageproject.org>

Raizen, S. (1988). *Increasing educational productivity through improving science curriculum.* Washington, DC: National Center for Improving Science Education.

Ralabate, P. (Aug. 2, 2006). NEA highlights No Child Left Behind Act's impact on students with disabilities. *National Education Association.* Retrieved 2-20-2009, from www.nea.org

Ralabate, P. (Aug. 2, 2006). Statement to the Aspen Institute's Commission on NoChild Left Behind. *National Education Association.* Retrieved 2-20-2009, from <www.nea.org> (PDF, 186 KB, 34 pages).

Rathmann, C., W. Mann, & G. Morgen (2007). Narrative structure and narrative development in deaf children. *Deafness Education International, 9* (4):187–196. Published online Nov. 1, 2007 in Wiley InterScience. (DOI: 10.1002/dei.228) Retrieved 2-20-2009, from <www.interscience.wiley.com>

Raymond, E. (2008). *Learners with mild disabilities: A characteristics approach.* (3rd edition). Boston: Pearson/Allyn & Bacon.

Redl, F. (1959). The concept of the life space interview. *American Journal of Orthopsychiatry, 29:* 1–18.

Reid, D.K., Hresko, W.P. & Swanson, H.L. (1991). A *cognitive approach to learning disabilities,* (2nd ed.). Auston, TX: Pro-ed.

Reutzer, R. & Cooter Jr., R. (1999). *Balanced reading strategies and practices.* Upper Saddle River, NJ: Merrill/Prentice Hall.

Reinert, H. (1980). *Children in conflict* (2nd ed.). St. Louis: Mosby.

Reyhner, J. (Dec., 13, 2008). *The reading wars: Phonics versus whole language* (revised). Retrieved June 2, 2008, from < http:jan.ucc.nau.edu/~jar/Reading_Wars.html>

Richland School District Two (1998). *Technology: Student benchmarks K-12 checklist.* Richland, SC: Author, 1998. Retrieved 2-20-2009, from <http://www. Richland2.k12.sc.us/tech/studentchecklist.htm>

Rivera, D.P. & Smith, D. (1997). *Teaching students with learning and behavior problems* (3rd ed.). Boston: Allyn & Bacon.

Robledo, S.J. (1997–2009). The top preschool programs and how they differ. *Baby Center.* Retrieved 2-20-2009, from: < http://www.babycenter.com>

Robinson, S. & Smith, D. (1983). Listening skills: Teaching learning disabled students to be better listeners. In E. Meyen, G. Vargason, & R. Whelan (Eds.) *Promising practices for exceptional children curriculum implications.* Denver: Love.

Roles of Children in Greek/Roman Culture (undated). Retrieved 5-20-2009 from <http://www.crystalinks.com/greekculture.html> and <http://www.crystalinks.com/romeducation.html>

Rose-Krasnor, L.: Social cognition (1988). In T. Yawkey & J.E. Johnson (Eds.), *Integrative processes and socialization: Early to middle childhood.* Hillsdale, NJ: Erlbaum.

Sadler, M. & Ward, G. (Oct. 2005). Supporting the narrative development of young children. *Early Childhood Education Journal,* Vol.33, No. 2.

Safford, P. (1989). *Integrated teaching in early childhood: Starting in the mainstream.* New York: Longman.

Scholastic Word Wizard Dictionary (1996-2009). *Primary grades vocabulary instruction with Word Wizard Dictionary.* Retrieved 2-07-2009, from <http://teacher.scholastic.com/dictionary/>

Sakiey, E. & Fry, E. (1984). *3000 Instant Words.* Providence, RI: Jamestown.

Salend, S. (2008). *Creating inclusive classrooms: Effective and reflective practices* (6th edition). Upper Saddle River, NJ: Prentice Hall/Pearson.

Salvia, J., Ysseldyke, J. with Bolt, S. (2007). *Assessment in special and inclusive education.* Boston: Houghton Mifflin.

Sargent, L. (1991). *Social skills for school and community.* Reston, VA: CEC-MR.

Schumaker, J., Hazel, J. & Pederson, C. (1988). *Social skills for daily living.* Circle Pines, MN: American Guidance Service.

Scheerenberger, R. (1983). *A history of mental retardation.* Baltimore: Brookes. School House Review (The) (On-line serial). Retrieved 2-20-2009, from <http://www.worldvillage.com>

Scruggs, T.E., & Mastropieri, M.A. (1995). Teaching science to students with disabilities in general education settings: Practical and proven strategies. *Teaching Exceptional Children, 27*(4), 10–13.

Scruggs, T.E. & Mastropieri, M.A. (2007). Science learning in special education: The case for constructed versus instructed learning. *Exceptionality, 15,* 57–74.

Serfass, C. & Peterson, R. (Sept. 1, 2007). A guide to computer-managed IEP record forms systems. *Teaching Exceptional Children.* Retrieved 4-07-2009, from <http://www.encyclo-pedia.com/doc/1P3-134602958/html>

Serna, L. (1997). Social competence and self-determination skills. In E. Polloway & J. Patton, *Strategies for teaching learners with special needs* (6th ed.). Columbus, OH: Merrill/Prentice Hall.

Serna, L. & Patton, J. (1997). Mathematics. In E. Polloway & J. Patton, *Strategies for teaching learners with special needs* (6th ed.). Columbus, OH: Merrill/Prentice Hall.

Shea, T. & Bauer, A. (1994). *Learners with disabilities: A social systems perspective of special education.* Madison, WI: Brown & Benchmark.

Sheinker, A., Sheinker, J. & Stevens, L. (1988). Cognitive strategies for teaching the mildly handicapped. In E. Meyen, G. Vergason & R. Whelan (Eds.) *Effective instructional strategies for exceptional children.* Denver: Love.

Shepherd, G. & Ragan, W. (1992). *Modern elementary curriculum* (7th ed.). Fort Worth, TX: Harcourt Brace Jovanovich.

Simon, C.S. (1979). *Communicative competence: A functional pragmatic approach to language therapy.* Tempe, AZ: Communi-Cog Publications.

Skeels, H.M. & Dye, H.B. (1939). A study of the effects of differential stimulation on mentally retarded children. *Program of the American Association of Mental Deficiency, 44,* 114–136.

Skolnick, A.S. (1986). *The psychology of human development.* San Diego: Harcourt, Brace, Jovanovich.

Skrtic. T., Harris, K. & Shriner, J. (2005). *Special education policy and practice: Accountability, instruction, and social challenges.* Denver: Love.

Slavin, R. (1994; 2005). *Educational psychology* (8th ed.) Englewood Cliffs, NJ: Prentice Hall.

Sloan, W. & Stevens, H. (1976). A century of concern: A *History of the American Association on Mental Deficiency 1876-1976.* Washington, DC: AAMR.

Smith, M., Schloss, P. & Hunt, F. (1987). Differences in social and emotional development. In J. Neisworth & S. Bagnato, *The young exceptional child: Early development and education.* New York: Macmillan.

Smith, T., Dowdy, C., Polloway, E. & Blalock, G. (1997). *Children and adults with learning disabilities.* Boston: Allyn & Bacon.

Spache, G. (1964). *Reading in the elementary school.* Boston: Allyn & Bacon.

State Compulsory Attendance Laws. (2004). National Center for Education Statistics, Department of Education Statistics, 2004.

Strang, R., McCullough, C. & Traxler, A. (1967). *The improvement of reading* (4th ed.). New York: McGraw-Hill.

Stephenson, M. (2008). *A Montessori homeschool story.* Retrieved 2-20-2008, from <http://www.montessori.edu/homeschooling.html>

Strickland, B. & Turnbull, A. (1990). *Developing and implementing individualized educational programs* (3rd ed.). Columbus, OH: Merrill.

SuperKids Educational Software Review (On-line serial) (2009). *SuperKids education for the future: Education software reviews.* Retrieved: 2-20-2009, from <http://www. superkids.com>

TampaReads. (2008). *ReadingKey Vocabulary Building Program.* Retrieved 2-07-2009, from <www.tampareads.com> or <www.readingkey.com>

The Portage Project. (2003). *The New Portage Guide Birth-to-Six: The Tool for Observation and Planning* (TOP). Retrieved 2-07-2009, from <www.portageproject.org>

Thomas, G. (1996). *Teaching students with mental retardation.* Englewood Cliffs, N.J.: Merrill/Prentice Hall.

Toth, M., Ragno, N., Gray, B. (Eds.) (1990). *World of language.* Morristown, PA: Silver Burdett & Ginn.

Turnbull III, H. R. (1993). *Free appropriate public education* (4th ed.) Denver: Love.

Turnbull III, H. R., Stowe, M. & Huerta, N. (2006). *Free appropriate public education: The law and children with disabilities.* (7th edition). Denver: Love.

Tyler-Wood, T.L. & Mortensen, M.J. (2006). Bringing Up Girls in Science. Conference Proceedings for the Society for Information Technology and Teacher Education.

United States Department of Education. (Oct. 2004). No Child Left Behind Overview. *A guide to education and No Child Left Behind Act of 2001: Improving the academic achievement for the economically disadvantaged (p.13) Preparing, training, and recruiting highly qualified teachers and principals (p.14) Making the education system accountable (p.17) Helping all children learn to read (p. 19); Helping children with disabilities (p. 20)* Retrieved 2-20-2009, from <ED.gov> (PDF 330 KB)

United States Department of Education. (March 2006). No Child Left Behind. *About ED initiatives: Helping readers achieve and succeed.* (PDF 120 KB) Retrieved 2-20-2009, from <Ed. gov>

United States Department of Education (Aug. 2006). No Child Left Behind. *Highly qualified teachers for every child.* (PDF 111KB) Retrieved 2-20-2009, from <ED.gov>

United States Department of Education. (Feb. 2007). No Child Left Behind. *President's FY 2008 Education Budget: Building on Progress.* (MSWord 226 KB) Retrieved: 2-20-2009, from: <ED.gov>

United States Department of Education. (2008). *Improve student performance, Early Reading First.* Office of Elementary and Secondary Education, No Child Left Behind. Retrieved 2-20-2009, from <ED.gov>

United States Department of Education (Feb. 4, 2008). Fiscal year 2009 Budget Summary Section II: Elementary and Secondary Education. Retrieved 2-20-2009, from <ED.gov>

United States Department of Education. (2008). National Center for Education Statistics. Digest of Educational Statistics (2007):
  1. *Student effort and educational progress;*
  2. *Elementary/secondary persistence and progress (Status Drop Out Rates);*
  3. *Learner outcomes: Academic outcomes (Reading Performance of Students In Grades 4, 8, 12);*
  4. *Students with Disabilities Exiting School with a Regular High School Diploma;*
  Retrieved Feb. 18, 2009, from http://www. nces.ed.gov/fastfacts.

United States Department of Education. (2008). Institute of Education Sciences (IES). Practice Guide Book: Dropout Prevention (publication number dp-pg-090308.pdf) Retrieved Feb. 18, 2009, from < http://www.dropout prevention.org/>

United States Department of Health and Human Services. (2003). *Head Start Child Outcomes Framework: Head Start Bulletin,* Issue No. 76. Administration for Children and Families. Retrieved 2-20-2009, from <www.headstartbulletin, No.76 contents>

University of Illinois at Urbana-Champaign. (1994). *Clearing House on Early Education and Parenting.* ERIC/EECE Digest Archive. The Project Approach. Retrieved 8-7-2009, from <http://ceep.crc.uiuc.edu>

Van Kleech, A. (1994). Metalinguistic development. In G. Wallach & K. Butler, *Language learning disabilities in school-age children and adolescents some principles and applications.* New York: Merrill/Macmillan.

Vaughn, S. & Haager, D. (1994). Social competence as a multifaceted construct: How do students with learning disabilities fare? *Learning Disability Quarterly, 17:* 253–266.

Vicker, B. (2000). *Building competency with figurative language one idiom at a time. The Reporter, 5* (3), 17–21. Retrieved 2-20-2009, from <http://www.lidc.indiana.educ/irca/IRCAarticles/ fcommunicationarticles.html>

Wadsworth, B.J. (1984). *Piaget's theory of cognitive and affective development* (3rd ed.). New York: Longman.

Wagner, L. (2003). *Building dictionary skills: Grades 4-5.* Columbus, OH: Frank Schaffer Publications.

Watts, E., O'Brian, M. & Wojcik, B. (Winter 2004). Four models of assistive technology consideration: How do they compare to recommended educational assessment practices. *Journal of Special Education Technology, v19,* n1, pp. 43–56. ERIC # EJ729598. Retrieved 4-07-2009, from <www.eric.ed.gov>

Weaver, C. (1996). On the nature of whole language education. In C. Weaver, L. Gillmeester-Kraus & G. Vents-Zogby: *Creating support for effective literacy education.* Portsmouth, NH: Heinemann.

Wheelock, W., Campbell, C. & Silvaroli, N. (2008). *Classroom Reading Inventory,* 11th edition. Dubuque, IA: McGraw-Hill.

Whelan, R. (1988). Emotionally disturbed. In E. Meyen and T. Skrtic (Eds.) *Exceptional children and youth: An introduction* (3rd ed.). Denver: Love.

Wiederholt, J. (1974). Historical perspectives on the education of the learning disabled. In L. Mann & A. Sabatino (Eds.). *The second review of special education,* (pp. 105–152). Austin, TX: PRO-ED.

Wiig, E. & Semel, E. (1984). *Language assessment and intervention for the learning disabled* (2nd ed.). Columbus, OH: Merrill.

Wilson, R. & Hall, M. (1996). *Programmed word attack for teachers* (6th ed.). Columbus, OH: Merrill.

Wolery, M. & Brookfield-Norman, J. (1988). Pre-Academic instruction for handicapped preschool children. In S. Odom & M. Karnes (Eds.) *Early intervention for infants and children with handicaps: An empirical base.* Baltimore, MD: Brookes. (Rolling Prairie Library System Horizon Information Portal)

Work, R. (1994). Articulation disorders. In S. Adler & D. King (Eds.) *Oral communication problems in children and adolescents* (2nd ed.). Boston: Allyn & Bacon.

The Wright Group. (1995). *Content Essentials for Science K-6.* Wright/McGraw-Hill publishers. Retrieved on 4-04-2009, from <www.WrightGroup/McGraw-Hill.com>

Wysocki, K. & Jenkins, J. (1987). Deriving word meanings through morphological generalization. *Reading Research Quarterly, 22,* 66–81.

Yarbrough, B. (2007, May 1). *Science textbooks too advanced for students? Hesperia Star.* Retrieved 4-10-2009, from <http://www.redorbit.com/news/education/921144/Science_ textbooks_too_advanced_for_students/index.html>

Young-Ihm, K. (Fall 2002). Changing curriculum for early childhood education in England. *Early Childhood Research and Practice, ECRP,* Vol. 4, No. 2. Retrieved 2-20-2009, from <http://www.ecrp.uiuc.edu/v4n2/kwon.html>

Charles C Thomas
PUBLISHER • LTD.

P.O. Box 19265
Springfield, IL 62794-9265

- Bryan, Willie V.—SOCIOPOLITI-CAL ASPECTS OF DISABILI-TIES: The Social Perspectives and Political History of Disabilities and Rehabilitation in the United States. (2nd Ed.). '10, 282 pp. (7 x 10), 12 il.

- Coleman, Janet R. & Elizabeth E. Wolf—ADVANCED SIGN LAN-GUAGE VOCABULARY—RAIS-ING EXPECTATIONS: A Re-source Text for Educators, Interpreters, Parents, and Sign Language Instructors. (2nd Ed.) '09, 206 pp. (8 1/2 x 11), 694 il., (spiral) (paper).

- Jones, Carroll J.—CURRICULUM DEVELOPMENT FOR STU-DENTS WITH MILD DISABILI-TIES: Academic and Social Skills for RTI Planning and Inclusion IEPs. (2nd Ed.) '09, 314 pp. (8 1/2 x 11), 50 tables, (spiral).

- Blomquist, Barbara Taylor—INSIGHT INTO ADOPTION: Uncovering and Understanding the Heart of Adoption. (2nd Ed.) '09, 212 pp. (6 x 9), $27.95, paper.

- Brooke, Stephanie L.—THE USE OF THE CREATIVE THERA-PIES WITH AUTISM SPEC-TRUM DISORDERS. '09, 348 pp. (7 x 10), 49 il., (13 in color), 1 table, $83.95, hard, $59.95, paper.

- Coleman, Janet R. & Elizabeth E. Wolf—ADVANCED SIGN LAN-GUAGE VOCABULARY—RAIS-ING EXPECTATIONS: A Re-source Text for Educators, Interpreters, Parents, and Sign Language Instructors. (2nd Ed.) '09, 208 pp. (8 1/2 x 11), 694 il., $39.95, (spiral) (paper).

- Hoffman, Cheryl M.—COMPRE-HENSIVE REFERENCE MANU-AL FOR SIGNERS AND INTER-PRETERS. (6th Ed.) '09, 404 pp. (8 1/2 x 11) $59.95, spiral (paper).

- Luginbuehl-Oelhafen, Ruth R.—ART THERAPY WITH CHRON-IC PHYSICALLY ILL ADOLES-CENTS: Exploring the Effect-iveness of Medical Art Therapy as a Complementary Treatment. '09, 220 pp. (7 x 10), 67 il., (12 in color), $37.95, paper.

- Stepney, Stella A.—ART THERA-PY WITH STUDENTS AT RISK: Fostering Resilience and Growth Through Self-Expression. (2nd Ed.) '09, 214 pp. (7 x 10), 16 il. (14 in color), 19 tables, $56.95, hard, $38.95, paper.

- Thompson, Richard H.—THE HAN-DBOOK OF CHILD LIFE: A Guide for Pediatric Psychosocial Care. '09, 378 pp. (7 x 10), 5 il., 15 tables, $79.95, hard, $55.95, paper.

- Wilkes, Jane K.—THE ROLE OF COMPANION ANIMALS IN COUNSELING AND PSYCHOL-OGY: Discovering Their Use in the Therapeutic Process. '09, 168 pp. (7 x 10), 2 tables, $29.95, paper.

- Bakken, Jeffrey P. & Festus E. Obiakor—TRANSITION PLAN-NING FOR STUDENTS WITH DISABILITIES: What Educators and Service Providers Can Do. '08, 170 pp. (7 x 10), 4 il., 25 tables.

- Coulacoglou, Carina—EXPLOR-ING THE CHILD'S PERSONAL-ITY: Developmental, Clinical and Cross-Cultural Applications of the Fairy Tale Test. '08, 364 pp. (3 x 10), 22 il., 41 tables, $78.95, hard, $53.95, paper.

- Jones, Carroll J.—CURRICU-LUM-BASED ASSESSMENT: The Easy Way to Determine Response-to-Intervention. (2nd Ed.) '08, 210 pp. (8 1/2 x 11), 59 tables, $35.95, (spiral) paper.

- Smith, Sheri, Rosalind Ekman Ladd & Lynn Pasquerella—ETHICAL ISSUES IN HOME HEALTH CARE. (2nd Ed.) '08, 258 pp. (7 x 10), $56.95, hard, $36.95, paper.

- Crandell, John M. Jr. & Lee W. Robinson—LIVING WITH LOW VISION AND BLINDNESS: Guidelines That Help Profess-ionals and Individuals Under-stand Vision Impairments. '07, 220 pp. (7 x 10), 14 il., $49.95, hard, $34.95, paper.

- Cowden, Jo E. & Carol C. Torrey—MOTOR DEVELOPMENT AND MOVEMENT ACTIVITIES FOR PRESCHOOLERS AND IN-FANTS WITH DELAYS: A Multi-sensory Approach for Profess-ionals and Families. (2nd Ed.) '07, 348 pp. (7 x 10), 195 il., 13 tables, $73.95, hard, $53.95, paper.

- Drummond, Sakina S.—NEURO-GENIC COMMUNICATION DISORDERS: Aphasia and Cog-nitive-Communication Disorders. '06, 246 pp. (7 x 10), 25 il., 17 tables, $55.95, hard, $35.95, paper.

- Goodman, Karen D.—MUSIC THERAPY GROUPWORK WITH SPECIAL NEEDS CHIL-DREN: The Evolving Process. '07, 318 pp. (8 x 10), 21 tables, $69.95, hard, $49.95, paper.